D1103778

A BRIEF HISTORY
OF KOREA

MARK PETERSON

WITH PHILLIP MARGULIES

Facts On File
An imprint of Infobase Publishing

To Don and Linda Clark

A Brief History of Korea

Copyright © 2010 Infobase Publishing

Facts On File, Inc.
An imprint of Infobase Publishing
132 West 31st Street
New York, NY 10001

Library of Congress Cataloging-in-Publication Data

Peterson, Mark, 1946–
     A brief history of Korea / Mark Peterson with Phillip Margulies.
        p. cm.
     Includes bibliographical references and index.
     ISBN 978-0-8160-5085-7
     1. Korea—History. 2. Korea (South)—History. 3. Korea (North)—History. I. Margulies, Phillip, 1952– II. Title.
     DS907.18.P49 2009
     951.9—dc22   2009018889

Facts On File books are available at special discounts when purchased in bulk quantities for businesses, associations, institutions, or sales promotions. Please call our Special Sales Department in New York at (212) 967-8800 or (800) 322-8755.

You can find Facts On File on the World Wide Web at http://www.factsonfile.com

Text design by Lina Farinella
Illustrations by Pat Meschino
Composition by Hermitage Publishing Services
Cover printed by Art Print, Taylor, PA
Book printed and bound by Maple Press, York, PA
Date printed: December 2009
Printed in the United States of America

10 9 8 7 6 5 4 3 2 1

CONTENTS

LIST OF ILLUSTRATIONS

LIST OF MAPS

INTRODUCTION

Home to more than 71 million people, Korea has been divided along the 38th parallel since the defeat of Japan (Korea's former colonial ruler) at the end of World War II. Outside of Korea, South Korea is better known than North Korea; a parliamentary democracy since its independence in 1948, South Korea has prospered over the last few decades. North Korea remains a secretive society, struggling to meet the needs of its people, and it remains something of a mystery to most outsiders. While the geographical and ideological divisions that now separate North and South Korea persist, the two countries share a long history and a uniquely Korean culture.

Geography

Korea is a peninsula, a term in Korean that means literally "half island," and it is indeed a peninsula—surrounded on three of four sides by water. The Korean Peninsula extends approximately 620 miles from north to south and is located some 124 miles from the Japanese island Kyushu across the Korea Strait. The Korean Peninsula's west coast is bordered by the Yellow Sea. The highly irregular coastline of Korea is 5,257 miles long.

The northern land border of Korea is formed by the Yalu (or Amnok) and Tumen Rivers, which have their sources in the region around Mount Paektu, an extinct volcano and Korea's highest mountain peak (9,003 feet). The Yalu River flows into the Yellow Sea, and the Tumen River flows east into the East Sea. The majority of rivers in Korea are short and flow from east to west. The longest river, the Naktong, is the one exception, flowing south from central highlands to a point on the southern coast near Pusan.

The total land area of the Korean Peninsula, including islands, is 84,943 square miles, of which 55 percent constitutes the territory of North Korea. North Korea occupies a total land area of 46,540 square miles, extending about 450 miles from north to south about 230 miles east to west. Its coastlines on the East Sea and the Yellow Sea run 1,550 miles. North Korea shares its total international boundary of 1,040 miles with three countries: China (880 miles), Russia

(12 miles), and South Korea (148 miles). The northern border with China follows the Yalu River for part of its course, according to an 1876 agreement, and the Tumen River for part of its course, accord-

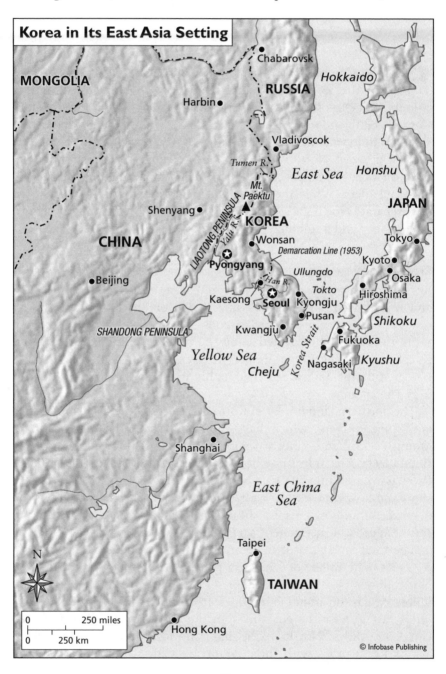

Korea in Its East Asia Setting

MONGOLIA

RUSSIA

Chabarovsk

Hokkaido

Harbin

Vladivoscok

Tumen R.

East Sea

Honshu

Mt. Paektu

JAPAN

Shenyang

KOREA

CHINA

Wonsan

Tokyo

Demarcation Line (1953)

LIAOTONG PENINSULA

Yalu R.

Pyongyang

Ullungdo

Kyoto

Beijing

Han R.

Osaka

Kaesong

Seoul

Tokto

Hiroshima

Kyongju

Pusan

Shikoku

SHANDONG PENINSULA

Kwangju

Fukuoka

Yellow Sea

Korea Strait

Cheju

Nagasaki

Kyushu

Shanghai

East China Sea

N

Taipei

TAIWAN

0   250 miles

0   250 km

Hong Kong

© Infobase Publishing

ing to a 1909 agreement. The border with South Korea is the Military Demarcation Line of 1953, which has not been formally accepted by either North or South Korea.

Mountains cover four-fifths of the Korean Peninsula. The major mountain ranges crisscross the country in northwest-to-southeast and northeast-to-southwest patterns. Almost the whole of north-central Korea is dominated by six mountain ranges: Machol-lyong, Hamgyong, Pujol-lyong, Nangnim, Myohyang, and Choguryong. Plains constitute only one-fifth of the land area in North Korea but contain most of the farmlands and human settlements. Farmland is found mostly in the broader valleys of the west coast areas. While only 15 percent of the land is arable, South Korea can feed itself through effective and intensive farming. The South does import food, but it is an option and a luxury more than a necessity. The North is not independent in food production and needs to import basic grains.

South Korea is bordered by North Korea to the north, the Yellow Sea to the west, and the East Sea to the east. The Korea Strait and the South Sea lie to the south of the peninsula. South Korea has a total land area of 38,023 square miles. The greatest distance north to south is about 400 miles, and east to west about 270 miles. The coastline along the East Sea and the Yellow Sea runs for 1,499 miles. South Korea shares its entire international land boundary of 148 miles with North Korea. This border, just north of the 38th parallel, includes a demilitarized zone.

South Korea is a rugged, largely mountainous country, with mountains and uplands constituting almost 70 percent of the total land area. The tallest mountain is Mount Halla (3,445 feet), an extinct volcano. (Mount Paektu, the 9,003-foot-high volcano mentioned above, is located in North Korea). Only 15 percent of the land in South Korea is made up of plains, and these are mainly along the coast. The major topographical feature is a chain of mountains, with the Taebaek Range at its core, running parallel to the eastern coast.

The four largest rivers within South Korea are the Han, with a length of 320 miles; Kum, 249 miles; Naktong, 326 miles; and Somjin, 132 miles. These rivers were once subject to great flooding in the summer, but now a series of dams control the summer monsoon runoff.

Climate

Korea has a continental climate with four distinct seasons. In contrast to the mild temperatures and variable winds of the spring and fall seasons, the winters are long and bitterly cold, especially in North

Korea, as a result of northern and northwestern winds blowing from Siberia. Winter temperatures, however, are subject to great variations, from far below freezing in the northern mountainous provinces to 25°F at Wonsan to the east. The daily average high and low temperatures for Pyongyang, North Korea's capital, in January are 27°F and 9°F. Average snowfall is 37 days during the winter. Although winters are less severe than in North Korea, snowfall is not uncommon in South Korea. The average January temperature varies from -5° in Chungcheong to 28°F in South Korea's capital, Seoul.

For both North and South Korea summer tends to be short, hot, humid, and rainy because of the southern and southeastern monsoon winds that blow from the Pacific Ocean. The summer monsoons, with their heavy rainfall, hit Korea in July every year. These occur in the middle of the summer because the wet clouds from the Tropics are blown north into Korea (and all of northeast Asia), where, when they meet cooler air, they drop their moisture. Korean agriculture is attuned to the monsoons, and the rain is welcome in the summer to water the rice crop and fill the reservoirs. There are also typhoons, which are associated with the monsoons. Typhoons affect Korea at least once every summer. The word *typhoon* means "great wind" in Chinese— essentially, a hurricane. Heavy downpours during typhoons can cause floods and widespread damage to crops.

In North Korea the daily average high and low temperatures for Pyongyang in August are 84°F and 68°F. Annual rainfall ranges from 22 to 60 inches, with the Tumen and lower Taedong River valleys receiving the least and the Imjin River basin and the upper Chongchon River valleys receiving the most. On the peninsula up to 85 percent of rainfall is concentrated in the summer months, especially in July. No region in South Korea receives less than 30 inches of rainfall annually, though serious droughts periodically occur. In most areas yearly rainfall is more than 40 inches.

Provinces

Traditionally, Korea has had eight provinces. With the division of Korea at the end of World War II, however, the south divided its provinces, and the north created new provinces so that each side now has nine. Regional differences can be seen in dialects; television dramas and movies often feature actors speaking in one dialect. Sometimes there are associations with the speakers of the dialect, such as implying the figure is from a rural area or is associated with

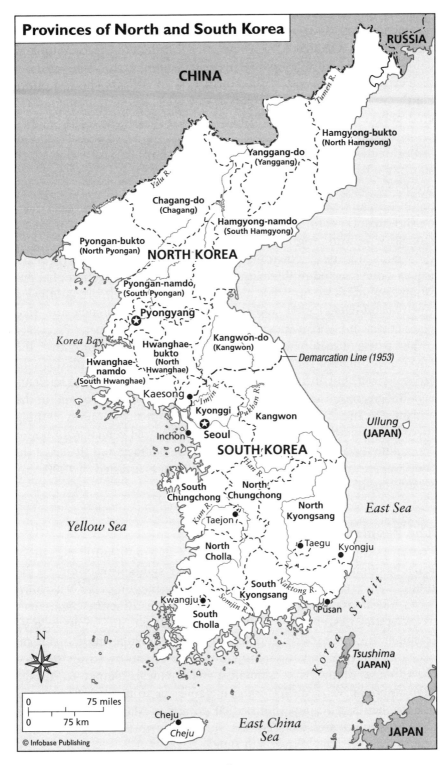

Provinces of North and South Korea

CHINA

RUSSIA

Hamgyong-bukto
(North Hamgyong)

Yanggang-do
(Yanggang)

Chagang-do
(Chagang)

Hamgyong-namdo
(South Hamgyong)

Pyongan-bukto
(North Pyongan)

NORTH KOREA

Pyongan-namdo
(South Pyongan)

Pyongyang

Korea Bay

Kangwon-do
(Kangwon)

Hwanghae-
bukto
(North
Hwanghae)

Hwanghae-
namdo
(South Hwanghae)

Demarcation Line (1953)

Kaesong

Kyonggi

Kangwon

Inchon

Seoul

Ullung
(JAPAN)

SOUTH KOREA

East Sea

South
Chungchong

North
Chungchong

North
Kyongsang

Taejon

North
Cholla

Taegu

Kyongju

Yellow Sea

South
Kyongsang

Kwangju

Pusan

South
Cholla

Tsushima
(JAPAN)

N

Korea Strait

0   75 miles
0   75 km

Cheju

Cheju

East China
Sea

JAPAN

© Infobase Publishing

Yalu R.

Tumen R.

Pukhan R.

Imjin R.

Han R.

Kum R.

Naktong R.

Somjin R.

a particular group that is up to no good (leaders of the two military coups in 1961 and 1980 were from the same region with a marked dialect). Sometimes one of the North Korean dialects shows up in a South Korean drama. Each region of Korea has its own unique food— cold noodles are a favorite throughout all Korea today but is known to be of North Korean origin.

Regionalism also shows up at the ballot box. In South Korea, the southwest has tended to vote as a bloc for their favorite candidates for president, whereas the southeast has liked other candidates. As the South Korean democracy has developed, both regions have been successful, in succession, in electing a president. Seoul, a city with many citizens who were originally from the countryside, is a microcosm of the whole country. At one time, from the 1960s to the 1980s, regionalism was divisive and problematic for Korea. With the election of opposition candidates in the 1990s, the formerly underprivileged southwest got its candidate elected, and the balance of power is such now that regionalism in not considered a major problem any longer.

The worst of regionalism occurred when the military took over the government in May 1980. Most of the country fell in line with the military takeover, but in the southwest, in the city of Kwangju, students and citizens took to the streets. The military cracked down, and in the end more than 200 were killed. To its credit, Korea has done everything it could to heal the wound by creating a memorial cemetery to honor those who died as martyrs to the cause of democracy, and the leader of the Kwangju resistance, Kim Dae Jung, who was arrested in 1980, was elected president in 1997.

The People

Koreans are proud of their racial heritage and uniformity of culture. Koreans often identify themselves using the symbolism of one of the foundation myths featuring an early king, Tangun, who was born when a bear prayed to become human. Koreans describe themselves as "We, the descendants of Tangun . . ." There are some records documenting migrations into the Korean Peninsula; most historical accounts indicate that the immigrants were of similar ethnic stock— the Chinese, Mongolians, Manchus, and Japanese. Numerous lineage groups, or clans, trace their founding ancestry to migrant Chinese. A few Jurchen and Khitan (both tribal groups in Manchuria) defectors and immigrants are also recorded, in addition to rare cases of immigrant Japanese, mostly in recent times.

Though Korea remains one of the most ethnically homogeneous nations in the world, contemporary Korea is more heterogeneous than it was in historic times. Because of overly successful population policies that have limited the size of families to one or two children—overly successful, because those policies have been reversed in recent years—there are not enough laborers and, even more critical, too few females for potential marriage partners for Korean men today, especially male agricultural workers. Partly as a result, large numbers of migrant workers have been welcomed to Korea. Often the migrant worker is tasked with difficult, dangerous, and dirty work—often abbreviated as the "three D's." These migrant workers sometimes stay in Korea for a few years before returning to their homelands. Others stay longer and in some cases marry Korean spouses and obtain Korean citizenship. Such migrant workers are sometimes racially the same as Koreans (i.e., mainland Chinese, Mongolians, or Vietnamese), though others are not (i.e., Filipinos, Southeast Asians, and South Asians), and in some cases immigrants are Caucasians from Russia. In any event, it is safe to say that the human landscape in Korea is changing. In addition to migrant workers the number of Filipino women in Korea has increased. It was once common for upper-class families to hire lower-class women as maids; now maids are hard to find, and significant numbers of Filipino women work as maids in upper-class Korean households. There are reports of Filipino women working in the same rural areas getting together to learn Korean and talk about child-rearing.

Language and Religion

The national and official language is Korean, a member of the Altaic family of languages. Korean is written in a largely phonetic alphabet called hangul, consisting of 14 basic consonants and 10 simple vowels. The letters are combined into syllables, some of which correspond to Chinese characters. Chinese loanwords form roughly half the vocabulary. The American presence in South Korea since the 1950s has stimulated the growth of English as the most prominent foreign language. English is taught in all South Korean schools.

In terms of the many tourist posters that often feature a beautiful Buddhist temple in a remote and scenic mountain retreat, one may begin to assume that Buddhism is the dominant religion of Korea, but Buddhism is one of four or five major religions in Korea today. Confucianism entered Korea with Buddhism between the third and fifth centuries; both came from China. Before the introduction of

Buddhism and Confucianism Koreans practiced shamanism in forms that probably included the king as a priest. Later, Christianity entered Korea. The Catholics came first in the late 18th century, and then the Protestants came in the late 19th century. The history of the Catholics and Protestants was so different, persecution of the Catholics and acceptance of the Protestants, that in the Korean language "Christian" means Protestant. At times, if Catholics are asked if they are "Christian," they will say "No, I'm Catholic!"

In more recent times, some Koreans have practiced various "new religions." These tend to be syncretistic—a blend of the major traditions—and to some degree nationalistic. Some of the new religions seem more Buddhist, some more Confucian, and some more like Christian sects. Others feature early Korean figures (mostly from mythology) in paintings hanging above an altar of the worship space.

Surveys rank the numbers of believers in Buddhism and Christianity as nearly equal in almost every case, some saying each claims numbers around 25 percent of the population, others saying each claims around 33 percent. Although there is competition between the two major religions, with only a few exceptions the two major traditions get along peacefully. With Buddhism and Christianity claiming more than half the population, what percentage of the people practice Confucianism? Here the answer is complicated. At one level, when a survey is taken, the number of Confucian "believers" is only 2 or 3 percent, but at another level, Confucianism is practiced by 100 percent of the people.

Confucianism can be classified as a philosophy rather than a religion, and indeed, by its nature, it is nontheistic. World religions specialists sometimes classify religions as "this-worldly" or "other-worldly." On that scale Confucianism is the classic "this-worldly" religion. As such, Confucianism is a set of social and political norms and guidelines on how to live in society. Great emphasis is placed on the family and education, and, indeed, these two values are primary in Korean society because of Confucian influence. Respect for one's parents and one's elders, loyalty to the state and to one's group (of various kinds), etiquette, politeness, and trustworthiness are all values in Confucianism that are easy to find in Korean society. In the school system students have one or two hours of ethics classes each week, and each school has a teacher who specializes in ethics. Although great efforts are made to be sure no single religion is featured in the public school system, much of the curriculum in the ethics classes comes from the Confucian classics.

Shamanism, like Confucianism, does not claim many believers in surveys because most of those who practice shamanism see themselves as part of the great Buddhist tradition, and, like Confucianism, at one level or another, shamanism shows up in Korean lifestyles such that one might suggest that 100 percent of Koreans practice shamanism. Although often criticized as *mishin* (superstition), shamanistic practices are observed for all to enjoy, such as at the dedication of a new building or a new car, truck, or bus. The little ceremony calls upon the spirits to protect the new building or mode of transportation and features ritual elements from a full-blown shaman's ceremony, specially featuring a pig's head or just a little broiled pork. Other aspects of shamanism show up in Korean life from time to time, such as praying to spirits or local gods.

Government

One of South Korea's greatest claims to fame is its example of developing a democracy. In the early years of the Republic of Korea, Korea was bogged down with authoritarian leaders, even dictators. The government was taken over on two occasions, in 1961 and 1980, by military leaders—in each case a two-star general. However, to Korea's credit, the seeds of democracy sprouted, and today a democracy with a peaceful transfer of power, a functioning legislature, and an independent judiciary is the pride of the Korean people. In some ways Korea might be more democratic than the United States. For example, universities now elect their presidents from among the faculty. At one point, under the authoritarian regimes, the minister of education had to approve the appointment of a president by the university's board of trustees.

The North Korean government is the last of the cold war–era communist states. Modeled after Stalinist Russia, the government controls almost every aspect of life in North Korea. Opposition to the single-party state is not tolerated, and offenders can be sent to correction camps, of which there are many. In foreign relations North Korea often runs into conflict with the United States.

North Korea's communist state has survived the fall of the Iron Curtain and the end of communism in Russia and Eastern Europe. The communist government of China has turned to a capitalist economy, leaving Cuba and North Korea the last of the cold war communist states. North Korea has been unique, however, in that transfer of power has been only from father to son. Kim Il Sung, who founded the state in 1948, turned power over to his son before his death in 1994. Now, Kim Jong Il has been rumored to be choosing one of his three sons to become his successor.

Economy

The economies of North Korea and South Korea could not be more different. South Korea is a showcase of capitalistic success. The North Korean economy is dependant on foreign aid to avoid widespread starvation in times of bad harvests.

The success story of South Korea began in the 1960s under the leadership of Park Chung Hee, who suppressed democratic movements, claiming that he first wanted to develop the economy. By the late 1960s the economy was booming with a growth rate of more than 10 percent per year. By the turn of the millennium, South Korea was hardly recognizable from the perspective of the 1960s. The South Korean economy today boasts world-leading production in shipbuilding, computer chip production, and cell phones. Other sectors of the economy are also strong, including automobiles, steel, and other manufactured goods. The strength of the economic development was at one time Korea's low wage, but as wages and standards of living rose, industry turned to robotics and other high-tech responses to remain competitive. With China's economy currently booming, South Korea is responding by investing in China by relocating factories to China and other overseas locations.

North Korea's economy, on the other hand, is not doing well. At one point in the 1960s, the North Korean economy was ahead of South Korea's. It had recovered more quickly from the war and had received significant aid from other Communist countries. With the end of communism in Eastern Europe, however, North Korea could no longer rely on aid or trade with Communist allies. In desperation it turned inward and developed its own philosophy called *juche,* or self-reliance. In order to raise more crops it began farming the upper hillsides. Unfortunately, the removal of the natural vegetation and the complex root structures of the shrubs and trees for the sake of planting corn and potatoes led to large-scale devastation when the heavy monsoonal rains came. Upland crops and soil were washed down into the lowland rice paddies, ruining both. The same rains fell on South Korea, but it did not have floods or the accompanying famine that North Korea suffered in the late 1990s and early 2000s. International aid has greatly helped North Korea. Aid has come from many sources, including the United States, despite the political tensions between the two countries.

1

FROM EARLY SETTLEMENTS TO THE SILLA UNIFICATION OF KOREA (PREHISTORY–668)

The story of the first Koreans began on the plains of Northeast Asia in an area sometimes called Manchuria, which today makes up the three northeast provinces of China. Related to early nomadic peoples, the first Koreans began migrating into the Korean Peninsula between 2,000 and 10,000 years ago. They did not come in a single wave. Rather, peoples of a similar culture and language, some earlier than others, gradually settled into areas north and south of the Yalu River, which forms the border between present-day China and North Korea.

Origin of the Early Korean Settlers

Since much of Korean civilization bears the marks of Chinese influence, it is easy to assume that Koreans descended from the Chinese. Among China's major contributions to Korean civilization are the use of Chinese characters, Buddhism, and Confucianism. Korea is clearly part of the Chinese cultural realm, but this was not always so. The earliest Koreans shared common traits with peoples in Northeast Asia, including similarities in religion, social organization, housing, and language. The Korean language shares some features with Mongolic, Turkic, and Manchu-Tungusic families, which is why some linguists classify it as Altaic, a language family quite different from the Chinese family. Chinese later came to have a dramatic influence on Korean: Today, as many as 60 percent of Korean words have Chinese origins. Korean structure, however, is very different from that of Chinese, indicative of a different origin and a separate language family.

Korean founding myths also indicate non-Chinese origin. The most popular Korean myth is that of Tangun, which was recorded in *The Samguk Yusa*, a Korean history written in 1285 C.E. It claimed that Tangun, the founder of Korea, who ruled the land wisely for 1,000 years, was born in the 50th year of the first emperor of China, 2333 B.C.E. Tangun was born when a bear and a tiger both wanted to become human. The heavenly being, Hwanung, told them that if they would live in a cave and eat nothing but garlic and mugwort for 100 days, they could become human. The tiger could not endure the confinement; the bear did, and its wish was granted. It was turned into a female human. Hwanung, finding her beautiful, took her to be his wife; she bore a son on the top of a mountain and named him Tangun. During the 1,000 years of his reign, the land was peaceful and prosperous.

Although the Tangun myth has similarities to the myths of the peoples of Northeast Asia, other Korean myths more closely resemble those found in Southeast Asia. These myths feature people being born from eggs or sailing in stone boats. While there is evidence that some people may have immigrated to the Korean Peninsula by sea from the south, if migrations in large numbers from the south had taken place, one would expect a larger influence from southern cultures on the Korean language, material culture, and religion than is evident today.

Another indicator of a northern origin of the Korean people can be found in religion. Religions, like myths, contain elements or symbols that can be traced to prehistoric times. The indigenous religion of Korea is shamanism. Although it is not highly structured and does not have a written corpus of belief, it has ceremonies and symbols that have been passed down since prehistoric times. One of its features is a ceremony led by a shaman (a spirit medium) to mediate with the spirit world. Symbols used in the ceremony include swords or knives, mirrors, and comma-shaped stones that resemble a tiger's or bear's claw. Mirrors and claws of jade are found in early Korean crowns buried with Silla and Paekche kings dating from the third through the early sixth centuries C.E. The kings were also buried with their swords. The royal regalia of the Japanese emperor also included the sword, the mirror, and the stone. Archaeologists theorize that these religious symbols originated in shamanism practiced in prehistoric Northeast Asia and that over time they made their way, with migrating people, into the Korean Peninsula and across the Korean Strait to Japan.

Physical anthropology provides other clues that Koreans originated in Northeast Asia. Physical anthropology is the study of humans as physical beings. Koreans possess several physical characteristics that tie them to Northeast Asia rather than to China, two of which are tooth shape and high incidence of a birthmark known as the "Mongolian spot." A large percentage of Koreans have ridges on the inside edges of the front teeth called "shovel-shaped incisors" by specialists. They share this trait with other peoples in Northeast Asia. Babies born by people from Korea and places in Northeast Asia also have the "Mongolian spot," a bluish-colored area of skin located low on the back. It is generally about the size of an adult hand, looks like a bruise, and fades away by the time a child is two or three.

Early Archaeological Findings

According to archaeologists several Paleolithic sites on the peninsula (dating 20,000 to 50,000 years old) and a very few Mesolithic sites (20,000–6,000 B.C.E.) predate the arrival on the peninsula of the first Koreans during the Neolithic period (6000–700 B.C.E.). It is unclear whether the earlier two stone ages were linked to the most recent one, the Neolithic Age, but it is quite certain that the Neolithic people were, indeed, the ancestors of the Korean people today.

The pottery of the Neolithic Age shows various styles and influences. One style, called the comb-pattern, shows a design on the side of the pots that looks as if it had been scraped with a comb. There was also a plain style of pottery, which is later found in combination with the comb-pattern. Archaeologists suppose that these styles originated with two different groups that migrated into Korea in prehistoric times and then joined together as one people. Early records from Chinese sources tell of a Ye people and a Maek people and later of a Yemaek people. Perhaps these historic and archaeological records both speak of the same event.

About the ninth century B.C.E. a bronze culture was evident in Korea. The earliest bronze technology was of the Scytho-Siberian style, a technology developed in Central Asia and refined in North Asia. The Scythians were great bronze workers, and as nomads they conquered other tribes thanks to their invention of a critical piece of equipment, the stirrup. Stirrups kept them on their horses while their enemies were falling off theirs. They were experts in other kinds of bronze work too. Later on, around the fifth century B.C.E., a different kind of bronze technology began to appear, influenced by Chinese culture. These bronze implements included mirrors as well as ritual vessels. The mirrors were handheld, circular objects about 6 inches in diameter with a highly polished side, the mirror side, and a decorated reverse side that often had a small handle surrounded by other designs. Ritual vessels included small pots and pitchers, apparently used in ceremonies. The record of these bronze artifacts points to early Chinese contact with Korea, and some historical records support this.

Among evidence of early contact with China is the myth of Kija, which tells of a refugee from China at the fall of the Shang dynasty, purportedly around 1122 B.C.E. (Shim 2002, 271). The Kija myth first appeared in the early Koryo period (918–1392), a time when the Korean court was

THE TANGUN MYTH IN PUBLIC LIFE

The first Pak ancestor came from an egg left by a flying horse, according to the founding myth of the Pak clan, and the first Kim came from an egg found in the forest, according to the founding myth of the Kyongju Kim clan. Koreans do not necessarily take these and other ancient myths at face value, but the Tangun myth is taken seriously by most Koreans. The Tangun story is accepted at the level of the national foundation charter and is considered an embodiment of the true story of the first Korean leader (Jorgensen 1998, 222). This point has ramifications for the generally accepted date of the origin of Korean history. Since Tangun was born in the 50th year of the Yellow Emperor of China, the equivalent of 2333 B.C.E., Korean history is widely assumed to date back 5,000 years.

Tangun is the object of worship by one sector of today's population, and some of the new religions that have arisen in the last 20 years feature an image of Tangun as the altarpiece. In 1993 North Korea reported finding the actual tomb of Tangun and his queen. The site has been built up and surrounded in recent stonework in a rather elaborate fashion. By asserting that the oldest Korean was a North Korean, North Korea reinforces its claim to legitimacy over that of South Korea.

Similarly, North Korea today claims historical primacy for its capital, Pyongyang. Pyongyang is more than 2,000 years old. Since it is older than the South Korean capital, Seoul, which is only 600 years old, North Koreans claim greater legitimacy for their capital and their state. The rivalry between the two states on the Korean Peninsula runs deep. Any claim that one may have over the other is used to bolster its status at home among its own people and abroad in the never-ending contest to encourage allies to accept one over the other.

cultivating close ties with China; this timing suggests that the myth may have been created as an alternative to the nativistic Tangun myth. In fact, each myth would be used at different times in Korean history and by different groups to support different political agendas. The Tangun myth became more popular with groups that wanted Korea to be independent; the Kija myth was more useful to those who wanted to show that Korea had a strong affinity to China. The degree to which the myth contains an

A recently built vintage cover protects the well where, according to legend, a horse flew into the skies and left an egg. When the egg hatched, a shining young boy emerged. About 12 years later this boy became the first king. It is believed that he is the ancestor of all the people named Pak (Park) in Korea, 9 percent of the population. (Academy of Korean Studies)

element of truth, in this case that there were Chinese immigrants, is open to question. However, there is evidence of Chinese immigrants in historic times, and therefore the myth of earlier Chinese immigrants may well capture some element of early migrations into the Korean Peninsula.

Another historical record indicates early Korean contact with China. About 700 B.C.E. Chinese records mention the name *Choson,* or *Old Choson.* The term was used again by a refugee from the Han dynasty named Wiman, who about 200 B.C.E. set up a kingdom in Korea called Wiman Choson. The name *Choson* is also used for a later dynasty when the term was revived in 1392 for the longest of the historic dynasties, which ruled for 518 years until 1910.

Kija Choson was a mythological dynasty about which little is known (Ho Jung Song 2004, 95). Wiman Choson left some traces, however, in Chinese records. The sophistication of the Wiman Choson society was evident in the legal code that survived. According to the record, murder was punishable by death; injury to another was compensated in grain; and theft was punishable by enslavement, the thief becoming a slave of the one whose property he stole. These laws delineate a fairly orderly and well-organized society. The historical record also tells of titles used by various officials in Wiman Choson, revealing a degree of social differentiation and sophistication.

Dolmens

One of Korea's claims to fame has been the number of dolmens found on the peninsula, large stone structures that date from the Neolithic and Bronze Ages. In Korea three types are found: a northern type, a southern type, and an intermediate type with features of both the northern and southern types. Those of the northern type are large, with stones more than two feet thick, 10 feet long, and six feet wide. Typically, the northern type looks like the Greek letter pi (π), a large stone sitting horizontally across two vertical stones. The social organization needed to create such a labor-intensive monument was quite sophisticated. It required an organized and fairly large population and the leadership of a strong ruler. In analyzing the stones, or megaliths, geologists have determined that many had been hauled for miles from their origins. The kind of technology required to move the stones was surely simple—a matter of rolling the stones on logs, digging pits for the vertical stones, covering the supporting stones with earth, rolling the top stone up the earthen mound, and then hauling away the earth to leave the horizontal stone perched safely atop the vertical stones. Nevertheless, it reveals a

More dolmens exist in Korea than in any other country. There are three forms of Korean dolmens, the larger—such as the one shown here—is identified as the northern style, the smaller version is called the southern style, and the intermediate type has features of both the northern and southern styles. There were once about 80,000 dolmens of both types in Korea. Now only about 30,000 survive. They have been listed as a UNESCO World Heritage Site. (Academy of Korean Studies)

degree of large-scale social organization that would have just become possible in the late Stone Age and early Bronze Age.

The southern-style dolmens are less impressive but much more numerous. They are small and built level with the earth, with the stone on top covering a stone chamber usually around two feet square.

The third style combines features of the other two styles. These dolmens tend to be built close to the ground, as in the southern style, but the stone on the top is large, somewhat like the northern style, although bulkier and cubic in shape.

In all three cases (the grander northern style, the humbler southern style, and the large-stoned third type) the dolmens appear to have been used as burial sites. Most have long since been robbed of their artifacts, but occasionally an archaeologist reports new findings. Some estimates say there were as many as 80,000 sites prior to the Korean War and about 30,000 sites today.

Korean dolmens received international recognition in 2000 when several of the dolmen collections, some set apart as national parks, were designated UNESCO World Heritage Sites.

Puyo and Koguryo in Early Chinese Records

Korea first appears in Chinese histories long before Koreans started writing their own history. Two early Korean states mentioned in Chinese records are Puyo and Koguryo. Little is known about them, but because they dared to confront their large neighbor China in battle, historians assume that they were not merely tribal federations but had developed into kingdoms.

Puyo, located north of the Yalu River, is first mentioned in Chinese sources as early as the fourth century B.C.E., and its name appears from time to time until the first century C.E., when the Chinese recorded that the Xiongnu, the Puyo, and the Koguryo were a threat to China from the northeast. By this time the Puyo were using the term *wang* (Chinese for "king") for their leader, which suggests that they had moved from tribal status to state. From 49 C.E. until the fall of the Han dynasty in 222 C.E., Puyo and China were allies, probably because of "leapfrog diplomacy": The Chinese liked to make alliances with the kingdom at the back door of their hostile neighbors. In this case, the hostile neighbor with which they shared a border was the Xianbei. Puyo was to the north and east of the Xianbei territory.

After the fall of the Han, Puyo assisted the Chinese state of Wei (or Cao Wei), situated to the north and east of the Chang Jiang (Yangzi River), in battles against Koguryo, their common enemy in the mid-third century C.E. Wei and Koguryo had started out at the fall of the Han with friendly relations, but war broke out in 244. At that point the Puyo-Wei alliance defeated Koguryo, only temporarily. Just as its own alliances helped keep it strong, alliances against Puyo destroyed it. In 285 Puyo was caught in a battle between the Xianbei and the resurgent Koguryo. The Xianbei armies toppled Puyo, and the king committed suicide. Some of his relatives fled to Okcho, a small state in the northeastern part of the Korean Peninsula, and others escaped to China. The Chinese propped up the kingdom for a time, but in 316, when the Xianbei drove the Chinese to the south, Puyo's last hope disappeared. Some of the remnants of Puyo were given refuge in Koguryo. There is some evidence that Puyo people settled in the kingdom of Paekche, which had developed in the southwestern part of the Korean Peninsula in the early third century.

The Koguryo first appear in Chinese records as the fierce tribe that was among the "barbarian" enemies of China in the northeastern borderlands in the first century B.C.E. By the first century C.E. they were already using the Chinese term for king, *wang*. Originally they prospered in the heartland of the region formerly called Manchuria.

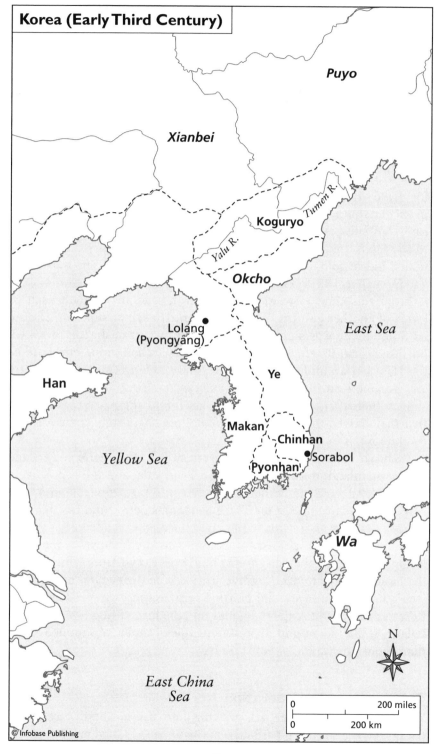

Korea (Early Third Century)

Puyo

Xianbei

Koguryo

Tumen R.

Yalu R.

Okcho

Lolang
(Pyongyang)

East Sea

Han

Ye

Makan

Chinhan

Sorabol

Pyonhan

Yellow Sea

Wa

East China
Sea

N

| 0 | | 200 miles |
| 0 | | 200 km |

© Infobase Publishing

9

The Koguryo gradually moved south into the Korean Peninsula and controlled the northern sections of it.

In 108 B.C.E. an emperor of China's Han dynasty sent troops to the empire's remotest border and set up four commanderies, or military outposts. Although three did not last long, the fourth survived, Lolang. It outlasted the Han dynasty, which fell in 220 C.E., and flourished as a center of advanced culture at the far-flung edge of Chinese civilization and the heart of Korean civilization. This Han dynasty outpost attracted the less-sophisticated Korean tribes, and Lolang became a great trading center. Its trading connections included even Sorabol, a settlement in the far southeast of the peninsula that later grew into Kyongju, the capital of Silla, one of the Three Kingdoms of Korea (ca. third century to 668) that unified the peninsula in the seventh century C.E. Koreans traded hides, gold, and other raw materials for Chinese manufactured goods, such as silk and bronze vessels.

From this time forward Korean culture had to evaluate itself in terms of another culture, one that presented itself as superior. During its time Lolang was a conduit of much cultural transfusion to Korea, but Korea had its effect on Lolang as well. When its parent dynasty, the Han, fell around 220 C.E., most of the Lolang Chinese stayed on and became Korean. Lolang was taken over by the Koguryo kingdom shortly thereafter, and Koguryo leaders found the place so attractive that they moved their capital to Lolang in 427, raising Koguryo's cultural quotient in the process.

Koguryo culture proved to be very resilient. Although it originated on the mainland, north of the Korean Peninsula, and the people were gradually squeezed out of that land down onto the peninsula, they later played a formative role in the Three Kingdoms period and beyond. The Koguryo state was resurrected at the end of the Unified Silla period (late ninth century), at least in name. It was then known as the Later Koguryo kingdom, then, beginning in 918, as Koryo, from which comes the modern name *Korea*. Koguryo has become the symbol of northern strength and legitimacy, and North Korea embraces it as such. North Korea asserts that its capital, Pyongyang, the former Koguryo capital of Lolang, could more rightfully claim the role of capital of a unified Korea than Seoul, the capital of South Korea.

The Samhan Confederation

When the Koguryo state was moving into the northern part of the peninsula, the southern parts had not yet formed kingdoms but rather functioned as three associations of tribes, or tribal federations. They were called the Samhan tribes: *Sam* means "three," and *han* was a Chinese loanword that probably meant "great."

After the fall of the Han, one of the northern Chinese states, the state of Wei, remained friendly with Koguryo. Relations were so good, in fact, that Wei ambassadors obtained permission to travel through Koguryo territory in the mid-third century to visit the southern half of the peninsula. These Wei dynasty travelers described their journey in what has come to be called the Samhan tribal confederations. These Chinese records give us a glimpse into early Korean life before the Koreans in the south started keeping records.

The Wei ambassadors told of three regions, and they described a number of city-states or walled towns in each. The Chinese character they used, a glyph with a border around the outside and people with weapons on the inside, can either indicate the border of a country or the wall of a city or town. The glyph is today always translated as "country," but at this time it was surely a city-state or walled town. In the southwest region, Mahan, the Wei travelers recorded 54 such city-states; in the south-central area, Pyonhan, 12; and in the southeast, Chinhan, also 12. In each of these regions, kingdoms later emerged. Paekche was

WRITING HISTORY

The chronology of the Samhan period is somewhat problematic. The travelers from the Wei dynasty clearly visited some time after the fall of the Han dynasty about 220 C.E., since the Wei dynasty came into being only after the fall of the Han, and the first reference to a Wei traveler to the area appears in the mid-third century. At that point the Three Kingdoms (Koguryo, Paekche, and Silla) had not developed, and the Samhan (tribal federation) was still in place. The Silla kingdom, the last of the three kingdoms to develop, eventually unified the peninsula, so it was also the one to write the history of the period. The problem is that Silla took some liberties with the historical record. Silla recorded the date of its origin as 57 B.C.E.—pushing it back 20 years before the founding of Koguryo. Many books, museums, and other places accept the Silla date without question and push back the date for the Samhan to times before 57 B.C.E., but the best account of the Samhan period comes, incongruously, from the late third century C.E.

established in Mahan sometime around the second half of the fourth century; Kaya appeared around the same time in the Pyonhan region; and Silla arose in the Chinhan region around the early fifth century.

Little is known about the Samhan tribes, but the Wei travelers described a people who were remarkably similar to Koreans of more recent times and even, in some ways, Koreans of today. They described them as wearing white clothing: Koreans of the Choson dynasty (1392–1910) and even the Japanese period (1910–45) also wore white clothing and at times called themselves the "white-clad people." The travelers described a people with great ceremonies, a people who enjoyed drums and dancing as well as drinking and singing. Like the Koreans of the Choson period, the Samhan people tied their hair up on the tops of their heads. Up to the turn of the 20th century, one of the rites of passage for a young Korean man was the "capping" ceremony: His long queue, which had dangled down his back as a youth, was ceremonially wound up and capped under the black, wide-brimmed horse-hair hat that was the mark of an adult male of the upper class. Indeed, many descriptions of the prehistoric Koreans of the Samhan period seem to foreshadow the culture that manifested itself later on, well into historic times.

The Three Kingdoms

In the first four centuries of the first millennium, Korea gradually entered the Three Kingdoms period (Jung-Bae Kim 2004). It may sound like a trick question: "How many kingdoms were there in Korea during the Three Kingdoms period?" The answer is "four." Koguryo continued to grow in power in the north. In the southeast Mahan gradually transformed into the kingdom of Paekche; Pyonhan developed into the kingdom of Kaya; and Chinhan became the kingdom of Silla. The kingdoms Koguryo, Paekche, and Silla survived into the seventh century, but from the third (or fourth) to the sixth centuries there were four kingdoms. Kaya, which fell to Silla in the mid-sixth century, is often overlooked, but it played an important role in the formation of Korea.

During this time Chinese cultural influences gradually seeped into the peninsula. Those areas closest to China developed them first while the more distant areas accepted Chinese culture and civilization later. History means literacy, and in Korea, literacy meant adopting Chinese characters. They were a poor fit, however. Korean is radically different from Chinese, yet the cumbersome set of Chinese characters was the only form of literacy available. As Koreans adopted Chinese literacy, they accepted the culture that came with it. That culture included Buddhism, Confucianism, and Chinese forms of government.

Chinese culture transformed Korea. The adoption of Chinese literacy and culture was felt in every area of human culture on the peninsula, yet beneath the Chinese veneer, Korean culture persisted. Through the next centuries Korea moved between the two poles of greater acceptance of Chinese culture on one hand and holding on to native Korean traditions on the other. Whether Korea lost more than it gained may be debated, but as far as most Koreans of the time were concerned, adopting Chinese culture represented progress.

Koguryo

Koguryo had developed out of the tribes of Manchuria into a state by the first century C.E. It had been described by the Chinese as filled with fierce warriors who had fought with the Chinese, the Xianbei, the Puyo, and others. Its own history states that the rule of its first king began in 37 B.C.E. Unlike similar beginning dates claimed by the other kingdoms, the date for Koguryo is probably fairly accurate.

Little is known about Koguryo from written records in the earliest periods, although they do appear often, but briefly, in Chinese records. Archaeology, confirmed by legend, tells more about early Koguryo. The most dramatic sites are the Koguryo tombs of royalty found in several

Painting from a Koguryo tomb depicting mounted warriors in full armor, including armor for their horses (Academy of Korean Studies)

13

The tombs of Kyongju. From Three Kingdoms Silla through Unified Silla, there are more than 300 tombs covering nearly 1,000 years of Silla culture. The tombs are partly the reason for naming the whole region of Kyongju a UNESCO World Heritage Site. (Academy of Korean Studies)

locations in northeast China. There are also city walls and mountain fortresses that survive in part also located in various places in what is today China.

Koguryo had suffered severe losses in battles with the Xianbei during the reign of King Kogugwon (r. 331–371), but the kingdom rebounded and restructured its institutions under King Sosurim (r. 371–384), who made two important decisions in 372: He established a Buddhist temple in the name of the state, and he set up a Confucian academy. Both were giant steps in adopting Chinese culture. Koguryo also adopted a Chinese-style bureaucratic structure and proclaimed a new code of laws.

The building years of the late fourth century were followed by the expansion years of the early fifth century, when Koguryo reached its zenith. A monument to King Kwanggaeto (r. 391–413), dated 414, commemorated his accomplishments. The stele is about 18 feet tall and five feet square, and its 1,800 characters are still mostly legible. It stands in China on the north side of the Yalu River, just across the border from today's North Korea, and there is an exact replica of it in the Independence Hall in South Korea. It is a magnificent document, perhaps the oldest lengthy document that survives from early Korean history. It tells of the conquests of King Kwanggaeto, whose name means "expander and opener of territory." According to the monument, he conquered 64 fortresses and 1,400 villages. His domain extended south along the east coast of Korea to a point about 100 miles from the Silla capital of Kyongju.

King Kwanggaeto's successor, King Changsu (r. 413–491), who ruled for 79 years, was also noteworthy. His name aptly means "long life," though most likely the title was given posthumously. (This was the case with later kings who were named posthumously according to their accomplishments, but were simply called "king" or "his majesty" when on the throne.) Changsu was a diplomat and successfully kept at bay contending Chinese dynasties, thus enabling a period of peace and prosperity. It was in his reign that Koguryo moved its capital to the former Han dynasty trading center Lolang and renamed it Pyongyang. Later in his reign Koguryo captured the heart of the peninsula, the critical Han River valley, by pushing Paekche farther south.

This was the height of Koguryo glory. In the Three Kingdoms Period control of the Han River valley was the single best measure of which kingdom was most powerful at the time. Koguryo had been an ally of Silla against Paekche in the early fifth century, but as Koguryo grew stronger and pushed against its two southern neighbors, Silla broke its alliance with Koguryo and made an alliance with Paekche. The ever-shifting alliances were one of the things that kept a balance among the triangular forces of the time and enabled three separate political entities to survive for three centuries in a relatively confined space.

Paekche

As Chinese influence increased in the south, the three separate but similar tribal federations called Samhan became more sophisticated. The federations were based in walled towns, each the center of a domain or region that the Wei dynasty travelers had called "countries." Those

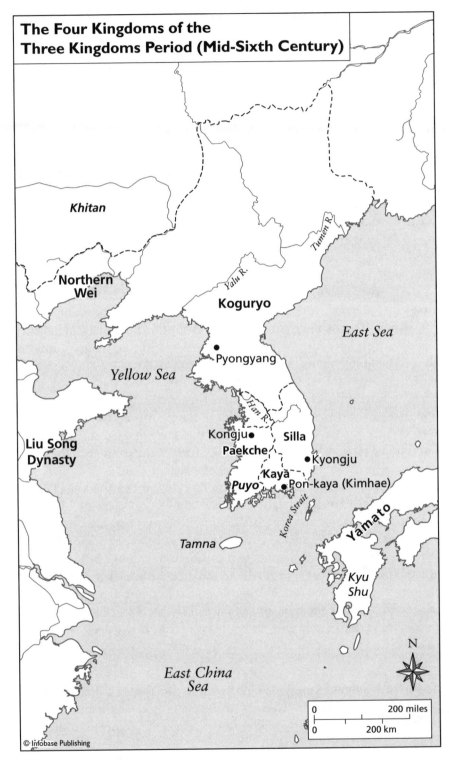

The Four Kingdoms of the
Three Kingdoms Period (Mid-Sixth Century)

Khitan

Northern Wei

Yalu R.

Tumen R.

Koguryo

East Sea

Yellow Sea

● Pyongyang

Han R.

Liu Song Dynasty

Kongju ●

Silla

Paekche

● Kyongju

Kaya

Puyo

● Pon-kaya (Kimhae)

Korea Strait

Tamna

Yamato

Kyu Shu

East China Sea

N

0   200 miles
0   200 km

© Infobase Publishing

16

alliances of walled towns developed into separate kingdoms, but the way Mahan-Paekche arose was different from how Pyonhan-Kaya and Chinhan-Silla developed.

Paekche was a conquered state. The name *Paekche* itself implies the process: It means the "hundred crossings"—referring to the many rivers the conquerors had to ford as they moved from north to south. There is evidence that the conquerors were the vanquished Puyo people who had once lived in northern Manchuria. In a series of defeats by the Wei, Koguryo, and Xianbei in the years 316, 346, and 380, the Puyo who survived were captured or scattered. Around the same time Paekche began to emerge as a powerful kingdom to the south, with a royal family named Puyo. It appears that some residents of the ancient Puyo kingdom fled to the south, conquered the less advanced people of Mahan, and created the Paekche kingdom.

The establishment of Paekche occurred in several waves. The earlier phase is sometimes called the proto–Three Kingdoms era. One of the first waves can be seen in a historical record from the year 246, when Chinese military forces that manned the Han dynasty outposts in Korea attacked the Han River area. The Chinese were beaten back, surprised by the strength of the defenses there. This is the first evidence that Mahan was making the transition to Paekche. Later historians pushed the horizon back as far as possible, to 18 B.C.E., as Paekche competed with Koguryo, whose founding date was legitimately in the first century B.C.E. The list of kings before King Koi (r. 234–286) is somewhat in question, but from Koi's time forward Paekche kings were powerful. It was he who defeated the Chinese in 246.

Information from later in King Koi's reign indicates reforms in government and the proclamation of laws. One of the new laws reveals a degree of sophistication requisite of a kingdom: Those officials who took bribes would have to pay compensation three times the amount of the bribe. More than the law itself, the degree of government organization necessary for bribery to exist implies a well-developed state, no longer a tribal confederation operating by the consensus of the member tribes.

King Kun Chogo (r. 346–375), a warrior king who presided over the final phase of the establishment of Paekche and the expansion of Paekche power, first drove southward and conquered the remnant of the Mahan people in 369, then turned northward against Koguryo in 371, killing the Koguryo king, Kogugwon. Now in control of the Han River basin and territory extending far to the north and the south, Paekche was the most powerful of the Three Kingdoms.

Paekche took advantage of its power to open contacts with the Chinese and the people of the Japanese islands who had formed the Yamato state. Paekche was to be a longtime ally of Yamato Wa (Best 1982, 443). When Paekche became a Buddhist state in 384, it became the most important conduit of the new religion to Japan, but the alliance went beyond Buddhism. In the early fifth century Paekche and Yamato Wa formed a military alliance to attack Silla. Their association was such that some 200 years later, in the unification wars of the seventh century, Paekche reached out to its old ally Yamato Wa for assistance once again before it succumbed.

In 475 Paekche suffered a major loss to Koguryo that forced them to leave the capital in the Han River valley and relocate about 100 miles to the south near present-day Kongju. The next two Paekche kings used contacts with the southern Chinese state of Liang to bolster their own sagging fortunes. Trade was apparently brisk, based on artifacts that have come out of tombs of that period. The tomb of King Muryong (r. 501–523) (sometimes written as Munyong), discovered in 1971, revealed so many Chinese artifacts that the archaeologist reported they would have thought they had a Chinese king's tomb on Korean soil were it not for specific stone inscriptions identifying it as the tomb of the Paekche king Muryong. The

An elaborate incense burner standing 25 inches (64 cm) tall depicting a mountainside teeming with animals and plants and crowned by a phoenix. It is a symbol of the artistry and refinement of the Paekche kingdom. This incense burner was excavated from a Buddhist temple site in 1996 near the ancient Paekche capital, Puyo. It is thought to be a sixth-century work. (Academy of Korean Studies)

king's trade strategy worked. Paekche recovered from its defeat at the hands of Koguryo and was soon to rise to the point of threatening Koguryo once again.

Before going against his enemies, however, King Song (r. 523–554) decided to move the capital to a more favorable location, only about 20 miles south to the modern city of Puyo. Indeed, he intentionally revived the memories of the glories of the once-mighty kingdom of Puyo, last seen on the Manchurian plains. For a time he called his kingdom "Southern Puyo."

King Song was ready to attack Koguryo, but this time, rather than face Koguryo alone, Paekche proposed to Silla that they combine forces to drive Koguryo out of the Han River basin. In 554 they succeeded, but Song's victory was to be short-lived. No sooner had the Paekche-Silla forces taken the Han River basin than Silla turned on Paekche, taking the territory that had once been Paekche's and driving Paekche forces south. King Song counterattacked, lost the battle, and was killed. Thereafter, Paekche considered Silla its worst enemy.

Kaya

It is unclear how Kaya emerged from the Pyonhan states. There were two centers for the developing walled towns of Pyonhan: One, inland and to the north, became known as Greater Kaya; and the other, near the coast, became known as Original Kaya. Some argue that Kaya never became a true kingdom but was just a barely developed tribal federation, which was why Kaya became the first state to be conquered by Silla. The existence of a historical record of a line of rulers who used the title *wang,* however, tends to contradict this claim.

An interesting foundation myth of the Kaya also survives. According to this myth the first king of Kaya was named Suro, with the surname Kim. He married a maiden who sailed into the harbor of Kaya (present-day Kimhae) on a boat made of stone. She is credited with bringing Buddhism to Kaya. She was from the royal family of a kingdom called Ayuta, a Southeast Asian kingdom that had adopted Buddhism. (Ayuta is the Korean transcription for what was the ancient Thai kingdom of Ayodhya.) King Suro and his queen had numerous sons, and they all took their father's surname of Kim. Feeling sorry that his wife's line was lost forever, he had his second son take the queen's surname, Ho. Their descendants are numerous in Korea today. Because the (Yangchon) Ho and (Kimhae) Kim families have the same ancestor, however, they could not intermarry then and do not today, with some exceptions.

The tomb of King Suro, the founder of the Kaya state. King Suro is ancestor to half of the Kims in Korea (the Kims from Kimhae), who make up about 10 percent of the population. (Academy of Korean Studies)

The two divisions of Kaya, Greater Kaya and Original Kaya, each fell separately to Silla. Silla conquered Greater Kaya in 532 and Original Kaya with the rest of Kaya in 562 (Young-sik Lee 2000, 1). Since Kaya fell in sections, some conclude that Kaya was never a fully developed state but a decentralized confederation of tribal powers in two or more places.

Perhaps setting a pattern for later conquests, Silla did not annihilate the royal line of Kaya but rather incorporated the Kaya royalty into the Silla aristocracy. A century later, when Silla attempted to unify the peninsula, the commanding general, Kim Yusin, was a "new Kim," that is, a descendant of the Kaya Kim line. The crown prince, Kim Chunchu, was of the "old Kim" line, a descendant of the Kyongju Kim line, and the two of them were brothers-in-law: Kim Yusin's sister married Kim Chunchu and became a royal princess. Kim Yusin, in turn, married the daughter of that marriage (his niece) in an example of how tightly interwoven the marriage patterns were for the aristocracy. It also shows that Kim Yusin, a "new Kim" from Kaya, was fully a member of the "old Kim" aristocracy. Later, at the fall of Silla and at the fall of Koryo, the aristocracy of these defeated kingdoms was welcomed into the aristocracy of the new kingdoms. This remarkable pattern of relatively peaceful continuity from one dynasty to the next may be unique in human history, and it began with the absorption of Kaya by Silla.

Paekche and Kaya both had strong ties with kingdoms in what is now Japan. Japan was not yet united as one political entity but was rather a series of smaller tribal federations. Kaya had an especially strong tie with the Japanese tribes in Kyushu, Japan's southernmost island. The archaeological findings of Kaya and Kyushu are strikingly similar. They clearly show that iron-making technology had moved from the mainland to the peninsula, to the islands. The inhabitants of Korea had learned more sophisticated metallurgy from China and North Asian tribes, and they passed that knowledge on to the peoples

KAYA LINEAGE AND LEGACY

Kaya, the fourth and least known of the early kingdoms, ironically has the largest lineage group in Korea today. Of 48 million people in South Korea, about 21 percent are named Kim. Not all of the Kims are related: There are Kyongju Kims, Andong Kims, Chongpung Kims, Chonju Kims, and others, but nearly 10 percent of South Korea's population claims to be Kimhae Kims—descendants of King Suro. The modern city of Kimhae is located on the site of the old Kaya capital. Two recent presidents of the Republic of Korea, Kim Young Sam (served 1993–98) and Kim Dae Jung (served 1998–2003), are members of the Kimhae Kim lineage.

The Kimhae Kim lineage is also the clan with potentially the largest numbers of false claimants to aristocratic status. Since the clan is so large, it is difficult to monitor descent accurately. As a result it likely has the largest numbers of former slaves and commoners who later claimed membership in a prominent clan. A legend exists about those who are true members of the clan and those who are imposters: All true members of the Kimhae Kim clan supposedly have a dot or freckle in the same secret place.

Besides the ubiquity of the name Kim, Kaya also left modern Korea with one other important cultural gift: the *kayagum*. This traditional stringed instrument, a kind of zither, is plucked as it lies across the lap of a musician who sits on the floor. The *kayagum* is similar to stringed instruments in Japan, the *koto,* and in China, the *guzheng*. The *kayagum* is a reminder of the heritage of the kingdom that flourished so many centuries ago.

who lived on the Japanese islands. Kaya was particularly adept at metallurgy and exported metal to the other Korean kingdoms and Japan. The iron cultures of Kaya and Kyushu are so similar that archaeologists have concluded that some of Korea's Kaya people must have crossed the waters to settle in Japan.

Some Japanese scholars reject this conclusion, however, and continue to support the position that the Japanese used to justify their colonization and takeover of Korea at the turn of the 20th century. According to this theory the Japanese tribes had established a settlement in Korea in prehistoric times. The theory is based on an early Japanese record, the *Kojiki* (712 C.E.), which mentions a place on the peninsula called Mimana (Grayson 1977, 65). Whether or not an early Japanese settlement existed, the evidence is clearly on the side of Kaya as the exporter of technology to Kyushu, not the reverse. Today nothing offends the Korean sense of nationalism and resurrects the images of the brutal Japanese takeover more than to hear of one of its former kingdoms referred to by the Japanese name, Mimana—it has become one of the symbols of Japanese abuses in Korea over the centuries.

Silla

Silla, the last of the Three Kingdoms states to be established, developed out of the Chinhan tribal federation in the third century C.E. Though the Chinhan federation consisted of 12 walled towns in southeast Korea, the Silla foundation myth features only six of them. These six tribes are associated with six villages in the area of Kyongju, which later became the capital of the state (Won-yong Kim 1982, 25). The six villages were located on four tributaries to a major river. They formed an alliance and made a member of the Pak clan, who may have come from outside the area, their first king. This was the first level of development and can be called the "small state stage." Hardly bigger than a city, the small state of Sorabol (to become Silla) began to consolidate power by taking over smaller city-states or walled town areas nearby, eventually controlling what is today most of the North Kyangsang Province, an area naturally bounded by mountains. One of the sources of the power of Sorabol was the superior weapons they had, both of bronze and of iron, weapons they had acquired through trade with the Chinese at Lolang. Sorabol is not far from the port cities of Ulsan and Pohang, and apparently Sorabol used both.

Separate from the six tribes was the royalty of early Silla: the Pak, Sok, and Kim clans. The succession of the early kings, which goes from Pak, to Sok, to Pak, to Sok, to Kim, to Sok, to Kim, shows a style of rotation that is more typical of a tribal federation than a state. In many ways Silla did not become a true kingdom until the time of King Naemul (r. 356–402), but the stages of development were in motion as early as the first century B.C.E. By the time of King Naemul and thereafter the kingship was well established and stayed in the Kim line, with one brief return to the Pak line at the end of the Unified Silla period (in 917). It was five kings later before King Chijung (r. 500–514) used the Chinese title for king, *wang,* which is one benchmark in the stages of developing a state. The use of the Chinese term *wang* probably does not imply adoption of Chinese institutions of government as much as it shows Silla's desire to appear as powerful or legitimate as the other kingdoms that had adopted the term. There was movement to adopt Chinese institutions, but the process was a long one, barely beginning at this point in Silla. Korean institutions persisted, and aside from a few exceptions, Chinese forms did not take over. One such native institution was the *hwabaek,* which apparently meant the "harmony of the white-headed," meaning a council of elders. A remnant of the tribal alliances from which the kingdom grew, the *hwabaek* continued to function well into the Silla kingdom.

Silla's capital, once called Sorabol, was later renamed Kyongju. It was a grand city with numerous sites that have survived to the present day (Youn 1998). At its pinnacle in the seventh and eighth centuries Kyongju was one of the three most prosperous cities in the world, along with Kyoto, Japan, and Chang'an, China. The city itself, with its many ancient relics, was named a UNESCO World Heritage Site in 2000. Two categories of sites are found in the city: those that predate the introduction of Buddhism, which occurred in the early sixth century, and those that are Buddhist in nature. Today Kyongju is called a "museum without walls" because of the numerous historical places there.

Among the pre-Buddhist artifacts two are particularly noteworthy: the numerous tomb mounds that dot the landscape, including the Flying Horse Tomb, and the astronomical observatory. The tombs are found in various sections of the city. They are rounded, somewhat natural-looking, grass-covered mounds, and some are the size of a three- or four-story building. The occupants of the tombs excavated thus far are not identifiable (Young-Duk Kim 1997, 35). Several elegant Silla gold crowns and other artifacts have been found inside the tombs. The gold crowns contain symbols that were significant in shamanism. Fixed to the stylized branches of the crowns were comma-shaped pendants of jade, most likely stylized bear claws or tiger claws. These symbols were probably

23

A *Silla crown, one of six excavated from archaeological studies of Silla tombs* (Academy of Korean Studies)

representations of actual animal claws that were years earlier worn by the tribal leader, who may have also had a shamanistic role in tribal society. Also dangling from the crowns were gold disks, symbolic of mirrors, another element in Northeast Asian shamanism.

In one of the excavated tombs, the one known as the Flying Horse Tomb, archaeologists discovered a unique and unusually beautiful artifact. On a piece of birch bark found with the equipment for a horse and chariot—assumed to be a mud flap—is a marvelous painting of a horse that seems to be flying. Its hooves, tail, and mane feather off into wispy clouds. Besides the painting of the flying horse and a gold crown, the Flying Horse Tomb held numerous additional artifacts.

Another important structure is an astronomical observatory built during the reign of Queen Sondok (r. 632–647) (Nha 2001, 269). A small but graceful structure, it resembles a large bottle. From the observatory the astronomers could observe stars and the moon and make accurate calendars, a necessity for the state. Farming could then be regulated, and eclipses could be incorporated into the royal record, so that such phenomena would not startle the people into believing that the monarch and court were out of sync with the heavens.

The reign of the queens is an interesting aspect of Silla rule. In all, three queens ruled Silla, including the last two rulers of the Three Kingdoms period. They did not rule in place of their husbands but were daughters or nieces of previous kings. Queen Sondok was on the throne when Silla conquered Greater Kaya. Queen Chindok (r. 647–654) was ruler when her cousin crown prince Kim Chunchu negotiated the alliance with Tang China that led to the unification of the peninsula. Later, in the Unified Silla period, the third of the three female rulers in Korean history, Chinsong (r. 887–898), followed two brothers to the throne. The

The depiction of a flying horse from a mudguard found below a king's saddle. It was found in the Flying Horse Tomb in Kyongju. (Academy of Korean Studies)

term *queen* was added in later records; it was customary while a monarch ruled to record only a royal title without the notation for gender. After the Silla period no other woman came to rule Korea in her own right.

Buddhism Arrives in the Three Kingdoms

Buddhism spread to the southern part of Korea later than it did to the northern kingdoms. The dates for the official acceptance of Buddhism—that is, the date when the court commissioned the building of a temple—are known for each of the Three Kingdoms. In Koguryo it was 372; in Paekche, 384; but in Silla, not until 527. These were the dates that marked the culmination of Buddhist efforts in each kingdom, not the beginning. It took time for the beliefs to be accepted by numbers of people and then the king.

The acceptance of Buddhism can be taken as a measure of the growth and development, and perhaps even military power, of each of the three kingdoms (Best 2002, 165). This is because the formal acceptance of Buddhism meant a great deal in areas beyond religion: With Buddhism came the Chinese writing system and literacy, and with literacy came many other ideas and items of Chinese civilization. By

This structure is described in the historical record as being an astronomical observatory built during the reign of Queen Sondok (ca. 581–647), late Three Kingdoms period, just prior to unification. (Academy of Korean Studies)

the time Buddhism was accepted and a state temple built in each kingdom, each kingdom also became familiar with Confucianism. These two great religions had dramatic impacts on the societies of the Three Kingdoms. Through them people began to see themselves as part of an international world tied to China and Japan as well.

The Three Kingdoms period, generally recognized as the fourth century through 668, was a time of war. At one time or another each of the three kingdoms was the most powerful. And at one time or another the other two formed alliances against the third. Each in turn broke alliances. It is not surprising that Buddhism was so successful at this time. Buddhism, a philosophy that transcends family and nation, answered the big questions: the meaning of life and death and the question of life after death. Confucianism, on the other hand, was concerned with earthly matters—society, good government, and ethics. At this time of warfare, when people lost their brothers, fathers, husbands, and sons, Buddhism helped the living to bury the dead.

The royalty and court ultimately accepted Buddhism, but not without opposition. Buddhist monks and lay members first had to spend some time proselytizing the religion. No details are known of how the process worked in Koguryo and Paekche, but a narrative, a kind of myth, indicates how Buddhism was finally accepted in Silla. According to this record the king personally favored Buddhism, and he had an adviser, a monk named Ichadon (501–527). Most of the king's court was not in favor of Buddhism, however, preferring instead the traditional religion of shamanism. Ichadon approached the king with an idea. He would write a decree naming Buddhism the state religion, and he would use the king's seal to make the decree official. He knew that the court would accuse him of forging the document and call for his execution. Ichadon would willingly submit to the accusation, he said, but before being executed he would make a prediction: Upon his death the sky would cloud over and rain flower petals rather than drops of water; the earth would shake; his severed head, rather than falling to the ground, would fly off to South Mountain; and milk, not blood, would spurt from his neck. The king agreed to the scheme. The document was written and proclaimed as if the king did not know. The court accused Ichadon of using the king's authority without permission, and he was executed. Just as he predicted, the heavens clouded over and rained flower petals, the earth shook, his severed head flew off to South Mountain, while milk, not blood, spurted from his neck. Everyone then knew that the Buddha had power, that Ichadon was a just martyr, and that the country should adopt Buddhism and establish a state-sponsored temple.

Aside from the question of what exactly happened at the execution of Ichadon, the story, if read between the lines, reveals certain facts. First, there was opposition to Buddhism. Although the king favored Buddhism, conservative members of the court did not. Second, through some mechanism, Buddhism was accepted over the objections of those who would have held on to a native religion rather than accept the foreign belief. The king at that time was Pophung-wang (r. 514–540); his name means "the raising of dharma"—dharma being the Sanskrit word for "the law," or the basic doctrine of Buddhism. The debate about the acceptance of Buddhism was the first of several over the ensuing centuries between those who wanted to accept Chinese cultural offerings and those who preferred a native Korean alternative.

Confucianism and the Code of the Hwarang

Like Buddhism, Confucianism spread to Korea from the outside. Even less is known about the acceptance of Confucianism, however, because architecture and icons are not as important to the Confucian faith as they are to the Buddhist faith. No buildings from the Silla period remain to record the adoption of Confucianism, but there is other evidence. The historical record tells of state scholars, implying they were well versed in the Confucian classics.

One of the noteworthy developments in Silla in the Three Kingdoms period was the corps of young people who studied martial arts and became the leaders of the military that would eventually unify the peninsula. They were called the Hwarang, literally the "knights of the flowers," a paradoxical term that implied preparation for battle while still honoring the gentle arts of humanity as symbolized by the flower.

The Hwarang knights had a code of honor that originated in the early 600s from the hand of a famous monk called Wongwang. Of its five points, three were Confucian in value: (1) loyalty to the king, (2) filial piety to one's parents, (3) trustworthiness to one's friends, (4) avoidance of indiscriminate killing, and (5) no retreat. The first three are taken directly from the Three Bonds and Five Relationships of Confucianism. The fourth is a reflection of Buddhism, and the fifth is a measure of the strength of the military spirit they developed (Tikhonov 1998, 318). This spirit lives on today in the Korean Military Academy; the road leading up to the academy is called The Hwarang Road, and the entrance to the academy is called the Hwarang Gate.

The Three Kingdoms and Japan

At the height of the Three Kingdoms period, cultural influences from China had a great impact on transforming the three states from tribal societies to sophisticated, literate, artistic, and wealthy kingdoms. Chinese influence did not end in Korea but was carried across the Strait of Korea to Japan. Subsequently, in the Asuka period (552–645), Japan enthusiastically adopted Buddhism.

All three kingdoms had had connections with Japan, but it was Paekche that left the greatest impression. Perhaps in a desire to secure an alliance to the rear of its rival Silla, Paekche was active in sending monks and artisans to Japan. Metalworkers helped pour large Buddhist images in bronze, and painters created scenes from the Buddhist sutras on the walls of the temple buildings. Some of the treasures of Japan from that period were developed through its contact with Paekche. For example, just outside the old capital of Nara, there is a Buddhist temple called Horyuji. The main hall was built in 607 C.E. with aid from Paekche visitors. That building, they claim, is the oldest wooden structure in the world. The temple complex was one of the first trea-

THE *HYANGGA*

One of the art forms that has survived from the Silla kingdom during the Three Kingdoms period is a form of poetry called *hyangga. Hyang* means "country" or "rural" (that is, indigenous as opposed to Chinese), and *ga* means "song"; thus, *hyangga* means "native songs." There are only 25 surviving poems, and they are hard to decipher, since they are written in a kind of *idu,* a Chinese-character script reformed to express pure Korean sounds and ideas. The *hyangga* often had to do with Buddhism and with death and warriors. The following poem is a prayer to Amitabha. Amitabha is one of the major Buddhist deity figures who, along with Sokyamuni (Siddartha Gautauma, the historic Buddha) and Vairocana, was worshipped in Korea and indeed throughout East Asia.

Oh, Moon.
As you travel to the West this night,
I pray thee, go before the eternal Buddha,
And tell him that there is one here
Who looks up to the throne,
Who is loyal to his vows,
Who chants with hands together, saying:
Oh, grant me eternal life.
Oh, grant me eternal life.
But alas, can any of the forty-eight vows be kept
While entrapped in this mortal frame.

Although this prayer, which is attributed to either a monk, Kwangdok, or his wife in the mid-seventh century, does not refer to him by name, it is clear that it is addressed to Amitabha because it speaks of the "West," and the Western Paradise is the home of Amitabha. The Western Paradise, or the Ultimate Paradise, was one of the better-known heavens for believers of Buddhism throughout East Asia. Amitabha appealed to the common people because he was more accessible than the other Buddhist deities. Indeed, one approach taught that a person needed only call on his name to achieve salvation. Many popular forms of worship grew up around him and the Western Paradise including simple chants. In this poem the repetition of the chant "Grant me eternal life" implies an endless repetition of the chant.

Source of the poem: Yang Chu-dong. *Koga yongu* (Research on Ancient Songs [hyangga]). Seoul: Ilchogak, 1965, rev. ed. 1983. Poem translated by Mark Peterson.

sures recognized as a UNESCO World Heritage Site in Japan. Inside the museum at Horyuji is a bodhisattva called the Kudara Kannon. It is a figure of the Goddess of Mercy (the bodhisattva Avalokitesvara, Kannon in Japanese, Kwanum or Kwanseum in Korean) made of wood. A bodhisattva is a follower of the Buddha who has gained the right to enter nirvana but stays back to assist fellow human beings. A seated figure 6.5 feet (2 m) tall, it is one of the oldest treasures in Japan. Unlike the stocky figures of the Buddha that are often seen in East Asia, this bodhisattva is elegant, thin, and lithe; seated with one ankle resting on the opposite knee, the figure has long, flowing hair. *Kudara* is the Japanese word for *Paekche*.

Paekche monks also carried books and literacy to Japan. Japanese, as an Altaic language, is very different from Chinese, and sometime after the importation of Chinese characters by Koreans, the Japanese modified the script, simplifying it to create the two forms of writing in the ninth century, *hiragana* and *katakana*, that are still in use today.

On the Eve of Unification

By the seventh century political entities in East Asia were becoming larger and more powerful. China had been reunified under the Sui dynasty (581–618), and Japan enacted the Taika Reforms in 645, which for the first time unified the country under a strong central government. In Korea the three main kingdoms struggled for dominance. One can measure which of the three kingdoms was the most powerful at any given point in two ways: One is to see which kingdom controlled the Han River basin; the other is to see which kingdom had an alliance with another. Koguryo, the first to form, was the largest and certainly the most powerful in the beginning, but it was Paekche, when it emerged as a kingdom, that first had its center in the Han River basin. As a military power, it was perhaps the strongest of the three when in 371 it drove the Koguryo armies back to the north and killed the Koguryo king.

Koguryo continued to grow in power, however, and in the early fifth century it responded to Silla's cries for assistance. Yet growing Koguryo strength frightened Silla and pushed it into an alliance with Paekche that endured from 434 to 554. In spite of the Paekche-Silla alliance, Koguryo then captured the Han River valley. In the end the newcomer and last kingdom to develop—the one that had requested aid from Koguryo and then an alliance with Paekche—became powerful enough to capture the Han River basin in 551. Silla now had an avenue to the Yellow Sea and access to China. This strategic advantage proved decisive because in the long run it was Silla's contact with Tang China that made the difference in its fortunes. From the fourth to the seventh centuries, alliances shifted, and the Han River territory was won and lost again. However, because of the Silla-Tang alliance, the triangular stalemate on the Korean Peninsula was about to change forever.

2

UNIFIED SILLA (668–935) AND KORYO (918–1392)

R eunification in China preceded unification in Korea. China had fallen into chaos after the fall of the Han dynasty in 220 C.E., but a powerful dynasty called the Sui (581–618) reunified all of China in 589. Like the short-lived Qin dynasty, which unified China but soon gave way to the long-lived Han, the ruthless Sui were not able to hold on to the unified empire and were replaced by the Tang in 618. These events in China had a ripple effect on the Three Kingdoms of Korea— Koguryo, Paekche, and Silla. Eventually, Silla, through its alliance with Tang China, conquered the other two and established the Unified Silla period, which lasted from 668 to 935. The unification of Korea brought about far-reaching changes in government, including the adoption of Chinese-style structures and an enlarged role for the king and the central government, accompanied by an increasingly wealthy aristocracy.

When Silla began to weaken in the ninth century, cracks in the body politic appeared along the lines of the former kingdoms. Though Kyongju was the capital of Unified Silla and for more than 200 years was the center of power for the whole peninsula, when it began to lose control of the outlying areas, the leaders of the resurgent forces drew on the memory of the former kingdoms. The rebels in the area that was once called Paekche called their new state the "Later Paekche" kingdom, and those inhabiting what was once Koguryo called their region "Later Koguryo."

The Later Koguryo, which was soon renamed Koryo, is the dynasty that eventually appeared on European maps and gave the West the name it still uses for Korea today. The Koryo court lasted for nearly 500 years, from 918 to 1392, enjoyed years of peace, but also withstood chaotic years of war. However, Koryo is better known for its cultural achievements than for its wars or politics. One of the greatest prizes of

Korean culture is the beautiful pottery known as Koryo celadon. The Koryo dynasty also saw two unique developments in the field of printing: The largest collection of Buddhist scripture was carved in the early 13th century on 80,000 wooden blocks for printing paper editions. At about the same time Korea was the first country in the world to develop metal movable typography, about 200 years before Johannes Gutenberg developed typography in Europe.

Warfare between Koguryo and China

Koguryo had been a longtime enemy of China during the time of the Han dynasty and continued to be an enemy of some of the smaller Chinese states after the fall of Han. When the state of Sui unified China, it reflexively looked to Koguryo as a serious threat to its northern border. Sui mounted a campaign against Koguryo. When this failed, Sui tried again and then a third time.

One of the greatest heroes in Korean military history was the general Ulchi Mundok (fl. early seventh century), who defended Koguryo against the Sui. Most of the fighting took place on the Liaodong Peninsula in Manchuria, not on the Korean Peninsula. In one of the battles with the Sui dynasty, however, the Chinese forces spilled into the Korean Peninsula and closed in on the capital, Pyongyang. General Ulchi Mundok devised a plan whereby the Korean soldiers would feign defeat. The Chinese, thinking a rout was on, pursued the Koguryo soldiers. Soon they came to a river, then called the Sal, now called the Taedong (Gabriel 1994).

There, the Korean forces waited for the Chinese army to spread itself out as it crossed the river. At the moment when the Chinese were not expecting it, the Koreans attacked and slaughtered thousands of the enemy. One account says the Chinese started with 300,000 men in their army and returned with only 2,700.

Little else is recorded about him, but Ulchi Mundok is remembered as a great hero. Although his family name was not passed down to the present day (unlike that of the Kims and others from Silla), still he is remembered. One of the major streets in downtown Seoul bears his name, Ulchi-ro. After the Sui founder died, the state was unable to maintain its dynasty. Sui's repeated attempts to conquer the Koguryo, which caused the deaths of thousands of Chinese soldiers and the bankruptcy of the royal treasury, led to its downfall.

The Sui dynasty was followed by the Tang dynasty (618–907), and they, too, tried repeatedly to conquer Koguryo. However, Koguryo proved remarkably resilient. It withstood six invasions from two of the most powerful dynasties China would ever know.

In the meantime, the southern part of the Korean Peninsula was locked in hostilities. Paekche attacked Silla, and Silla turned to Koguryo for an alliance to beat back the invasion. The competing three kingdoms had endured from the third to the seventh centuries through a balance of power. Like an equilateral triangle, a strong geometric structure, the three-sided political configuration remained well balanced. Whenever one side seemed strong enough to take advantage of a weaker side, the weaker side would form an alliance with the third side, and the result was a stalemate and a continuation of the Three Kingdoms. By the mid-seventh century, however, these dynamics began to change because China had been reunified. Koguryo, preoccupied with invasions from China, turned down Silla's request for an alliance after 642.

The Tang-Silla Alliance

Silla now made the decisive move. The Silla crown prince, Kim Chunchu (later to be King Muyol, r. 654–661), personally visited Chang'an, the Tang capital, and presented a proposal to the emperor: If China would first aid Silla in battles against Paekche, then Silla would assist China in a combined attack on Koguryo. China accepted the alliance. In 660 China sent its naval forces across the Yellow Sea, and Silla forces poured

THE PAEKCHE COURT WOMEN

Although Silla emerged as the winner (and in most accounts the hero), the virtue and noble heroism of the Paekche court women were immortalized in a legend. According to the legend when Silla forces were about to enter the Paekche capital, Puyo, and the palace was about to fall to the conquering army, the women of the palace fled. They ran to the edge of the capital where a high cliff overlooked a river. There, rather than submitting to the Silla soldiers and being carried off as slaves of the conquering army, the women jumped off the cliff to their deaths in their colorful court costumes. From that time forth the rocky outcropping overlooking the river has been known as Nakhwa-am, "the cliff of the falling flowers." The story of the virtuous Paekche women is retold as a moral ideal for women today. Even in defeat, Paekche is still seen as a symbol of goodness and valor.

Reportedly the tomb of Kim Yusin, located on the outskirts of Kyongju. Kim was a Hwarang knight who later became a general and led the Silla armies in conquering Paekche and Koguryo, unifying the Korean Peninsula in 668. He was a descendant of the Kaya Kim aristocracy that survived and intermarried with the Silla aristocracy. (Academy of Korean Studies)

over the mountains, trapping Paekche soldiers between them. Paekche fell the same year. Just before its fall Paekche called on its ally Japan for aid. However, Japan was not in a position to respond.

With Paekche conquered by the combined forces of Tang and Silla, the alliance turned its attention to Koguryo. The stage was set for what should have been one of the greatest battles in history. Mighty Koguryo, which had successfully fought off six major invasions from China and had contributed to the fall of the Sui court, would now have to face enemies on two sides. Would Koguryo withstand the assault? In anticipation of a difficult battle, Silla forces marched north as Tang forces marched east.

However, during the relative peace that ensued when Tang focused its attention on Paekche, Koguryo had turned on itself. Dissension within the ruling elite on how to face their enemies led to a divisive palace coup in 666. Forces loyal to the old king remained in control of some areas, and the country split. When the forces of Tang and Silla marched in, they discovered that the anticipated great battle was not to be. The Koguryo forces were so overwhelmed and divided that hardly an arrow flew before the Koguryo kingdom fell in 668. Many soldiers fled and later became part of a new kingdom that formed on the far

35

borders of Silla and Tang called Parhae (*Pohai* in Chinese) (Ki-ho Song 1999, 104).

Except for the most remote eastern section where the Parhae kingdom was later established, most of the Koguryo territory fell to the conquering allies. The victors then proceeded to quarrel with each other. The fighting between the Tang and Silla ended fairly quickly, however, in favor of a diplomatic settlement in 676.

The Tributary System

Under the terms of their treaty, Silla became a part of the Tang tributary system. The Chinese system of demanding tribute was very different from that of other empires. Typically in history, a conquering empire exacting tribute from a subordinate state would demand as much as possible, often impoverishing the conquered people. Sometimes the subordinated people would provide slaves or court women for the empire. This was not the case with China. Although it fluctuated in its generosity, often showing more exploitative trends at the beginning of a dynastic period, the Chinese court generally made modest demands for tribute. When the tribute was delivered, the Chinese court benevolently responded by giving gifts in return. At times the Korean court would send tribute missions when it was not required because of the economic benefit to Korea. The side trade, called "tribute trade," that accompanied the missions was often beneficial to the diplomats themselves, and as a result Korean diplomats pushed for any good reason to send a tribute mission to China. This system began with the Tang and Silla and continued during most of the dynasties to follow.

In the early years of the Silla-Tang relationship, the recent warfare marred the relationship. As time went by, however, a peaceful and prosperous tributary relationship took root. Silla did not control the entire peninsula. Tang, by right of its role in the conquest of Koguryo, demanded the northern third of the Korean Peninsula. For a time Tang even maintained military bases in former Paekche territory. Eventually, the Tang forces left Silla territory and retreated to the line on the northern third of the peninsula, where they had some problems with the Parhae.

As time passed the Chinese court took on a "big brother" attitude, and Korea took great pride in its "little brother" role, especially as acceptance of Confucianism grew. One of the five basic relationships of Confucianism is the relationship between older and younger, and that relationship is often cast in terms of brothers. Korea, proud of its younger brother status, considered itself a loyal (another Confucian virtue) member of the Chinese realm.

Unified Silla

Unified Silla (668–935) was prosperous. Its capital, Kyongju, was a crossroads of trade between China and Japan (Farris 1996, 1). Silla was mentioned both in Arabic sources of the time and in the famous Japanese book *Tale of Genji*. There were reportedly 35 mansions in Kyongju, some with separate quarters for each of the four seasons. A late ninth-century census records more than 175,000 households. One report states that there were no thatched-roof houses in the city—all were tile-roofed. That report may have been exaggerated, but Kyongju clearly was an opulent city. One Tang source tells of the wealth of the ruling class and says that the highest officials had as many as 3,000 personal slaves.

Another measure of the glory of Silla is the art, architecture, stone carvings, and Buddhist temples that survive. Only a small fraction of the 203 temples that archaeologists say existed in the Kyongju area at the height of Silla rule remain, but they do suggest how wealthy the kingdom was.

One of the Buddhist remnants of note is the Emille Bell, created in the mid-eighth century, one of the largest bells in East Asia. The bell is rung by a wooden battering ram from the outside, not by a clapper inside the bell, as in the West. Its sound reverberates over and over for several seconds and carries a long distance. The bell's purpose is to call all sentient beings to worship the Buddha. The Emille Bell gets its name from an old Korean word that means "mother" or "mommy," because the reverberations of the bell suggest the sound of a small child calling its mother. This haunting sound gave rise to a legend about the difficulties the metalworkers had in pouring the bell from molten bronze: After several failures, one of the foundry workers offered his young daughter as a human sacrifice. Then the bell worked. But the haunting voice of the young girl can be heard each time the bell is rung. The legend raises the question of whether human sacrifice was practiced in early Korean history. The legend is an isolated case, however. Because there is no other evidence of such practice from early history, scholars conclude that human sacrifice was not practiced and that the legend represents merely a folktale explaining the haunting sound of the bell.

Some of the best art pieces of the time were stone carvings, which still survive. The granite Buddha sitting in a man-made cave high on

Early Unified Silla (Mid-Eighth Century)

Khitan

Yuexi

Parhae

Tumen R.

Yalu R.

East Sea

Yellow Sea

Silla

Tang

Han R.

●Kyongju

Korea Strait

Heian

East China
Sea

N

0   200 miles
0   200 km

© Infobase Publishing

the hills east of Kyongju overlooking the East Sea was carved at this time (751). The Buddha figure, known as Sokkuram ("the Buddha in the stone cave") was designated a UNESCO World Heritage Site

HWARANG SEGI, A HIGHLY CONTROVERSIAL DISCOVERY

In 1989 a manuscript that was allegedly a copy of the *Hwarang Segi* was found in a small South Korean town. It was purportedly transcribed by a Korean clerk who had worked in the Japanese imperial household and had had access to the imperial library. The *Hwarang Segi* is a detailed biography of 16 Hwarang knights, describing the life and activities of Silla aristocracy. Allegedly written by Kim Taemun in the early eighth century, it speaks of the personalities alive at the time of the unification under Silla. The oldest existing history of Korea, the *Samguk Sagi* of 1145, written by Kim Pusik centuries after Silla unification, mentions both Kim Taemun and the document.

The original document is not available, reportedly because some of the account is not favorable to Japan. One such event was a record about the gift of a princess given by the Japanese king to the Silla king, but the Silla king in turn bestowed the gift on one of his advisers, a degradation of the Japanese princess and an insult to the Japanese.

The account is interesting in that it is a detailed and personal narration of life in the palace and the interaction between royal and aristocratic people in the early eighth century. All previously known accounts have been of an official nature, far removed from the day-to-day interactions of real people. If the *Hwarang Segi* account is authentic, the insights into early Korean behavior and attitudes are remarkably revealing.

Most scholars have dismissed the document as a hoax, but there are some factors that the skeptics have not explained very well. For example, the *Hwarang Segi* describes a moat around the old Silla palace, for which no evidence existed at the time the document surfaced. After the document was found archaeologists unearthed the moat. More than isolated incidents, though, it is the internal evidence and account of the relationships between the royalty and aristocracy as a whole that is most convincing to the scholars who think the record is authentic.

Source: McBride, Richard D. "The Hwarang Segi Manuscripts: An In-Progress Colonial Period Fiction." *Korea Journal* 45:3 (Autumn 2005): 230–260.

Pulguksa Temple, the temple of the Buddhist Land, built in 751, Kyongju. This temple was one of the first three UNESCO World Heritage Sites designated in Korea in 1997. (Academy of Korean Studies)

in 1997. The image apparently was inspired by travelers and artisans from Central Asia. The walls surrounding the Buddha contain bas-relief sculptures of the disciples of the Buddha, many of whom have Caucasian features, long faces, and big noses. There is some evidence that artisans from Central Asia posed for the sculptures. There are also clearly non-Korean guardian figures at some of the tombs of kings, again attesting to the cosmopolitan nature of Silla society.

Silla monks and others traveled to Chang'an, the Tang capital. Some even journeyed to India. A notable example was a monk named Hyecho (704–787), who made at least two pilgrimages to India. We know his story because his diary was discovered in the 1930s behind a false wall in one of the Tunhwan caves in western China along the silk route. The diary gives details of visits to the various kingdoms of India and some kingdoms in the territory west of India. He made one trip by land through China and one by sea through Southeast Asia.

One of the most important travelers was a monk who never made the trip to China or India. In fact, he could not even get beyond the borders of Silla, yet he became one of Korea's most important figures in Buddhism. His name was Wonhyo (617–686). Wonhyo tried to go to China once by land through the northern territory but was stopped at

Carved from a single piece of granite and standing 10 feet tall, this magnificent stone Buddha is located inside a human-made cave high on the hill above Pulguksa Temple. The depiction of Buddha's disciples on the walls show Caucasian features, implying perhaps that artisans from Central Asia helped with the project and posed for the artists who carved the stone. (Academy of Korean Studies)

the border by Chinese guards, who said his description matched that of a criminal, a smuggler they were looking for. He tried again later to go by sea. He traveled across the Korean Peninsula from Kyongju on the east coast by land to the west coast to book passage on a ship in a port city. As the travelers neared the coast a storm blew in, and they had to take refuge in a cave in the hills overlooking the port. Thirsty and tired, they fumbled in the darkness and found broken pottery pieces that were large enough to catch rainwater dripping at the mouth of the cave. When they awoke the next morning, they found that they were in a crypt and that the "pottery" was a skull. Wonhyo took this as an omen that he should not make the journey to China. His decision to stay home proved providential for him. Whereas other monks would go and return to advocate the teachings of one school and one master, Wonhyo combined the teachings of several travelers and synthesized the various beliefs into a common belief system that became the core of Korean Buddhism. Wonhyo became known as the "Father of Korean Buddhism."

Though a Buddhist monk, Wonhyo was also the father of another important historical figure. Through a brief relationship with a princess, Wonhyo became the father of Sol Chong (660–730), who became one of the first Confucian scholars in Korea. In fact, he was the first to be enshrined in the National Confucian Shrine, and some refer to him as the "Father of Korean Confucianism." Consequently, Wonhyo was not only the father of Korean Buddhism but also the grandfather of Korean Confucianism.

Sol Chong was an important historical figure for an additional reason. Although his scholarly work was mostly in classical Chinese, he also saw the need to write in Korean. Since the Korean alphabet was not invented until 1446, Koreans at the time modified Chinese characters to reflect uniquely Korean aspects of language, such as grammatical particles and inflections. It was a cumbersome system, given that Chinese and Korean were so different. Before Sol Chong many different and inconsistent systems existed side by side. Sol Chong's contribution was his proposal for a uniform and systematic use of specific characters for specific usages. The system of using Chinese characters for writing Korean, called *idu*, literally "clerical readings," was used by government clerks for daily record keeping. Classical Chinese was the lingua franca of most of Asia, and Korean scholars were as proficient in the language as the Chinese. The situation was not unlike that of medieval Europe, where the educated used Latin, whether they lived in England or on the Continent.

IDU, A WAY OF WRITING KOREAN WITH CHINESE GRAPHS

Using Chinese graphs to write Korean words, grammatical suffixes, and verbal endings—all phonetic elements—was a difficult match. Chinese script is actually based on pictures, called pictographs, and on interpretations or extensions of the pictures' meanings to create abstract ideas, or ideographs. Linguistically, Chinese is a mono- and duosyllabic tonal language with a simple grammar. Korean, on the other hand, could not have been more different. It is a polysyllabic, nontonal, agglutinative, highly inflected language. The result of using Chinese graphs to write in Korean was a cumbersome system that was nonetheless used for more than 13 centuries, until 1900. In spite of its awkwardness, it was used even after the Korean alphabet was invented in 1446.

When Koreans first started using Chinese characters—the only script known to them—they looked for ways to modify the script to write uniquely Korean sounds. The various systems were consolidated and standardized by Sol Chong in the early eighth century.

To understand the issue, a simple sentence may serve as a sample: "I am going home" is *wo hui jia* in Chinese and *nanun chibe kamnida* in Korean. Some of the words in Korean can use the equivalent Chinese character: I = *wo* = *na*; go = *hui* = *ka*; home = *jia* = *chib*. The other parts of the sentence are structural elements: -*nun* is a subject marker; -*e*, a dative marking; and -*mnida,* a declarative, polite, formal sentence ender. Each of these elements, however, would use a Chinese graph for its pronunciation, ignoring the inherent meaning of the graph.

Since all Chinese graphs have meaning, using a character for its pronunciation only is problematic. How would the reader know which graphs were used for their meaning and which were used for the pronunciation alone? The answer Sol Chong devised was to designate a limited number of graphs for the most common grammatical affixes used in Korean. For example, for the graph used phonetically as a subject marker in the sentence above, *nun,* Sol Chong suggested that Korean writers always use the Chinese graph for "shadow" and none other. Similarly, for each of the common grammatical particles, they should consistently use only one graph for each sound. The graphs assigned for this purpose were usually seldom-used graphs. Thus, a system was developed that could be used to write Korean sentences even though the linguistic structure of Korean was so completely different from Chinese.

Buddhism and Confucianism

Buddhism and Confucianism have had a complex relationship over the centuries. They entered Korea at roughly the same time (between the fourth and sixth centuries), but it was Buddhism that had greater appeal in the Silla period and indeed through much of the Koryo period (918–1392). Confucianism grew in power throughout the Koryo period and then came to completely dominate the Choson dynasty (1392–1910).

Once Silla's ruler adopted Buddhism in the early sixth century, the religion received official royal patronage. It remained largely limited to the social elite until the Unified Silla period, when two monks, Uisang (625–702) and the above-mentioned Wonhyo, helped to turn it into a popular movement. Each social strata in this highly stratified society soon had its own designated temples—there were royal temples, many levels of aristocratic ("head rank") temples, and various lower-class or commoner temples at the bottom of the hierarchy. Buddhism continued to flourish throughout the Koryo period. Eventually, by the late Koryo period this strong Buddhist presence comes to be described as excessive and corrupt. The Choson founders criticized what they saw as an over-grown Buddhist institution. By then monasteries controlled large tracts of land and even owned slaves, many of whom had been impoverished free men who sold themselves into slavery to ward off starvation during the hard years of the Mongol invasions and thereafter in late Koryo. The monasteries also employed armies. The support of the numerous temples and monasteries, which were exempt from taxation and thus attracted large numbers of monks and nuns seeking to escape taxation and government services, had become a serious burden on the national economy.

The late Silla period, at the height of Buddhist achievement in Korea, also witnessed one of the greatest scholars of Confucianism, Choe Chiwon (859–ca. 910). He first made a name for himself by going to Tang China and passing the civil service exam, which provided him entry into Chinese government service. After serving in several positions, he returned to Kyongju, expecting a high position. The Silla court, finding him too qualified for a central government position, kept him at arm's length by assigning him to a series of provincial positions. Finally, despairing of ever finding a significant position in his home country, Choe retired to the countryside. Although he never reached high levels of government power, in his retirement he instead served as an important Confucian scholar and teacher who taught numerous disciples. Later, with the fall of Silla and the rise of Koryo in 918, many of his disciples and their students came to play important roles in the new dynasty. For his contributions Choe Chiwon became the second man named a "sage" in the National Confucian Shrine.

Economy

The economy of Silla was primarily based on agriculture. The reservoirs that existed at this time indicate that flooded rice paddies had been developed. Intensive rice agriculture that featured transplanting of seedlings was not developed until sometime later, but rice sown by broadcasting was cultivated (Nelson 1982, 531).

One of the reasons the Kyongju area came to dominate first the Silla territory of the southeast of the peninsula and later the whole peninsula was its external trade. With ready access to the sea, the Kyongju aristocracy was able to sail around the south coast of Korea and up the west coast to the port of Lolang, where they could trade local products for iron implements and weapons from China, giving Silla an advantage over its neighbors, who at the time had only bronze. By the fifth century and after, Silla merchants traded directly with China and Japan. Items from West Asia appeared in the tombs of Silla royalty at Kyongju, indicating that Silla participated in the silk route trade.

In addition to traders and farmers there were numerous artisans. There must have been a large sector of the population involved in the making of ceramics. Numerous examples of pottery and records of roofs covered in tiles survive from the Silla period. Artisans worked in wood, leather, gold, iron, and bronze.

The large number of Buddhist temples—there were 203 temples in Kyongju alone—must have played an important role in the economy. They required laborers for their upkeep, farmers to tend the temple lands, and artisans to create buildings, paintings, sculptures, and bronze bells.

The central government must have imposed a high tax payment on conquered peoples. No records of the tax rate survive, but it was sufficient to maintain an army, navy, and luxurious lifestyle for the aristocrats. Taxes were collected in three forms: rice and other crops; specialty items such as animal skins, medicinal herbs, various kinds of ore, and other unique products from each area; and manufactured items including woven cloth and other handicrafts.

ENNIN: INSIGHTS FROM A TRAVELING MONK FROM JAPAN

In the mid-ninth century a Japanese monk named Ennin (794–864) traveled to China and kept a detailed diary that not only tells much about Japan and China but also provides surprising insights into Korean history. He departed Japan for China by sea in 838, where he stayed for nine years and amassed a collection of more than 500 scrolls and artifacts.

Ennin's diary reveals the extent of Korean shipping and trade in his reference to the coastal villages along the route of his journey: There were many Korean villages along the coast of China and along the shores of the Chang Jiang. Ennin tended to rely on the Silla Korean sailors and traders on his travels. Evidently, Koreans were active in the China trade in the late Silla period and were considered the best sailors with the best ships of the day. Finally, Ennin reported that not only were there Korean villages along the coasts but that there were Korean Buddhist temples built for their own worship services. This implies more than a temporary residence and speaks of the openness of the Tang system.

Source: Edwin O. Reischauer. *Ennin's Diary: The Record of a Pilgrimage to China in Search of the Law.* New York: Ronald Press, 1955.

Society

One custom from Korea's tribal heritage that did not disappear in the new order was the tradition of status by birth. Indeed, one of the hallmarks of Silla society was its rigid, almost castelike social hierarchy. Royalty could come only from the top two ranks, known as the "holy bone" rank and the "true bone" rank (Ki-dong Lee 1980, 31). The holy bone rank was so exclusive that it died out, and the remaining kings of the dynasty came from the true bone rank. Below the bone ranks were the head ranks, the highest being the "six-head" rank, then the "five-head" rank, and so on. The highest government positions were reserved for those from the six-head rank. A six-head rank candidate could also serve in lower offices and work his way up. A lower-head rank official had a ceiling; he could serve only in the position matching his rank and could never move up.

Beneath the bone ranks and the head ranks were the commoners, and below the commoners were the slaves. In the late Silla period and then in the early Koryo, Korean society became less stratified under Confucian influence. The Confucian ideal was a society with four classes—the official (or scholar-official), the farmer, the artisan, and the merchant. Elsewhere the adoption of the Confucian social order led to greater social stratification; in Silla, on the other hand, pre-Confucian social classes had been so rigid that the new philosophy pushed society toward less stratification. The official class, once the bone and the head ranks, simplified into a two-rank class of civilian scholar/officials on one hand and the military on the other. The artisan-farmer-merchant ideal of Confucianism came to be interpreted as the commoner class. And at the bottom—off the chart of the Confucian ideal—were the slaves. Slavery never played an important role in Chinese society. However, from the Silla period until the 20th century, slaveholding was one of the hallmarks of Korean society. Despite the Mongol invasion in the 13th century and the Japanese in the 16th century, there was never sufficient social upheaval to unseat the slaveholding system. Rather, hereditary slaveholding through several dynasties became part of the longest unbroken chain of slavery of any country on Earth. The children of slaves became slaves, and over the centuries little happened to change the pattern of slaveholding (Patterson 1982, 143). Manumission was possible, but rare, even in times of war; in times of famine, some commoners would sell themselves into slavery and the care and keeping of a wealthy owner. Slaves were primarily held by aristocrats, some of whom owned hundreds of slaves. When an aristocrat married he would double his slave holdings in that sons and daughters, and therefore husbands and wives, each inherited a portion of their respective family's slaves, and at the time of marriage, each side brought slaves into the new household.

There were two categories of slaves, privately owned and publicly owned, or in other words, government slaves. Government slaves were held by various offices in the central government as well as at each provincial office. Public schools and later private schools all had a staff of slaves to serve the young students. Privately held slaves were also divided into two categories and registered as such on the regular census documents: domestic slaves and field slaves. Domestic slaves lived in the house of the owner, while field slaves lived on land held by the owner, sometimes located far from the owner's house. Sometimes field slaves were rented out to other landowners, in which case the field slave would submit his tribute, a share of his yield, to the absentee owner. There were also slaves held by Buddhist temples and appeared in the census documents as such. Estimates of the percentage of the populace that were slaves hover around one-third until the 18th century, at which point wage labor became more advantageous to farm owners and the newly emerging factory owners.

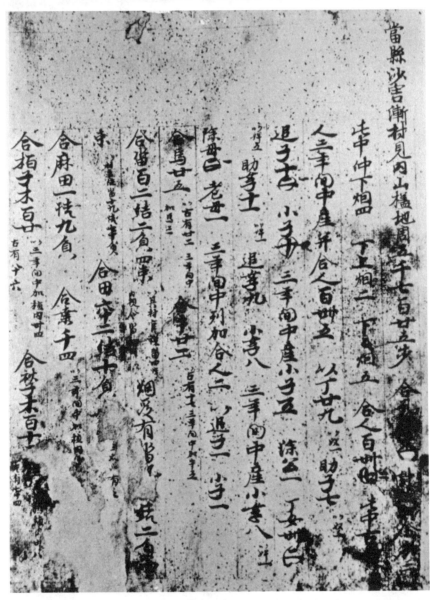

A page of the Silla period census preserved in Japan. One household in this census registry recorded 3,000 slaves. (Academy of Korean Studies)

Government

In terms of political developments, Silla was situated at a pivotal time. At the beginning of this period, the culture was not far removed from its tribal heritage: Ascribed status was more important than status by merit, and leadership by hereditary lords was more important than central government authority. This gradually changed—to a point. In 651 a central government office, called the Silla Chancellery, replaced the *hwabaek,* the council of elders, which represented the old order. Remnants of the older order persisted in the provinces, where Silla could not initially appoint its own officials. Rather, it recognized the local strongman. In time, however, the local leader was given central government rank, and later, central government officials could be appointed.

One method Silla used to keep local leaders in line was the hostage system. To ensure the local leader's loyalty, he was required to send his eldest son and heir to Kyongju. There the heir would be educated, treated royally, and subsequently develop loyalty to the throne, but if the strongman decided to revolt against the Silla leadership, it could use his son to pressure the provincial leader to either give up or else see his son executed. The hostage system was an effective method of ensuring centralized authority, and it was used elsewhere in East Asia and other parts of the world.

The influence of Silla elitism can be seen in the life of a colorful character named Chang Po-go (d. 846), a local ruler who controlled maritime trade along the Korean and Chinese coasts. In Chang's time Koreans lived scattered along the Chinese coast, as recorded in the diary of the Japanese monk Ennin (794–864). Chang had gone to China as a young man and become an officer in the Tang army. Later, enraged at the capture and enslavement of fellow Koreans along the coast, he petitioned the Silla court to establish a naval garrison on Korea's southwest coast to protect the sea-lanes and coastlines. He was highly successful and became a powerful leader of the China trade.

Meantime, loyalties were shifting in the capital, and the Silla royal court was rocked by a series of coups in which each claimant succeeded to the throne by assassinating the reigning king. In one contest for the throne, a prince made an alliance with the powerful Chang, and together they successfully secured the throne for the prince. In reward Chang asked that his daughter be married to the new king. For the status-conscious Silla court this was too much. Chang was assassinated, and that was the end of one of the few who dared to climb beyond his prescribed status.

The palace coups that plagued the Silla dynasty in the late ninth and early 10th centuries were one important reason the dynasty began to decline. Another key reason was the dissatisfaction of the provincial rulers, who were tired of exorbitant tax levies and who still remembered stories of bygone days when their territory was not part of the Silla kingdom but was independent or allied to one of the three kingdoms. Plus, given the political instability in the capital, it was hard for the court to keep control of the provinces. By the mid-eighth century local rulers began to form regional alliances. Through alliance or conquest some rulers came to control more territory.

Eventually, two centers of power developed: one loyal to the old Koguryo court, which called itself the Later Koguryo kingdom, and one loyal to the old Paekche court, which called itself the Later Paekche kingdom. Therein were seeds sown for the eventual destruction of Silla.

The Later Three Kingdoms Period

Silla had kept control of the leaders of Paekche and Koguryo by use of the hostage system, and it had levied taxes on all the territory. In the end these mechanisms broke down. The hostage system no longer kept the provinces under control, and tax revenues declined.

In the early Three Kingdoms period, the throne had rotated among various "holy bone" representatives from the Kim, Pak, and Sok clans, a remnant of the tribal confederation days. For the last 100 years of the Three Kingdoms period and the first 150 years of the Unified Silla period, the kings had come from a single lineage within the Kyongju Kim clan, but the unity this once represented began to break down. During the last century of the Unified Silla period, assassinations and rivalries reemerged between not only various segments of the Kim clan but also the old Pak clan. Trouble at the center was all the excuse some warlords needed to test the strength of the periphery.

The most powerful of these warlords was a Silla royal prince who, disillusioned at not getting his chance on the throne, left for an area to the north. His name was Kungye (d. 918), of the Kim clan. He fled Kyongju for Kangnung, at that time on the northeast border of Silla, and declared himself king of the Later Koguryo kingdom.

Kungye was later toppled by one of his generals. This ultimate act of disloyalty, otherwise intolerable in a Confucian society, was justifiable in the eyes of later historians because of the alleged cruelty of Kungye. After suffering several acts of vicious behavior at the hand of Kungye, the people came to Kungye's trusted general, Wang Kon (877–943), and asked him to overthrow his lord. Wang Kon rejected their first request, in good Confucian form. When asked a second time, he rejected them again. The third time, moved by their pleas, he rose up and killed the hated Kungye.

The truth probably lies somewhere between the extreme descriptions of the arch-evil Kungye on one hand and Wang Kon the traitor on the other. Since Wang Kon won, he had the privilege of writing history, and in his account he was the hero. In any case, Wang Kon became the king of Later Koguryo in 918.

The notion that the history may have been doctored a little is reinforced by Wang Kon's name. It means "setting up the king." Though it is not likely he was born with that name, he apparently liked his surname because he bestowed it on his loyal supporters. If it was good enough to be manufactured for him, he could manufacture it for others. Several of those who allied themselves and their territories to Wang Kon were also given the surname "Wang."

The Founding of Koryo

In 918 Wang Kon took a decisive step that has affected Korea to the present day. He changed the name of the kingdom by shortening it from the four syllables that meant "later Koguryo" (Hu Koguryo) to a two-syllable, Chinese-sounding name, Koryo. The name change put Korea inside the Chinese system: No longer were Koreans barbarians with a multisyllabic name; they were beginning to be an integral part of the tributary system of China, with all of the rights and privileges of a tributary state. Koryo not only moved its capital closer to China geographically, it moved closer to China politically as well.

Wang Kon established the capital for the new dynasty in Kaesong just north of present-day Seoul and eventually recruited Silla aristocrats to join him and move to the northern capital. He continued to recognize Kyongju, the capital of Silla, by calling it the "Eastern Capital," although it was located in the southeast part of the peninsula. Pyongyang became the "Western Capital," although it was located north of Kaesong.

In 918 Wang Kon's new kingdom was only one of three kingdoms on the peninsula. "Later Paekche" had emerged in the southwest, and Silla still had a king on the throne in Kyongju. Wang Kon was not anxious to destroy Silla. Rather, in good Confucian form, he gave Silla time and respectfully allowed the last king to serve out his term. Wang Kon even

Early Koryo Period (Tenth Century)

Liao

Jurchen

Parhae

Tumen R.

Yalu R.

Pyongyang●

East Sea

Yellow Sea

Koryo

Kaesong●

Han R.

Song

Later Paekche

Silla
●Kyongju

Korea Strait

Heian

N

East China Sea

© Infobase Publishing

| 0 | | 200 miles |
| 0 | | 200 km |

defended Kyongju when it was attacked by the Later Paekche (Hurst 1981, 1).

The leader of Later Paekche was a former Silla subject who rose to power in Paekche territory, a man named Kyon Hwon (ca. 867–936). As king of the Later Paekche kingdom, he attacked both Koryo and Silla. In 927 his armies sacked Kyongju, killed King Kyongae, took hostages, and hauled off treasures. However, Kyon Hwon did not cause the fall of the Silla dynasty. Instead, Wang Kon led an army of rescue and drove the Later Paekche forces back. Wang Kon won the respect of the people of Silla, and his respect for the old but dying kingdom was also reinforced.

Kyon Hwon was a capable ruler in some respects: He established the Later Paekche kingdom, ruled for nearly 30 years, and made alliances with one of the Chinese dynasties, the Liao (907–1125), at a time of disunity in China. In other regards he was despotic, ruthless, and capricious. After being beaten back from what had appeared to be the sure conquest of Silla, he decided to name his fourth son, Kumgang, his heir. This enraged his elder son, Shingom, who took over the kingdom, murdered his brother Kumgang, and imprisoned his father in a remote Buddhist temple. Kyon Hwon escaped, however, and sought refuge in the court of his erstwhile enemy, Wang Kon. Wang accepted Kyon Hwon and allowed him to lead an army against his own son and former kingdom. Kyon defeated Shingom in battle in 936 but in the process destroyed the kingdom he had set up, bringing Korea closer to unification under the new house of Koryo.

In the meantime, the last king of Silla, Kyongsun (r. 927–935), had surrendered to Wang Kon in 935. His territory and power shrinking, Kyongsun sought a role in the new Koryo kingdom. Wang took a wife from the Silla royal house, made the last king, Kyongsun, a member of the new Koryo aristocracy, and recruited many of the officials of Silla to come to Kaesong to serve in his court. Thus it was that the dates for Unified Silla, 688 to 935, overlap with the dates for Koryo, 918 to 1392.

In spite of the generation or two of turmoil, the transition from Unified Silla to Koryo hegemony was relatively smooth. Koryo's vengeance was reserved for Later Paekche; it had great respect for Silla. As in Silla's conquest of Kaya, the royalty of the defeated Silla kingdom were welcomed into the aristocracy of the victorious Koryo dynasty, avoiding a bloodbath (Duncan 1988, 39). In present-day Korea the historic integration of conquered dynasties is reflected in the fact that the largest surname groups in the country, Kim, Yi, Pak, Choe, and Chong—names of Silla aristocracy—compose 55 percent of the population. In addition to the Kims of Silla, there are the Kims who are descendants of the Kaya aristocracy, today called the Kimhae Kims. The Kimhae Kims are the largest lineage group in Korea, numbering about 4 million people.

KOREAN SURNAMES

There are only about 250 traditional Korean surnames. In recent years about 150 additional names have appeared, but these names are those of naturalized citizens originally from other countries. According to the 2000 census released by the government, 21.6 percent of South Koreans today are named Kim. The next four most common names are Yi (also spelled Lee and Rhee), 14.8 percent; Pak (or Park), 8.6 percent; Choe (or Choi), 4.7 percent; and Chong (or Chung, Jung, Jeong), 4.4 percent.

These five surnames bear a close connection to the six villages that formed the earliest Silla state. The six names of the Silla villages were Yi, Choe, Chung, Pae, Son, and Sol. In addition, there were the three royal families of Silla: Kim, Pak, and Sok. All these surnames survive in modern Korea, and, as noted, five of them dominate the percentages. By contrast, virtually none of the names of eight aristocratic families of Paekche—Sa, Yon, Hyop, Hae, Chin, Kuk, Mok, and Paek—survives today. Five of the eight have a homophone that exists as a surname today (Sa, Yon, Kuk, Mok, and Paek), but each of the Paekche names was written with a Chinese character different from the one now used. One name, Chin, survives today with the same Chinese character (one of four characters used for the surname pronounced Chin in Korea), but it is also a common surname in China and is probably not connected genealogically to the Paekche surname.

The survival of Silla surnames and the extinction of Paekche surnames illustrate the continuity of traditions from Silla, the winner of the Three Kingdoms warfare, and the eclipse of Paekche traditions. More important, the continuity of Silla culture for 1,300 years, through the intervening Koryo and Choson dynasties, speaks volumes about the resilience of Korean culture. In spite of two episodes of catastrophic warfare, Korea's subsequent history was relatively tranquil; dynasties were long-lived; and when a dynasty changed, the transition was not tumultuous but relatively peaceful. Thus, Silla surnames and many other remnants of Silla culture continue to the present.

Koryo's consolidation of power was not limited to the former Three Kingdoms. In the meantime, a new power in Manchuria, the Kitan, who had founded the Liao dynasty in 907, attacked the northern kingdom of Parhae in 926. Many of the ruling class of Parhae were descendants of Koguryo refugees from the unification war, and they decided to join Koryo for protection (U-song Yi 1977, 28). Consequently, the northern border of Koryo extended farther north from where it had been under the Unified Silla rule. It now included the Yalu River estuary on the northwest.

The Koryo Period
Wang Kon's Reign

Wang Kon was a remarkable alliance builder. One of his techniques in securing an alliance was to marry the daughter of the chieftain or general of a newly allied territory. He had more than 20 such marriages. Early in his reign he cultivated ties with northern Chinese dynasties. When the Song dynasty unified China in 960, Koryo became part of the Song tributary system. Koryo maintained peaceful relations with Japan, including trade and continued exportation of Buddhist technology. Koryo's relations with its northern neighbors, the Kitan, however, were marked by tension and conflict.

To assure the success of his new dynasty, Wang Kon drafted a document called the "Ten Injunctions" just before he died. It was a list of orders to advise his successors on how to govern Korea. Religious concepts dominate the document. He admonished his descendants to honor the Buddha, and he also encouraged respect for the teachings of Confucius. For good measure he added advice that his descendants follow the principles of feng shui, or geomancy—the belief that constructing buildings and burying the dead should be done in accordance with the forces of the Earth. *Feng* (or the Korean *pung*) means "wind," and *shui* (or Korean *su*) means "water," symbolic of the forces of nature:

1. Respect Buddhism; the kingdom is based on its teachings.
2. Build Buddhist temples according to the geomantic concepts taught by Toson.
3. The eldest son should succeed to the throne, unless he is unworthy, then the second, or if he is unworthy, then the third.
4. Honor the Tang dynasty; do not follow the ways of the barbaric Kitan.
5. Follow good geomancy; visit Pyongyang every four years, for there the geomancy is good.

6. Maintain the state festivals.
7. Follow the example of the ancient sage kings of China (Confucianism).
8. Do not appoint to office men from the southeast (former Paekche).
9. Be fair and treat the army well.
10. Study the Confucian classics.

Wang's successors obeyed most of these orders, and the injunctions have had tremendous impact on Korean history. In the years to come, aspects of religion, geomancy, and state ceremony followed Wang Kon's advice closely. Unfortunately, his negative view of the former Paekche people translated into a prejudice against people from the Cholla provinces that persisted for centuries.

The area that was most problematic was that of succession. As Wang Kon indicated, some flexibility was possible in the choice of an heir. Yet, with so many sons who wanted to be king, the potential for instability was great. Indeed, when Wang Kon died the next two sons to take the throne were killed in plots to establish yet another son as king. But the fourth king of the dynasty, Kwangjong (r. 949–975), reigned for 26 years.

Kwangjong's Reign

Kwangjong was an innovator. One of his most important decisions was to strengthen Koryo's ties with China and to reinforce Confucianism. Late Silla had already introduced some aspects of the Chinese centralized bureaucracy, and by the time Wang Kon's third son, Kwangjong, took the throne in 949, the government was centralized in Kaesong. All appointments—central and provincial, ministers and magistrates—were ordained by the king. Kwangjong moved Korea even closer to China by instituting a Chinese-style civil service exam in 958. This primed Korea to develop a government bureaucracy based on merit rather than ascription, making Koryo more competent and stable than the Silla dynasty had been, with its reliance on local power bases.

The move to recruit officials solely on the basis of merit was not completed in the Koryo period, however. Even toward the end of the dynasty in 1392, most officials were appointed because they held power in a particular region or on the basis of heredity—sometimes offices were passed from father to son, or father to son-in-law, or uncle to nephew, or other relationships. Still, Koryo took a giant step away from this narrow method of recruitment. Although Kwangjong broke with the rigid "bone rank" system of Silla, Koryo society was far from egalitarian. Social stratification settled into three major classes: the aristocracy, the commoners, and the slaves.

Technically speaking, Kwangjong was not the first leader in Korea to use the civil service examination. It had been tried briefly in the late Silla period on a limited basis, but at that time it was so restricted in its application and so few were qualified to apply that it was hardly recognized as an open recruiting device. The Koryo system, though an improvement, still suffered from one limitation not found in the Chinese system: The candidate had to prove his genealogical worthiness before he could take the exam. In China the examination system did not impose any restrictions on applicants. In Korea only those who could prove they were members of the aristocracy could sit for the exam. Koryo Koreans believed that certain bloodlines were nobler than others, and some of the doctrines of Confucianism reinforced this idea, helping to justify Koryo institutions of hierarchy, such as permission to sit for exams and slavery.

The main hall of the Sunggyungwan, the Confucian Academy in Kaesong, capital of the Koryo dynasty. Founded in the 10th century, it is one of the oldest academies, or "universities," in the world. (Academy of Korean Studies)

Koryo adopted Chinese-style government organization with only a few modifications. There were six main bureaus: personnel, rites, finance, punishments, military, and public works. There were two cross-cutting divisions in the organization—one between central and provincial positions, and one between civilian and military positions. The central positions were considered higher in status than the provincial ones, and civilian officers were generally considered to be of higher status than military officers. (Tension between civilian and military offices would afflict Koryo later in the dynasty.)

Kwangjong did other things in a Chinese way, such as adopting the Chinese calendar. The calendar had two manifestations. First, the years were reckoned in terms of the year of reign of the Chinese emperor—for example, the 25th year of Emperor Kaotsung. Most Korean documents were dated in the same manner. The other manifestation was used in conjunction with the first but did not change with every emperor. This was the 60-year cycle. This system consists of two lists: 10 "stems" and 12 "branches." The 12 branches are a list of 12 zodiacal animals. The rotation of the cycle of 10 and the cycle of 12 results in 60 pairings, and thus 60 years became the hallmark for

The six bureaus (ministries)	Tasks
Personnel	Oversees appointments to offices, recommends appointments to be made by the king
Rites	Conducts state rituals including ancestor ceremonies by the king, supervises educational system and schools throughout the country, administers exams to recruit candidates for office
Finance (also called (Households)	Collects taxes and provides funding for the state, oversees triennial census
Punishments (or Justice)	Agency of police, justice system, and prison
Military	Supervises recruitment, training, and deployment of soldiers
Public Works	Sees to the construction and maintenance of government buildings, roads, bridges, reservoirs, and irrigation systems

THE CHINESE ZODIAC, THE 60-YEAR CYCLE

The Ten Heavenly Stems	The Twelve Heavenly Branches					
	Korean	Animal Represen- tation	Sample Years			
1. kap	1. cha	rat	1972	1984	1996	2008
2. ul	2. chuk	ox	1973	1985	1997	2009
3. pyong	3. in	tiger	1974	1986	1998	2010
4. chong	4. myo	rabbit	1975	1987	1999	2011
5. mu	5. chin	dragon	1976	1988	2000	2012
6. ki	6. sa	snake	1977	1989	2001	2013
7. kyong	7. o	horse	1978	1990	2002	2014
8. sin	8. mi	sheep	1979	1991	2003	2015
9. im	9. sin	monkey	1980	1992	2004	2016
10. kye	10. yu	chicken	1981	1993	2005	2017
	11. sul	dog	1982	1994	2006	2018
	12. hae	pig	1983	1995	2007	2019

The 10 stems rotate six times, one stem per year, to make 60 years. The 12 branches rotate five times, one branch per year, to make 60 years. At the beginning of a cycle, kap and cha will match up, and they will return to the original pairing in another 60 years.

Every year fits into one of the 60 possible pairings. Some major historical events are known by the pairs that indicate the year in this system. For example, imjin (or imchin) is the date of the Japanese invasion of 1592; pyongja (or pyongcha) is the date of the Manchu invasion of 1636; and kabo (or kap-o) is the date of the late Choson dynasty reforms of 1894.

Years as well as months, days, and time of day were all measured in this system. For example, there were 12 hours (each lasting the equivalent of two Western hours) in a day, not 24, each named after a zodiacal animal. Midnight was chasi, "rat hour"; noon was osi, "horse

(continues)

THE CHINESE ZODIAC *(continued)*

hour"; morning was *ojon*, "before horse hour"; and afternoon was *ohu*, "after horse hour."

Fortune-tellers, called *saju-jaengi*, used the "four pillars" *(saju)* to tell one's fortune or to determine if a proposed marriage would be successful. The four pillars were the 60-cycle symbols of an individual's birth: the year, month, day, and hour.

---

major events in one's life. The 60th birthday was and is a major celebration, and a 60th wedding anniversary is a rare but grand event. A certain degree of fortune is implied by the year in which one is born, and individuals are said to resemble certain personality and character traits of the animal of their birth year. Marriage arrangements sometimes reflected this belief: Girls born in the year of the horse had difficulty getting married because women from this year were supposedly headstrong and did not make good wives.

The Kitan and the Jurchen

Throughout the first half of the Koryo period, the dynasty had trouble securing its northern border. In the early Koryo period, during the mid-10th century, the northwest neighbor was the Kitan, a coalition of northern tribal peoples, including some of the Magal people who had once been part of the Parhae kingdom. When Koryo was founded, it took some of the territory of Parhae, but the balance joined the alliance to the north that would become the Kitan tribes, which eventually allied to form the Liao dynasty (907–1125). The Kitan attacked Koryo along their common border on several occasions. In 1018 they mounted a large attack but were annihilated by a massive Koryo counterattack led by General Kang Kamchan (948–1031), one of Korea's great military heroes.

The Kitan were replaced by the Jurchen, who founded an even more powerful dynasty to the northeast called Jin (1115–1234). The Jurchen similarly caused border problems for Koryo in the early 12th century, but Koryo was able either to beat back the Jurchen or to recognize them and submit tribute to them. In the late 11th century Hanpu, the ancestor of the founder of the Jin dynasty, had taken refuge from the Kitan in the northern province of Koryo. This inspired a degree of closeness between the Jurchen and Koryo that mitigated some of their hostilities. The Chinese-style Jin dynasty quickly grew in power. By 1125 the Jurchen kingdom had captured the northern portion of China, forcing the Song dynasty into the lower half of China and inaugurating the period known as the Southern Song dynasty (1127–1279).

The Koryo court tried to maintain relations with both the Jurchen Jin dynasty and the Southern Song dynasty. Though the Southern Song controlled only the southern half of China, their rule was a time of great cultural developments. The Neo-Confucian movement, a revival of Confucianism among Chinese, Koreans, and Japanese, was founded by Zhu Xi (1130–1200), the Cheng brothers, and others during the Southern Song dynasty. Koreans came to revere this philosophy, and Neo-Confucianism would have a dramatic impact on Korea in the centuries that followed.

The Myochong Rebellion

Not everyone in Koryo applauded the far-reaching adoption of Chinese systems and philosophy. Among those opposed to the new developments were Buddhist monks, who were troubled by the rising influence of Confucianism. In 1135 a monk named Myochong (d. 1136) gained the ear of the king. He argued that the court and the country had become too Chinese and too Confucian. He urged the king to break with the pro-China bureaucracy based in Kaesong and move his court to Pyongyang. Myochong argued that not only was Pyongyang the heir to the old city of Lolang, but that it had been the capital of Old Choson, the earliest (though mostly mythical) kingdom of Korea. He added that the geomancy of Pyongyang was better, as Wang Kon himself had said in his "Ten Injunctions." The king was persuaded, but when he presented his decision to the bureaucracy, he was overruled. Myochong would not give up that easily, however. He returned to Pyongyang, raised an army, and declared a new state in open rebellion against Koryo.

The Kaesong court dispatched an army under the command of Kim Pusik (1075–1157) to quell the rebellion. Kim was a high government official, and although he was on the civilian side of the bureaucracy, he was the one given the military task. Kim successfully quelled the rebellion, returned to Kaesong, and took up his civilian duties, which came to include writing the official version of history. His work, called *Samguk sagi* (Historical record of the Three Kingdoms), was published in 1145.

The *Samguk sagi* was apparently based on an earlier work called the *Samguk ki*, no longer extant. Thus, Kim Pusik's *Samguk sagi* is the oldest comprehensive history of Korea. A didactic history written in

Confucian style, it emphasizes the moral lessons of history and judges the actors of that history over time by their character and adherence to Confucian values.

The Confucian view of history was not to go unchallenged. In 1285 a Buddhist monk named Iryon (1206–89) wrote an alternative history that emphasized more of the domestic uniqueness of Korea—a non-Confucian–style history called the *Samguk yusa* (Remnants and reminiscences of the Three Kingdoms). Iryon's purpose was to preserve the unique culture of Korea and to tie it to Buddhism. He included in his history the Tangun foundation myth, other myths, and *hyangga* (Silla poetry).

These two great histories provide not only alternative views but also a symbol of the convergence and divergence of Buddhism and Confucianism in Korea. The two belief systems could not be more diametrically opposed. On the other hand, they form a perfect symbiosis: What one religion does well, the other does not; questions unanswered by one are answered by the other. In spite of the tension between the two religions apparent in Myochong's rebellion and the histories written by Kim Pusik and Iryon, during most of Korean history both religions were practiced side by side. In the Koryo period Confucianism was growing in influence at court, while Buddhism was losing the official sponsorship it had once enjoyed.

Military-Civilian Conflict

The tension between Buddhists and Confucians did not rise to the level of hostilities very often, and when it did, as in the Myochong rebellion, the scope was narrow and the losses minimal. Another tension built into the fabric of early Koryo society and politics turned out to be more potent—the tension between military and civilian officials at court. According to Confucian doctrine, as one does not use one's best metal for swords, one does not use one's best men in the army. Acting on this belief, early Koryo put its civil officials on a pedestal and consistently knocked military officials off theirs.

In the ninth of his Ten Injunctions, Wang Kon had encouraged fair treatment for the military, an admonition that was at times ignored, as records of the time attest: The record indicates that families of high military officers were starving. Other records tell of poor treatment of the generals and other military men by the civilians, who at times treated the generals as servants.

In addition, whenever the court had a serious military problem to deal with, it often put a civilian official in charge of the army dispatched to the front. Two such cases already mentioned were Kang Kamchang, who drove the Kitans out in 1018, and Kim Pushik, who quelled the Myochong rebellion in 1136. The fact that they were successful reinforced the idea that the military was not really as competent as the civilians, even in military affairs. This schism, more than that between Confucians and Buddhists, was to create major problems for Korea in the middle of the Koryo period.

One of the critical events that pushed the military over the edge and into action was an incident on a royal outing, an excursion to a Buddhist temple in 1170 (Shultz 1999, 31). On the pilgrimage a whole retinue of soldiers and civilian officials were in tow, as was the case when a king traveled. Displaying a new level of disrespect, one of the civil officials, Kim Tonjung (d. 1170), lit a general's beard on fire as a prank. Kim Tonjung was none other than the son of the famous civilian scholar-official Kim Pusik. The general was Chong Chungbu (d. 1179).

The humiliation was the last straw for General Chong, who began seeking the time and place to get his revenge and stage a revolt. At the next royal outing he and his men were waiting at the place where the entourage was scheduled to stop to rest. They descended on the group, shouting, "Death to all civilian officials!" and then carried out their pronouncement with horrible efficiency. Kim Tonjung and countless other civilian officials were killed. Chong banished the king, Uisong (r. 1146–70), to Koje Island and the crown prince to Chin Island, establishing the king's younger brother, Myongjong (r. 1170–97) as the new king. Myongjong was manipulated as a puppet at the hands of the military, first by Chong Chungbu and then by a series of other generals.

Myongjong's "rule" was marked by a series of assassinations. Two other generals had helped Chong Chungbu carry out his takeover, Yi Uibang (d. 1174) and Yi Ko (d. 1171). For a time the three ruled together, but the triumvirate was short-lived. Yi Uibang tried to take over by first killing Yi Ko in 1171 and then trying to marry his daughter to the crown prince, thus securing his position through marital ties to the royal family. This threatened Chong Chungbu. Chong killed Yi Uibang in 1174 and thereupon ruled alone. Chong was in turn assassinated in 1179 by a young general named Kyong Taesung (1154–83), who took over the government. In 1183 he mysteriously took ill and died at the age of 29. Kyong was disliked by many of the military because of his aristocratic background. Thereafter, another general, Yi Uimin (d. 1196), seized power. Yi Uimin came from the other extreme end of the social hierarchy: He was born a slave. Inspired by one of their own rising to the top, other slaves rose up in rebellion in various parts of the country under Yi's rule. Yi became more and more ruthless in reaction to the criticism he received for breaking with the rules of social hierarchy. Finally, he was killed by yet another general in 1196, Choe Chunghon.

The Choe Military Dynasty

Shortly after seizing power, General Choe Chunghon (1150–1219) killed his brother, Choe Chungsu (d. 1197), who had assisted in the assassination of Yi Uimin, and then the cycle of assassinations stopped. The Choe family held power for a total of four generations, establishing a military dynasty within the Koryo dynasty. This period is referred to as the time of the Choe military government.

Choe Chunghon was able to break the cycle of assassinations and hold on to power by implementing several changes. He diminished the power of the king even further by controlling the succession to the throne. He deposed Myongjong in 1197 and set his brother, Shinjong (r. 1197–1204), on the throne. When Shinjong died, Choe placed Huijong (r. 1204–11) on the throne, then replaced him with Kangjong (1211–13). When Kangjong died, he was followed by Kojong (r. 1213–59). Thus, Choe Chunghon deposed two kings and buried two kings. Shinjong died at age 60 and Kangjong at age 61, both of natural causes (as far as we know).

Another reason for the success of the Choe military government was that it made peace with the civilian officials. Indeed, the Choe military government recruited many civilian officials to serve at levels high and low. While some members of the Koryo bureaucracy retired to the countryside, others accepted and served the military court. One of those who served and eventually rose to the highest civilian position in the government was Yi Kyubo (1168–1241). A true example of the scholar-official, he was actually better known as an author and scholar than as the prime minister. He left a large collection of writings, as was typical of Confucian scholars of the Koryo period and characteristic of those of the subsequent Choson dynasty. This is how the class of the Confucian scholar-official that was to play such an important role in the years ahead came to power and prestige during this period of military rule. The military that had taken power from the scholar-official class in retaliation for being degraded by them ended up relying on them and even providing the platform for launching the scholar-official into a position of dominance that would last for the next 600 years.

COMPARISON TO THE JAPANESE *BAKUFU*

A t the time of the Choe military government in Korea, the *bakufu* military rulers governed Japan. The Japanese *bakufu* ruled for more than 700 years, while the house of Choe was in control for only four generations (62 years). Both transitions to military rule, however, occurred within 10 years of each other.

The Japanese *bakufu* came to power in 1160, 10 years before Chong Chungbu's takeover in Korea. It governed from 1160 to 1868, from the Taira period (1160–85) through the Kamakura shogunate (1185–1336), through the Ashikaga shogunate (1336–1573), to the Tokugawa shogunate (1600–1868). The word *shogun* means "general," and the term *shogunate* is used in the place of "dynasty." The imperial family of Japan was never deposed; only the house of the shogun changed. It was the generals, however, who wielded power.

Korea returned to civilian rule after 62 years in 1258, but Japan remained under the control of military overlords. This changed in the late 19th century, when the emperor was restored to power during the Meiji Restoration.

Source: Shultz, Edward J. "Ch'oe Chunghon and Minamoto Yoritomo." *Japan Review* 11 (1999): 31–53.

The Mongol Invasion

Korea was under the control of the military when the greatest challenge to its independence came: the invasion of the Mongols. Koryo's first contact with the Mongols, in the early 13th century, was as an ally. The Mongols had beaten the Jurchen state of Jin in 1212; with the Jurchen in disarray, the Kitan, whom the Jurchen had controlled, rose up in resistance. When pressed by the Mongols, the Kitan retreated into Koryo, the land of their traditional enemy. A combined Mongol-Koryo force had defeated the holdout Kitan in a battle near Pyongyang in 1219.

Unfortunately for Koryo, the Mongols then demanded tribute as the price of being an ally. The demands for tribute were too costly, and Koryo did not always comply. Their relationship was deteriorating when in 1225 a Mongol envoy was killed. The Mongols used this incident as an excuse to launch their first of six invasions against Koryo in 1231 (Ledyard 1964, 1).

The Mongols had risen to power under Genghis Khan (1162–1227), who was able to unify a diverse group of tribes located on the plains of North Asia. He conquered lands and people to the west, south, and east, but it was his grandson, Kublai Khan (1215–94), who conquered China, both the Southern Song and the Jin (Jurchen) in the north. Kublai's new dynasty was called the Yuan (1271–1368).

In 1231 the Korean court, under the control of the Choe military family, left Kaesong and took refuge on Kanghwa Island to the southwest, in the estuary of the Imjin and Han Rivers. The Choe family's army of retainers escaped with them. While they hid in the relative safety of their island fortress, the common people of Koryo were left to fend for themselves. Peasant armies rose to defend their lands and families, but they were no match for the Mongols. The devastation was extreme and the results catastrophic.

On the island the Choe military leadership and the king and his court built a palace and a miniature city in replica of the capital, Kaesong. They carried on as if oblivious to what was happening on the mainland.

Tradition holds that the rulers-in-exile were safe on the island because the Mongols, as horse riders, were not capable sailors. Although the stretch of water between the island and the mainland is only as wide as that of a large river (a bridge crosses the span today), legend says the Mongols were not able to cross the water. The story is not convincing in light of the fact that the Mongols, when they decided to invade Japan, mounted an armada: They simply loaded their horses on the ships and sailed off to conquer the island nation, albeit with Korean help. Surely they could have conquered the Koryo court had they wanted to. Having control of the peninsula, however, they took the position of waiting the court out.

A Koryo military unit named the "Three Special Forces" continued to fight and toward the end, in 1271, was driven to Cheju Island for safety. The Mongols, however, were able to sail to Cheju and quash the last of the holdout army in 1273. In the process the Mongols discovered the herds of horses kept on the island. One of their demands for tribute thereafter included a supply of horses from Cheju.

The Mongols established a different form of tribute system from that of the Chinese. No longer were the tribute demands reasonable. No longer was there reciprocation of tribute goods. No longer was

JAPAN AND THE *KAMIKAZE*

In one of the least successful Mongol campaigns, Koreans were forced to build ships for the Mongol invasion of Japan. Although the Mongols did not bother to mount an attack on Kanghwa Island, where the Koryo court was hiding out, they did want to attack and conquer Japan. They forced Korean shipbuilders to prepare a sufficient number of boats—boats large enough for the soldiers as well as their horses—and launched their attack in the summer of 1274.

Just as the Mongol armada was approaching the Japanese coast, a terrific typhoon blew in, wrecked the ships, and prevented the invasion. The Mongols, however, were not so easily dissuaded. They prepared another armada in 1282, again at the expense of Korean shipbuilders and sailors. Again, just as they reached Japanese soil, the winds blew in, ruining the invasion. A few soldiers reached the shore, only to be quickly dispatched by the soldiers of the Kamakura shogunate.

The Japanese called the winds that protected Japan "the winds of the gods," or *kamikaze*. Thereafter, the myth developed that Japan was inviolable: It had never been invaded, and when invasion was attempted, it was protected by the gods. Thus, the gods would never allow Japan to be invaded. This was why at the end of World War II, when Japan was about to face its first invasion, their defending suicide bombers were called the *kamikaze*.

there the advantage of accompanying a tribute mission in order to conduct some trade at a private level. Rather, as part of their tribute, the Mongols demanded an asset the Chinese had never asked for: slaves. It is estimated that the Mongols hauled off at least 200,000 slaves during the time they controlled Korea, from 1231 to 1368 (Ledyard 1964, 1).

Tributary of the Mongol Yuan Dynasty

With the assassination of the last of the Choe military dictators in 1258, the rule of the Choe generals, who had been in power for four generations (62 years), was over, and the king was free to make a treaty with the Mongols. As part of the treaty, King Kojong (r. 1213–59) agreed to a new hostage arrangement: His son would be taken to

Beijing, marry a Mongol princess, and be educated until his turn came to rule in Korea. Thereafter, for eight generations, each Korean king relinquished his son, the crown prince, allowing him to be raised in Beijing, and each king had a Mongol mother and a Mongol wife. No Chinese dynasty dominated the Korean court as thoroughly as did the Mongols.

Korean women were delivered to the Yuan court as well. Many were lost to history as nameless slaves and concubines, but some were given to the emperor's court to be part of the imperial harem. One of the sons of these court women became the emperor. Yuan dynasty China called Korea a "son-in-law kingdom," since the emperor's daughters would marry the Korean king. But at the same time, Korea was also the "mother" kingdom, or at least the kingdom that provided the mother of the emperor. This closeness of relationships was one beneficial outcome of the conquest. Although the devastation wreaked by the Mongols was nearly total, once the dust settled, Korea became part of a vast international empire that brought products and ideas to Korea.

Particularly important was the idea of Neo-Confucianism, which had been developed by the Southern Song but was just starting to filter through the Yuan court to Korea. As dramatic as the Mongols' impact was on Korea, with all of its war and chaos, it would be eclipsed by the revolution in thought brought by Neo-Confucianism.

Cultural Achievements

In spite of the destruction and chaos caused by the warfare during the invasion of the Mongols, in its aftermath Korea saw great cultural innovation. In some cases innovation was stimulated by contact with the Mongols and the Chinese, in other cases innovation was indigenous, and in some cases it was developed out of fear of the Mongols. A case in point is the invention of metal movable type technology. Although the Chinese had developed printing using movable fonts made of wood and ceramics some time before, it was the Koreans who first created movable type printing fonts made of metal. The oldest book printed using metal movable type that survives is a 1377 document called the *Jikji*, a Buddhist text explaining the teachings of a Korean monk. A record exists that indicates that the technology was used as early as 1234, but none of the earlier books survive.

More important than movable type at the time, however, was printing with carved wooden blocks. At the same time that some Buddhist temples were experimenting with movable type, another temple was

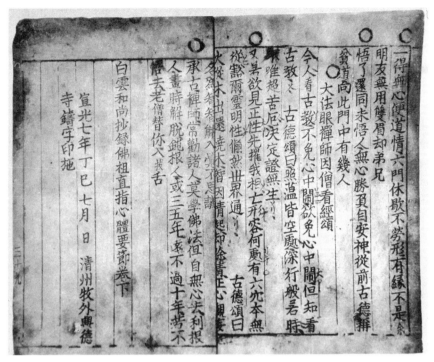

Jikji, the Buddhist text summarizing the teaching of one great monk, printed in 1377. Jikji
is the oldest surviving sample of printing on paper with metal movable type. A museum
devoted to this book and movable type technology is located in Chongju, North Chungchong
province. (Academy of Korean Studies)

engaged in a massive project, that of printing the entire Buddhist
canon, which required carving more than 80,000 wooden blocks. The
monks completed the project once in the early 13th century, only to
have it destroyed by a Jurchen invasion. As an act of devotion to the
Buddha whose protection they sought, this time from the Mongols,
monks repeated the feat a second time. Although it did not stop the
Mongols from invading, the edition survives—it is housed today in a
remote mountain temple called Haein-sa, located not far from Taegu.
The blocks and the buildings that house them were named in 1997 as
a UNESCO World Heritage Site.

The highest art form from the Koryo period is the Korean adapta-
tion of Song celadon ceramics, among the finest in the world. Ceramic
art experts say that the Koryo celadon surpassed its Song exemplars in
the quality of the color of the glaze, a turquoise that is at once delicate
and deep. It is found sometimes on very simple ware and other times

A section of the buildings that house the more than 80,000 blocks used for printing the complete text of the Buddhist scriptures, which were printed in the 13th century to ward off the invasion of the Mongols. The blocks and the buildings that house them were one of the first three UNESCO World Heritage Sites named in 1997. (Korean Overseas Information Service)

One of the 81,257 wooden blocks carved with the most complete text of the Buddhist canon (Academy of Korean Studies)

on very elaborate works. The shape might be as important as the glaze for some works, often incorporating themes from nature, such as ducks, lotus blossoms, peaches, and dragons.

In scholarly matters Confucianism came to slowly eclipse Buddhism. Confucian historiography, as seen above in the *Samguk sagi* (Korea's first history), is one manifestation of this development, but it is also found in biographies, eulogies, essays, and memorials to the throne. If deemed worthy, the writings of a scholar-official would be collected and published as the complete works of a scholar after his death. The first of these anthologies was published in the mid-Koryo period, and they continued to be published for the next 800 years. One example is that of

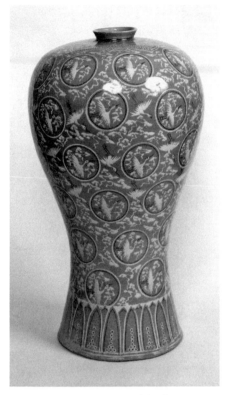

A Koryo celadon vase, one of the finest examples of ceramics in the world (Academy of Korean Studies)

Yi Kyubo, whose collected works include about 2,000 Chinese poems as well as letters, court memorials, biographies, and essays, short compositions that were often humorous and always insightful.

Toward the end of the Koryo period, Neo-Confucianism, which had emerged in China in the early 11th century, gained traction in Korea. Influenced by Buddhism and Daoism, this Confucian revival would come to dominate the political, social, and philosophical landscape of the Choson dynasty.

Decline of Koryo

The story of the Koryo dynasty is remarkable. It lasted nearly five centuries, making it one of the longest dynasties in world history. During this time the name of the country came to be known as Korea in the

A Koryo celadon incense burner showing the intricate carving as well as the delicate glaze that make this art form one of the finest in the world (Academy of Korean Studies)

West, and the West has retained that name despite changes of the name within Korea in the intervening centuries. (Inside Korea today the country calls itself "Hanguk" in the south and "Choson" in the north.) Koryo had noteworthy internal strength such that it survived an internal military takeover on the one hand and external domination by the Mongols on the other.

By the mid-14th century the Yuan dynasty of Mongol China began to totter. Internal rebellion in China, led by pro-China/anti-Mongol

YI KYUBO, "DESTRUCTION OF THE CELLAR"

Yi Kyubo was a remarkable scholar-official, and a prolific writer and essayist, who also served as prime minister. He wrote numerous poems in the Tang Chinese style. Below is one of his lighter-hearted essays that speaks to the Confucian view of nature and how one should not interfere with the natural order.

I returned from a trip to the capital to find a mound, like a tomb, in the center of the courtyard. I called forth my sons and demanded to know what this was about.

They explained that it was not a tomb, but rather a cellar.

I grew angry and asked what they meant by a cellar.

They explained that inside the chamber under the ground, fruit and vegetables can be kept cool in the heat of the summer, and in winter it provides shelter and the women folk can spin and weave without getting their hands raw and chapped.

I grew doubly angry. Heaven has provided furs for us to wear in the winter and linen to wear in the summer. That there are four seasons is the decree of heaven. To act counter to this runs against the natural order. Keeping fruit for untimely pleasures violates nature. And for human beings to live in the ground as if they were snakes and toads is an extreme violation. I will not stand for this.

I told my sons that if they did not tear the cellar down immediately I would beat them mercilessly.

Well, they tore it down and used the support beams for firewood.

And then my heart was once again at rest.

Source: Yi Kyubo. *Tongguk isang kukchip.* Vol. 21, p. 3.

groups, began to spread. Soon the Mongols were driven out (1368), although they maintained a government in the northern border territory, their homeland. The ouster of the Mongols from China had major implications for the future of the Koryo dynasty, whose royal and aristocratic families had intermarried with the Mongols. Although they survived for another quarter century there, a weakened court ultimately gave way to a new dynasty, the Choson.

3

THE EARLY AND MIDDLE CHOSON (1392–1636)

The founders of the Choson dynasty set out to create a dynasty that would last as long as that of their predecessors, the Koryo, and they succeeded. The transition to the new state was smooth and peaceful, accompanied by modest reforms rather than revolt and social upheaval. There was great continuity between the two dynasties as the new state was founded by members of the old elite, men who had passed exams and held office in the Koryo period and whose reforms were inspired by Neo-Confucianism, a new interpretation of the same doctrines that the elite had relied on for centuries.

Reforms focused on the pro-Mongol faction at court and the Buddhist establishment. Especially hard hit were the vast and numerous Buddhist monasteries that had acquired large monk and slave armies during the late Koryo period. The armies had helped defend the country during the Mongol invasions but were now perceived as a challenge to central rule and thus disbanded by the central government. Their land was confiscated and divided among those who had helped in the founding of the Choson state.

The early years of the dynasty saw great prosperity and innovation, and the dynasty experienced its golden age under the grandson of the founder, King Sejong. Some 200 years into the Choson state the dynasty faced its greatest challenge in the Hideyoshi Invasion of 1592. Although the devastation was great, the Japanese did not stay. Indeed, Choson survived and flourished for another 300 years.

The Fall of Koryo

Despite Koryo's ties to the Mongols, the fall of the Mongol Yuan dynasty of China in 1368 did not cause the immediate fall of Koryo. That Koryo held on for another 24 years, until 1392, is a measure of the inherent loyalty of the Korean people and their reluctance to overthrow the incumbent dynasty, then nearly 500 years old. Nevertheless, the Koryo court was so weakened by its marriage ties to the Mongols, and so many of the high officials had amassed fortunes and power through their collaboration with the Mongols, that it would eventually prove impossible for the dynasty to hold on.

The king at the time of the fall of Yuan was Kongmin (r. 1351–74). In a surprise move he asserted Korean independence from the Yuan dynasty. When the new Ming dynasty was declared in 1368, Kongmin was ready to turn on the Mongols and recognize the new rulers of China. He took several radical steps. He abolished the office of cooperation with the Mongols, he attacked Yuan military positions, and he officially recognized the Ming. The Ming responded by restoring traditional tribute relations with Koryo, and in addition they established a formal military alliance. At home Kongmin tried to purge the bureaucracy of pro-Yuan officials and replace them with lower officials untainted by ties with the Mongols.

King Kongmin's actions were remarkable in light of the facts of his life: He was the eighth in a line of kings who had been raised in the Yuan court, had married a Mongol princess, and had a Mongol mother, and by bloodline he was 127 out of 128 parts Mongol. However, when the time came to break with the Mongols, Kongmin did not hesitate. Clearly, he would have been in peril if he had remained loyal to the fallen Yuan court, yet if he went too far in seeking reforms he would risk a revolt. The latter was what happened.

In his efforts to rebuild his kingdom, Kongmin turned to an unlikely source, a Buddhist monk named Sin Ton (d. 1371). Although Sin Ton was one of his most trusted advisers, a Buddhist monk had never before been appointed prime minister. Sin Ton embarked on an ambitious program of confiscating land that pro-Yuan officials had acquired during Mongol rule and returning it to its former owners. He also freed great numbers of slaves. These moves, while extremely popular with commoners and the lower aristocracy, were threats to the high aristocracy. To protect their interests, members of the high aristocracy arranged the assassinations of Sin Ton in 1371 and Kongmin in 1374. Later histories did not treat either man well. The Neo-Confucians who came to dominate the court, and therefore historiography, wrote of a corrupt Buddhist monk who meddled in politics. As a result many Koreans today regard Sin Ton one of the great villains of their history. Had he been successful and survived, however, he would probably have been one of Korea's greatest heroes. Kongmin was tarred with the same brush: Nothing good could come of a king who would deign to appoint a Buddhist monk prime minister, it was argued. In recent years some historians who criticize the pro-Chinese position of Korea for so much of its history have burnished Kongmin's image. They see Kongmin as a romantic hero who, had he prevailed, might have helped Korea lead a more independent course less subservient to China.

General Yi Songgye

In its decline the Koryo court faced another problem besides the ouster of their Mongol overlords. Japanese pirates were attacking and robbing coastal areas, leaving large areas of the coast depopulated. Korea initi-ated military campaigns against the pirates in which two powerful generals emerged—Yi Songgye (1335–1408) and Choe Yong (1316–88). The two, who were both successful in the Japanese campaigns, also proved pivotal in the new fights on the Chinese front.

The new Ming court was not as loyal to Koryo as Koryo was to Ming. Koryo was quick to recognize the Ming as the rightful successor to the alien Yuan dynasty. The Ming court, however, was suspicious of its "little brother," a loyal tributary among the barbarians. Ming laid claim to the territory the Yuan had held in the northern part of the peninsula. Koryo counterclaimed the territory, which it had held prior to the Yuan confiscation.

The two generals, Choe and Yi, differed on how to deal with the problem. Choe wanted to attack the Ming forces to the north of Korea, while Yi opposed the attack. However, King U (r. 1374–88) chose to attack, and as a kind of test of loyalty he put Yi in charge of the expedition. Yi obediently led the march north. In the middle of the Yalu River, on the islands in the estuary of the river, Yi Songgye was caught in the mid-summer monsoon rains, and there he made a momentous decision. He decided it would be better to take over the kingdom of Koryo rather than pursue a basically suicidal mission against the Ming. He turned his forces around and successfully marched on Kaesong. The year was 1388.

For the next four years Yi controlled the court from behind the scenes. He deposed King U and installed U's son, Chang (r. 1388–89). Then, claiming that King Chang was tainted by Mongol blood, Yi placed King Kongyang (r. 1389–92) on the throne, a distant royal relative who was descended from an early Koryo king. Yi banished his military rival, Choe Yong, and then had him executed. He was paving the way for the establishment of a new ruling dynasty.

New dynasties in Korea were rare. The Koryo dynasty had survived a military coup and the Mongol invasion, and it was in the process of recovering from the fall of the Yuan dynasty. To set up a new dynasty was potentially a violation of tributary agreements with China, and it was certainly a violation of Confucian ethics: "There is only one sun in the sky; there is only one king on the throne." Yi Songgye's new dynasty had to be set up very carefully. When he proclaimed the new dynasty four years later, in 1392, he set up a line of rulers that was to last for 518 years. Only the third of the Korean dynasties, it was also to be the last.

Founding of the Choson Dynasty

Yi Songgye had waited for four years after his return from the northern border to Kaesong before he declared the new dynasty. Having replaced the king with a puppet king he could control and use to deflect any possible countercoup attempts, Yi made his preparations behind the scenes, deciding who would be loyal to him and who would not. Then he announced his new dynasty in 1392.

Four years after the establishment of the new dynasty, the court was moved to a new capital, Hanyang, today's Seoul, capital of South Korea. The new rulers gained several advantages by moving. The first was geomantic auspiciousness: One of the king's advisers, a specialist in geomancy, claimed that the setting of Seoul was ideal. The second reason was to get away from anyone in the old capital who might still be loyal to the old court and who might cause problems for the new dynasty. The move to Seoul made it all the more difficult to restore the Koryo court should anyone want to try. In the process Yi Songgye made it clear that he was going to set his own course.

The founding of the new dynasty was only partially based on military might. Though Yi Songgye was a military man, his supporters included a large group of officials, most of whom had passed the Confucian civil service examination (Clark 1982, 17). Not only were they Confucian scholars, they had been influenced by the revival of Confucianism led by the famous late-Song scholar and commentator on the classics Zhu Xi (1130–1200). These Neo-Confucian scholars supported the new rulers and provided much of the rationale and intellectual justification for setting up the new dynasty. Taking a dim view of Buddhism, they argued for its disenfranchisement. Laws were enacted that restricted Buddhist temples to remote mountainous areas, and monks were not allowed to enter Seoul, the new capital. The vast lands held by Buddhist temples were confiscated and distributed to those who had helped Yi Songgye. With Neo-Confucianism came not only laws restricting the activities of the Buddhists but an unswerving acceptance of Chinese culture, including the point of view that Chinese culture was superior and should be emulated. That emulation began with a centralized government structure, then extended to rituals, both public and private, and eventually came to dictate family matters and interpersonal behavior. The process had already begun in the late Koryo period: Besides Chinese-style government organization and the exam system for recruitment of officers, Koryo had adopted the National Confucian Academy and other trappings of Chinese or Confucian institutions (Duncan 1998). The completion of the "Confucianization" process was to take another 200 to 300 years, but once the Neo-Confucians set it in motion at the founding of the dynasty, there was no turning back.

Neo-Confucianism

Neo-Confucianism relied on the original teachings of Confucius but added a metaphysical element that attempted to explain the mysteries of life. The key concepts in Neo-Confucianism are *li* and *qi*. Translated often as "principle" and "life force," respectively, the two concepts became the basis for understanding life both in a biological sense and in a spiritual sense. For example, a pine tree is a pine tree because it has the *li* of a pine tree, which is different from that of a maple tree or an apple tree. *Qi* is that which gives the pine tree life and enables it to grow and flourish. In the spiritual realm human personality develops from the interaction of *li* and *qi* of the person and is expressed in the seven emotions common to humans—desire, hate, love, fear, grief, anger, and joy. These attributes need to be controlled and refined with the goal of becoming a noble person or sage, the ideal in original Confucianism. The two fundamental principles of Confucian statecraft are virtue and merit. In order to govern one must first be able to successfully govern oneself. Thus, authority is most effective when it is waged by good example. Whole treatises were written on these subjects, often in the form of commentaries on earlier writers. Zhu Xi, the preeminent figure in the founding of Neo-Confucianism, wrote commentaries on the works of Confucius. Korean Neo-Confucian scholars wrote commentaries on the commentaries of Zhu Xi, and later scholars wrote commentaries on their predecessors' works. Confucian thought stresses learning as an integral component of not only better governing oneself but also improving one's chances for success within society.

CHONG MONGJU (1337–1392)

Chong was a member of the group of Neo-Confucian scholars associated with Yi Songgye in the last days of the Koryo dynasty. He was committed to Confucianism as the best alternative to the alleged corruption of Buddhism in late Koryo. The group of Neo-Confucian scholars worked to revive the "fallen society," but unlike the others, Chong did not see the need for a new dynasty. In the end he declined to give his support to Yi Songgye. Yi's son, Pangwon, asked Chong to join, but Chong refused and was executed on a stone bridge in Kaesong called the "Good Bamboo Bridge." The stain of his blood on the bridge is said to be still visible today—such was the power of his morality. He is one of the 18 sages enshrined in the National Confucian Academy.

As a martyr Chong Mongju is a great symbol of loyalty in Korea today. His unswerving loyalty was captured in a poem he wrote to the Yi house in response to the invitation to join the new dynasty. The phrase "one red heart" is a symbol of undying loyalty that is often repeated in poems, plays, and stories in Korean literature.

The poem is a *sijo*, a three-line poem with four segments in each line, which had come into fashion just before Chong Mongju's time. *Sijo* were popular throughout the Choson period and are still written today. Chong's *sijo* is memorized by practically all Koreans and is foundational in understanding both the structure of a *sijo* and the concept of loyalty.

Song of Loyalty

Though I die, and die again, though I die a hundred times,
Long after my bones have turned to dust; whether my soul
   exists or not,
How can the loyalty, to my Lord, of this one red heart, ever fade
   away?

Source: Chong Mongju. "Song of Loyalty." Available online. URL: http://blog.ohmynews.com/jeongwh59/231064. Accessed February 13, 2009. Poem translated by Mark Peterson.

The Confucian classics and the commentaries became the subject of the all-important examination system that determined who would be recruited to serve in the government. Thus, the government was run by Confucian scholars, the so-called scholar-officials.

The Role of the Examination System

The role of the examination system in late Koryo and all of Choson cannot be overemphasized. The examinations determined almost all recruitment to government offices (Choe 1987). The few exceptions were for sons of certain high officials, who could at times be appointed to office without having passed the exams. In such a case, however, the father had obtained his office by passing the exams. Government positions were virtually the only source of power, wealth, prestige, or recognition in Choson society.

There were three levels of exams: Those for lawyers, physicians, and accountants (as well as translators and geomancers-astronomers) were considered third tier. Second were exams for military officials. The first-tier exams, consisting of two levels of tests, were for civil office.

In the 518 years of the Choson dynasty, 14,564 men passed the highest civil service exam, an average of about 30 per year—an elite group indeed (Seongmu Lee 2004). These were the men who occupied the prime positions in the government. Starting at a lower or middle level, they worked their way up over the course of their careers. About 50,000 men passed the military exams and became military officers. Some civilian posts were open to military officers as well. For instance, certain county magistracies were saved for military officers. Nevertheless, it was clear that the civilian officials were higher in the pecking order.

The term for "aristocrat" or "gentleman" in Korean is *yangban*, meaning "both" or "two" (*yang*) and "sides" or "ranks" (*ban*). The two sides were the military and the civilian (Taik-kyoo Kim 1989, 87). This reflects the fact that power resided in those who had passed the two exams: both the civil service exam and the military officer's exam.

Those who passed the exams to become lawyers, physicians, accountants, translators, and geomancers-astronomers were considered technicians, skilled people necessary for running the government. These exams were collectively called the *chapkwa*, literally "the miscellaneous exams." Lower in prestige than the civil exam and the military exam, the miscellaneous exams were used to recruit highly skilled professionals to assist in the work of the central government. Only those whose fathers or grandfathers had served in such positions could take these exams. These skilled workers constituted a relatively small, intermarrying class called the *chungin*, literally "the middle people." One might assume that these "middle people" constituted a middle class in sociological terms, but that was not the case: They derived the name *middle people* from the fact that they all lived in the center of Seoul. The hereditary control of the exam within these lineages was such that succeeding generations could specialize in other *chungin* professions. For example, suppose a man passed the exam in law. One of his sons might also pass the law exam, but another son might become a translator. In the third generation there might be another translator, but then another grandson could become a doctor. In the fourth generation there might be some who passed the exams their father or grandfather did, and some who might not pass any exam, but in the fifth generation perhaps someone might again pass one of the exams. In this way, the "middle people" kept control of the lesser positions of the government.

Although in some ways they were looked down upon by the aristocracy, the *chungin* were part of the elite of society. While they were indeed lower than the aristocracy, with their position and power they were nonetheless well above the common people. They held the trappings of the upper class, including secure positions with good stipends and tile-roofed houses instead of the thatched-roofed houses of the lower classes, and they owned slaves. They also kept genealogies printed in expensively bound books similar to those held by the aristocrats.

Social Structure and the Census System

The census was conducted every three years. Everyone was required to report to the county magistrate's office, where the census registers were updated. Each family had a copy of its previous census for the individual household that would be examined, and any changes (births, deaths, or marriages) were added to the new document for that year.

The census clearly labeled each household head and adult members according to their social status, which fell into three large groupings: aristocrat (including the *chungin*), commoner, and slave. Aristocrats were the most typical owners of slaves, although occasionally a commoner would own a slave, and, strangely, sometimes a slave would own a slave (Palais 1984, 173).

Some aristocrats had titles and offices that made them part of the ruling elite, but many were simply descendants of office-holding aristocrats who themselves had only the title of *yuhak*, which literally means "juvenile scholar." Scholars would be registered by this designation throughout their lives, even when they were 70 or 80 years old. After a *yuhak* died his title would change in the registers to "deceased scholar." The term for this was *haksaeng*, the very term used today for "student" in Korea, China, and Japan, literally meaning "a scholarly life." (In the case of the deceased Korean ancestors, the term must have been used in the past tense—"had lived a scholarly life.")

The census registers not only recorded those living in the household but gave the genealogy of the husband, wife, daughters-in-law, and others who lived in the house. The genealogy was construed as the "four ancestors"—the father, grandfather, and great-grandfather in the male line and then the maternal grandfather. Agnatic relationships, those tracing male ancestry and kinship, were the ones recorded.

After the aristocrats the census listed the commoners and then the slaves. Commoners also had occupational titles by which they were registered. Many were in the military, some with specialized positions such "beacon fire tender," and others were foot soldier, sailor, and artilleryman. Other commoners were recorded as carpenters, metal craftsmen, leatherworkers, herb collectors, and many other specialties.

Slaves were mostly just recorded as "slaves," but some slaves had specialized duties and in practice did not look much different from the commoners. Some slaves lived in the households of their owners, and others lived separately, sometimes far away.

Transition to the Choson Dynasty

The Choson dynasty was established by elite members of the dynasty it replaced, and the military action to support the takeover was minimal; there was little loss of life or blood (Duncan 1988, 39). Even so, the downside of such a smooth transition is its effects on the lower side of the social scale. Without social upheaval, the lowest class—the slaves—had no opportunity to escape their servile situation. When the new dynasty was established, it published a list of "merit subjects," government officials who had helped to establish the new dynasty. Those on the list included some military men, but most were scholar-officials who were now advocates of Neo-Confucianism. For their merit they were rewarded with land and slaves. The land and slaves were confiscated from the previous ruling class, those tied to the Mongols, and from Buddhist monasteries that had grown large with the consent of the Koryo court. Slaves owned by aristocrats, armies, and monasteries saw no release from their bondage—they became the slaves of the aristocracy of the new dynasty.

Although domestically things went smoothly for Yi and his new dynasty, this was not the case in foreign relations: China's new Ming dynasty, one that had just ejected the foreign Yuan dynasty, was wary of the new leaders on the Korean Peninsula. Seeking the approval of the Chinese and the reestablishment of the tributary relationship, the new Korean court sent word of the new dynasty to China, and as part of its "big brother–little brother" relationship asked the Chinese emperor to choose the name of the new dynasty (Clark 1998). Of the two options presented by Korea, China selected "Choson," but China had some serious reservations about recognizing the new dynasty. It did not like Yi Songgye because, the Chinese claimed, his genealogy included some questionable ancestors. It was not until well into the new dynasty that it relented and extended unreserved recognition to Choson.

The dynasty was well set up, but it was not without its problems. Yi had two wives and eight sons, six by the first wife and two by the second. His sons by the first wife, particularly the fifth son, Pangwon, were old enough to have fought alongside him. Pangwon held the rank of general and was a principal adviser to his father in establishing the new dynasty. It was he who was most disappointed when Yi named the crown prince: It was to be the younger son of his second wife. Unwilling to sit by and watch that happen, Pangwon killed his 15-year-old half brother and the boy's older brother as well. The king, sickened by the killing among his sons, abdicated to Panggwa, his second son. It appears, however, that Pangwon was actually in control, because after two years Panggwa stepped aside to allow Pangwon to become the king. In the cautious style of his father, Pangwon had his brother sit on the throne to take any slings and arrows, and then when it was clearly safe he took the throne himself.

Yi Songgye is better known to history as King Taejo (r. 1392–98), the "temple name" for kings in the Chinese fashion. The Silla kings had not adopted the Chinese system of naming kings, but all the Koryo dynasty kings except for the four discredited kings at the end of the dynasty had had such names. The names were chosen after the king died and in some way described his reign. By tradition the founder of a dynasty was given the title *Taejo*. Very often the second king was named Taejong. In the Choson dynasty it was Pangwon, the de facto second king, who was titled Taejong (r. 1400–18). The insignificant king in between, Panggwa, was titled Chongjo, the "settled king," (r. 1398–1400).

Taejong (Pangwon) proved to be a capable ruler. He did much to firmly establish the dynasty, such as publish a code of laws that would govern the country for the next 500 years. It was his son, however, who was unquestionably the greatest king of Korean history. Taejong must have recognized the extraordinary talent of his third son because he abdicated his throne while still able to ensure that it passed peacefully and securely to his choice of heir. The man who had killed two brothers and forced a third off the throne in order to become king himself gave up his power early so that his sons could not do what he had done to get the throne. The new king was to be known as Sejong (r. 1418–50).

Sejong

Sejong's accomplishments are legendary. He commissioned research and publications in medicine, pharmacology, and agronomy (agricultural land management), making the latest advances in each field widely available. He supported the advancement of calendrical science and timekeeping (for example, during his reign a highly accurate water clock was developed), he standardized weights and measures to assure and encourage fairness in trading, and he improved laws and lightened punishments (Kim-Renaud 1992).

PAK YON (1378–1458)

The life of Pak Yon is an excellent example of the concern for correct ritual and ceremony in the Sejong court. King Sejong wanted the court music and ceremonies to be authentic and true to the Confucian classics. When Pak visited Ming China, he found that the music had changed from that of the time of Confucius and that the instruments played in the Ming court were not the same as those described in the classics.

At King Sejong's urging Pak began research on the texts, and from them he created authentic musical instruments. He wrote more than 40 reports to the throne that are recorded in the historical record presenting his findings and requesting approval to use them to compose the court orchestras and to create musical instruments.

One example of Pak's painstaking thoroughness was his quest to recreate an authentic bamboo flute like that to which Confucius would have listened. The ancient ritual text gave the measurements of the flute in terms of grains of rice: It was to be 100 grains long, and the size of the barrel was to be such that it could hold 300 grains of rice. Pak made such an instrument, but it did not sound right. He theorized that perhaps the grain at the time of Confucius was different, so he began to experiment with different sizes of bamboo shafts, measured by different kinds of grains. Pak found that a certain size of millet gave just the right ratio for a flute 100 grain long with a capacity of 300 grains. When he played that flute, the sound was sweet and true.

He also commissioned new maps of Choson's borders, recently expanded and secured by his father and grandfather, which were particularly important to the military men charged with defending them. He launched an attack against Tsushima, the island in the Korea Strait between Korea and Japan, to wipe out pirate bases, and then he negotiated an agreement with the So family, the lords of Tsushima, to control pirates who had been raiding Korean coastal towns.

Court ceremonies and other rituals were of utmost importance to King Sejong. He sent a delegation to Ming China to learn about their court ceremonies. His ambassadors returned to report that they were shocked at how far the imperial ceremonies in China had strayed from those described in the Confucian classics. King Sejong decided that Choson should follow the classics, and thus Korea was set on a course that was to make it more orthodox, more true to the Confucian texts, in actual practice than the Chinese.

Hangul, the Korean Alphabet

Of all of Sejong's accomplishments, by far his greatest and the one for which he is best known was the creation of hangul, the Korean alphabet. Observing that the people did not have their own script—they could use Chinese characters only awkwardly—Sejong wrote a declaration in 1446 that he would introduce an alphabet for common use. His stated objective was to provide a means of literacy for the common people. At the time only the upper class were literate because only they were conversant in Chinese, both in the way the Chinese themselves used it and in the specialized way that Koreans had developed it (*see* sidebar on *idu*, page 43). The scholar-officials who composed the elite class were well educated in written Chinese, the lingua franca of Asia, and could write correspondence for the Chinese court, arguments about Neo-Confucian philosophy, poetry, and anything else that a well-educated Chinese person could. They could also write Korean in the modified Chinese script, *idu*, but it was so difficult and cumbersome that only the well educated, those who knew classical Chinese, could use it.

The new alphabet was originally called *hunminjongum*, which means "to teach the people correct sounds." Clearly the alphabet had a prescriptive purpose, and a concern for the common people seems to have been foremost in King Sejong's mind. Today the alphabet is known as hangul.

Unlike the writing system of Japan, which is also influenced by Chinese, hangul is not a syllabary. For example, the two writing

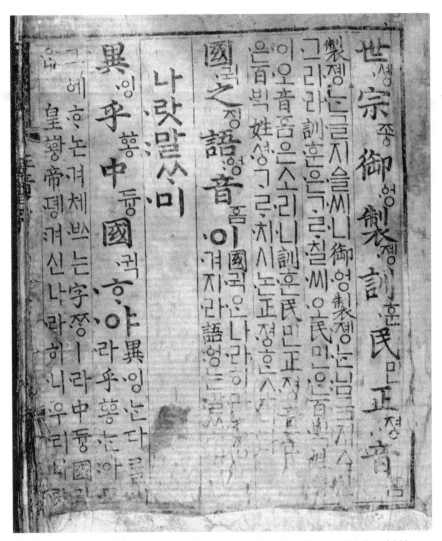

The first page of the declaration announcing the creation of the Korean alphabet, 1446
(Academy of Korean Studies)

systems used in Japanese, both hiragana and katakana, are based on syllables, that is, the consonants and vowels are not separable. The syllable *ka,* for instance, cannot be broken down into a "k" and an "a." Korean hangul, on the other hand, is a true alphabet, with 24 letters (10 vowels and 14 consonants) that can be combined in various ways to create just about any sound a person can pronounce. The words are arranged in syllabic units, mirroring Chinese to some extent, rather than being written in a simple line. Traditionally the syllables were arrayed vertically in columns that were read from right to left, but today they are arrayed horizontally and read from left to right. The structure of the syllables accommodates the inclusion of Chinese characters, if desired. The Korean language includes many words from Chinese coupled with grammatical parts that are pure Korean.

King Sejong commissioned his scholars to write an epic poem using the new alphabet. To the chagrin of the Confucian scholar-officials, he also had them write a biography of the Buddha, again showing his interest in the common people, many of whom were Buddhist.

The committee of scholars who helped with the alphabet and wrote other scholarly works were in a special office called the Chiphyonjon, meaning the "hall of the assembly of the wise." To it Sejong appointed his brightest scholars. He assigned some to travel to China to learn of other languages and scripts, but with all the help he had, remarkably, it was the king himself who was most concerned about the alphabet and who made the decisions about how it should be. Unlike many aspects of human endeavor, in which the one in charge gets the credit for work delegated to others, in this case the record shows it was the king himself who was directly involved in the creation of the alphabet.

The alphabet was not well received by some scholar-officials who were committed to Confucianism and Chinese scholarship. They judged the alphabet silly, too simple, and something that no serious person would ever use. Some renounced it, but the alphabet was useful and has stood the test of time. (Its widespread usage had to wait until the beginning of the 20th century, however, when hangul emerged in newspapers and other popular media in response to Western influences.)

The greatest challenge to hangul's survival came from Sejong's son, King Sejo. Because Sejo (b. 1417) usurped the throne, people wrote criticisms of him in hangul. In response Sejo outlawed the use of the alphabet and burned the books already printed in it.

Thereafter, the alphabet was seen as somewhat subversive and was used only clandestinely for the rest of the dynasty, from the late 15th century until the late 19th century. Though forbidden, it was still used privately, and a marvelous and large variety of literature circulated in handwritten copies. This large collection of handwritten stories and poetry has long been associated with female writers, but some experts believe that men also participated in the writing, copying, and circulation of this underground literary movement.

Sejo, the Usurper

King Sejong did not live to an old age. He died at the age of 47, leaving the throne to Munjong (r. 1450–52), his oldest son and, as the fifth king of the dynasty, the first to succeed to the throne in the prescribed fashion: The oldest son, he was named crown prince and then king, but this succession, too, was not to be normal, because Munjong died prematurely after only two years on the throne. His son, 12-year-old Tanjong (r. 1452–55), took the throne. After three years his uncle Sejo staged a takeover, claiming that the boy-king was being manipulated by evil advisers. Sejo arrested Tanjong and sentenced him to internal exile. After another two years—time to see what opposition might surface—Sejo ordered the execution of the boy (he was poisoned) and the arrest and execution of six former advisers, high officials whom Sejo accused of plotting to restore Tanjong to the throne.

As in the palace coup dramatized in Shakespeare's *Richard III,* a power-hungry uncle killed a nephew on the throne. Just four years earlier the six officials who were executed had been part of the court of Sejong, some having even served in the Chiphyon-jon, where hangul was invented. To their sympathizers they became known as the Six Martyrs. These "best and brightest," though discredited in life, lived on in glory in the memory of their descendants, while those who supported the usurper, Sejo, were regarded as corrupt and evil. Even so, it was Sejo's supporters who won control of the kingdom, and their descendants likewise gloried in the accomplishments of their ancestors. This split in the bureaucracy was a scar that was to mark the Choson period for the rest of its existence.

Yonsangun

Though he took the throne illegally, King Sejo (r. 1455–68) turned out to be an otherwise good ruler. His bloodstained beginning was not to mar the remainder of his reign. Like his brother, who ruled for only two years, Sejo's son Yejong (r. 1468–69) ruled for only one year. Sejo's grandson, Songjong (r. 1469–94), who ascended the throne at age 13, had a long and uneventful reign, but such was not the case for his son, Yonsangun.

Yonsangun (r. 1494–1506) was one of two kings who were not awarded the honorific posthumous title of *-jong* or *-jo.* Both had been deposed. Yonsangun and later Kwanghaegun were deemed unworthy of the title *king.* Rather, they retained their title of a prince, *-gun,* even after death.

SONG SAMMUN (1418–1456)

One of the Six Martyrs was a scholar-official named Song Sammun. Born the year Sejong ascended the throne, he became one of the young scholars in the Chiphyon-jon, or Hall of the Assembly of the Wise, and thus was one who assisted Sejong in the development of hangul. He was also one of those accused of plotting the restoration of the boy-king Tanjong and sentenced to death.

Before his death Song, also a poet, composed a four-line poem in Tang Chinese style. Korean scholars from Silla times onward had excelled in Tang poetry. They revered the famous Tang masters Li Pou and Tu Fu and wrote poems inspired by the masters.

The poem Song Sammun left is a gallows poem, one he allegedly wrote on the way to his death:

> The beating of the drum calls for a life.
> I turn to see the sun is about to set.
> On the road to hell, is there a tavern?
> At whose house will I rest my head tonight?

Song's poem is dark and guilt ridden, yet it may be meant ironically: Song knew his death was unjust and that his reputation was likely to be restored posthumously, which it was. He is heralded as a great martyr who died for his principles and was unjustly murdered by an unrighteous king.

Source of poem: Song Sammun. Untitled poem. Available online. URL: http://k.daum.net/qna/view.html?qid=3HUEm. Accessed February 13, 2009. Translation by Mark Peterson.

Yonsangun's crimes were numerous (Wagner 1975). He was capricious and violent, he killed servants who displeased him, and he was sexually abusive and paranoid. The most critical of his offenses were his purges: wholesale banishment or execution of officials. Yonsangun saw a structural conflict in the relationship between the king and the bureaucracy. He justified striking at the bureaucracy as necessary to protect the authority of the king. Indeed, Choson Korea's very structure fostered antagonism between the government and the king. There were checks and balances in that the government had control over certain aspects of the king's power, and these were the things that irritated Yonsangun.

To understand the nature of the dispute that had developed by the late 15th century, one must understand the constraints on the king implicit in Confucian government. Confucius taught that a virtuous ruler listened to remonstrance, which was defined as rightful criticism; the good king sought review and criticism of his actions. Korea's Confucian-inspired government structure included several offices that institutionalized the practice of remonstrance and made sure that the king would receive his daily allotment of it. In this arrangement the remonstrating official was guaranteed immunity from royal recrimination.

The three offices for remonstrance were collectively called the Censorate. The role of the first was to watch the king; the second watched the bureaucracy; and the third, which was originally a library—a kind of lecture hall for the king—took on censoring duties in that the high officials there had frequent contact with the king. Although each had a distinct and separate duty, in fact, they all tended to do the same thing. After all, if there was a problem in the bureaucracy, it became a problem for the king, since he made all appointments. In addition to the three offices of the Censorate, there was also the Royal Lecturate, an office that would meet with the king almost daily to study the Confucian classics. The young scholars who would teach young kings, debate with middle-aged kings, and be lectured to by old kings would occasionally criticize the king. Far from being an autocrat or dictator, the king was constantly being reviewed and criticized by government officials. This system worked for all the kings except Yonsangun.

The first purge unfolded in 1498, four years after Yonsangun became king. The issue was the writing of the history of Songjong, his father. A scholar named Kim Chongjik had written that Songjong's grandfather, Sejo, was a usurper. Because the legitimacy of Yonsangun's great-grandfather reflected on the legitimacy of Yonsangun himself, the king was enraged to find a criticism of Sejo. Although the author of the history had died six years earlier, Yonsangun struck out at Kim's disciples who were holding government offices. The purge was a series of executions and banishments. Not only were the living punished, the dead were persecuted as well. Kim Chongjik's body was exhumed and his body parts scattered. Criminal punishment often involved cutting the offender's body into eighths, so that one body part could be sent to each of the eight provinces and there posted with a sign identifying the criminal and his crime. This punishment was carried out on Kim Chongjik's body. (Just as people could be tried and "executed" after they had died, so they could be restored or exonerated. Later Kim was exonerated.)

Yonsangun was not finished. In 1504 he learned that his mother, who had died when he was three, had been persecuted and forced to drink poison. This sent him into another rage, and he purged several dozen more officials whom he had identified in the persecution of his mother. The second purge prompted the government to undertake the difficult and perilous task of deposing the king. The government successfully arrested Yonsangun, stripped him of his powers, and sent him into exile. Choson practices of punishment often included banishment, which was always internal. Often the banishment was lifted after a few years, but at other times the case was reheard and a more severe penalty decreed, including the death penalty; this was the case for the boy king Tanjong, in 1455, but Yonsangun did not stand for a second trial. He was banished to an island in the Yellow Sea, where he died a few weeks later. The record does not say how he died, but one can assume it was not a natural death.

Cho Kwangjo

The government installed the king's brother, Chungjong (r. 1506–44), as the next king. His reign was long and peaceful, but he did enact one purge in 1519 (Sung Moon Kim 2002, 233). This purge was quite different in nature from those conducted under Yonsangun. In this case a bright and ambitious young scholar who had passed the civil service exam was the center of the problem: Cho Kwangjo (1482–1519). Cho found the king open to new and liberal ideas and argued that the exams were too philosophical, too detached from the practical needs of the government. Their basic idea was that good men make good government, a "good man" being one who understood the classics; by administering a test to see who knew the classics, one could identify good men and establish good government. Cho basically agreed with the need for an exam to determine which candidates were best qualified, but he argued that some of the questions ought to deal with practical matters and not just Confucian philosophy. The king agreed, and Cho was allowed to administer the next exam. He thus recruited a corps of young scholar-officials to help him in leading the government in a new and more practical direction.

In his idealism, however, Cho also attacked the conservative elements close to the king. The king had rewarded a large group of more than 100 men with lands and slaves for helping him secure the throne. Cho was able to convince the king that 76 of those men should be eliminated from the rosters of merit. This, of course, enraged those cut off from power and wealth, and they in turn convinced the king that Cho was dangerous and ambitious. The king accepted their indictment, and Cho and several of his closest allies were executed, with several others exiled.

The way the enemies of Cho Kwangjo got the king to turn against him is one of the more unusual stories in Korean history. His accusers found leaves of trees on the palace grounds chewed through by insects, leaving holes arranged in such a way that they seemed to spell out the words "Cho would be king." Cho's enemies were able to convince the king that it was an omen. In reality, someone had written on the leaves with honey, and insects had eaten away the sweetened areas, thus creating the holes and the message.

At only 37 years of age, Cho was executed by poisoning in 1519 along with a handful of his colleagues. In Choson Korea, however, issues surrounding an individual and what he did, right or wrong, did not end with his death. In subsequent years Cho was restored posthumously. His offices and honors were all restored to him, meaning that his descendants got the benefits of their ancestor's position. Above and beyond restoration, Cho Kwangjo was one of those selected for enshrinement in the National Confucian Shrine, one of 18 to be named a sage.

The fourth in the series of purges unfolded in 1545. King Chungjong died in 1544 and was replaced by his son Injong (r. 1544–45), who chose as his advisers allies of Cho Kwangjo, but King Injong died after eight months as king. He was replaced by his half brother Myongjong (1545–67), who was only 11 years old. Injong and Myongjong, sons of Chungjong, were born of different mothers; coincidentally, both women were named Yun. Each also had an uncle, known as "Big Yun" and "Little Yun," with tremendous influence over the king and the court. Injong and Big Yun leaned toward Cho Kwangjo's supporters, but Myongjong and Little Yun were on the side of those Cho had removed from the merit roster. They led the purge of 1545 in which more of Cho's young Neo-Confucian idealists were banished.

Yi Hwang and Yi I

The balance of the 16th century was a time of great peace and progress, particularly in regard to Neo-Confucian philosophy. From 1545 to 1592 the major landmarks on the historical scenery of Korea were the two giants of Neo-Confucian scholarship, Yi Hwang and Yi I.

Yi Hwang (1501–70), also known by his pen name, Toegye, was the older of the two, but his work overlapped that of Yi I, also known by his pen name, Yulgok (1536–85). The two scholars met only once but exchanged letters from time to time. More important than the things they discussed with each other, however, were the issues they discussed with their disciples. The issues were extremely arcane, dealing with philosophy as developed by the great Chinese Song dynasty scholar Zhu Xi. He, with other scholars, was responsible for the revival of Confucianism called Neo-Confucianism. Zhu Xi had worked in the realm of previous scholars who wrote commentaries on the classics, but his approach was so comprehensive that it was a virtual reconstruction of Confucianism. Yi Toegye and Yi Yulgok made their contributions by commenting on Zhu Xi's commentaries.

The two great 16th-century Korean scholars agreed more than they disagreed, but they and their disciples were known for what they disagreed on. The important issue was that by that point, with 200 years of experience with Neo-Confucianism behind it, Choson-dynasty Korea had become an orthodox, thoroughly committed Confucian society, at least philosophically. Although most of their discussion centered on arcane aspects of Neo-Confucianism, such as whether *li* or *qi* dominates, Yi Hwang and Yi I famously disagreed during these discussions. At the outset of the dynasty, there were court records of complaints that certain officials were not carrying out the ceremonies; later, however, the prestige associated with being able to carry out the ceremonies seems to have been sufficient motivation for those who could afford it. Since the proper performance of the ceremonies was an expensive affair, only the upper class could afford such luxury. This and the printing of one's genealogy, another expensive enterprise, thus became proof that one belonged to the upper class. The genealogies recorded the important dates on which ceremonies were to occur as well as the gravesites, the places where such ceremonies took place.

One of the more practical issues Yulgok raised was military preparedness and a possible invasion from Japan. He warned of the need to raise a larger army; this went unheeded, and he died in 1584. By 1592 the people of Choson Korea must have wished they had been better prepared: The Japanese invaded.

The Japanese Invasion of 1592–1598

Korea was to be forever changed by what happened in 1592. Again, it was events outside Korea—this time in Japan—that impacted Korea. The 16th century in Japan was a time of political turmoil and unending warfare. When one warlord, Toyotomi Hideyoshi (1536–98), was finally able to unify the island nation under his control, he looked for other lands to conquer.

The Japanese objective was not Korea, however, but China. Toyotomi Hideyoshi sent a note to Korea in 1591 asking for an "imperial road" to China through Korea. Ever loyal to "older brother" China, Choson Koreans were insulted by the request and reacted with outrage: How could this insignificant island kingdom dare to invade the great empire of China? More to the point, how could the island of "dwarfs"—the Korean pejorative for the Japanese—ever think that the Koreans would turn their backs on China? Still greater insults were about to be inflicted on the people of Korea.

In response to the letter asking for passage to China, the Korean court sent an embassy to Japan. Upon his return the ambassador reported that the Japanese threat was groundless and the Korean court need not worry about a possible invasion. The deputy ambassador, however, offered a dissenting opinion. He reported that he had left the official delegation and looked around in Japan, had seen soldiers and their arms, and had concluded that the threat was credible. The king, choosing to accept the ambassador's report and ignore the deputy ambassador's warning, made no special preparations for the defense of the country.

It may not have made a difference. Korea probably could not have prepared for the invasion in time because, unlike the Koreans, the Japanese were experienced in warfare—Hideyoshi's forces had just conquered the other warlords of Japan to unify the empire—and the Japanese had superior weaponry. Japanese contact with Europeans, which began in 1543, had led to the purchase and manufacture of muzzle-loading firearms. The Koreans had cannon and gunpowder, but they had not developed the smaller weapons that could be carried, hoisted to a shoulder, and fired.

In addition, the Japanese were highly trained. They had been at war for a century and knew warfare. The Koreans had been at peace for exactly 200 years—since the founding of the dynasty, which had been done with minimal warfare. Before that Korea had been at peace for an additional 100 years or so. Koreans had had border skirmishes with Jurchens in small bands and had fought Japanese pirate bands along the coast, but Choson Korea had virtually no combat experience. On balance, Koreans were not prepared to fight the powerful Japanese army.

The Japanese landed a large force near Pusan on May 25, 1592, and quickly overwhelmed the minor resistance there. They then marched and fought their way to Seoul, arriving in less than three weeks. One

Japanese invasion of Pusan on the southeast coast, 1592 (Academy of Korean Studies)

could hardly walk that far in that time, let alone fight and conquer, but the Japanese did. They almost completely overwhelmed the Korean forces. The slaughter of Koreans continued for another seven years.

When the Japanese reached Seoul, the residents panicked; many fled, including the king. King Sonjo (r. 1567–1608), otherwise a popular and capable king, was jeered and pelted with debris as his royal entourage

Japanese invasion overcoming the inland fortress of Tongnae in 1592. The riders at the top of the painting are heading off to warn other areas that the Japanese armies have arrived. (Academy of Korean Studies)

left for the Chinese border. Some outraged slaves burned government buildings ahead of the Japanese soldiers to destroy the records of their servile status.

The salvation for Korea came in the form of Chinese intervention on land and Korean naval success at sea. The Chinese court had debated whether they should intervene in Korea. There were clearly "hawks" and "doves" in the debate. The hawks argued that the Chinese had a tributary relationship and duty to go to Korea's aid and that it was better to fight the enemy abroad than to be forced to fight on home soil (an argument not unlike that heard at various points in 20th-century America). The doves argued that it was not their fight and judged that the Japanese, barbarians who had never posed a threat before, could not possibly be a threat to the great "Middle Kingdom."

The Chinese response, when it came, was strong and full: The Chinese sent both foot soldiers and ships. Together with the Korean forces that were able to regroup and fight for the homeland, they were able to stall the Japanese invasion by early 1593.

Admiral Yi Sunsin

Korea's naval strategy was one point of success in the country's struggle against the Japanese invaders. Led by a remarkable admiral, Yi Sunsin (1545–98), the navy was able to cut off Japanese supply lines, which extended from Seoul to the Chinese border, by repelling Japanese ships sailing around the southern and western coasts. Admiral Yi had prepared a strong navy whose fleet included some "turtle boats," ships with a protective covering of metal plates to make them impervious to the fire arrows of the enemy. These turtle boats were the first ironclad warships in the world. More than the ships, however, Admiral Yi's knowledge of the Korean waters and skill in planning an attack were the decisive factors in Korea's naval victories.

Having reached a stalemate, the combatants entered a protracted period of negotiations from early 1593 to 1597. During the break in fighting, officials at court turned to faultfinding. One of the tragedies of the war was that one of Yi Sunsin's rivals at court raised an indictment against him that for some reason the king accepted. Yi was arrested, relieved of his command, and reduced in rank to a foot soldier. When the war resumed, the new commander, Won Kyun (d. 1597), believed a spy's false report that the Japanese forces were marshalling near a certain island. Admiral Won sailed into the trap and lost nearly every ship. Admiral Yi was then restored to the command, and the naval battles went once again in Korea's favor. In the final battle of the war, Yi Sunsin died at the helm of the command ship in a story as dramatic as any story of heroism in combat found in history or fiction: He was mortally wounded but had his nephew, who was fighting at his side, keep him upright so the sailors would not be disheartened by seeing the loss of their commander.

The renewed warfare was occasioned by a breakdown in negotiations between the Chinese and the Japanese; the unfortunate Koreans, on whose territory the war was fought, were powerless at the side of the superpowers at the negotiating table. The sticking points of the negotiations were largely symbolic. Having given up on their dream of conquering China, the Japanese wanted to be recognized as an empire of rank equal to that of the Chinese. In the worldview of the Chinese and, of course, the Koreans, such a thing was impossible. The war raged again until Hideyoshi, who had never left Japan, ordered the retreat from his deathbed in 1598. The Chinese and Korean ships had formed a blockade, which the Japanese broke through to land onshore and load the last foot soldiers on the ships. Then the Japanese ships had to break out of the blockade to sail home to Japan, and in this naval battle Admiral Yi died. The Koreans and Chinese could have let them go without a battle, but they did not. Rather, perhaps fearing that the Japanese

COMBAT COMPENSATION

The Korean and Chinese forces pursued the Japanese, although they knew the enemy was retreating. One reason they might have done so involves soldiers' compensation. Soldiers were paid for each confirmed kill that they made; a soldier confirmed his kill by presenting the dead man's right ear. Each ear submitted yielded the soldier a payment in silver. Not just the Koreans but also the Japanese and Chinese structured solders' payments in this way. At one point soldiers began mutilating the left ear to claim it was actually a right ear, and the government changed its policy to that of compensating soldiers for bringing in noses rather than ears.

No one knows what happened to the Japanese ears and noses taken by the Korean and Chinese forces. The Japanese collection of Korean ears and noses, however, was thrown onto a pile near the center of government in Japan's capital, Kyoto. That mound, taller than the houses surrounding it, is still found in Kyoto today.

might return again, the combined forces fought the retreating Japanese forces vigorously in this last battle of the war (Ledyard 1987, 81).

Aftermath of the War

The war left 2 million to 4 million Koreans dead and destroyed most of the homes and farms of the countryside. Very few buildings made of wood or documents made of paper that predated the Japanese invasion are to be found in Korea today. The destruction and chaos must have been nearly total. Amazingly, the court survived, and the social order remained intact. The king returned to Seoul, and the rebuilding process began, though slowly. All five palaces in Seoul had been burned; the main palace was not rebuilt until 1865. In a sense the Choson dynasty limped through the remainder of its tenure, as symbolized by the slowness to restore its palaces to their former glory.

Japan lost soldiers and sailors, but its people and land were not affected by the war. After the death of Hideyoshi, the Japanese soldiers returned home, alas to more warlord confrontations. Hideyoshi's heirs were not able to maintain power, and eventually one of Hideyoshi's rivals, Tokugawa Ieyasu (1543–1616), succeeded in uniting the islands once again. He founded the final shogunate of the Japanese line of shogun dynasties, which ended in 1867.

The Europeans, who first arrived in Japan in the mid-16th century, brought with them technology, goods, and missionaries. The relationship had a great impact on Japan, especially in terms of economic and technological developments. The following years came to be called Japan's "Christian Century" until the missionaries were expelled by the Tokugawa shogunate in the first half of the 17th century. Among the Catholic converts at the time was one of Hideyoshi's generals, Konishi Yukinaga; in the invasion he took with him in his entourage a Portuguese priest, Gregorio de Cespedes, who is believed to be the first European to set foot in Korea. For Korean Catholics it is a bitter piece of history that the first Catholic arrived with a murderous invading army.

In addition to physical objects the Japanese took from Korea living treasures—potters, whom they carried off as captives to Japan. For centuries thereafter to the present day, the finest ceramics, teacups, and teapots for the tea ceremony, a symbol of Japanese culture, were produced in the villages where the Korean potters were forced to settle. There were four such villages, one of which, a place called Okawachi, a part of present-day Imari city, was famous for the porcelain ware it produced.

China did not fare well in the war's aftermath. The Ming dynasty had spent so much of its capital and manpower in the war with Japan that it became vulnerable to its northern neighbors, the Manchu. The Manchu toppled the Ming dynasty and set up their own rulers, the Qing dynasty, in 1644. China's weakness can be attributed, in part, to one of the last Ming emperors, Wanli (r. 1573–1620), who was derelict in his duties, leaving his eunuchs to run the country while he devoted himself to his pleasures, particularly eating. He became so obese that he could not walk without assistance, coming to personify the corruption and incompetence of royalty, but it was the war with the Japanese in defense of Korea that set up China for the Manchu takeover.

The war's greatest legacy may be the resilience of the Choson state and people. Of the three warring states, Choson Korea lost the most people, including a large number of civilians, unlike the Chinese and Japanese. Koreans also lost nearly all developed property. Some palaces were not restored for another two and a half centuries. Although Japan saw a change of shogunate and China was soon conquered by the Manchu, the state of Choson, unquestionably the greatest victim of the war, did not fall.

The Manchu Qing Confrontation

The Manchu were descendants of the Jurchen who had troubled Korea earlier. They conquered China, but they also attacked Korea on their way into China to secure their flank against a possible attack from China's indebted ally. They attacked Choson in 1627 and quickly secured Korea's pledge of loyalty in Chinese tributary fashion. The Koreans, too battered to resist, secretly contacted Ming China and planned a combined attack on the Manchu. The Ming-Choson alliance never coalesced, however, and the Manchu attacked Korea again in 1636. This time, in order to secure Korea's alliance, they took the crown prince and his two brothers captive, reestablishing the hostage system seen earlier in the Yuan-Koryo relationship, but unlike the Mongols, who held each successive generation of crown princes, the Manchu did not continue the practice beyond the first generation. Once they had secured the Chinese court and proclaimed the Qing dynasty in 1644, they released the three Korean princes.

The degree of devastation in Korea at the hands of the Manchu was insignificant compared with that wreaked by the Japanese a generation earlier. The Manchu were not interested in the goods of Korea, they only demanded its loyalty in their pursuit for the greater prize—China.

The eldest of the three princes taken by the Manchu died mysteriously after returning to Seoul. The second son later became Hyojong (r. 1649–59), who throughout his reign harbored great hatred for the Qing court. He planned a "Northern Retaliation," but it never came to be. Gradually, the Korean court came to accept the Qing and used the Qing calendar in all public documents, but in private discourse, letters, bills of sale, and the like many continued to use the reign date of the last Ming emperor. Because the calendar was based on a 60-year cycle, what to do in years 61 and after was a problem, but this was solved by referring to the second appearance of a year in the cycle as the second *kapcha* ("first year"), for example. Since the Qing dynasty continued for another 250 years, some Korean documents were dated the third, or the fourth, or even the fifth *kapcha*. Aside from being a quirky method of recording years, it was a measure of Korean loyalty to the "true" Chinese court and their displeasure with the aliens who had usurped the Chinese throne.

This usurpation of the Ming court posed a philosophical and religious problem for Choson. How could they show the same respect to the usurpers, the barbarian Qing? Ming was the "older brother" in Confucian terms, but the Qing was not worthy of elder brother status. This moral dilemma pushed Choson toward increased orthodoxy in their practice of Confucianism. Since older brother was gone, it was up to younger brother to maintain Confucian standards. Cultural compromises that Koreans had heretofore routinely made in adopting Confucianism would no longer be acceptable, with great consequences for society. Ritual practices and inheritance laws began to change over the next century. More immediately, what should have been a minor issue in the interpretation of the ritual requirements became a major confrontation with deadly consequences for the losers.

The conflict began at the death of King Hyojong in 1659. His son King Hyonjong (r. 1659–74) ascended the throne at age 18. The question was how long the king's stepmother should mourn for King Hyojong. She was advised to mourn for one year, the time period stated in the ritual texts. However, she had previously mourned three years for the king's elder brother who had died young. One faction at court argued that those who advised her to mourn only one year were lessening the stature of the king who had just died. This had implications for the legitimacy of the new king, Hyonjong. Nonetheless, Hyonjong stuck with his decision to support those who said one year was correct. In spite of resentments on the part of those who argued for three years, the issue passed.

The next occasion for a mourning ritual, however, reignited the issue. This time it was a question of how long the king's step-grand-mother should mourn for her step-grandson's queen, Hyojong's wife. The particular issue was not as important as the fervor with which the officials at court took sides in this debate on correct Confucian ceremony (Haboush 1998). There were five degrees of mourning, ranging from three years to one month: Three years were reserved for parent or child; one year was for grandparent, grandchild, or stepchild; and nine months, three months, and one month of mourning were prescribed for more distant relatives. Some at court argued that the grandmother should mourn for one year, as for a grandchild, and others that she should mourn for nine months since she was a step-grandmother. In this case those who had earlier argued for three years argued for one year, and those who had argued for one year now argued for nine months. The debate battle lines were drawn in the Choson court. Powerful officials asserted each side of the debate, and younger officials lined up behind each. It was a dramatic showdown, with the king in the position of deciding which side was correct. The winning side would remain in the court; the losing side would have to resign, or worse, they could be banished or executed for giving the king wrong advice. The king chose the one-year option, the more con-servative choice, and not only reaffirmed the position of the deceased step-grandmother—treating her like a birth grandmother—but also set Korea on an even more orthodox track in the application of Confucianism in politics and society.

The showdown was pivotal in the history of the late Choson court. Some historians have concluded that the ceremonies were not really the issue, arguing that philosophy was only a cover for a fight for power between factions at court. However, more recently, historians have made the case convincingly that philosophy was at the heart of the conflict: Confucianism became so important that an exact analysis of proper ceremonies was important in Korea, which had become the repository of orthodox Confucianism now that China was under the control of barbarians.

A shrine on the outskirts of modern Seoul is another testament to the fervor of Korean Confucianism. At the foothill of a mountain is a shrine to the imperial family of the Ming dynasty where Confucian-style ceremonies are still offered. Such offerings are not found in China or Taiwan, but in Korea, ever loyal, the ceremonies are still practiced. This is an interesting statement on the Confucianization of Korea and the depth of feeling for the core Confucian concept of loyalty.

After the devastating Japanese invasion at the end of the 16th century and then the invasions by the Manchu in the early 17th century, the Korean people settled into a long period of peace and recovery. Gradually, the population began to grow again, mourning for the dead became more institutionalized and was passed on to the next generation, and the economy moved toward recovery. Even so, in the relatively tranquil years to come, deep and permanent changes were going to take place—changes that would mark the traditional family and social order in uniquely Korean ways.

4

LATE CHOSON
(1636–1910)

The final years of Korea's Choson dynasty present themselves as a tragic drama with a clarity that is unusual in history. In hindsight it seems obvious that in the 1800s Korea faced a challenge that it failed to overcome due to weaknesses in Korea's social order, especially in the conservative and (by the 1800s) highly inept Confucianism that the Choson dynasty had adopted from China.

Korea would confront a phenomenon that had previously been faced by China and Japan—the advent on its shores of modern, Western-style imperialism complete with superior weaponry, steamships, an endless supply of cheap trade goods, and a demand that Korea "open" itself to diplomacy and trade. It was a new style of imperialism that grew out of the Industrial Revolution, as Western nations, equipped with unbeatable modern weaponry and manufacturing capacity, sought new places to sell their goods and used force to demand favorable trade terms. In each of the three East Asian nations—China, Japan, and Korea—the challenge from the West initiated an internal power struggle between modernizers and traditionalists. In each case the struggle had a religious dimension as people reexamined their most basic beliefs.

Korea, when its time came, had the examples of Japan and China before it. Korea, too, had its reformers, its power struggle between modernizers and traditionalists, and its religious revival. Ultimately, none of the factions achieved their aims; Korea lost its sovereignty and change came to it on terms imposed by foreigners. It was colonized by the Japanese, actually before the official end of the Choson dynasty in 1910, and later it was dragged into World War II by its Japanese hosts. Upon Japan's defeat in 1945, Korea was split into two countries and became the bloodiest battleground of the cold war. While half of Korea is today a prosperous free nation, the other half is arguably the world's cruelest and strangest totalitarian state. These events cannot help but cast a backward shadow on the Choson dynasty, the society that failed to preserve Korea's independence. What went wrong?

Korea Changes within Sealed Borders

In the early 17th century, reeling from a series of devastating foreign invasions by its immediate neighbors, Korea's leaders banned foreign travel and foreign visitors. A strictly limited trade was permitted with Japan, and occasionally Korean envoys were sent to the court of the shogun at the Japanese capital of Edo. Though Korea acknowledged its subordination to China and the legitimacy of China's new Qing (Manchu) dynasty, it kept the border along the Yalu River closed. The description "hermit kingdom" really does seem to fit Korea in this period, though in fairness it should be noted that Japan was following exactly the same extreme isolationist policy. It was partly because of this self-imposed seclusion and partly because it offered the least tempting target that Korea was the last East Asian country opened to the West.

John K. Fairbank, a leading Western scholar on East Asia, observed that despite their great differences "in historical experiences, social structure, and worldly situation," the ruling class in the China of the Qing dynasty and the Korea of the Choson dynasty both "felt themselves to be conservators of a great tradition, not innovators" (Fairbank 1965, 462).

Societies never truly stand still, however. Within its sealed borders Korea continued to change, sometimes fussing over the details of court ritual or the rules of inheritance to bring them into line with Confucian orthodoxy and at times giving birth to intellectual ferment that analyzed society and human relations in a fresh way. Factions, named for the place in Seoul where each leader lived—the Northerners, the Westerners, the Southerners—vied for power with intrigues over succession. Toward the end of the 17th century, as it recovered from invasion, Korea's agricultural productivity improved, leading to an increase in population. Agriculture then declined throughout the late Choson period, most steeply in the 19th century (Park 2007). In the late 17th and early 18th centuries a series of works written by out-of-power aristocrats proposed novel, rather democratic political theories. Their efforts are collectively known as the Sirhak ("practical learning") movement. Though the existence of these works demonstrates that the Korean ruling class could show remarkable creativity and insight into the problems of their times, they ultimately had little effect on the actual structure of society. Meanwhile, Korea's economy evolved and diversified, but the majority of its people lived in grinding poverty that became worse during the last two centuries of Choson rule.

Korea was even influenced by the West because despite its government's best efforts, Western ideas managed to trickle in in the form of Western books translated into Chinese, brought into Korea by Korean envoys to the Chinese imperial court. Many Koreans were attracted to the doctrines of Christianity in the form of Catholicism, which Koreans called "Western Learning" and saw as a more egalitarian religion than Confucianism. By the end of the 18th century, Catholicism became popular enough for the state to ban it, but it continued to grow in the face of active persecution.

Confucian Orthodoxy

At the outset of the Choson dynasty in 1392, the Yi royal family and their supporters had consciously chosen Neo-Confucianism as the ideology for the new dynasty. Confucianism had been influential in Korea for a thousand years, but previous dynasties were somewhat divided in their allegiances to Buddhism and Confucianism. With the new group that took power at the end of the 14th century, Confucianism and specifically Neo-Confucianism became the only orthodoxy acceptable.

In the early years under King Sejong, the court and the state reformed court rituals and state ceremonies to put them in line with the Confucian classics, but the early dynastic reforms affected only the court and government; the ordinary person, even an aristocrat, could take it or leave it. An event from the royal annals of Sejong's time illustrates this casual attitude. It was a complaint from an official that a certain other high official was not carrying out ancestor ceremonies. Such a complaint would never have been raised in the mid-Choson period or thereafter, because by then all aristocrats proudly carried out ceremonies for their ancestors as a mark of their higher status.

Changes in Inheritance, Marriage, and Adoption Customs

For centuries, because of the difference between what Koreans practiced and what was written in the Confucian classics, society functioned under the terms of a kind of compromise between the ideal and the real. The classics spoke of the role of the eldest son as the primary heir, but Koreans were dividing property equally and conducting ceremonies

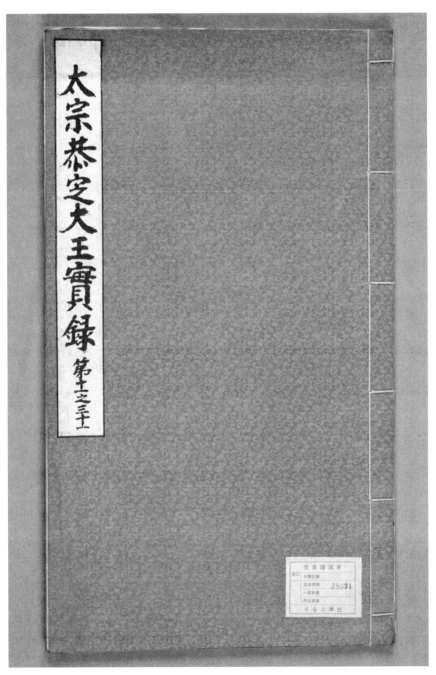

There are hundreds of volumes of royal annals from the Choson dynasty now designated a UNESCO World Memory. The cover of one volume is shown here. (Academy of Korean Studies)

for the ancestors on a rotational basis, with all sons and even daughters participating equally. This compromise continued for centuries, even after the founding of the Choson dynasty, a court founded on Confucian principles, but when the Confucian values of primogeniture (the eldest son's exclusive right of inheritance) and eldest son preference caught on, their impact on the family was dramatic. In the first half of the dynasty, people wrote wills outlining which child inherited which parcel of land and which slaves, but as the transition to primogeniture took place, fewer and fewer wills were written: There was no point in writing a will when the eldest son inherited control of all the property.

These changes started to unfold in the late 17th century. One by one, as families were faced with dividing the inheritances of the father and mother between the children, they began to break with the tradition of dividing property equally between sons and daughters and started to give more to the eldest son and less to the daughters. In one case the family elders wrote in the inheritance document that since the daughter had married into a family that lived so far away, she could not return to carry on the ceremonies properly, and therefore she would be given only half as much as was given to the sons. In another case the family cited the Confucian classics: Since the sons mourned for three years at the passing of a parent but the daughter mourned for only one year, the daughter would be given only one-third as much as a son. Gradually, case by case, daughters were disinherited, younger sons got small parcels, and the eldest son came to inherit the largest, controlling share of an estate. Although younger sons' portions were usually large enough to live on, sometimes the eldest son would have to assist the younger sons or their children. The eldest son's estate would then become a center for the extended family. The resources of the estate would be used for carrying out the ceremonies and for assisting all the extended family should the need arise.

Ceremonies became more and more elaborate. Huge feasts became part of the ceremonies for the dead, and since all the descendants of the deceased would meet together on those occasions, they became large family reunions. Relatives renewed family ties and took the chance to discuss issues of common concern, such as marriage arrangements of family members with other lineage groups or the success of the next generation in studying for the all-important state examinations.

This change in inheritance practices brought about changes in marriage practices. Before the transition a daughter would sometimes move into her husband's household, while sometimes a son would move into his bride's house. A couple who had only daughters would certainly have a son-in-law move in. With the disinheritance of daughters and the new emphasis on a son inheriting the line, however, a couple without a son would no longer let the property go to a daughter and son-in-law. Instead, they would adopt a son.

Legally, the adoption of a son was allowed only if the "son" to be adopted was already a member of the lineage group, a member of the bloodline. The son-elect had to be a member of the lineage carrying the same surname, and he had to belong to the next lower generation—for instance, a nephew to the adopting parent. Adoption did not mean bringing up an orphan. The focus of the adoption was not the son, but the father. It meant the care and keeping of the ancestor—the adopting father, who would at some point die and become an ancestor who needed offerings in the ancestor ceremonies. In fact, as this practice of adoption took hold in the 18th and 19th centuries, about half the time the adopting father was already dead by the time the adoption was submitted to the government for approval, and the adopted son was not a baby; he was often 20, 30, or 40 years old.

The Choson government had a Ministry of Ritual whose function it was, among others, to monitor adoption procedures. Its officials kept a register of requests for adoption. Dating from 1618, the register is kept in 18 large books wherein handwritten entries detail the facts of each request and whether it was authorized. Most were.

The adopted son was a party to the process of agnatic adoption (adoption to continue the male line) and had to submit documents showing that he agreed to the procedure. Two lineage elders, one from "both sides of the family," as well as the adopting father and the biological father also had to submit affidavits affirming that the proposed adoption was appropriate. Until the late 17th century the term *both sides of the family* was interpreted to mean the heads of the lineage of the adopting father and the adopting mother. Afterward, *both sides of the family* came to mean the family of the adopting father and that of the biological father. This signifies that in the early and middle 17th century, "both sides" included two different surnames; from the late 17th century on, the "both sides" clause indicated two men with the same surname, since agnatic adoption means adoption from within the same surname group. Matters evolved further in the late 18th and 19th centuries, as recorded toward the end of the register. In some cases, despite the formula that called for representatives from "both sides" of the case to agree to the adoption, only one lineage elder is listed as agreeing to the procedure. That single lineage elder would have been the senior family representative for both the adopting father and the biological father, both in the same segment of the lineage.

With the daughters marrying out and the sons staying in the same house or building a new house nearby, there developed villages of families with the same surname, all members of the same lineage group or extended family. Particularly for aristocratic families, single-surname villages became the norm.

These changes—primogeniture, marrying out of daughters, adoption of bloodline male relatives, ancestor ceremonies conducted by the eldest son, and single-surname villages—all became part of what Koreans today think of as their "traditional" values. Research on this subject is fairly new, however, and most Koreans today do not realize that this "traditional family" and the system associated with it are really only two or three centuries old. These Confucian-based changes permanently changed Korean society starting in the middle of the Choson period, that is, from the late 17th century onward.

Decay of the Examination System

One of the great strengths of the Confucian system was that it was, in theory, a meritocracy, a civil service system into which entry was based on an examination in the Confucian classics. There were three categories of examinations, civil, military, and technical, and civil was considered the most important; those who passed the civil examinations were Korea's hands-on rulers. In reality only the wealthy could afford the extensive study that was necessary to succeed in the examination system; this usually limited participation to the top tiers of Korean society. Training for the civil examinations was limited to the landowning Korean aristocracy, the *yangban*. Since the government also required the services of people with knowledge of technology, science, and foreign languages and because the *yangban* considered such activities to be beneath them, students trained in these subjects were drawn from the hereditary class of petty officials that formed Korea's "middle people," the *chungin*.

Hence, the examination system, unlike its iteration in China, was hardly egalitarian—as an expression of Confucianism, which strongly supports class differences, one would not expect it to be. However, while it worked honestly, it gave an intellectual cast to Korea's upper classes by emphasizing learning and competence. Knowledge of the Confucian classics was the path to prestige and power.

From the outset, there was a tension in Korea between the Confucian system, with its emphasis on competence and justice within the limits of an inherently unequal, hierarchal society, and the traditions of the landowning *yangban* who administered the system. As good Confucian administrators, they were expected to act according to the dictates of virtue. As landowners, they had obligations to their family and their clan, and they tended to use their power to increase their family holdings. The power that came with success in the examination system resulted in the corruption of the system. Whatever political faction happened to be in power was able to see to it that those on its side had access to the examination questions and to deny posts to enemies even if they had passed the exams. In the 1800s access to high office was regularly achieved by bribery, a process that led to corrupt government, since those who had acquired their posts by bribery used their positions to squeeze profits out of the common people (Eckert 1990, 179). By its end the examination system had become a formality, and bribes for certain posts were such a regular feature of the system that regular prices were set for them.

Increased Factionalism in the Wake of the Invasions

The identification of the ruling elite with the interests of their own clans or regions also led to increased political factionalism, a key weakness of the Korean state during the late Choson period, according to the 20th-century Korean historian Han Woo-keun. The factions that formed as a result of these regional alliances struggled to control Korea by controlling the throne. When the northerners were in power, they excluded the westerners and southerners. Factionalism increased after the invasions. According to Han, factionalism intensified in the postinvasion period, "the old factions splitting and multiplying at a bewildering rate. They often centered around succession to the throne or points of Confucian ritual and etiquette, especially the proper period of mourning on the death of a royal personage, but their actual motivation was for the most part pure and simple greed for power" (Han 1970, 300).

The chronic factionalism of the late Choson period had large and mostly bad effects on the country. Struggles over the succession often put incompetent leaders in power. Factions, once in power, ruled to suit their own interests, not necessarily the interests of the state. *Yangban* excluded from power for long periods had to find other occupations, some building up their estates, some developing into a Korean intelligentsia, and some engaging (mostly covertly) in the despised activity of commerce.

The Tax System

In the tax system as well as in the examination system, there came to be a great gulf between theory and practice. Under a system developed in the 17th century, the government collected taxes through local officials in the form of grain, then paid contractors in grain for whatever special products the government required. The amount of tax required was based on an assessment of the amount of arable land. Farmers were also required to pay for exemption from military service: The amount required was two rolls of cloth for each man of military age,

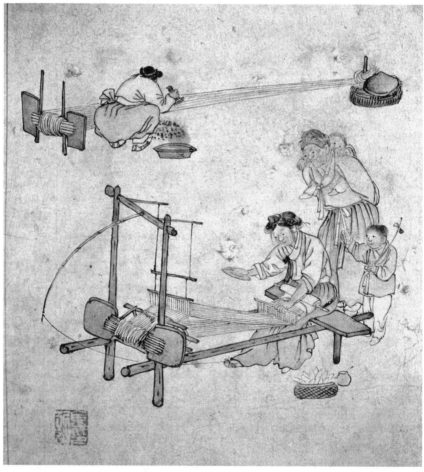

Weaving was a cottage industry in the Choson period. The women of the family spun the thread (shown in the upper section) and then wove the thread into cloth (shown in the lower section). A family wove its own cloth of cotton, hemp, and silk and then wove more for submission of taxes. (Academy of Korean Studies)

that is, between 16 and 60. *Yangban* families were exempt from this tax. Farmers did everything they could to evade it, sometimes going to the length of leaving their homes at collection time. Local officials did everything they could to maximize the tax, sometimes falsifying the ages of children to make them seem qualified or counting dead men eligible for military service (and making their families therefore responsible for two rolls of cloth for each dead man).

Wasteland, newly reclaimed land, land subject to drought or flood, and land belonging to the royal clan were exempt from tax (Han 1970, 341). These loopholes in the tax system were originally instituted as measures to offer peasants relief, but like all such loopholes they were ripe for abuse. As time went on corrupt local officials, who had found ways of diverting the lands' products into their own pockets, managed to have much of the land they controlled reclassified as tax-exempt under one or another sort of provision. The result was that a smaller and smaller percentage of the land provided the government with its finances. The burden on all farmers became greater as they found themselves supporting both the government and an ever-enlarging aristocracy. The evils of the tax system were recognized, and on occasion strong kings attempted to reform it (for example, the military tax was cut in half in 1750 by King Yongjo). Over the long run, however, the burden on the common people only became worse.

Yongjo and Chongjo

The epitome of the Confucian ruler was King Yongjo (r. 1724–76), who reigned 52 years, the longest reign in Korean history. In all ways he was the exemplary king. He knew the classics better than his officials did, and he seemed to relish the opportunity to debate Confucian philosophical issues with them. Confucianism, of course, was the only serious philosophy of the day.

The strong leadership of Yongjo and his immediate successor, Chongjo, gave Korea the closest thing it ever had to a golden age during the late Choson period. The tax system was made more rational. The law code was revised and supplemented. Factionalism was reduced through the direct action of the monarchy, which saw to it that posts were given to members of more than one faction. Some of the most interesting works of the Sirhak school were written during this period. These thinkers proposed democratic and egalitarian principles that were in sharp opposition to Korean practice. One leading Sirhak thinker, Yi Ik (1681–1763), a polymath who wrote about astronomy, geography, law, and mathematics, advocated the abolition of class barriers (Han 1970, 326).

Yongjo was faced with an acute problem regarding his successor. He had two sons, but one died young, leaving him only one heir to the throne. One heir would have been sufficient had he not had a mental illness. The crown prince, Sado, was severely ill, erratic, and violent in his behavior. He wantonly killed people both inside and outside the palace and was given to extremes in sexual behavior as well. In all ways he was the opposite of his circumspect and proper father. Yongjo tried everything, including abdicating the throne to his son, to give him a chance to become serious, rule on his own, and thereby become a fit king, but that did not work either. Thus, Yongjo had to face the unthinkable—to see to the death of his son. Sado had a son who could become the next heir to the throne.

On several occasions Yongjo told his son to commit suicide, but Sado would not. The king could not bear to inflict the fatal wound himself, nor would he allow any court member to kill his son. He could not try his son in court for crimes, although they were numerous, because his grandson would be tainted by having a father who was judged a criminal. The only solution was the enforced "suicide" of his son. Not knowing how long he himself would live, Yongjo saw to his son's death in 1767. Yongjo ordered a wooden rice chest large enough to hold a man if he sat with his legs folded to be placed in the middle of the courtyard on a hot August day. He ordered Sado to crawl into the chest, which he did, perhaps thinking that his father would relent, as he had in the past. After eight days in the rice chest, Sado died of suffocation. Yongjo lived another nine years. By that time Sado's son Chongjo was old enough to rule on his own.

Chongjo (1752–1800) ruled from 1776 to 1800, spending much of his reign trying to repair the legacy of his father. Believing his grandfather had been manipulated by some of his advisers, he led a purge of those who had been strongest in understanding and supporting his grandfather's action in the death of his father. Chongjo built a secondary palace 50 miles south of Seoul in Suwon to be closer to his father's tomb. The wall he built around the city is an outstanding example of architecture of the late premodern period and has been listed as a UNESCO World Heritage Site.

Spread of Roman Catholicism

Christianity, a belief system that had earlier excited the curiosity but not the enthusiasm of the Sirhak thinkers, began to make serious inroads in Korea during Chongjo's reign. In 1784 a *yangban* notable named Yi Sung-hun, who had been to China as part of a diplomatic mission, was baptized in Beijing by a Catholic priest. Over the next few years the number of converts to Christianity grew, particularly among the *chungin* class of technical specialists. In *Korea Old and New,* the Korean historian Ki-baik Lee notes:

> These early believers had, as it were, converted themselves, through reading treatises brought back from China. What they seem to have sought in Catholicism was a means to grapple with a host of evils that then beset the Choson's social and political order. . . . Accordingly the acceptance of Catholicism may be seen as constituting a challenge to the grasping and predatory nature of the Choson state and the intellectual rigidity of Neo-Confucianist orthodoxy. (Eckert 1990, 170)

The growing importance of Christianity led to its persecution, partly because Roman Catholic doctrine was in direct contradiction to some of the central tenets of Confucianism—in 1742 the pope had ruled that ancestor worship was incompatible with Christianity. In 1785 Chongjo declared Catholicism a heresy. The following year he forbade the importation of books of any kind from Beijing.

As was often the case in the Choson dynasty, what happened officially was different from what happened in fact. Until Chongjo died Catholicism was tacitly permitted. As soon as Chongjo died, the threat of Catholicism became an issue in one of the factional disputes that so often accompanied the succession in Korea. A persecution of Catholics began immediately, and within a short time about 300 of Korea's several thousand Catholics were executed or died in prison. Among those executed in 1801 was a Chinese Catholic, Chou Wen-mu (James Chou), the first ordained priest ever to enter Korea. That same year, in response to these events, a Catholic name Hwang Sa-yong tried to send a secret letter to the French bishop in Beijing requesting that a battleship be sent to Korea to protect Korea's Catholics. The letter was intercepted and used thereafter as an additional justification for the persecution of Catholics. Catholicism nevertheless continued to spread in the face of periodic persecutions; Catholics would number more than 23,000 by 1865 (Han 1970, 349).

The Kings of Late Choson

King Chongjo died in 1800 at the age of 48. The next three kings did not have heirs—the dynasty was literally and symbolically running out of energy. Furthermore, royal in-laws interfered in politics for the first time since the mid-Koryo period. In fact, the 19th century is often called "the time of in-law politics."

Each of the three successors of King Chongo—King Sunjo (r. 1800–34), King Honjong (r. 1834–49), and King Cholchong (r. 1849–63)—was married to a woman from the Andong Kim clan; Honjong's mother, who was his regent, was from the Pungyang Cho clan. The in-law clans Kims and Chos dominated key government appointments, and the father-in-law of the king in each case was considered one of the most powerful men in the country.

Honjong and Cholchong both became king through adoption from branch lines of the royal family. When Cholchong likewise had no heir, the court again had to find someone to adopt into the king's line. This time they settled on a 12-year-old boy. He was not yet married, and the royal court determined that he would not marry a Kim or Cho in order to free the court from the domination of the powerful in-laws. The boy-king, who became known as Kojong (r. 1864–1907), was not to be free from in-law problems, however, and he was to have an additional level of interference in his rule—his biological father. Adopted posthumously as the son of Cholchong, Kojong had a living father known as Taewongun, a title for the father of a sitting king who himself had not been the previous king. This was an anomalous situation, since the father of the king would ordinarily be dead. Korea had had other Taewongun in its history, but Hungson Taewongun (his formal title) was unlike all the others. Since Kojong was only 12, a regent had to be appointed, and the court chose Queen Dowager Cho, his adoptive grandmother. But Hungson Taewongun stepped in, and by dint of his unassailable authority as father of the king, he started running the government. Although he was never legally appointed as such, he was de facto regent, and some histories even refer to him as the regent when, in fact, he had never been legally appointed as such.

The Decade of the Taewongun (1863–1873)

The Taewongun ruled for 10 tumultuous years. Because the dynasty was declining, he considered it necessary to move decisively to restore it. He began to tax the *yangban* (the aristocracy), who heretofore had been tax exempt. Over the 470 years of the dynasty to that point, the *yangban* class had grown, and the tax base had narrowed. The Taewongun also cut into the *yangban* class, dividing the aristocracy and delineating the "true" *yangban* from the "lesser" *yangban* by attacking the symbol of their scholarly status, their schools.

The educational system of the Choson dynasty was twofold, consisting of a government system and a private system. The government-sponsored schools were called *hyanggyo* (country schools); there were about 250, one in each county. Beginning in the late 16th century, a private school system began with a school in the heart of north Kyongsang province, modeled after the school at which the Chinese master Zhu Xi taught. These schools, called *sowon* (private academies), proliferated to the point that many counties had three or four. In 1871 the Taewongun closed all but 47 of them. He chose which *sowon* to support and which to shut down based on their signboards.

Historically, a *sowon* was established to enshrine a noteworthy scholar. If the scholar happened to be an adviser to the king, and if that king chose to honor him with his own calligraphy, then the *sowon* had the king's calligraphy on its signboard. A king would personally write the title of such a *sowon* with his own brush. Thereafter, the king's calligraphy, written on paper, would be carved onto a wooden plaque and hung from the eaves of the main hall of the academy. Some *sowon*, on the other hand, had signboards signed by prominent scholars. Such schools functioned in a manner similar to the royally recognized schools until the Taewongun outlawed them. *Sowon* with a king's calligraphy were considered approved and allowed to continue to function. Those without that honor were closed. The members of the 47 sanctioned *sowon* supported the closure of the other schools; these scholars appreciated recognition as members of the inner circle.

Both private (*sowon*) and government (*hyanggyo*) academies had two main buildings—a lecture hall in the center of the courtyard and a shrine toward the rear or innermost part of the complex. In front of the lecture hall, to each side of the main courtyard, were dormitories. The shrine building contained the "spirit tablet," a wooden plaque about a foot tall with the name of the person honored as a sage inscribed thereon.

The enshrinement process was important in Confucianism. One of the ideals in Confucianism was to become a sage, a scholar. When a man reached exceptional heights in scholarship or government service, he would be made a sage. His spirit tablet would be kept for endless generations in a shrine. All ancestors could have a spirit tablet, often of paper, but ancestor ceremonies honored the tablet for only the first four generations after the person's death. To retain a spirit tablet beyond four generations required permission of the king, and such a process was tantamount to making the ancestor a "sage."

The *hyanggyo* all held the tablets of Confucius, his four disciples, the 16 Chinese sages, and, by the end of the Choson dynasty, 18 Korean sages. The *hyanggyo* was a replica of the National Shrine, the Songgyungwan, in Seoul. Each *sowon*, however, was dedicated to a specific individual, such as one of the 18 in the National Shrine or some other scholar of Neo-Confucianism. Those *sowon* deemed unworthy by the Taewongun also housed spirit tablets of ancestors who were outstanding scholars. The destruction of those places at the order of the Taewongun was an act far more severe than tearing down a number of schoolhouses; each demolition was a renunciation of the scholar-ancestor enshrined in a Confucian hall of worship. It meant the repudiation of the scholar and all his worshippers, who were both literal descendants of the man and scholarly descendants, the descendants of his disciples.

The Taewongun, in his determination to restore the dynasty, also rebuilt the main palace in Seoul in 1865, which had been destroyed during the Hideyoshi invasion 270 years earlier. To him it was an important symbol, and it was an embarrassment that the government and royalty were housed in lesser palaces in Seoul. He would rebuild it at any cost. When, two years into the rebuilding effort, he started running out of money to pay the workers, he printed paper money without support, and its use set off a spiral of inflation that damaged the economy for years thereafter.

Contact with Western Countries

Though at the time Koreans may not have realized it, nothing in the eventful Taewongun decade was more significant than the direct contact that Korea began to have with Western countries. During the preceding few decades China, the greatest Asian power and the first to face Western encroachment, had been weakened in ways that shocked its neighbors, to whom China's might had been a fact of nature. In the 1830s the Chinese threatened to expel the British from China if they did not cease importing opium, a highly addictive narcotic, which British merchants purchased in India (already under British control, though not yet officially a colony) for the Chinese market. In the Opium War (1839–42) the Chinese were easily defeated and forced to sign a humiliating treaty very advantageous to England. Other Western powers soon demanded and received similar terms from China. Within a few years China was almost torn apart by a religiously inspired uprising, the Taiping Rebellion (1850–64), which aimed to expel foreigners and overthrow the Qing dynasty. The Chinese government was able to defeat the Taipings only with the help of the French and British. Korea knew about the Western incursions into China and had followed the events of the Opium War, after which China had reluctantly agreed to open its markets to the British. But the West's attempts to initiate trade with Korea had thus far failed. Korea's borders were closed to trade with nations other than China and, to a limited extent, Japan.

America made its first attempt to open the Korean market for trade in 1866. An American commercial ship, the SS *General Sherman,* sailed up the estuary of the Taedong River to a point where they met Korean officials. The foreigners said they wanted to trade and were told by Korean officials to wait for orders. Heavy rain and a high tide allowed the ship to steam farther upward, to the outskirts of Pyongyang, where, when the waters receded, the ship was stranded. By this time the response arrived from Seoul that the sailors were to leave or be killed. Since they were stranded, they could not leave, and thus hostilities began. The Koreans sailed several burning barges into the *General Sherman* and eventually caught it on fire. As the sailors attempted to flee, they were killed.

There is some controversy about what happened. One report says the Americans held hostage the Korean official who came to negotiate with them and who agreed to provide them with some food for their onward voyage. There is also a question about whether the ship was truly a commercial ship; it had been a gunship and still had reinforced armor on its sides. However, there is little question about the result. The ship was burned, and nothing was left of it but the metal frame and anchor chain; the latter would be used for years as the chain that opens and shuts the main gate to Pyongyang at night and dawn. All the crew was killed, and the incident provoked several American investigations, including one that resulted in some fighting on Kanghwa Island a few years later in 1871.

Later in 1866 one of the strangest episodes in Korean history came to pass. A Hungarian adventurer named Ernst Oppert, sailing a German ship, hatched a plot that he hoped would make him the sole broker of trade in and out of Korea. Oppert had learned that Korea was not open to trade and had no interest in opening its borders and ports to outsiders. Oppert had spent enough time in China to learn of the East Asian belief in geomancy, also called *pungsu* in Korean and *feng shui* in Chinese, a system of controlling fortune. Chinese and Koreans believed that the descendants of a man would have good or bad fortune depending on where his ancestors' bones were buried. Oppert reasoned that if he could kidnap the bones of the Taewongun's father and hold them hostage, he could blackmail his way into controlling the Korean trade the way some Westerners already were controlling trade in Hong Kong. He knew he could not break into the tomb of a king—the royal tombs were large stone and earth mounds, but the father of the Taewongun was not royalty; his tomb was ordinary. Oppert took his chances. He was able to locate the tomb near the coast, and he came ashore with some paid Korean guides. He was actually digging into the tomb when they were discovered. It turned out grave robbing was a bigger job than he thought, and it took too long to get into the tomb. Oppert and his band ran off when the local authorities came to investigate.

These two experiences reinforced the Taewongun's conviction that the barbarians were indeed barbarous but could be defeated and kept off shore. The events of 1871 only confirmed his judgment. U.S. authorities sent a small expedition to inquire into the fate of the missing merchant ship the SS *General Sherman,* and the French sent a small expedition to inquire into reports of the execution of French priests in anti-Catholic purges. First they had to get to the capital, Hanyang, or Seoul, located a safe 20 miles up the Han River. Kanghwa Island, with its fortifications, served as the defensive outpost for Seoul. Both expeditions had similar outcomes: They sailed close to Kanghwa Island, in the estuary of the Han River. Though heavily fortified for its time, Kanghwa's defenses were easily overcome by the advanced firepower of each of the Western powers in turn. Each delegation found what it had come for (verification of the deaths of their countrymen), and each sailed off for its homeland.

Japan's Intentions

Knowing what is known now, it seems clear that the Koreans would have been better off to invite the attentions of the Americans or even the French or British, whose imperialism in East Asia was basically commercial—they wanted trade on terms highly favorable to them, but they were not interested in actually colonizing, still less annexing, Japan, China, or Korea. America or Britain might have exploited Korea, but they would not have conquered it. The Japanese did eventually conquer Korea. They were considering the possibility by the 1870s, less than 20 years after their own opening to the West at the hands of the Americans. The method they eventually used closely echoed the means by which Japan itself had been opened to the Western world by Commodore Matthew Perry (1794–1858). In 1854, to persuade Japan

JIKJI, THE WORLD'S FIRST BOOK PRINTED WITH METAL MOVABLE TYPE

While the French were on Kanghwa Island in the position of conquerors, they engaged in a bit of pillaging. In an intriguing sidelight, they took some books from the government offices there. Kanghwa Island, it should be remembered, was the place where the Koryo court had taken refuge for 80 years during the time of the Mongol invasion in 1231. Some Koryo-period relics were still kept on the island.

It is doubtful that the men of the French expedition knew of the significance of one of their acquisitions at the time. Years later, when these documents were studied, it was found that one of the plundered books was a copy of volume two of a Buddhist text called the *Jikji,* meaning "pointing out the truth." As it turns out, it is the only extant copy of any of the books printed with the first set of metal movable type fonts made in history. All other copies of that text and other texts printed at that time have apparently been destroyed. This invention predates Johannes Gutenberg's invention of movable type in the West by 200 years.

Despite the great value of the book to Korean cultural history, it remains in the National Library of France. Korean delegations' repeated negotiations and appeals that the book be returned to Korea have not yet been successful.

In Chongju, 95 miles south of Seoul, there is a museum dedicated to displays of old Korean printing. It is built on the site of the ruins of the Buddhist temple where the first books were printed using metal movable type.

of the benefits of trading with the United States, Perry had brought with him a miniature steam locomotive and a section of track. The United States had been sure that Japan's isolation was irrational and that its opening, though made under duress, would eventually benefit both parties. The Japanese opened Korea with a similar mixture of self-interest, altruism, smugness, and aggression, but the nearness of Korea to Japan increased the ingredient of aggression.

Some 15 years later Japanese bureaucrats were debating ways of restoring the national honor, which they felt had been tarnished by their brush with America's gunboat diplomacy and the trade agreements with the West, treaties whose inequality the Japanese came to understand as they had more contact with Europe and the United States. Some Japanese were also aware that colonies were a part of the Western formula for success, which they were determined to imitate. They had been infected with the anxiety that afflicted the industrialized countries of Europe and the United States by the late 19th century—they worried that if they did not hurry, there would be no more underdeveloped countries available for colonization.

As early as 1869 Miyamoto Okazu, a lower-level official in Japan's foreign ministry, is on record as fretting that Russia and Western powers had their eyes on Korea and might acquire it, to Japan's "everlasting harm." He suggested that since Japan was not yet strong enough to annex Korea, it ought to send an emissary (backed by gunboats, like America's 1854 emissary to Japan) and to negotiate a "fraternal alliance," joining Korea to Japan in a "united federation." Okazu proposed that Japan take control of Korea's diplomacy and reform its calendar, finances, and armed forces. All this would help to "wash away the stain of outmoded customs" in Korea (Duus 1995, 34).

In late 1869 Japan sent Sada Hakubo, an official who favored an aggressive Japanese foreign policy, to Korea on a peaceful, fact-finding mission. On his return Sada advocated a military expedition to force the opening of Korea. His advice, which was unrealistic at the time—Japan was not ready to mount the invasion he proposed—summed up several of the motives that would ultimately lead Japan to annex Korea: to preclude its colonization by some enemy of Japan's; to benefit economically; to find an outlet for Japan's military class, the samurai, which had been disgruntled by the Meiji Restoration; and to restore the national honor.

> If Imperial Japan passes this great opportunity to the foreigners we will lose our lips [i.e., Korea] as a consequence, and one day our teeth will surely suffer from the cold. . . . Korea is a gold mine, and rice and wheat are abundant. With one sweep we can mobilize the manpower, the mineral resources and the grain [in Korea] and use them in Hokkaido. . . . [Japan] is suffering from the problem of too many military men rather than a shortage thereof. . . . The belligerent, when discontent, contemplate revolt. At this time when there is fear of civil war in our country, if we undertake the Korean expedition and make the bitter cup of samurai grievance spill [in Korea] we can massacre Korea in a single stroke, polish our military system, and demonstrate to the world the imperial glory. (Duus 1995, 35–36)

Japan's next move was much more modest than the one Sada proposed. Traditionally, the very limited amount of trade that Korea permitted between itself and Japan was conducted in the *waegwan,* a small trading post in Pusan, which was invariably run by a representative of a single Japanese family, the So family. In 1873, in a calculated violation of this precedent, a Japanese foreign minister in charge of Korean relations was sent to Pusan for the purpose of transferring control of the trading post to the Japanese foreign ministry. As the historian Peter Duus notes in *The Abacus and the Sword: Japanese Penetration of Korea, 1895–1910,* this move had a symbolic value that both the Japanese and the Koreans recognized. "No longer a symbol of traditional subordination of the So family to the Korean court, the *waegwan* had become a foothold for the new 'civilized' set of institutions through which the Japanese intended to conduct their formal relations with Korea" (Duus 1995, 37).

In late May 1873 local Korean authorities posted a wall notice on the residence of the chief guard of the *waegwan* that condemned Japan's illegal actions and called on it to honor the established rules and regulations. This Korean response to Japan's latest maneuver sparked a debate in Japan on the feasibility of a policy that would enable Japan to "subdue Korea." According to Peter Duus, the Japanese who used this phrase were not yet thinking of colonization but merely of a commercial opening of Korea on terms favorable to the Japanese (Duus 1995, 38).

The Taewongun's Reaction

The Taewongun misunderstood the significance of the French and American invasions. He had heard of China's travails and its loss of territory to several European powers—the British in Hong Kong, the Portuguese in Macau, and the French and Germans in the northern areas. With the retreat of the Western forces, the Taewongun celebrated his victory in the French War and the American War and sent a message to the Chinese emperor to that effect. Of course, from the point of view of the French and the Americans, there had never been a war, let alone one lost. When the Taewongun was forced out of power in 1874, he had little idea of the actual geopolitical situation in the world. His actions were bold, but he was essentially a conservative ruler who did not understand the threats that Korea faced in the new world of 19th-century imperialism. Though he reduced corruption and centralized political power during his time in office, he also bankrupted Korea at the worst possible time. His very strength as a politician had

King Kojong's father, the Taewongun, ordered that stone markers urging the rejection of foreign influence be placed all around the kingdom in 1871. They stated, "Western barbarians are invading; we must fight them and not seek peace; appeasement is selling out the country." (Academy of Korean Studies)

tragic consequences for Korea, since his policies, which were continued by his son, King Kojong, did not prepare Korea for its encounter with modernity, with the West, and with Japan (Palais 1991).

King Kojong

When Kojong was 22 he was able to take over the throne for himself, and the bureaucracy and king were able to sideline the Taewongun. However, Kojong was not without problems from within his own family. One reason Kojong had been selected king was that he was not yet married, and the royal family made sure that he did not marry a woman from either of the most powerful clans, the Kims or the Chos. In 1866 a marriage was arranged with a young woman from the Min clan of Yohung who had no brothers—an ideal choice, it would seem. In the late Choson period, however, there was no such thing as a *yangban* man without a son; if he had no children or only daughters, he would surely "adopt" a nephew. Later, Queen Min's father adopted a son from within patrilineal lineage (agnatic adoption was well established in Korea at this point). Thus, Queen Min suddenly had a brother, and that brother had brothers. The court was once again plagued with in-law problems. Apart from this, Queen Min herself turned out to be the most powerful of all the queens of Korean history. Her role in the crucial events of the next few decades, a time of foreign pressure and internal disorder, was to be pivotal.

The Kanghwa Treaty of 1876

In 1875 an incursion from the West Sea was to change Korea forever. Korea was opened not by a Western nation but its neighbor to the east, Japan. On the morning of September 20, 1875, Japan sailed an armed naval vessel, the *Unyo*, near Kanghwa Island; the *Unyo* was supposedly on a peaceful surveying mission. No surviving records prove that it was not, but in the judgment of most historians, the mission was meant to provoke an incident that would lead to a changed Japan-Korea relationship. As described by Peter Duus:

> When Korean shore batteries fired on the Un'yo, the Japanese response was swift and severe. After bombarding the Korean fortifications, the Un'yo landed a shore party that torched several houses on the island and exchanged fire with Korean troops. The Japanese, armed with rifles, made quick work of the Koreans, who carried matchlock muskets, and thirty-five Korean soldiers were left dead. News of the incident did not reach Tokyo until September 28, but the next day [the Japanese government] decided to dispatch gunboats to Pusan to protect the Japanese residents there ... (Duus 1995, 43–44)

As an outcome of this provocation, the Japanese were able to force court officials to meet and sign a treaty of "amity and trade." The treaty declared that Korea was an "independent state," meaning that it was no longer even in theory subordinate to China. Later supplements to the treaty contained provisions that privileged Japanese commercial interests, much as Japan's treaties after its opening had privileged Western commercial interests. Japan had its foot in the door.

Other powers soon signed similar treaties: the Americans in 1882, the British and Germans in 1882 (ratified in 1884), the Russians and Italians in 1884, and the French in 1886. The Chinese, too, moved to establish closer ties with Korea. As other powers, especially Russia and China (enfeebled but still a concern for Japan), began to take a greater interest in Korea, the Japanese became nervous. Korea, with its backward military technology, would be a pushover for invasion and takeover. Then, instead of having a hermit kingdom for its nearest neighbor, Japan would look across the sea or Korea Strait at the outpost of some hostile, battleship-possessing modern power. In the words of a German military adviser to the Meiji government, Korea was "a dagger pointed at the heart of Japan" (Duus 1995, 49).

Thus, when Japan's leaders and representatives spoke of the need for a strong, modern, independent Korea, this was not mere rhetoric to dress up aggressive plans. At least at times, the Japanese were genuinely interested in modernizing Korea, including its armed forces. If Korea could take the path that Japan had taken and do it quickly, then Japan need not worry about the dagger aimed at its heart. Korea would be a younger partner in Asian modernization, dependant on its teacher, Japan. But if Korea were too slow to modernize or if Korea were to show signs of collapsing, then Japan's best move might be to take over Korea before some other nation did it (Deuchler 1977).

A small group of forward-thinking Korean officials agreed that their country needed to modernize and looked to Japan as an example and guide. Encouraged by the existence of this group, in the 1880s the Japanese invited several of them to Japan, where they went on a tour of Japanese military facilities, schools, government ministries, factories, libraries, post offices, museums, arsenals, hospitals, and shipyards—much as Japanese officials had done in their tour of Europe 10 years earlier. While they were in Japan they were given a study written by Huang Tsun-hsein, a Tokyo-stationed Chinese diplomat, who believed that both China and Korea could best strengthen themselves by adopting Western technology and also the political institutions that underlay Western success. The study was later passed on to King Kojong, who seems to have been persuaded by it. Meanwhile, Japan sent a military mission to Korea headed by Lieutenant Horimoto Reizo to train an elite new Korean military unit, which, it was hoped, would lead to the strengthening of Korea's armed forces along Japanese lines.

The Military Uprising of 1882

Resentment of Horimoto's mission led directly to the Military Uprising of 1882, which strengthened the antiforeign, antimodern forces of reaction within Korea. Those excluded from the new uniforms and status eventually attacked the new military and its Japanese advisers. Horimoto Reizo was killed. To settle the issue and help restore order, King Kojong recalled his father, the Hungson Taewongun, out of exile and returned him to power. This was too much for Queen Min. To counter her father-in-law's renewed influence, she sent an envoy to China seeking military aid. China responded by sending more than 1,000 soldiers under the command of Yuan Shikai (1859–1916), who later became the first president of the Republic of China. The Chinese soldiers arrested the Taewongun and deported him to Tientsin, China.

With the Min faction making policy in Seoul, the advantage in the great power game that was being played over Korea passed temporarily

YUAN SHIKAI

Yuan Shikai is one of the most scurrilous figures in Chinese history. After spending years representing Chinese interests in Korea from 1882 to 1894, he went on to become a powerful warlord in China. At first loyal to the waning Qing court, he obtained funds from Chinese and foreign sources and became the general of the most powerful army in China. Then, betraying the Qing, he joined forces with the revolutionaries who sought the end of the dynasty and the establishment of a modern state.

In 1911 Sun Yatsen (1866–1925), the man heralded as the founder of Chinese democracy by both the Republic of China on Taiwan and the People's Republic of China on the mainland, needed Yuan's military to topple the Qing dynasty. Sun allowed Yuan to become the first president of the Republic of China in 1912 as part of their agreement. Yuan then betrayed the republic by announcing the formation of a new dynasty with himself as the emperor. His dynasty lasted only four months, however, and three months later he died of kidney failure. It did not bode well for Korea to have a man like Yuan Shikai as an adviser representing China at such a critical time in history (Lew 1984, 63).

to China. Historian Young Ick Lew describes the immediate effect on Korean policy:

> With a strong military force firmly entrenched in Seoul, the Ch'ing [Qing] government began to interfere boldly in Korea's internal affairs, claiming the authority to do so on the basis of the traditional suzerain relationship.... The Chinese recommended the appointment of two special advisors on foreign affairs, a Prussian diplomat, Paul G. von Mollendorff ... and the Chinese diplomat Ma Chien-Ch'ang.... creating two offices to plan and coordinate Korea's self-strengthening measures.... The Ch'ing government also sought to expand Chinese economic interests in Korea with a view to offsetting the growing influence of Japanese merchants. On the heels of its armed intervention China imposed on Korea a set of Regulations for Private Maritime and Overland Trade, whereby Chinese merchants obtained the right to reside, conduct business and to travel freely within Korea. (Eckert 1990, 207–208)

The Chinese show of force prompted the Japanese to increase their military strength in Korea. In the settlement of the 1882 affair, the

Japanese sought reparations and an agreement that in the future the Chinese and Japanese would not intervene in Korean military affairs. China and Japan agreed that neither side would send additional troops to Korea without informing the other, so that the military balance could be maintained. (This latter provision was to have disastrous consequences for Korea 12 years later when Japan invoked the clause to justify a large-scale dispatch of Japanese soldiers.)

Now Japan and China each had their clients within Korea, each identified with a different path to modernization with the help of a different Asian partner. China encouraged a faction within the Korean government led by Kim Hongjip, Kim Yunsik, O Yunjung, and the royal in-law family led by Min Yongik in what was called "enlightenment thought," a conservative approach to modernization. On the other side was the Progressive Party, a pro-Japanese group of reformers led by Pak Younghyo, Kim Okkyun, and So Kwangbom. Kim Okkyun and So Kwangbom were among the group invited by the Japanese to visit Japan in 1884. Pak Younghyo was King Kojong's brother-in-law; he had close ties to Kim Okkyun and So Kwangbom. These two factions, one pro-China and one pro-Japan, were each to have its ups and downs in the next few years until Japan defeated China decisively in 1894.

The Attempted Coup of 1884

In 1884 Kim Okkyun and the others in the group returned from Japan full of ideas about how Korea needed to modernize. Having seen the rapid industrialization in Japan, they were eager to see Korea follow suit. Frustrated by the Min faction, Kim Okkyun decided to assassinate the key members of the faction, blame the assassination on the Chinese, and tip the court to a pro-Japanese stance. He selected December 4, 1884, when the new post office, built to incorporate the existing domestic mail service with international mail service, was to be dedicated.

In attendance were two of the Min brothers and most of the diplomats in Korea at the time. Those present included Paul Mollendorf, a Prussian working for the Chinese government; Lucius Foote, the head of the American legation; and William Aston, the head of the British legation. There were also three Japanese delegates and three Chinese delegates at the table. During the dinner party celebrating the post office opening, Kim's allies were to set a nearby thatched-roof house on fire. In the ensuing chaos other conspirators hiding outside the post office would then stab the Min brothers. The plot did not go according to plan. Kim's men could not get the fire going, and in the delay Kim

Kim Okkyun, a young scholar sent to study in Japan, returned in 1884 to report to King Kojong. When the king's advisers rejected his call to modernize along Japanese lines, Kim plotted to assassinate the king's advisers. (Academy of Korean Studies)

stood up twice to look outside, perhaps tipping off the Min brothers that something was afoot. When the fire alarm was finally sounded, there was not as much chaos as the conspirators anticipated. They were

129

able to wound only one of the Min brothers, Min Yongik. Unaware of the assassins' failures, Kim Okkyun ran to the king to tell him that the Min brothers had been killed. When the king learned three days later that they were alive, Kim fled. He boarded a ship for Japan, where he lived in exile for 10 years. In 1894 he moved to China for another 10 years, until he was assassinated there (Cook 1972).

Protestant Christianity

The wounded Min brother became the central figure in the drama that opened the door for Christian missionaries in Korea. Min Yongik was treated by Korean herbal doctors but failed to recover. The Korean court knew that the American delegation in Seoul included a physician, a surgeon named Horace N. Allen (1850–1927). Allen, a Methodist minister, was also the chaplain to the delegation.

Dr. Allen was able to treat Min Yongik successfully, and in gratitude King Kojong granted his request for permission to establish hospitals, schools, and churches in Korea. The following year Protestant missionaries arrived in Korea, including Horace G. Underwood (1839–1916), who established Yonsei University, and Dorothy Scranton, who established Ewha University. Catholic Christianity had entered a century earlier but suffered persecution and martyrdom. Now Protestant Christianity entered with the blessing of the king and began to prosper. Oddly, in Korean the word *Christian* connotes the Protestant church and its members, to the exclusion of Catholics; in Korea today, one is asked whether one is "Christian" or "Catholic," as if they were mutually exclusive terms. Their separate paths of entry, the Catholics with a heritage of persecution and the Protestants with a heritage of official patronage, have marked them as distinctly different varieties of Christianity. Ultimately, the Protestant practice, particularly Presbyterianism, has become widespread in Korea, but Catholics make up a significant percentage of the populace as well.

The Tonghak Movement

It was the Catholics who were the catalyst for the creation of the first modern domestic religion in Korea in 1864 called Tonghak. A purely religious movement at the outset, it became the focus of a peasant uprising in 1894. The uprising, known as the Tonghak Rebellion, had as one of its aims the end of foreign influence. Ironically, it had the opposite result. It led to war between the Chinese and Japanese on Korean soil and did a great deal to hasten the loss of Korean sovereignty.

In 1864 a man named Choe Cheu (1824–64), who belonged to an impoverished branch of a *yangban* family, had a vision and began teaching a new doctrine. The doctrine was a blend of Confucianism, Buddhism, shamanism, Taoism, and magic and was called Tonghak, meaning "Eastern Learning," a direct contrast to "Western Learning"—the Korean term of the day for Catholicism.

Tonghak came into being as a foil of Catholicism, and though it was a syncretism of Eastern philosophies, it did pick up some traits of the religion it set out to counter. For example, followers met for weekly worship service in buildings that resembled chapels. Perhaps this feature alone made the government think that they were more similar than dissimilar to the Catholics. Although Tonghak was not political, the orthodox Confucian government saw it as not merely heterodox but threatening. The government had already led several purges and persecutions of the Catholics, and it regarded Tonghak, though in name the opposite of Catholicism, as a threat to social stability. After a time Choe was arrested, tried, convicted, and executed in 1864, ironically for being a Catholic (Young 2008).

The death of its founder was not the death of Tonghak, however. In subsequent years it flourished in clandestine cells across southern Korea (Young 2008). Though it began in the southeast, it grew and spread to the southwest. By 1894 peasant discontent and the outlawed religion had melded. Chon Pongjun (1854–95), a Tonghak member though not a religious leader, used the network of Tonghak churches as a means of building a peasant uprising. Tensions had been building in North Cholla Province, a place that supplied more than its share of government revenues. In 1892 a typically corrupt official named Cho Pyonggap had been appointed the district magistrate of Kobu in Cholla Province, and (in the words of Korean historian Han Wookeun) "set about lining his pockets in the usual manner, but with unusual energy."

> Farmers were encouraged to bring waste land under cultivation by promises of tax exemption, and then taxed. The well-to-do were blackmailed by false accusations of crimes. Farmers were forced to work on irrigation projects without pay, the money they should have got going to Cho.
> The people complained to Cho's superiors up to the provincial governor, but without success, the petitioners being dispersed by force. (Han 1970, 406–407)

The injustices suffered by the peasants under Cho Pyonggap were typical of life in rural Korea, which was therefore ripe for a widespread revolt. In February 1894 Chon Pongjun, convinced by now that appeals to the government were useless, led nearly a thousand farmers in a large-scale attack on government offices, including the armory and the warehouse that contained tax grain, which Chon subsequently distributed to the needy. The revolt spread quickly. Chon led peasants in the North Cholla province to take over the government granaries located at county magistracies. There they drove off county magistrates, whom they charged with greed and tax gouging—collecting more taxes than required and keeping the extra for themselves. They continued to distribute the stored grains to the impoverished people. The method of taking control of county offices and granaries spread like wildfire, and other Tonghak rebels took over other granaries throughout North Cholla province and parts of South Cholla and North Kyongsang Provinces. By the end of May Chon Pongjun and the Tonghak rebels were in control of much of the important agricultural heartland of the southern region of Korea.

The New York Times took note of the revolt and described it in sympathetic terms in a July 1, 1894, article, noting in headlines that "OFFICIAL CURRUPTION IS THE CAUSE OF THE REVOLT: The People, Having Been Long Oppressed and Robbed by Those in Power—Sympathize With the Insurrection" (New York Times, July 1, 1894). A later article, written when Chinese and Japanese intervention in the conflict had led to the first Sino-Japanese war, reported that the revolt had turned ugly and firmly took the side of the Japanese as the vanguard of modernity and sensible government in Asia: "Tonghak Rebels Burn Villages and Slaughter Men and Women. TAX OFFICIALS BURNED TO DEATH. Japan Will Put an End to the Revolt if the Corean Dynasty Will Reform Its Administration." Arguing that "Japan is at present the only power which can put [the rebels] down," the Times wrote: "Japan is pledged to introduce a more peaceful, upright, and stable administration than has prevailed in Corea for the past ten years, but so far she has met with much double-dealing from the Corean officials" (New York Times, January 20, 1895).

The Sino-Japanese War of 1894–1895

The government in Seoul sent a large army to the southeastern province to retake the county-level government offices and granaries, but the Korean army was not successful, no more successful than China had been in quelling the Taiping Rebellion in the 1850s, and like China then, Korea was forced to rely on foreign assistance. In desperation it sent word to China asking for troops. The move played into Japanese hands. The Japanese invoked the article in the 1882 military treaty between China and Japan that stated that military deployments by one side would be met by corresponding deployments by the other side; Japan sent troops. The Chinese troops barely had time to quell the Tonghak rebellion before they had to defend themselves against the Japanese, who swept in with a better-trained and better-armed force and quickly pushed China out of Korea. This conflict became known as the Sino-Japanese War of 1894–95.

Much of the fighting was naval. Japan had spent a great deal of modernization effort building a large navy of small vessels designed to move quickly and efficiently around the narrow passages and jagged coastline of Japan's islands. China had done the same, but its modernization efforts were not as successful as Japan's. In 1895 the dowager empress Cixi (1835–1908) diverted China's entire navy budget to the building of a stone boat—a picnic pavilion—to decorate the pond of the summer palace, arguing that it was a part of the navy. When the naval budget was not diverted, the Chinese approach to modernization was to build a few large ships to patrol its long and even coastline. When the battle in Korea was over, all the large Chinese vessels sat on the bottom of the Yellow Sea, and Korea was firmly under Japanese control. Japan even laid claim to China's largest island, Taiwan.

In Korea, without China, her longtime ally and "big brother," the Japanese began to expand their interests. Under Japanese pressure the Korean government began to reform. In 1897 Korea declared itself an empire, and the hapless King Kojong declared himself an emperor. Symbolically, Korea was no longer under the protection of China but on equal footing with China and Japan. In reality, it was just one step closer to being subsumed by Japan.

The Murder of Queen Min

One of the more remarkable events of this turbulent period was the Japanese murder of the Korean queen by Japanese soldiers. Queen Min was King Kojong's only queen, a powerful personality who in many ways influenced the king and the court. Her pro-China/anti-Japan position kept Korea firmly loyal to China, its longtime ally, and deflected any progressive influences by the rapidly modernizing Japan. Japan's leaders knew of her influence and thought it best to eliminate her. There was an attempt on her life in 1882, but she survived by fleeing the palace and allowing one of her ladies-in-waiting to dress in the queen's robes

Queen Min, often referred to by her posthumous title, Empress Myeongseong, was assassinated on October 8, 1895, in the palace by Japanese samurai for her pro-Chinese stance. (Academy of Korean Studies)

and be killed. In the second, successful, attempt the Japanese assassins killed not only the queen but all her ladies-in-waiting to be sure that they were not fooled again. Then they dragged her body to a nearby wooded area, where they burned it. This needless act of savagery was perhaps retaliation by the soldiers whom she had tricked before, a symbolic act to make sure that she was truly dead.

THREE MONUMENTS TO A MARTYRED QUEEN

Korea has revisited the murder of Queen Min in attempts to rec-oncile its modern diplomatic relations with the state with which it has had such an unhappy relationship. Marking the spot where the queen was killed inside the large palace compound in downtown Seoul are three monuments. Each says basically the same thing, but each was built for a different reason.

The first monument was erected by Syngman Rhee, president from 1948 to 1960, as a postliberation reminder of the dark days of the Japanese occupation that had just ended. This rather small monument simply states that the queen was killed by Japanese assassins on that spot. The second monument was built during the reign of Park Chung Hee just after the "normalization" of relations with Japan. From 1945, the time of the liberation from the Japanese occupation, until 1964, Korea did not have diplomatic relations with its former overlord. Park, however, regarded normalization—the exchange of ambassa-dors and the establishment of an embassy in the other's capital—as an essential part of his economic development plan. Park sought and obtained loans and investments from the Japanese. To counter argu-ments that he was too *sakura* (literally "cherry blossom," a phrase meaning pro-Japanese), Park pursued a program of building shrines and monuments to heroes of the anti-Japanese resistance in 1592 and in the 20th century. As part of that program, a new monument, about five feet long carved from granite with a sculpture of a woman's head with a Korean queen's headdress, was erected to the side of the small Syngman Rhee–era monument.

The third monument is a large pair of paintings, the size of a bill-board and protected by a Korean-style roof, created during the Chun Doo Hwan administration, 1980–87. Chun, like Park before him, faced the need to obtain large-scale financial assistance from Japan, and, like Park before him, in order to compensate on the domestic front for the loss of face caused by relying on Japan, Chun built a number of anti-Japanese monuments. The paintings depict two of the crucial scenes in the murder of the queen. In one a woman sitting on the floor in her room stares up defiantly at a Japanese soldier brandishing a samurai sword. All around her, dead and bleeding on the floor, lie the bodies of her loyal ladies-in-waiting. In the second painting ghoul-ish figures of a half-dozen Japanese soldiers surround a body-sized

(continues)

THREE MONUMENTS (continued)

bonfire, a depiction of the burning of the queen's body after she was murdered.

Queen Min was a powerful figure at court in her day and a tragic symbol of the loss of life and nation during the time of occupation. In death she is a symbol that is used to remind today's Koreans of the tragedy of those bygone years. Her story was told in an opera that opened in Seoul in 1997, called *Myeongseong Hwanghu, The Last Empress,* after her posthumous imperial title. The opera played briefly in New York City as well.

Independence Movements

Despite the continued erosion of Korean sovereignty associated with the Japanese victory, Korea's most promodern, prodemocratic, and even proindependence forces still looked to Japan to lead Korea into the modern world. One leader in such efforts was Philip Jaisohn, born So Chaepil. So Chaepil had been part of the student delegation sent to study in Japan along with Kim Okkyun. Tainted by being part of the pro-Japanese faction, So left Korea and ended up in the United States, where he studied medicine and became a medical doctor, practicing in Philadelphia (and adopting the Western name Philip Jaisohn). A naturalized American citizen, he is often referred to as the first Korean American. When he received word of the Chinese defeat in Korea, he returned in 1895, hoping he could help Korea modernize by following examples he had seen in Japan and the United States. His first effort was to help organize the Independence Club, which built the Independence Arch. Modeled after the Arc de Triomphe in Paris, it was built on the spot where arriving Chinese ambassadors used to rest their final night in a hall called "Welcoming Pavilion" before putting on ceremonial robes to make the final half-day's trip to the palace and present themselves at the Korean court. Etched into the stone on the side of the Independence Arch that Chinese ambassadors first saw was "Independence Arch" in Chinese characters; on the opposite side, where commoner Koreans would pass, were the same words in the Korean alphabet. Philip Jaisohn also edited the *Independent News,* a new daily newspaper published in *hangul* and English. It was the first widely circulated use of the Korean alphabet since the year after its invention in 1446 (Chandra 1988).

136

Though Jaisohn and his fellow Independence Club members were sincere proponents of modernization, democracy, and Korean sovereignty, their efforts in the 1890s tended to promote the interests of Japan. At the time the Japanese were fostering governmental reforms the Independence Club favored. In 1896 the Korean government accused Jaisohn of wishing to make Korea a republic. He was once more forced into exile and returned to the United States. Jaisohn remained a lifelong activist for Korean independence and later, in the United States, founded the League of Friends of Korea in support of the March First Movement (1919), which protested Japanese rule in Korea. In 1945, after Japan's defeat, Jaisohn returned to Korea, where some 3,000 Koreans, including the young prodemocracy activist Kim Dae Jung (b. 1924, South Korean president, 1998–2003), requested that he run for the presidency. Jaisohn ultimately decided in the interest of unity to stand aside, leaving Syngman Rhee to become South Korea's first president.

The Russo-Japanese War of 1905

With the defeat of China in its war with Japan in 1894, the only other major power in the region was Russia. Russia had set up Port Arthur (Chinese: Lushun) on the Liaodong Peninsula as a base for its own expansion southward, connecting the city with Siberia via the South Manchurian Railroad that ran through Manchuria and the city of Mukden (Chinese: Shenyang). Japan and its European ally, Great Britain, did not want to see Russia, under Czar Nicholas II (1868–1918), further expand its influence in the area, and although Great Britain did not get involved in the hostilities, it encouraged Japan in the war. On February 8, 1904, Japan launched a surprise attack on Port Arthur, one of the largest armed conflicts the world had ever witnessed. It saw the first large-scale use of automatic weapons and was the first time in modern history an Asian country defeated a European power. Most of the battles were naval battles; only two were close to Korea, the Battle of Chemulpo (the old name for Inchon) and the Battle of the Yalu River. Once the Russians were driven out of Port Arthur, they retreated to Mukden, where they were surrounded and defeated at great cost (more than 26,000 Russians killed, 25,000 wounded, and 40,000 captured). The final battle was another naval battle, this time in the straits of Tsushima between Korea and Japan, where the Russian navy was completely destroyed, including eight battleships.

Russia did not have the will to pursue the war any longer, largely because of domestic unrest. Widespread demonstrations all across Russia required the czarist government to pull back from any external dispute to try to control the unrest at home. Thus, the Russians were amenable to a quick settlement. The peace talks were held at Portsmouth, New Hampshire, under the auspices of U.S. president Theodore Roosevelt (1858–1919). After the war Korea had no allies to turn to. Japan declared Korea its protectorate, meaning that it took over Korea's foreign relations. In reality Japan began to control Korean domestic issues as well, leading to outright annexation in 1910.

The Japanese takeover of Korea was gradual. The protectorate was proclaimed in 1905, but Kojong refused to sign the required document agreeing to the move. Koreans were split in their reaction to the Japanese overtures. Some took up armed resistance; the movement was suppressed by the Japanese military and eventually pushed off the Korean Peninsula into Manchuria. Some welcomed the Japanese and tried to find a place for themselves in the new order. Later to be called collaborators, they appreciated the news that an Asian power had defeated a European power, seeing it as an encouraging sign of Eastern

THE TREATY OF PORTSMOUTH

The peace treaty ending the Russo-Japanese War of 1905 was signed in a rather unlikely location, Portsmouth, New Hampshire. U.S. president Teddy Roosevelt brought the combatants to the negotiating table. For his efforts he was awarded the Nobel Peace Prize, the sixth one given.

The Nobel Peace Prize notwithstanding, many Koreans over the years have considered Roosevelt's negotiation of the Portsmouth Treaty, which gave Japan a free hand to do what it liked in Korea, a betrayal by the United States. Certainly the treaty did not serve Korean interests. In fact, Dr. Horace Allen, the U.S. minister in Seoul, had urged his government to intervene to stop Japanese aggression, but Roosevelt believed that Japanese control of the Korean Peninsula would be useful as a break to Russian expansion. In addition, the treaty ratified a secret agreement between William Howard Taft, the U.S. secretary of war, and Katsura Taro, Japan's prime minister: The United States agreed not to interfere with Japan's role in Korea as long as Japan did not interfere in the U.S. role in the Philippines.

autonomy. To them Japan represented progress and modernization, while the lingering Choson royalty represented stagnation, corruption, and poverty. The majority of Koreans were somewhere between the two poles, just trying to get by.

In 1907 Emperor Kojong made his last desperate move to restore Korean sovereignty. Learning of an international meeting, the second World Peace Conference, to be held that year at The Hague, Netherlands, he sent a secret delegation—secret, at least, from the Japanese, who would have blocked their participation had they known. At the conference the delegation presented itself as the true representative of Korea with credentials from Kojong. It was an open repudiation of the Japanese protectorate. The June 30, 1907, *New York Times* reported that it had been a dull day at the conference except for the appearance of Yi Sangsol, former premier; Yi Chun, former judge of the supreme court of Seoul; and Yi Wijong, former secretary of the Korean legation at St. Petersburg:

> The protest says ... the Japanese are violating [Korea's] rights and trampling on international law, depriving them of their national independence and even resorting to violence. It adds that the Korean Emperor gave the delegates full powers which they will put at the disposal of the delegates to the conference, asking their intervention for admission to the conference. They wish, the protest says, to defend their rights, and expose the Japanese methods....
>
> One of the Korean delegates said in an interview today:
>
> "The Japanese are behaving in Korea like savages. They are committing all kinds of barbarities against property and against the people, especially the women. [The conference's] refusal to receive us was astonishing and painful, as our relations with Russia, as well as with America, are so good that we thought they could not refuse to assist us. We intend to go to America to appeal to the generosity of that noble country for help ...."
> (New York Times, June 30, 1907)

When Kojong's representatives appeared at The Hague, asking to be seated at the conference as the delegates from Korea, their credentials were rejected by the other delegates, who were bound by the Treaty of Portsmouth. To show their displeasure the Japanese forced Emperor Kojong to abdicate the throne. His son, who was reportedly mentally deficient, became Emperor Sunjong (1874–1926, r. 1907–10). His primary duty was to do the bidding of the Japanese, a humiliating task but one that would last only three years. The Choson dynasty was all but over.

The Japanese governance in Korea was under the leadership of a resident-general, and the first resident-general was none other than Ito Hirobumi (1841–1909), a former prime minister and one of the fathers of Japanese democracy. His is one of only four statues today in the main hall of the Japanese diet (parliament building). Until recently his image was on the smallest denomination and most-used unit of currency in Japan, the 1,000 yen note. Ito had liberal ideas for his time. He had been one of a small group of former samurai who created the constitutional monarchy and parliamentary democracy in Japan. While some Japanese argued for the annexation of Korea, Ito initially favored a kind of confederation in which Korea would have a degree of autonomy. His policy changed as a wave of violent resistance swept Korea.

Upon the abdication of Kojong, when the Japanese had disbanded Korea's military forces, an angry crowd clashed with Japanese guards outside the palace, and another crowd destroyed the building of a pro-Japanese newspaper. Soldiers from the disbanded Korean armed forces fought a pitched battle with the Japanese in Seoul. They were defeated, but the survivors joined the rebels who were already fighting Japanese rule in the provinces. Korean guerrillas based in inaccessible mountain regions raided Japanese installations, damaging railroad tracks and telegraph lines. "The Japanese response," writes Han Woo-keun, "was indiscriminate slaughter and destruction" (Han 1970, 453). The Japanese themselves estimated that there were 69,832 Korean guerrillas in 1908, with nearly 1,500 clashes that year between Korean irregulars and Japanese troops. The number fell to 25,000 in 1909, and to 2,000 in 1910 (Cumings 2005, 146). As the Japanese solidified their military control of Korea, the guerrillas moved their bases across the border into Manchuria.

In 1909 Ito Hirobumi made a trip to Manchuria to discuss the possibility of Korean annexation with Russian diplomats. At the train station in Harbin he was shot and killed by a Korean assassin. On August 22, 1910, Korea officially became a part of the Japanese empire. The last Yi ruler was forced to abdicate. Not only did the dynasty end, Korea as an independent nation ceased to exist.

5

THE JAPANESE COLONY
(1910-1945)

A s the Choson dynasty ended, Korea began 35 years as a colony of Japan. The conditions of subjugation were not always the same. Generally, the Japanese colonial occupation is divided into three phases: the Military Period, also called the Dark Age (1910–19); the Cultural Policy Period (1919–31); and the Assimilation Period (1931–45). The first decade was characterized by harsh military rule, but the Japanese also brought with them modernization and new ideas and products. During this phase the resistance elements, both on the left and the right, were squeezed off the peninsula; armed resistance fighters hid in the hills of Manchuria, while others tried to set up governments in exile in Shanghai and elsewhere. On the other end of the spectrum, the collaborators sought advantages for themselves and their country by pragmatically recognizing that Japan was in charge and a new world order was in effect. Most of the farmers and workers tried to make the best of the situation. The second decade was remarkably open, and censorship and suppression were subtle. Armed resistance continued in Manchuria, but governments-in-exile had abandoned any practical hope of obtaining recognition; the ordinary citizen continued to look for reasons to hope for a better day. Japan's economy was growing, and some Koreans enjoyed new products from the outside world. Much of the Korean populace accepted, to some degree, Japan's concepts of an "Asian Greater Co-prosperity Sphere" and "Asia for the Asians." Cultural creativity flourished, with short stories and poems published in an array of newly created magazines; the world economy of the 1920s was booming; and the average Korean was swept along in a flood of development and prosperity. The subtle emergence of "thought police" and the first political arrests were a foreshadowing of darker days to come. The third decade and a half was marked by war that brought untold hardships to the colony. Life became difficult for the average Japanese citizen, but matters were even worse for the residents of the colony, the second-class citizens.

The Military Period (1910–1919)

Japan had had its eyes on Korea since the 1870s. Its influence in Korea had grown in fits and starts, and Japanese policy was not always consistent. There were differences between military men and democracy advocates, who argued about using military power. Japan's influence grew gradually. Its decisive invasion of Korea occurred as a by-product of the war with Russia in 1904, when Japanese troops landed at Inchon, marched into Seoul, and forced the Korean government to accept Japanese "protection." From that point on only outside intervention could have removed Korea from Japanese control, and the Treaty of Portsmouth confirmed that those with the power to intervene were content to let Japan have Korea. Every move the Japanese made after 1905 served to strengthen their control, efforts that included the suppression of a vigorous Korean guerrilla movement. When Korea was annexed to the Japanese empire on August 22, 1910, it was largely because the groundwork had been laid.

Though the term *annexation* is commonly used to describe Japan's actions, the Korean people did not become citizens of Japan with the rights of Japanese, nor did they have any real representation in their own government or control of its policies. Japan took control of Korea, retained control with the help of a large military and civilian police force, and ruled it through a series of governor-generals appointed in Japan.

It was an age of imperialism. Japan had already taken control of Taiwan as a result of the Sino-Japanese War of 1895, and it was now looking at Manchuria and the mainland of China. The Japanese observed that the world was being carved up by imperial powers. Their choice, it seemed, was to be carved up or seize the carving knife—to be colonized or to become an empire. Japan's successes—defeating the Chinese and then the Russians—probably surprised the Japanese as much as it did other Asians and, for that matter, the rest of the world. Japan was the first and only non-Western empire in the age of imperialism and the first to defeat a European power. Once Japan began to succeed at imperialism, it could not easily turn back. Japan was on the road to becoming one of perhaps three or four countries that would rule the world. At least that was the way it looked to the imperialists at the time.

Military Regime

The first Japanese governor-general was Terauchi Masatake (1852–1919). He had been appointed resident-general in 1909 to succeed the assassinated Ito Hirobumi (1841–1909) and became governor-general at the point of annexation. Terauchi held the post until 1916, and his tenure was one of ruthless military rule. The first phase is called the Military Period because of the increase in numbers of soldiers and military police that Japan brought into the peninsula to combat the resistance movement that had gained strength after 1905, when Japan declared Korea its protectorate. Before 1905 a Japanese political takeover had not seemed plausible. After the Korean army was dissolved in 1910, many who had been in the military joined the guerrilla fighters, leading to a sudden increase in armed anti-Japanese activity. Yet the Korean resistance remained scattered and poorly organized. Within a few years the overwhelming force of the Japanese army and police had eliminated the armed resistance by killing Korean resistance fighters, arresting them, or squeezing them out of the country. Those committed to armed resistance mostly left the peninsula. Many gathered in Manchuria and Russia, from where they fought a guerrilla war against Japanese forces at the Chinese-Korean border. During the administration of Governor-General Terauchi, thousands of Koreans were killed: Official numbers say 17,000; unofficial estimates are higher.

While some Koreans gave their lives in the fight against occupation, others accommodated themselves to it. In an effort to diffuse resistance in Korea's traditional aristocratic ruling class, the colonial government gave special treatment to members of the former Korean royal family and to high-ranking pro-Japanese officers. Some eminent Koreans were offered titles of nobility, others were given pensions, and elderly Confucian scholars were given "age grants" (Han 1975, 406). An essentially powerless privy council was staffed with pro-Japanese Koreans. Thanks to the existence of the privy council, which employed 15 pro-Japanese Korean first-class advisers and 55 pro-Japanese Korean councilors, the Japanese could tell the world that Koreans were participating in their government (Kang Man-gil 2005, 6).

Koreans were also employed in large numbers in the lower echelons of the military and civilian police force, by means of which the Japanese controlled Korea. The military police force, which was widely used for nonmilitary and noncriminal matters, was a special feature of Japanese rule in Korea. In the words of Korean historian Mang-gil Kang,

> *The military police were involved directly or indirectly in every aspect of colonial rule, from the collection of intelligence to the extermination of anti-Japanese guerilla units, the summary disposition of criminal affairs, the mediation of civil suits, the serving of processes, the collection of taxes, the protection of forests, the compilation of populations registers, the provision of escorts for postal officers, the enforcement of quarantines and the prevention of epidemics, the measuring of rainfall, the control of economic activities including smuggling, the oversight of labourers, and the diffusion of the Japanese languages, and projects for improving farming. (Kang Man-gil 2005, 7)*

Economic Exploitation, Modernization, or Both?

The Japanese changed Korea forever, and ever since the end of their era in Korea in 1945 outsiders have been debating whether there was anything good in these changes. In Korea, where the whole period tends to be remembered as a time of Japanese exploitation and patriotic Korean resistance (with the occasional traitor and collaborator), the point seems much less debatable. Professor Bruce Cumings describes the view among contemporary Koreans he has met:

> *Among Koreans today, North and South, the mere mention of the idea that Japan somehow "modernized" Korea calls forth indignant denials, raw emotions, and the sense of mayhem having just been, or about to be, committed. For the foreigner even the most extensive cataloging of Japanese atrocities will pale beside the barest suggestion of anything positive and lasting that might have emerged from the colonial period. Koreans have always thought that the benefits of this growth went entirely to Japan and that Korea would have developed rapidly without Japanese help anyway. (Cumings 2005, 148–149)*

Other observers have found Koreans who say that the Japanese presence brought benefits as well as oppression. The American writer Hildi Kang, in *Under the Black Umbrella*, an oral history derived from interviews with Koreans who lived through the colonial period, quotes a Korean elder, Yi Sangdo, who recalls that the Japanese built dams and bridges that brought flood control to his village. "I must say, their organization impressed me. I think it was probably good in the long run," while another Korean just as strongly—and perhaps just as accurately—insists, "They had sinister plans . . . to eliminate any vestiges of Korean consciousness" (Hildi Kang 2001, 2).

While the Japanese encouraged—actually forced—Korea to grow economically, it stifled Korea politically. The Japanese outlawed political organizations, shut down newspapers and magazines it deemed threatening to their rule, and prohibited and confiscated books at will, including school textbooks that told young Koreans too much about themselves and their possibilities, books such as *Elementary Korean History, History of Korea, the Biography of Yi Sunsin,* and *History of the French Revolution* (Kang Mang-gil 2005, 9).

It is impossible to know how Korea might have changed without the Japanese. Undoubtedly its economy and industry would have modernized, with less grief for Koreans. Certainly the Japanese seem to have sped up the process. They had to do this in order to retain control of their unwilling colony and to make it a bulwark of their hurriedly assembled empire, which they saw as always threatened with destruction. Japan made Korea efficient to make it more useful to Japan. In place of the relatively decentralized traditional Korean state of the Choson period, the Japanese put in place "a powerful state that penetrated to the lowest levels of Korean society," notes historian Michael Robinson in *Korea Old and New.* "Power was centralized in a large bureaucratic order backed by impressive coercive force" (Eckert 1990, 257). Very few colonies in the history of imperialism were as thoroughly and tightly controlled as was Korea by such a large and ever-expanding bureaucracy. By 1910 about 10,000 officials were employed by the colonial bureaucracy; by 1937 the number was 87,552 (52,270 Japanese and 35,282 Koreans), and according to Robinson, "if a broader calculation of all public and private positions important to the colony is made, the totals for 1937 would be 246,000 Japanese and 63,000 Koreans" (Eckert 1990, 257); the population of Korea at the time was about 23 million. To give an idea of how intense a style of colonial government this was, Robinson points out that the French ruled a Vietnamese population of 17 million with only "2,920 administrative personnel, 10,776 regular troops and about 38,000 indigenous personnel."

Virtually all histories of Korea suddenly bristle with precise statistics as soon as they reach the period of Japanese control, because the Japanese kept such complete records. This fact in itself says a lot about the nature of Japan's rule, its intrusiveness, and its efficiency. In the colonial period government control reached down to a level that under Korea's traditional Confucian administration had virtually escaped government. Now an edict from the governor-general's office immediately affected life in the village, and those at the top knew, if they cared to, what was going on in the village. The Japanese did this in order to overcome resistance and get the most out of their colony, and they did it, additionally, because it was what they were doing at home.

Back in Japan itself they were establishing a modern state of a rather regimented, authoritarian variety. The difference was that in Korea this process was being carried out by foreigners for the benefit of the foreigners. To whatever degree the Japanese believed their words about their mutually beneficial partnership with the Koreans—and the memories of some of the Koreans interviewed by Hildi Kang suggest that some Japanese did believe it—their policies in Korea were designed to strengthen and enrich Japan. If the Koreans benefited, that was all very well from the Japanese point of view—it proved that their empire was good for everyone, but when sacrifice was called for, it was the Koreans who were made to sacrifice for the Japanese. The Korean historian Han Woo-keun gives an illustration of the process. In 1920 the Japanese instituted a 15-year plan to increase Korea's annual rice crop by 45 million bushels, 25 million of which were to be exported to Japan.

> This proved to be an unrealistic goal, but nevertheless the planned quantity of rice was exported to Japan every year. By 1933 more than half of the annual rice crop was being sent to Japan, while rice consumption by the average Korean dwindled in proportion. By the end of the 1920s, the average Japanese consumed almost twice as much rice as the average Korean, who had to supplement his diet with millet, maize and barley, mostly imported from Manchuria. (Han 1970, 480)

Governor-General Terauchi, while expanding the police force and clamping down on any sign of resistance to Japanese rule, actively pursued his country's economic goals as well. Korea received a railroad, a developing industry, and improved harbor facilities, much of which was geared to exporting raw goods to Japan and importing manufactured goods from Japan. Mining, fishing, and agricultural output all increased, and a manufacturing sector started to prosper.

The landscape changed for the whole country. The railroad, the ultimate symbol of modernization, cut a path from Pusan to Seoul to Sinuiju and went on to China, Manchuria, Siberia, Russia, and the rest of Europe. In the process railroad towns supplanted the other, once-prominent towns in the area. Taegu, for example, was a fairly insignificant town until the railroad came. It soon became the third-largest city in Korea. Originally, Sangju, to the north of Taegu, was a major market town and government center; after the emergence of Taegu as a railroad town and center of commerce for the area, Sangju faded into obscurity. The next major stop from Pusan to Seoul was Taejon, also an inconsequential city before the railroad came. Thereafter, it became the fifth- or sixth-largest city in the country.

In many traditional societies railroad lines have engendered opposition from native populations. In East Asia the opposition was expressed in terms of geomancy. Railroads, which cut through the countryside, leave scars: The straight lines of the railroad stand in stark contrast to the natural curves of the Earth, the outlines of the hills, and the flow of the rivers. On the basis of geomancy many Chinese and Koreans objected to the railroad when it first appeared.

When the Japanese laid out the course for the railroad through Pusan, they were confronted with a problem. The straight-as-an-arrow course would have taken the railroad right through the tomb of the founder of the Tongnae Chong lineage. The Chong surname group has four major branches, Tongnae, Kyongju, Yonil, and Hadong. The Chongs of Tongnae were important *yangban* figures in society, and the Japanese would have been politically unwise to run a rail line across the first ancestor's grave. So the Japanese quite politely curved the line around the grave and avoided conflict with the Tongnae Chong. In the process they engendered considerable goodwill for their caring and flexible attitude. The incident improved relations between the Japanese authorities and many of the Tongnae Chong, along with those intermarried with them.

However, these examples notwithstanding, Japanese residents in Korea and the Koreans themselves did not benefit equally from the technical and economic innovations. The government's own reports reveal that the Japanese residents in Korea prospered at a much higher level than the Koreans. Indeed, the Japanese population burgeoned as hard-pressed Japanese immigrants arrived and made use of their advantages to gain an economic foothold. Japanese entrepreneurs, farmers, miners, and fishermen found great success in Korea, much more than native Koreans achieved. For example, in fishing, Korean fishermen numbered four to five times as many as Japanese fishermen in Korea, with more than twice as many boats, but they caught fewer fish and made less money, about 80 percent of the Japanese level. Mining figures showed a similar trend. At the time of annexation, Korean-owned mines produced about a third of the colony's mining output; at the end of the first decade of occupation, they contributed less than a tenth. In manufacturing Koreans had nearly as many factories as the Japanese, but the output was 10 to 1 in favor of the Japanese; some industries were almost completely dominated by Japanese owners, such as food, beverages, and tobacco. Koreans had more factories in traditional areas such as ceramics, metalwork, and rice production.

One of the reasons behind this disparity in economic development was a law called Company Ordinance that went into effect in
December 1910. This law increased the bureaucratic requirements
for a Korean to set up a new company while facilitating the process
for a Japanese. High on the list of oppressive laws hated by the native
population, the law was revoked in 1920 in the period of general
liberalization. However, the damage had been done. The policy had

JAPANESE ARCHITECTURE IN SEOUL

There are three buildings in Seoul today that are prominent
remnants of the Japanese colonial period: City Hall, the Bank of
Korea, and the Seoul Railroad Station. All were built in a grand style
that is not traditionally Japanese but rather a borrowing of European
style. Seoul City Hall, built in 1926, is still used. One of the most
prominent buildings in downtown Seoul, it overlooks the City Hall
Plaza, which is often used for major public gatherings.

Not far from City Hall is the Bank of Korea building. Built in 1912,
it was once the headquarters of Japanese banking operations in Korea
and is now the centerpoint of Korean banking.

The original Seoul Railroad Station is today eclipsed by an ultra-
modern structure, mostly of glass, that serves the new high-speed
rail line, but the old station, built in 1925, has not been torn down.
It sits, somewhat majestic and somewhat forlorn, next to the shining
new Seoul Station.

The most impressive of all the Japanese structures, the Central
Government Capitol, completed in 1926, was torn down in 1994 after
a lengthy debate. Called the Capitol of the Government-General during the Japanese period, the building was expensive to tear down: It
was made of 2-meter cubic blocks of granite. Those who viewed the
building as the last vestige of the colonial legacy eventually prevailed,
however, and it was demolished.

One reason the building was so galling to Koreans was that it sat
in front of the old palace complex to the north of downtown Seoul,
blocking the view of the beautiful rooflines of the traditional palace
buildings, but there was another, subtler, reason the building was
hated. The outline of the building was in the shape of the Chinese
graph for Japan. In effect, the building was a giant symbolic stamp

put limitations on the development of capital by Koreans while fostering the formation of capital in the hands of Japanese individuals and corporations.

There were other forms of legal discrimination as well. Koreans, for example, could be flogged because, they were told, Korea had a tradition of flogging and torture; therefore the traditional punishments could be used on Koreans, but not on the Japanese. This obviously took

on Korean soil, a statement that Japan was there and there to stay. Tearing the building down, though a great expense, provided a kind of catharsis, a final reaffirmation of Korean independence.

In September 1945, within a month of liberation, this photo was taken by a member of the U.S. Army military government in Korea. Dominating the landscape is the Japanese-built capitol building that served as headquarters for the U.S. military government for three years and then the South Korean government for more than 30 years. The building was used as a museum for the following 10 years until it was finally torn down in 1994. (Academy of Korean Studies)

149

the wind out of one justification for the Japanese takeover: the elimination of archaic practices in Korea.

Another egregious aspect of Japanese policy was the land survey, which began even before annexation. Beginning in 1908 Japan conducted a survey of all farmland at great expense in order to extend ownership opportunities to Japanese citizens and corporations. Large Japanese companies soon bought or confiscated large tracts of land. In the process hundreds of thousands of Korean farmers eventually became tenants, in some cases on the very land they had once owned. The Oriental Development Company, founded in 1910, soon had 300,000 tenant farmers working its land. Forestland was confiscated in a similar manner beginning in 1918. All forestland held by villages and lineage organizations had to be registered, and thereafter the ownership was transferred to Japanese lumber companies. The abuse of the forests is one of the most often retold stories of the Japanese exploitations. The resulting erosion of the hillsides and devastation wrought by deforestation were impossible to overlook.

By 1918, under a policy of colonial development that encouraged Japanese settlement in Korea, no fewer than 98,000 farmers had taken up residence in Korea. There were about 30,000 Japanese fishermen living in Korea, and three times that many fished in Korean waters from ports in Japan. Businessmen from large companies and small-scale entrepreneurs flocked to Korea as well. Certain sections of Seoul and other cities came to be dominated by the Japanese. The landscape changed as Japanese-style homes, business buildings, and, of course, the dominant government office buildings were built.

Educational Changes

The philosophy underlying the Korean education movement of the 19th century was a belief that a strong country was rooted in a well-educated populace. This system included foreign language training. Language schools for teaching Japanese, English, and French were opened in 1895; for Russian in 1896; and for Chinese and German in 1900. In the early 1910s schools also developed new curricula for scientific and technical studies. Around the same time many schools started to teach nationalistic concepts. For many the concept of "Koreanness" and the concept of a modern nation-state were new ideas that were just beginning to be discussed and explored. The school system was key to this development.

Education took on a new role under the Japanese. With the Western missionary-sponsored innovations begun in 1884, the educational system had started to open to a nonelite public, a popular reform. Although some of the recently founded missionary schools survived the Japanese era, many were shut down, some as early as 1908, others in 1914, and still others in the 1930s.

In 1908 Resident-General Ito Hirobumi issued a decree that placed private schools under the same control as the public school system and closed some schools in the process. (This occurred during the protectorate, when Japan allegedly controlled only Korea's foreign relations.) For many Koreans the Japanese changes continued to improve the educational system. Most important, the Japanese continued to offer greater opportunity for more people. The improvements were relative, however. The Japanese had developed a parallel system, with one set of schools for the Japanese and another for the Koreans. The system provided schooling for more Koreans than had ever been educated before, which engendered some popular support, but nevertheless only a small percentage of Koreans were educated, whereas education for the Japanese in Korea was nearly universal. The government allowed the brightest of Korean students to study in the Japanese schools, creating allies among Koreans at an elitist level. A small percentage who performed very well or were especially well connected were even admitted to colleges in Japan. By 1912 there were 3,171 Korean students in Japan. This particular strategy, however, could have backfired on the Japanese. Many of the Koreans who studied in Japan became leftists and nationalists. "Living together and studying subversive political literature available in Japan, Korean students became increasingly radicalized," notes Michael Robinson. "In addition, the bonds between Korean and other foreign students were intensified by first-hand experience of ethnic discrimination in Japanese society. They also forged ties with leftist Japanese students who were alienated by the politics of the older generation" (Eckert 1990, 275).

World War I

On August 23, 1914, Japan entered World War I on the Allied side. It played a relatively minor role in the war, securing the sea lanes in the South Pacific and Indian Oceans against the German navy. Japan used its participation in the war to strengthen its position in China, first by occupying the German-leased territory on the shore of Jiaozhou Bay on the Shandong Peninsula. To China Japan posed a military threat even stronger than it had in 1895, when Japan had defeated China in the Sino-Japanese War. In 1911 the Qing dynasty had fallen at last, and

China was now the Republic of China, but it was weaker and more divided than ever. In 1915, with the other great powers distracted by the war, Japan presented China with an ultimatum of Twenty-one Demands, which amounted to a demand that Japan be allowed to dominate the Chinese territories of Manchuria and Mongolia. Also included were demands that China discontinue leasing territory to foreign powers, a demand aimed at giving Japan a monopoly of power in China and one that therefore threatened the interests of Japan's supposed allies, the United States and, especially, Great Britain. China agreed to the terms in May. By the end of the war, Japan's well-placed alliances and military might had gained it enough international prestige that it was welcomed at the conference at Versailles, where territorial and other claims were settled. However, some of its gains were annulled at the Washington Naval Conference, conducted between 1921 and 1922 among nine nations with interests in East Asia. The victorious allies, who had their own interests in China, were not eager to let it become a Japanese colony. Japan's designs on China threatened Western interests, and gradually, from this point on, the British and the Americans, who had admired Japan, began to see it as a threat.

From 1910 Manchuria had been used as a base by Korean guerrillas against Japan, and many Koreans had emigrated to Manchuria to escape the Japanese or simply to survive after having lost their land. By the end of World War I, Korean nationalists at home and in exile were aware of Japan's incursions into China as a serious threat. At the same time they saw other events in the world as opportunities. Like many other colonized peoples, Koreans took hope in the ideas of U.S. president Woodrow Wilson. His Fourteen Points, a plan for the imminent postwar world, called for reduced armaments, freedom of the seas, self-determination for all peoples, and foremost, "a general association of nations . . . for the purpose of affording mutual guarantees of political independence and territorial integrity to great and small states alike."

The occasion of the peace conference to be held in Versailles in 1919 galvanized the various Korean independence movements that had already grown up or were beginning to form among Korean exiles in Japan, China, Russia, and the United States. The victors of World War I were about to redraw the map of the world, supposedly on the principle of national self-determination. Korea was a nation with its own language and culture and a long history of independence, colonized against the will of its people. Now was a good time to bring this logic to the attention of the Western democracies. The Korean National Association, formed in 1909 in the United States by Syngman Rhee (1875–1965), who would later become the first president of South Korea (1945–60), voted to send Rhee to the peace conference. As a colonial subject of imperial Japan, Rhee was refused a passport by the U.S. government, but the New Korea Youth Association, founded in 1919 in China by Yo Un-hyong (1885–1947), was able to send Kim Kyu-sik (1881–1950) to Paris to lobby for Korean independence. In Japan Koreans studying in Tokyo formed the Korean Youth Independence Corps and passed a declaration dated February 8, 1919, demanding immediate independence for Korea.

The March First Movement, 1919

Within Korea the more radical and active nationalists were in hiding or in prison. However, since the Japanese permitted their colonial subjects to assemble for religious purposes, proindependence political activity centered around religious organizations—Christian, Buddhist, and Chondogyo (Religion of the Heavenly Way), the last an outgrowth of the Tonghak movement that had been at the core of the peasant uprisings of 1894. Leaders of all three of these religious groups were in contact with young Korean nationalists and were inspired by the Tokyo declaration of the Korean Youth Independence Corps. With their help plans for a large demonstration of Korean unity spread through the colony (Eckert 1990, 277). Nationalists clandestinely drafted a declaration of independence and 33 men—16 Christians, 16 Chondogyo followers, and one Buddhist—prepared to read and sign the document in a downtown Seoul park. Copies of the document were distributed around the country and overseas using the church network.

In Korea the movement gained strength and visibility when it turned the funeral for the last Choson king, Kojong, who had died on January 22, 1919, at age 71, 12 years after his abdication, into a huge public protest against the occupying power. It was widely rumored in Korea that Kojong had actually been murdered by the Japanese. Though historians do not believe this to be true, the rumor aroused the emotions of Koreans who ordinarily would not have taken part in political demonstrations. In life Kojong had not been an able leader. In death he became a powerful symbol of Koreans' yearning for independence. The demonstrations' organizers made use of these emotions.

Setting the date for the declaration was critical, and the occasion of the king's funeral seemed ideal, as the organizers expected people to gather in large numbers. His funeral was set for March 3, 1919, but fearing a leak, or perhaps a traitor who might turn them in, the planners moved the date up to March 1.

An indigenous Korean religion, Chondogyo (once known as Tonghak) was created in 1864 and survives in both North and South Korea today. Shown here is the headquarters in Seoul. Though Chondogyo was created as a response to Catholicism, it shares several Catholic features, such as church buildings. (Academy of Korean Studies)

Demonstrations supporting the declaration of independence quickly spread throughout the country. It is estimated that more than a million of Korea's 20 million people participated in street demonstrations. Their cry was "Manse!" (pronounced *mahn-seh*, literally meaning "ten thousand years" and often translated as "long live"—in this case "long live Korean independence!"). The Japanese indeed referred to it as the "Manse Movement." There were demonstrations in all but a handful of Korea's 218 counties. Kim Sunok, interviewed for Hildi Kang's *Under the Black Umbrella*, was a 10-year-old boy living in a village near Seoul at the time; he remembers seeing people in a tram wearing Korean clothes but Western hats and that they took their hats off and waved them in the air, "screaming at the top of their lungs, 'Independence now!' I asked the grownups what was happening. They said they wanted to get their country back. Those people on the tram were going to Seoul to join a demonstration" (Hildi Kang 2001, 17).

Another of Kang's interviewees, also a boy in 1919, remembered going to a demonstration in Osan city: "I pushed my way into the crowd, and heard whispers that someone had a Korean flag. This was the first time in my life I ever saw a Korean flag." The same man remembered that in Osan there were many Japanese stores, "and as we passed these stores, they were all shut tight" (Hildi Kang 2001, 17).

The Japanese colonial authorities, under the direction of Hasegawa Yoshimichi (1850–1924), who was governor-general of Korea from 1916 to 1919, attempted to suppress the movement with any force necessary. Since men, women, and children were all demonstrating, women and children were beaten and killed with the men. One famous martyr was Yu Kwansun (1904–20), a 15-year-old schoolgirl who passed out copies of the declaration and led demonstrations in her hometown area south of Seoul. She was arrested, imprisoned, and tortured, and after a year she died in prison. Yi Chae-im, a Korean housewife who was born in 1919, the year of the March First Movement and the Japanese response to it, remembers growing up hearing about Yu Kwansun. "Such a young girl! Her story caught the imagination of everyone. It became a rallying cry" (Hildi Kang 2001, 23).

One of the more brutal atrocities occurred when a group of people meeting at a church to read and discuss the declaration were confronted by the Japanese police. The police told them to disperse and go home, but the people refused, citing the sanctuary of the church. The Japanese police, in effect, took their dare, and in spite of the sanctuary of the church—or perhaps in anger at the church's role in providing the network of support for the movement—burned the church to the ground with all those trapped inside, including women and children. Altogether, more than 7,000 people were killed in suppressing the movement by the Japanese government's own count. There may have been many more.

Despite the swift response, the movement spread; copies of the declaration were read in major cities around the world. The word was out. Korea did not want to be part of the Japanese empire.

The Provisional Government in Exile

The March First Movement unified and energized the Korean resistance, which decided in 1919 to form a provisional government in exile to lead and, to the degree possible, coordinate Korea's national liberation movements. In fact, to begin with, three separate provisional governments were formed, and their origins give a presentiment of the conflicts of postindependence Korea. One government was formed in Vladivostok, Russia (a port city in easternmost Russia, not far from Korea, and thus a natural base for Korean exiles); another in Shanghai, China; and another in Seoul. Among the Korean exiles, all passionately devoted to Korean independence, were left-wingers and right-wingers. There were people who looked forward to a Korea as a Western-style republic with a Western emphasis on the rights of property, and there were communists who wanted justice for the poor and thought (as many intellectuals and workers around the world believed in 1919) that a wonderful new classless society was being created in the Soviet Union. In the 1920s Korean communist and anticommunist irregulars in Manchuria would often take time off from fighting the Japanese to fight each other (Kim Young-sik, 2003).

For the present these forces set aside their differences in the interests of a united front. A single unified provisional government was officially formed in April 1919 in Shanghai. Its president was Syngman Rhee, who had formerly headed the Seoul provisional government, and its prime minister was Yi Tonghwi (1872–1936), who had been the former leader of the Vladivostok government. Kang Man-gil describes its early activities:

> The Shanghai Provisional Government's diplomatic campaign for independence initially focused on the League of Nations. The Shanghai government sought to join the League and to gain the League's support for Korean Independence. When this failed, the government shifted its efforts to gaining support from individual powers such as China, the US, Great Britain and the Soviet Union, setting up offices in Paris, Washington, DC, London, Beijing, and Ussuri. The only office able to engage in sustained activities, however, was the one in Washington, DC, which came to be called the Europe-America office. (Kang Mang-gil 2005, 32)

In time the liberation movement split again over the issue of whether to pledge itself primarily to diplomatic action or to armed struggle such as the one being conducted in Manchuria. Kang Man-gil suggests in *A History of Contemporary Korea* that this was because Syngman Rhee could control the diplomatic efforts but had little control over events in Manchuria (where eventually many Koreans fought the Japanese side by side with Mao's communists). Under Rhee the provisional government declared armed resistance to be a "last resort." Rhee alienated other supporters with a proposal to entrust the rule of Korea to the League of Nations. Eventually the provisional government impeached Rhee, abolished the post of president, and created a looser form of organization that attempted to embrace all facets of Korea's liberation movement. Despite these efforts, the provisional government was unable to retake control of the movement as a whole.

Syngman Rhee, president of the Republic of Korea from 1948 to 1960 (Academy of Korean Studies)

One of Syngman Rhee's left-leaning cofounders of the Korean Provisional Government in exile was Yo Un-hyong. Yo grew up in an impoverished *yangban* family with a long history of resistance to foreign incursions and demands for social justice; his grandfather had participated in the Tonghak rebellion. In 1927 Yo was imprisoned by the Japanese. Upon his release three years later he became the editor of *Chungang Ilbo,* a newspaper in Seoul, and gained fame as a populist leader who advocated socialism as well as democracy.

The future leader of North Korea, Kim Il Sung (1912–94), was seven years old at the time of the March First Movement. The son of Protestant Christians and grandson on his mother's side of a Protestant minister, in 1920 Kim emigrated with his parents to Manchuria, where he attended Chinese schools. In the early 1930s Kim became the leader of a group of Chinese partisans fighting the Japanese and led them in raids against Japanese outposts in Korea. Kim's later position as premier of North Korea, surrounded by a mythologizing cult of personality, made his early career controversial. North Koreans see him almost as a god, while South Koreans dismiss his importance as a fighter. However, there is good evidence that Kim Il Sung was taken seriously by the Japanese as a formidable opponent. Two Japanese Guandong Army colonels who tracked Kim in Manchuria later described him as "the most famous" of Korean guerrilla leaders and as "particularly popular among the Koreans in Manchuria," who "praised him as a Korean hero and gave him, secretly, both spiritual and material support" (quoted in Cumings 2005, 161). In 1941, the year the Soviet Union signed a "friendship pact" with Japan, Kim Il Sung moved to the Soviet Union, where he received additional military education. He returned after World War II with Soviet support, eventually becoming the leader of the Democratic People's Republic of Korea (DPRK, North Korea).

Cultural Policy (1919–1931)

The 1920s were remarkably different from the decade before and the decade to follow. The March First Movement had embarrassed Japan in front of the world community. The large-scale Korean resistance and the harsh Japanese suppression were at odds with the image of enlightened colonialism Japan wanted to project. Japan had violently suppressed the movement, and thousands had been killed and injured; many more had been arrested. In the aftermath Japan reexamined its policies and initiated a softer approach to its colony. They called their new approach the "Cultural Policy" (Bunka Seiji), a label that denoted a relaxation of controls over the cultural life of Koreans. Koreans began to enjoy freedoms in many areas of their lives.

Japan between Militarists and Advocates for Democracy

The early 20th century in Japan was a time of a struggle between militarists on one side and prodemocracy groups on the other. Those who wanted to emulate Western models of democracy were winning the day in the late 19th century and again in the 1920s, while the militarists were stronger in the last decade of the 19th century (after defeating China in 1895) and the first decade of the 20th century (after defeating Russia in 1905). In the 1930s the Japanese war machine rolled into Manchuria (1931) and China (1937), again putting the militarists in control of the Japanese government.

The Taisho Period (1912–26) in Japan was a time of peace and liberalization. In 1918 Hara Takashi became Japan's first commoner to serve as prime minister, elected in open, fair elections, though only men meeting minimum tax qualifications could vote. As prime minister in Japan during the Korean March First Movement, he changed policies in Korea and appointed a more liberal administrator, Saito Makoto. As elsewhere in the world, Marxism, communism, socialism, and even anarchism attracted interest and followers in Japan, and diverse view-

TWO AUTHORS, TWO PATRIOTS: HAN YONGUN AND CHOE NAMSON

Han Yongun (1879–1944) was a remarkable man. He was the only signer of the declaration representing the Buddhist sector, the other 32 signers being evenly split between Christian and Chondogyo representatives. Han, a monk, was also an author. He wrote an early draft of the declaration. Han was arrested after signing the declaration but was released from jail the next year. In 1926 he wrote one of the more important pieces of literature of the Japanese era: *The Silence of My Beloved* is a collection of poems that appear to be love poems at one level but can be interpreted by their deeper symbolism as patriotic poetry.

Choe Namson (1890–1957) was one of the first major literary figures of the modern era. He founded Korea's first literary magazine, *Youth,* published from 1908 to 1911. It was he who wrote the declaration of independence even though he was not one of the 33 signers.

Choe agreed to write the document as long as his identity was kept hidden. Active in literary circles, he later made his peace with the Japanese and was appointed to the National Historical Society by the governor-general in 1927. Late in the colonial period Choe left Korea and found work teaching in Manchuria. Returning to the peninsula after liberation, he was arrested and accused of being a Japanese collaborator in 1949. He was pardoned only for reasons of poor health and died two years later. His legacy was indeed mixed—a great patriot and a pioneer author and publisher, yet a collaborator.

points were expressed. This eclectic political left countered the strength of the militarists and the right wing.

However, Japan's efforts to establish a modern liberal democracy were greatly hindered by the loss of its leaders to assassination, three of them prominent prodemocracy leaders. Ito Hirobumi, who had drafted the Meiji constitution (adopted 1889) and served as the first prime minister of modern Japan (four terms, 1885–88, 1892–96, 1898, 1900–01) and first resident-general of Korea (1905–09), was assassinated by a Korean nationalist in Manchuria in 1909. Hara Takashi was assassinated in 1921 by a man described as a lunatic. Hamaguchi Osachi, who served as finance minister, home minister, and then prime minister of Japan (1929–30, 1931), was shot. He survived to run for reelection but died a few months later. Finally, Saito Makoto, who served twice as the governor-general of Korea (1919–27, 1929–31) and once as prime minister (1932–34), was assassinated by militarists in 1936. The next prime minister, Okada Keisuke (1868–1952, in office 1934–36), left office after a failed coup attempt by the military in which he narrowly escaped assassination. Thereafter, the military was in control of the government and plunged Japan headlong into war.

A New Governor-General

The first signal Koreans had that a new liberal administration was in place was the appointment of a new governor-general. Though an admiral, Saito Makoto (in office 1919–27) was considered a moderate and one who had ideas less draconian than his two predecessors, Terauchi Masatake (1909–16) and Hasegawa Yoshimichi (1916–19).

The position of governor-general was closely intertwined with the position of prime minister, the highest office of Japan. (The emperor remained largely a figurehead.) For instance, Terauchi's predecessor as resident-general, Ito Hirobumi, had been prime minister just before his assignment to Korea. Terauchi reversed the process—he became prime minister immediately after returning from Korea. Hasegawa was the exception; he never served as prime minister, but his replacement, Saito Makoto, became prime minister after his term as governor-general in Korea. It is clear that Japan considered Korea important.

Upon his arrival in Korea, Saito made great efforts to show that repressive policies were a thing of the past. Indeed, Koreans began to exercise new freedoms. Saito abolished beatings and torture, and he pulled the police out of the marketplaces and other places where they once interfered. He pledged that more Koreans would be employed in government positions and that Koreans would be appointed as judges. He promised more schools and more educational opportunities for all Koreans, and he put Korean civil servants on the same pay scale as Japanese.

Although Saito's reforms improved the lives of Koreans, subtle measures were implemented at the same time that offset these liberalizations. Eventually, freedoms were lost, and the increased public controls implemented behind the scenes during the time of liberalization came to the fore and dominated the society of the 1930s. For example, the governor-general's promise of more schools was realized, and education was available to common people on a wider scale than ever before.

However, during the same period the government built more new police stations than schools. Japanese control of Korean opposition became more covert according to Michael Robinson: "Using an army of informers and intelligence officers, the Japanese police worked to subvert and crush political opposition before it took shape, thus to prevent a repeat of incidents such as March First" (Eckert 1990, 284).

Likewise, more Koreans were hired as government workers, as pledged, and salaries were set at parity for Korean and Japanese officials. Still, Japanese officials qualified for an overseas hardship bonus— unlike Koreans. Publications in the Korean language were permitted, and these flourished. Yet Japanese authorities established a new censoring organ, the Special High Police, in 1928 to monitor such publications and other social activities. Eventually, this body started to arrest Koreans on charges of "thought crimes." A typical example of what the Japanese punished under this term was a prosecution waged against the Chindon Society, suppressed for engaging in "activities deleterious to the promotion of harmony between Japan and Korea" (Eckert 1990, 314). Later, in the 1930s, when the Japanese began to see communism as a special threat to their rule in Korea, workers and leftist intellectuals were subjected to extended interrogations similar to those that were later called "brainwashing" when practiced on American prisoners in North Korea. The subjects of these programs were tortured until they repudiated their "impure" thoughts, confessed their political sins in writing, and joined special groups for those who had "reformed their thoughts" (Cumings 2005, 177).

Another new freedom enjoyed by Koreans under the term of Governor-General Saito was the freedom to form associations. All kinds of new groups could organize and meet for the common interest of the group. Koreans seized this opportunity and formed church-based groups, youth groups, tenant-farmer groups, patriotic groups, and many others. The government, however, required each group to register. Much is known of the nature of society at the time, because the colonial records are filled with minute details of what was authorized. The Japanese used the registration law to encourage more organizations that were supportive of the state and the colonization, although they did allow other kinds of groups to exist and function as well. While Koreans appreciated the freedom, the record of associations set the stage for an effective future crackdown by the Japanese. Indeed, in the 1930s, when the colonizers decided certain organizations were good but others were subversive, they had in hand the list of "troublemakers," the roster of membership of groups that were suddenly no longer allowed.

The Era of the Short Story

Among the more important of the organizations allowed to register and organize into common interest groups were literary associations. These groups not only met and encouraged members to write, they were allowed to publish their writings. Literary associations flourished. Never before had writers had such freedom. Korean literature blossomed, and numerous short stories and poems were published. No longer suppressed by decree and by social convention, King Sejong's hangul alphabet was used to great effect in the 1920s. Newspapers, magazines, and journals opened for business and began feeding a population anxious to read and learn of the modern world that had almost passed them by.

Literary journals started up at the rate of several each year for the first years of the 1920s. The names of the journals signaled both their optimism (Creation, Dawn of History, White Tide, for example) and their pessimism (such as Ruins). Similarly reflecting the times, Korean literature oscillated between optimism and pessimism, hope and despair.

The literary organizations were vibrant and full of life and optimism despite the dark and pessimistic stories members wrote. The leadership was young—most of the writers were in their 20s, and most had studied for a year or two in Japan. Each literary group had its own journal, and each had a slightly different purpose. Yet many of the same writers belonged to several different organizations. The line separating one organization from another was very thin. Young writers of these overlapping constituencies were selecting one another's works for publication. It was a heady time for young writers, who could publish their works; decide which of their colleagues' works would be published; and discuss writing, style, symbolism, influence from other countries, and influence from other Koreans as well as issues of nationalism and other schools of thought. Writers exchanged ideas openly and freely in their groups of like-minded writers. They were also free because there was no established hierarchy to please.

The favorite genre was the short story. The short story movement was led by a group of young authors who had studied in Japan, where the short story was the favorite form of literature at the time. Japanese and Korean writers were influenced by recent trends in European literature. Works of European writers such as Émile Zola (1840–1902) were being translated into Japanese and were inspiring Japanese and Korean writers. Korean writers experimented with Zola's naturalism, with its grim subject matter, realistic settings, and mechanistic explanations of human behavior, and with a Korean version of the fin de siècle decadence that had recently passed out of fashion in Europe.

A more up-to-date group of left-leaning writers worked to create proletarian fiction that would address the problems of workers and inspire the masses, as many writers in Europe and America were then attempting to do. By this time the ideas of socialism had gained ground with many young Koreans, perhaps as a result of the changes in Korean society, wherein modernization was creating a genuine class of factory workers, and because Koreans studying abroad had been exposed to radical thinkers and left-wing organizations. Following the Russian Revolution of 1917, the Bolsheviks had taken control of Russia, and Marxist ideas were beginning to gain ground elsewhere in East Asia. The Chinese Communist Party was founded in 1921 and the Japanese Communist Party in 1922, and these influences spread to Korea as well. Left-wing writers organized their own literary association in 1925. They gave it the unlikely name Korea Artista Proleta Federatio (The Korean Federation of Proletarian Artists), better known by its acronym, KAPF, in Korean pronounced "Kapu." KAPF writers believed literature should serve the social movement, while other writers argued the merits of literature for literature's sake. Although many stories predating the KAPF bore social messages, with the formation of KAPF, the social message of short stories became more overt. Many such stories met their end under the pen of the Japanese censors.

The Japanese police also censored the newspapers and the literary journals; the game, therefore, was to get things past the censor. Many stories and poems of the day were written in allegory such that the censors, reading the surface story, saw no problem, but the Korean reader, looking for symbolic meaning, saw a different story. At the outset the censorship was fairly loose, and even transparently critical pieces were approved for publication. For example, one of the best-loved poems of the early 1920s was entitled "Will Spring Come to Stolen Fields?"—an obvious reference to the Japanese occupation. Despite the ever-present Japanese censor, there was still a feeling of freedom in the air.

The relative freedom of the age, coupled with the inspiration from Europe via Japan, made the 1920s a watershed for the development of Korean literature. Indeed, this period produced dozens of major works that have found their way into every anthology of modern Korean literature. Literary output dropped off dramatically in the 1930s, however.

YI SANG AND "WINGS"

One of the more colorful writers of the period was a man named Kim Haegyong, who wrote under the pseudonym Yi Sang. His choice of pen name was based on an incident early in his life. He was working in an office where the boss was Japanese. One day the boss called him to come over, but rather than calling him Mr. Kim, "Kim-san," he mistakenly called him Mr. Yi, "Yi-san," which in certain dialects is more nasalized and sounds like "Yi-sang." Kim ignored his Japanese boss, since it seemed he was not calling him. Aggravated, the boss raised his voice and repeated, "Yi-sang!" Kim still thought he was calling someone else. Finally, the boss walked over to Kim and shouted in his face, "Yi-sang, I'm talking to you." Thereafter, in a kind of protest of the powerless, Kim used the name Yi Sang for all his writings.

One of Yi Sang's more notable short stories was "Wings." The story opens with a man living in the inner room of his home, while his wife is prostituting herself in the adjoining room. The man cannot leave his small room but contents himself to play with the cosmetics jars his wife has left for him. In the end he gets out onto the street and says he wishes he could grow wings and fly away.

The value of the story lies in its symbolism. The man represents the people of Korea, his wife the land of Korea, and the patrons of the prostitute-wife the Japanese colonizers. For the Korean reader who grasped that symbolism (which was successful in slipping the story past the Japanese censors), the story was overpowering: It was a clear condemnation of the reader, the average Korean; fascinated with the new technology of the time, symbolized by the makeup and perfume jars, he was standing by while his land was used and despoiled by the foreigner. Koreans got the message. It was not so much a call to arms as a statement of the frustration of a subjugated and powerless people. It was a kind of passive protest or a lament. Yi Sang's "Wings" is a picture of a reality that was too cold and depressing to discuss in real terms but, when described in symbolic terms, was more powerful than reality.

Yi Sang's literature was creative and innovative, certainly avant-garde for the time. His life, however, was tragic. He was imprisoned on the charge of anti-Japanese activities, and in jail he contracted tuberculosis and died. He was only 29 at the time of his death, yet he left a distinctive mark on Korean literature.

The 1940s were so chaotic that little was published, and the 1950s were disrupted by the Korean War and the chaos of the postwar era. It was not until the 1960s that the literary scene caught up to the heights that Koreans had briefly achieved in the 1920s.

Increasing Intolerance

In 1923 one of the worst earthquake disasters in the history of the world unfolded in Japan. On September 1 an earthquake measuring 7.9 on the Richter scale shook the Kanto region of Honshu. The natural disaster, known as the great Kanto earthquake or the great Tokyo earthquake, was horrific in terms of deaths, injuries, missing people, and property damage: About two thirds of Tokyo was destroyed and much of the region around Tokyo as well. After the quake fires broke out causing even more destruction. In all, about 140,000 people died.

For the 30,000 Korean residents of Tokyo, the disaster did not end with the earthquake and fires. Responding to rumors that the Koreans were looting and rioting, Japanese civilians, apparently in some cases aided by the military and the police, began to take out their frustrations on the Koreans. About 6,000 Koreans were massacred. Rightist Japanese vigilantes also killed notable Japanese leftists and communists as well as around 600 Chinese workers and members of other minority groups (Mai 2005).

Both the liberalization and the attacks on the left that were practiced by the Japanese administration in Korea were influenced by Japan's policies at home. In the early 1920s Japan, in common with other industrialized countries (the United States included), was haunted by the specter of the 1917 Russian Revolution, terrified of a similar uprising in Japan. This worry was grounded in reality; many Japanese workers and intellectuals were leftists, while in 1918 many of the common people all across Japan had rioted in response to food shortages and inflation. As noted earlier, Japan's own Communist Party had been founded in 1922, only a year after the founding of the Chinese Communist Party. Japan's rulers, even its most liberal, sometimes reacted to left-leaning dissent with brutal repression while heeding calls for liberal democratic reforms. The two-sidedness of the Japanese approach is perfectly expressed by its passage in 1925 of two laws: first, the Peace Preservation Law, which gave broad powers to the police to suppress political dissent, especially leftists, communists, and anarchists; and second, the Male Suffrage Act, which extended the franchise to all male citizens over the age of 25, eliminating the tax-paying requirement that had previously restricted the right to vote to about 1.2 percent of the population. While the election law benefited those on the political left, the Peace Preservation Law was enacted to suppress left-leaning groups in Japan. The Communist Party was banned and driven underground by 1926. However, the wording of the law, which criminalized participation in, instigation of, or assistance to any scheme undertaken "for the purpose of changing the national policy or of denying the private property system," was ambiguous enough to give the police maximum flexibility in arresting all their perceived enemies (Totman 2000, 364–365).

The new law was used effectively in Japan and even more so in Korea. Gradually, the freedoms gained were lost in the late 1920s. KAPF members soon found themselves targets; suppression and censorship gradually increased until 1935, when Japanese authorities arrested many of the KAPF members in two successive waves. Others escaped to the mountains and to Manchuria. Though disbanded and scattered, the KAPF writers were not forgotten. Decades later many emerged as cultural heroes in North Korea.

Opposition in Korea

The last so-called emperor of Korea, Sunjong, the hapless son of Kojong, died in June 1926. His funeral, like that of his father, became an opportunity for demonstrations against the Japanese colonization. This time the authorities were prepared. There was no written declaration to give focus to the demonstrations, and its organization was inferior to that of the March First Movement in other ways as well, reflecting the increasingly tight control over society. Unlike the March First Movement, this movement did not spread widely but was controlled and suppressed by the Japanese police.

A few years later a rather obscure event in the southeastern provincial capital of Kwangju became the catalyst for the second-largest demonstration against the Japanese rule. On November 3, 1929, a number of students were riding a train between Naju and Kwangju. It was the birthday of the emperor of Japan, and the students were returning from worship at the local Shinto shrine, which was dedicated to the emperor. By coincidence, November 3 on the solar calendar was October 3 on the lunar calendar, Korean Foundation Day. Perhaps the Korean students were struck by the irony of the date when they should have been celebrating Tangun, the first Korean ruler. In any case, when Japanese students began teasing a Korean female student, Korean boys came to her rescue. The scuffle between the two groups spilled off the train, into the city, and around the country.

Many of the organizations that were chartered and allowed to function in the early 1920s became the conduit of information about the student uprising in Kwangju. These organizations helped spread word of the protest to the far corners of Korea, and this helped spread the demonstrations. At the time the Special High Police were tightening their grip, and the newly enacted Peace Preservation Law was further restricting the day-to-day freedoms of Koreans. Perhaps demonstrators saw the protests as their last chance before the impending crackdown.

The demonstrations lasted for days and spread to schools all across the peninsula. Thousands of students were arrested and expelled from schools, but the demonstrations were successful in one respect: They became the second-largest protest against the Japanese colonial rule in Korea.

The power of the military gradually increased in Japan until there was an incident in 1931 that vaulted it into leadership, which it would not relinquish until the end of World War II. The Cultural Administration period ended with the explosions in the Mukden Railroad yard, ushering in the last period of Japanese occupation, the "Assimilation Period."

The Assimilation Period (1931–1945)

In the early 1930s Japan's imperial ambitions led it to take a series of increasingly risky gambles that involved it in 14 years of war, known in East Asia as the Pacific War. Eventually, all of East Asia was drawn into the conflict, as were Great Britain, the United States, and the Soviet Union. Japan's attempt to conquer northern China was condemned by its former allies, and Japan became internationally isolated. Meanwhile, its resources were stretched to the limit. At last in 1941, when the United States refused to sell Japan the oil it needed to keep its war machine running, Japan upped the ante by conquering the Dutch West Indies, and the logic of war demanded that Japan simultaneously attempt to cripple any possible opposition to its actions by attacking Pearl Harbor, the Philippines, Singapore, and Hong Kong.

Though time would show that Japan's survival was not really at stake, its government and its people seemed to feel, during much of this period, that it was and that its predicament justified drastic action. This paranoia empowered the most reactionary and militaristic forces on Japan's home islands. Abroad it motivated widespread atrocities and wanton massacres by Japanese troops who had been taught in school to regard other Asians as subhuman. It also led to a cruel but futile attempt to eradicate the culture of Korea. This period is known in Korea as the Forced Assimilation Period.

The Mukden (Manchurian) Incident

The *Mukden Incident* or *Manchurian Incident* are the names given to the event that on September 18, 1931, led to a sharp increase in Japan's military operations in northern China and eventually to the Pacific War. Extremists in Japan's Kwantung army, stationed in Manchuria under the terms of treaties that allowed Japan to use troops to protect its railroads and ports, wanted Japan to conquer the province once and for all. The civilian government back in Tokyo was reluctant to take the step, which had no justification under international law, so local commanders staged a bombing and blamed it on the Chinese. The conspiracy was enacted without the knowledge or authorization of Japan's prime minister or even its military high command in Tokyo. However, the conspiracy's aim—the military occupation of Manchuria—had been widely debated in Japan. The Japanese public, which had for decades learned from their schools and government-censored newspapers to admire the army, despise the Chinese, and see control of northern China as Japan's manifest destiny, was overwhelmingly in favor of the action.

The Japanese government had never established adequate civilian control over its military forces and was now led into a war by them. Japan quickly conquered the entire province of Manchuria, which, though recognized internationally as a part of China, at the time had been in the hands of a local warlord. In September 1932 Japan established a puppet government in the province it had conquered, which it promptly recognized as the supposed independent state of Manchukuo. No one was fooled. Manchukuo was a colony of Japan.

From Manchuria to Nanjing

At the time China was engaged in a civil war. The Nationalists—that is, the Republic of China forces commanded since the mid-1920s by generalissimo Chiang Kai-shek (1887–1975)—had been relatively successful in defeating the warlords who had defied the central government in the years following the collapse of the Qing dynasty. Now the greatest internal threat facing the Nationalists were the Chinese Communists under Mao Zedong (1893–1976), who in 1931 had established the Soviet Republic of China based in the mountains on the Hunan-Kiangsi border. In *The Pacific War: World War II and the Japanese, 1931–1945*, the

Japanese historian Saburo Ienaga explains how the civil war between the Nationalist and Communist forces weakened the Chinese response to Japanese aggression:

> The Chinese, of course, did not recognize the phony state of Manchukuo. Nevertheless, the Nationalist government, giving its first priority to the civil war with the Communists, had little enthusiasm for simultaneously attempting to recover Manchuria. . . . Thus, in July 1935, the Manchukuo-China Transportation Agreement restored regular communication and transportation between the two areas. Japanese aggressors seemed to have realized their dream—control of the vast spaces of Manchuria. . . . But they wanted more. They expanded military control to Mongolia and North China and overreached themselves. (Ienaga 1978, 67)

After its relatively easy conquest of Manchuria, the Japanese found it much tougher going, and the bloodiness of the campaign kept rising, climaxing in 1937 in the taking of Nanjing (Nanking), where Japanese troops massacred 300,000 civilians, according to Chinese figures, and committed many other well-documented atrocities. Before it was over the war begun in 1931 by the Mukden Incident had killed an estimated 20 million Chinese (Roy 1998, 164).

Forced Assimilation

Japan's new acquisitions on the Asian mainland changed the role of Korea within Japan's imperial system. Korea had become a stepping stone; to a great degree, Japan would colonize Manchuria *from* Korea. The worldwide economic crisis of the 1930s also influenced Japan's policy in Korea. Japan responded to the bleak international conditions with a program of heavy, government-directed investment in its colonies; it hoped to make its empire a self-sufficient economic system, safe from the fluctuations of the world market. The labor of Koreans, skilled and unskilled, willing and unwilling, would be essential to these plans. Korean textile mills would supply cheap clothes to Manchuria. Koreans themselves would go to Manchuria to build industrial plants, railways, and telegraph lines, mine the ore, and cultivate the rice (the Japanese believed the Koreans grew rice more efficiently than the Chinese). After 1938 there would be Koreans in the Japanese military forces as well, and Koreans would be brought to Japan to replace Japanese men serving in the army and navy. To achieve its ambitions the Japanese required "active support and participation in their economic and military plans," writes Michael Robinson, "not the indirect support of a portion of the

169

elite and the grudging, sullen passivity of the Korean common man." A new ultranationalist governor-general, Ugaki Kazushige (1868–1956), arrived in 1931, signaling an end to the velvet-gloved cultural policy of the 1920s. According to Robinson,

> Japan set in motion policies in the 1930s to mobilize the Korean population to support its economic, political and military campaigns. By 1945, the ensuing massive mobilization led to the uprooting of millions of Koreans from their homes and to a disastrous program of cultural oppression that attempted to obliterate the very identity of the Korean people. (Eckert 1990, 306)

In 1934 Ugaki introduced a new curriculum in Korean schools that featured increased instruction in Japanese language, ethics, and history. The new curriculum eliminated the study of Korean and the use of Korean in general instruction. Eventually, the colonial government would insist that only the Japanese language be used in all public offices, and by the 1940s all businesses and banks were forced to keep records exclusively in Japanese (Eckert 1990, 315). "Korean culture was simply crushed," observes Bruce Cumings (Cumings 2005, 182). Starting in 1935, students and government employees were required to attend Shinto ceremonies, although, as Cumings points out, "Shinto was a strictly Japanese religion, imbued with nationalist and essentialist ideas."

The Christian community in Korea led the resistance to the shrine order, which led in turn to a persecution of Korea's Christians. Several thousand Christian ministers were arrested between 1935 and 1938 for their role in resisting the shrine order. The intensity of the forced assimilation policies increased as Japan marched toward its disastrous collision with the United States. In 1936 a new governor-general was appointed, Minami Jiro (1874–1955; governor-general of Korea 1936–42). A former minister or war, Minami had been one of the leading generals of the Mukden Incident. After 1937—the beginning of large-scale war in China and the year of the Japanese massacres in Nanjing—Minami began to shut down Korean organizations of all types, while the colonial government created organizations to mobilize the population and indoctrinate Koreans with Japanese ideology. Some were directed at children and adolescents, with names such as Korean Federation of Youth Organizations, Local Youth Leadership Seminars, and Training Institutes for Children's Organizations. Other government-sponsored organizations were aimed at Korean intellectuals (for example, the

Korea All Writers Federation), laborers, tenant farmers, and fishermen. Organizations such as the Korean Defense Association, the Association for the Study of Policy Dealing with the Critical Situation, and the Korean Association for Imperial Rule Assistance were used to assist recruitment to Japan's armed services, which began accepting Korean volunteers in 1938. Virtually every Korean came to be associated with at least one mass organization by the 1940s (Eckert 1990, 316).

In 1939 the governor-general promulgated the Name Change Order, which "graciously allowed" Koreans to change their names to Japanese style surnames and given names. Though the program was supposedly voluntary, Koreans working for the government and for the many organizations closely associated with the government such as the Manchurian Railway Corporation found themselves under intense pressure to change their names. By 1945 more than 84 percent of the population had complied (Eckert 1990, 318).

Conceivably, there might have been a positive aspect to some of these changes—at the price of suppressing their own identity, Koreans could have achieved equal rights as citizens of the Japanese empire. This certainly seemed to be the promise of the new policy, but the Japanese proved to be extremely reluctant to fulfill it. Even after the 1939 Name Change Order, all public records carefully noted nationality distinctions so that Koreans could never "pass" as Japanese. Korean workers were paid at less than half the rate of Japanese workers for the same work at the same skill level (Cumings 2005, 169). Pro-Japanese Korean organizations, with Minami's encouragement, conducted a campaign to enfranchise Koreans—to win home rule (direct rule by the Japanese government rather than by a colonial governor) and representation in the Diet, Japan's parliamentary body, but these efforts were stymied by Japan's ruling oligarchy. Only at the war's end, with Japan's back against the wall, were Korean representatives chosen to sit in the Diet. They would have taken their seats in 1946 if the war had ended differently.

The Comfort Corps

Perhaps the worst situation of all the Koreans conscripted into the service of the emperor was that of the young women of the "comfort corps," the euphemistic term for those forced to serve as prostitutes for the soldiers of the Japanese empire. Among them were Japanese women as well as those of conquered lands, including Chinese, Filipinas, Burmese, Pacific Islanders, and even a few Dutch women captured when Japan took over Indonesia, but the largest contingent of women in the comfort corps were Korean, as high as 80 percent by some estimates. It is impossible to tell how many women were forced into serving the empire in this degrading way, but estimates range from 80,000 to 200,000.

The Japanese imperial army first developed its system of "comfort stations" at the request of Okamura Yasuji, vice chief of staff of the Shanghai Expeditionary Force. Soldiers who occupied Shanghai in 1932 had raped Chinese women. In response Yasuji had asked the government to set up brothels for his men, asserting that this would help prevent such rapes in the future. The program was greatly expanded after the battle for Nanjing in 1937, where the Japanese soldiers suffered the heaviest casualties of any battle to that point. When they finally took the city, many soldiers raped Chinese women. To bolster military discipline and reduce the spread of disease, Japanese military authorities thought it best to provide sexual services for the soldiers.

Many of the women conscripted into the comfort corps were already prostitutes, some picked up in impromptu recruiting drives, but many other women were ordinary civilians, tricked into prostitution, forced into it by greedy or desperate relatives, or simply kidnapped by soldiers who drove trucks into villages and picked up any young woman they happened to find in the streets.

George Hicks's book *The Comfort Women,* making use of extensive interviews with the survivors, includes the story of Yi Sang Ok, who was born in Inchon to a large family of independent farmers. Yi Sang Ok worked for a man named Kim Un Sik who ostensibly ran an employment agency for young girls. On the instructions of one of Kim's employees, Yi Sang Ok boarded a ferry at Pusan with 20 other girls, all under the impression that they were bound for a scrubbing brush factory. Instead they were taken to a "comfort station" on Palau Island. There was a long barracks building and 20 rooms without blankets or mattresses. "Soldiers began coming from about 4 or 5 P.M. When she tried to refuse service, she was beaten so savagely her hearing was permanently impaired" (Hicks 1994, 51). She was paid a fixed rate of 30 yen a month.

Another young woman, Yi Bok Sil, was kidnapped at her home by Japanese officials. After a three-day journey she found herself with 15 other Korean women in a Chinese house in Tientsin (Tianjin) in rooms about five square meters in area with a dirt floor covered with rush matting. She was violently deflowered while hearing screams from other rooms where the other women were undergoing the same ordeal. "After the first night," writes Hicks, paraphrasing Bok Sil's own account of her experiences, "the whole group discussed suicide, and two of

172

REPARATIONS FOR THE SUFFERING OF THE COMFORT CORPS WOMEN

The issue of reparations to comfort corps victims lingered on for nearly 50 years after the close of World War II. The first settlement came soon after the close of the war in Indonesia, where the Dutch pressed the claim in war crimes trials in 1948. Several Japanese military officers were found guilty of forcing 35 captured Dutch women into comfort stations (brothels for the Japanese soldiers), but the Japanese army did not face legal claims for similar treatment of Indonesian women nor was it charged for abuse of Koreans, Chinese, or women of any other nationality.

The desire to hush up shameful things rather than embarrass family members, a concept typical in most Asian societies, may account for the women's long silence, but in the late 1980s the silence was broken. At that point, while many of the so-called comfort women were still alive, women's organizations in Korea and China brought the case to the public and asked their governments to demand reparations from Japan. The Japanese government denied any knowledge or involvement at first, but in 1992 Yoshiaki Yoshimi, a professor of history at Chuo University in Tokyo, published documents proving that the highest levels of government had authorized the program. In 1995 the Japanese government issued an official apology and set up the Asian Women's Fund, a reparations fund to which victims and their families could apply for compensation.

them hanged themselves in their rooms. The others, including Bok Sil, resigned themselves to their fate" (Hicks 1994, 50).

The Japanese Legacy in Korea

There is bitter disagreement between Koreans and Japanese on the overall value of—or damage done by—Japanese colonialism in Korea. Some Japanese scholars argue that Korean historiography treats Japan too harshly and that their countrymen did good things in Korea that should be recognized. Koreans respond that even the so-called good things were done for Japan's advantage, not Korea's. Undoubtedly, Japanese colonization had lasting material effects for Korea. Like other modern colonizers, but more intensively than most, the Japanese built things for their own purposes that would be useful when they left. The better to move goods and troops, the colonizers built more than 6,000 kilometers of rail lines and 53,000 kilometers of automobile and country roads in Korea (in 1945 China, though many times vaster and more populous, had only twice as many rail passengers and twice as many roads.) "In short," notes Bruce Cumings, "by 1945 Korea had a much better developed transport and communications infrastructure than any East Asian country save Japan: this sets Korea off from China and Vietnam . . ." (Cumings 2005, 167). Once renowned for its isolation, Korea was linked to the world.

The Japanese also industrialized Korea. It began to do so early in the occupation, and the pace picked up as Korea became a supplier of manufactured goods to Japan's new colony in Manchuria. In the early 1940s the Japanese moved especially advanced industries to Korea to escape Allied bombing—the Chosen Aircraft Company near Seoul, the product of a joint venture between a Japanese industrial combine and a rich pro-Japanese Korean entrepreneur, built kamikaze aircraft in 1945. Japanese banks and industrial combines poured money into Korea, building textile mills, hydroelectric power plants, chemical plants, mines, and oil refineries.

The colonial period also saw the development of a modern civil service, a postal system, newspapers, banks, corporations, and trade associations as well as capitalism and the response to capitalism, including trade unions and leftist organizations. Korea during this period changed from a society largely dependent on the peasantry to one that became dominated by an industrial class and wage work. It saw the waning of a landed aristocracy and the rise of a middle class used to creating and running business enterprises.

Some Korean entrepreneurs who profited during the Japanese occupation, such as the banker and agricultural magnate Kim Song-su (1891–1955) and the adaptable Korean capitalist Pak Hung-sik (1903–94) were reviled by other Koreans as collaborators. Certainly they were not patriots, but their expertise in running modern business enterprises would be important for the future of Korea (Cumings 2005, 171–172).

No potentially positive outcome of the Japanese occupation goes unchallenged. For instance, the average life span of Koreans actually increased more than 60 percent, from 26 years to 42 years, during the 35-year Japanese rule. Koreans respond to this by citing the unknown number—at least in the tens of thousands—killed at the hands of the

Japanese. In addition at least 22,000 Koreans who were forced to serve fighting for Japan in World War II are known to have been killed. Some 700,000 Koreans were forced to work in Japan, and of these at least 50,000 were killed in the U.S. bombing of Hiroshima and Nagasaki.

In *A History of Contemporary Korea* the Korean scholar Kang Man-gil moves beyond lists of Japanese crimes to make a more sophisticated case for the damage caused by the colonial period. In Kang's view, though Korea modernized under the Japanese, it remained socially and politically backward, contributing to the long period of dictatorial rule that has only recently ended in South Korea and continues in North Korea. By seeing to it that Japanese firms did most of the investing and profiting in Korean development, the Japanese "inhibited growth of Korean capital and of the Korean bourgeoisie," while "Japanese policies of suppression hindered the growth of an organized and trained proletariat." Further, Kang argues that the colonial period caused Korea lasting political damage by interrupting a movement toward democracy that was evident in the last decade of the Choson era.

> Once Korea was colonized ... no form of political activity was allowed. Thus, throughout the entire colonial period the people inside Korea were unable either to gain any training for democratic politics or to produce political leaders with democratic traits. The thirty-five years of colonial rule were the period when Korean history should have liquidated the old system of autocratic monarchy and established a democratic political system. But, under Japan's militaristic colonial rule, the Korean people were deprived of any opportunity to learn democratic. politics (Kang 1976, 4)

The Japanese period has also left cultural legacies that are not always recognized. Many aspects of daily life have distinct Japanese roots, such as bath houses, tearooms, and even the subway system, which is laid out on tracks that run the opposite way of the streets: Traffic on the streets is like that of the United States and Europe, with vehicles driving on the right-hand side of the road, whereas on the subway system, developed with Japanese technical assistance, trains run on the left-hand side of the two-track way. This combination of systems is a little confusing when it comes to catching a ride: Buses and taxis run in the same direction on the street, but subway trains entered on the same side of the street go in the other direction. To add to the mix, on the stairs coming out of the subway is a sign that says "Those in a cultured society walk on the left."

The role of the many Koreans who worked with the Japanese and gave varying degrees of support to their rule—whether as workers in the colonial bureaucracy or police, aristocratic members of the Privy Council, landowners who increased their holdings as a result of the same policies that forced many other Koreans into tenancy, businessmen who benefited from Japanese sponsorship, editors and writers of pro-Japanese Korean-language newspapers and pro-Japanese organizations, or the more ambiguous category of Koreans who sincerely participated in Japan's Cultural Policy after 1919—is one of the touchiest aspects of the colonial experience. In the immediate aftermath of liberation, Koreans moved to punish the most prominent collaborators, and it is possible that a large-scale reckoning would have occurred were it not for the intervention of the U.S. occupation forces. Koreans who had served in the colonial government and landowners who had prospered under the Japanese were put in positions of authority by the U.S. occupation, which feared that a popular revolution would be taken over by communists and manipulated by the Soviets. Thousands of Korean colonial police who had been in hiding when the Americans landed were put back to work by the United States. Subsequently, in Syngman Rhee's Republic of Korea, leftists of all types were considered a more dangerous enemy than former collaborators; trade union mem-

Celebrating liberation from 35 years of occupation by Japan (Academy of Korean Studies)

bers, socialists, communists, and social revolutionaries of all types were violently suppressed, while people who might otherwise have been punished for their cooperation with the Japanese were able to thrive in the new regime.

Besides, in the 35 years during which the Japanese had ruled Korea, it had been impossible for large segments of the population to escape some involvement with the Japanese, often with mutual profit, so for decades after liberation, Koreans did not often broach the subject. Many thought it best to let sleeping dogs lie. However, after the passage of 50 years of healing time, Koreans now openly discuss the subject of collaboration. It is the subject of papers and historical conferences, and it is published in books. For most of the years since the Korean War, the North claimed that all the collaborators were thriving in the South, but the South denied that such was the case. It is now openly admitted that many who had collaborated with the Japanese were living in the South, having faced few negative consequences for their roles.

The Emotional Legacy of Colonialism

Koreans today have a complex love-hate relationship with Japan. On one hand they respect the economic power and innovative energy in Japan, but on the other hand they remember the legacy of colonial exploitation. That memory itself is complicated.

In the Korean collective memory today, Japan represents the invasion of 1592 and the colonial takeover in 1910. Koreans talk of how they had to change their names to Japanese names and emphasize that they could not use their own language or write in their own alphabet. Such talk gives the impression that those heavy-handed policies came with the Japanese in 1910, even though the name law and language prohibition were not implemented until 1939. The earlier days of the colony, with the collaboration of many sectors of society, are forgotten.

When Koreans today speak of the colonial experience, they often remember the last phase of the occupation, a time of war and extreme deprivation. In fact, memory of the experience is becoming mostly secondhand; the generation who lived through the Japanese experience is dying. Those who lived through it, however, often tell of the softer side of the colonial experience—of knowing Japanese as neighbors, classmates, and friends. Members of that older generation, now almost gone, speak of a strange love-hate relationship with the Japanese. They often describe the Japanese of that time as *mosoun saram,* or "frightening people," a term used in respect as much as derision: The Japanese

ANTI-JAPANESE
SENTIMENT TODAY

Few things spark the fires of nationalism faster than reports, which surface from time to time, that the Japanese government has sponsored a new history textbook that soft-pedals the war in Asia. Korea makes immediate diplomatic protest and demonstrations unfold in front of the Japanese embassy in downtown Seoul. Similarly, few sights inflame a Korean's nationalistic feelings more than a map that labels the body of water between Korea and Japan the "Sea of Japan." Korea argues vehemently that that body of water should be called the East Sea.

The last outpost of vigilance against a possible resurgence of Japanese colonialism are the tiny, once-uninhabited islets called Tokto (Takeshima in Japanese). Midway between Korea and Japan, and claimed by both, the islets now have permanent settlements, and Korean naval forces stand guard over the two rocky outcroppings. They do not guard the islets as much as they guard history. The Korean claim to Tokto and Korea's occupation of the islands by force are not so much to keep Japanese from fishing as they are a message from the government of Korea to the Korean people that the nation is independent and free and will not be occupied by Japan again.

were "frightening" in the sense that they knew how to get things done and that they were capable, intelligent, and creative, but they were also frightening in that they demanded obedience and compliance.

Subsequent generations who know the Japanese only vicariously from the stories handed down to them typically have stronger negative feelings toward the Japanese than the Koreans who lived among them. Gradually, the better aspects of colonial life were discussed less often than the sadder stories, and over time it became less acceptable to say anything good about the experience. Consequently, the younger generations passed on the worst of the stories and in a sense were more anti-Japanese than those who experienced the oppression firsthand.

6

LIBERATION, DIVISION, AND THE KOREAN WAR (1945–1953)

Many Koreans were dislocated by World War II and the accompanying economic deprivations. Some had volunteered or were drafted to serve the Japanese imperial army. Some were compelled to serve in the women's comfort corps. Other Koreans had volunteered to work in factories in Korea, Japan, or Manchuria. Still others left their homes out of economic necessity to find some way to feed their families.

Koreans served throughout Japan's far-flung empire. To the west and south Koreans were found on work projects in Burma and Indonesia. To the east they were scattered as far away as the islands of the Pacific, working on airfields and ports. Many Koreans serving the Japanese empire abroad were killed as the Americans started their "island hopping" strategy; this was the U.S. effort to gain control of the Pacific island by island. The largest number of Korean fatalities, some 30,000, occurred in Hiroshima on August 6, 1945.

Korea was liberated from Japan when Japan surrendered on August 15, 1945. The war did not damage the Korean Peninsula in the sense of bombing or other war-related destruction of homes and infrastructure. There was no combat on Korean soil. Korean people, however, were killed and wounded because they had been scattered to places where fighting did take place as well as places where the most dangerous labor was being performed. The other loss Korea sustained as a result of World War II was the loss of its unity. In the middle of the night, on August 10–11, as Soviet troops moved into Korea, a major and a colonel working for the U.S. State Department were given 30 minutes to decide on a boundary between Soviet and U.S. zones of occupation.

For more than 60 years Korea has been divided, roughly along this hastily drawn line that was never intended to be permanent. Korea was divided into north and south, soon leading to another war, this time on Korean soil.

Hardening Lines

Like the war it led to, the division of Korea after 1945 had complicated causes. It was not planned in advance. It was not desired by the Koreans themselves. Neither was it simply imposed upon them by the mutually suspicious recent allies, the Soviet Union and the United States. Like the divisions of Germany and Vietnam, it was both a product of the cold war and of long-building internal conflicts.

The birth of the two modern Korean states has long been a subject of intense dispute of fact and interpretation. For decades American politicians and writers maintained that the side the United States supported, led by the elderly, Christian, American-educated anticommunist Syngman Rhee, represented a democracy-loving majority battling a communist insurgency fomented by infiltrators from the Soviet-controlled North. Few serious historians say this today. In the words of the American journalist and historian David Halberstam, Rhee was a democrat, "as long as . . . no one else was allowed to challenge his will" (Halberstam 2007, 67–68). Besides, the revolutionary ferment in Korea was a home-grown response to old injustices. Instead of denying these facts, defenders of U.S. policy point out how much worse life is now in North Korea than in South Korea. Others such as Bruce Cumings, whose two-volume *Origins of the Korean War* is the longest and most authoritative study of the period, have wondered if it would have been better for everyone if Korea had been allowed to have the violent social revolution it was ripe for. Far fewer would have died than died in the Korean War, and by today a unified Korea might have come a long way toward being normalized like China and Vietnam—there would be no North Korean "rogue state" (Cumings 1990, 443).

Plans for postwar Korea were made without the participation of Koreans during and immediately after the war at a series of international conferences of the major powers. At the Cairo Conference (November 1943) U.S. president Franklin D. Roosevelt (1882–1945), British prime minister Winston Churchill (1874–1965), and Chiang Kai-shek (1887–1975), leader of China's ruling Chinese Nationalist Party, met to discuss the war with Japan and to plan for a postwar Asia. The conference concluded that Korea should be a free and independent state "in due course"; an earlier draft of the conference state-ment had specified "at the earliest possible moment," as proposed by Chiang, who represented the Korean Provisional Government in Exile. Roosevelt recommended the more conservative phrase in the final declaration. He believed that colonies would take as much as 10 to 40 years to prepare for autonomy (Cumings 2005, 190). The powers were not at this point thinking of a division of Korea. A little over a year later, in February 1945, when the war in Europe was near-ing its conclusion but American soldiers were paying a high price to wrest one Pacific island after another from the Japanese, Roosevelt and Churchill met with Soviet leader Joseph Stalin (1879–1953) at the Yalta Conference. Stalin accepted the idea of a trusteeship for Korea. Established nations would temporarily administer the country; as far as Stalin was concerned, however, the period of the trusteeship should be "as short as possible" (Kang Man-gil, 182). In addition, it was agreed that the Soviet Union would engage Japan in Manchuria and Korea once the European war was over to relieve pressure on the United States, which would focus on Japan and perhaps invade Korea from the south. As promised, the Soviet Union invaded Manchuria, encountering far less resistance than had been expected. The Soviets moved troops into Korea on August 11, 1945, and landed more troops in Korean ports on August 12 and August 13. The Japanese armed forces in Korea offered no resistance, and the Soviets moved swiftly southward. The United States, though its victory over Japan was assured (the atomic bomb had been dropped on Hiroshima on August 6 and Nagasaki on August 9), began to worry that the Soviets would occupy the whole peninsula and stay there. The United States was not yet prepared for its part in the proposed occupation, nor at this point was America ready to fight to keep Korea out of Russian hands. Even so, there seemed to be no harm in asking the Russians to go along with the arrangements discussed at Yalta.

J. Lawton Collins in *War in Peacetime: The History and Lessons of Korea* described the fateful decision. "After midnight, August 10–11, Colonel Charles H. Bonesteel (1909–77) and Major Dean Rusk (1909–94) . . . began drafting part of a General Order that would define the zones to be occupied in Korea by American and Russian forces." With only 30 minutes to complete their draft, the two men decided to make a boundary of the 38th parallel; this would put into the American zone Korea's capital city, Seoul, in addition to two major ports, Inchon and Pusan, which would facilitate the landing of troops (Collins 1969, 25–26).

It so happened that the Russians and the Japanese had discussed dividing Korea at the 38th parallel in 1886 and again in 1903. Bruce Cumings speculates that in the light of these precedents Stalin may have interpreted the choice of this particular boundary as a hint that it would be all right with the United States if Korea were permanently divided into Russian and American zones. "Like the Americans, the Soviets might have preferred a unified, friendly Korea, but a divided Korea would well serve the basic security interests of the Soviet state— assurance that the Korean peninsula would not provide venue for an attack against Russia" (Cumings 1990, 121). Somewhat to American surprise, the Russians agreed to the proposal and ceased their southward advance at Kaesong, just below the 38th parallel.

The United States had given little thought to Korea prior to 1945. The U.S. attitude would change with the victory that put Japan under American control and with the worsening of U.S.-Soviet relations during the late 1940s. Eventually, Korea would be seen as a potential strategic threat to both of the superpowers. Korea was dangerously situated between Russia and Japan. A unified, neutral Korea, standing like a wall between American and Russian spheres of influence, would have been acceptable to both the Soviets and the Americans, and it was certainly the outcome desired by most Koreans. It turned out to be impossible, because the Korea that the Soviets and the Americans found was profoundly disunited, ripe for revolution and civil war.

Power Struggle

Neither the Koreans nor the Japanese in Korea waited passively for the arrival of the Allied armies. The Japanese feared revenge of the Koreans and sought mainly to get out of the country safely. Koreans who had cooperated with the Japanese—big landowners, businessmen, colonial police, and Koreans employed by the colonial government—had to worry about the privileges and property they might lose in the new order following liberation and about possible trials as collaborators or summary punishment without the benefit of a trial. Other Koreans had to prepare for the power struggle that might follow liberation: Who would be in charge? What kind of a country would the new Korea be? Would it be independent at last, or would it be dominated by some new foreign power?

Even before the occupation, Korea had been a country of great inequalities. Koreans on the left wanted to change that. They did not all have the same sorts of change in mind. Their ideas ranged from mildly reformist and democratic to rigidly communist, from those who wanted land reform, democracy, and trade unions to those who wanted state ownership of property and took the Soviet Union as a model.

The popularity of leftist ideas in Korea had special, uniquely Korean causes. Not only had the introduction of capitalism caused difficult changes in people's ways of life (as it had in the West), but it had been imposed brutally and suddenly by the Japanese. Capitalism was thought of as something foreign. Most Koreans of all classes still had a Confucian disdain for commerce, seeing profit-taking as a form of theft. Korean businessmen had little prestige. Most Korean industrial workers had once been farmers and wanted to return to the land. Prosperous businessmen, whether or not they had been active collaborators, were suspected of being traitors, since they had profited from the occupation and participated in the Japanese war effort.

Koreans on the right feared and despised communism, but even milder left-wing programs threatened their interests. The anticommunists in Korea had an additional problem: Many of them had cooperated with the Japanese. A few anticommunists who had left Korea during the occupation—such as Syngman Rhee, the former president of Korea's government-in-exile in Shanghai—had good nationalist credentials, but the natural constituency of the right, the people who would work with Rhee, were landlords, businessmen, bureaucrats, and policemen who had prospered in Japan's Korea. The staunchest, most steadfast Korean nationalists were men such as Kim Il Sung, who had fought the Japanese in Manchuria until 1941 and come back as a Soviet protégé, and Yo Unhyong, who was willing to share power with communists.

End of Japanese Rule and Formation of the Korean People's Republic (KPR)

At the time of the Japanese surrender, the Japanese governor-general in Korea did not know of the arrangements that had been made for two occupation zones. The Japanese expected the Soviets to take the whole peninsula. In addition to their worries about the aroused Koreans, they feared the Red Army, whose undisciplined soldiers wantonly looted, killed, and raped in all the countries they liberated (Millett 2005, 49). To minimize this risk, they decided to hand over the reigns of government in advance to Koreans in exchange for a promise of protection. Since pro-Japanese Koreans had no credibility with most Koreans, the Japanese approached Korean nationalists. They met first with a conservative leader, Song Chin-u (1890–1945), who refused them, possibly for fear of being seen as a collaborator. The Japanese then asked for the help of Yo Unhyong, a respected, left-leaning nationalist who had spent years in Japanese jails.

Yo Unhyong saw the offer as a chance to lay the groundwork for an independent Korea. He agreed to form the Committee for the Preparation for Korean Independence (CPKI) and to assure the safety of the Japanese in Korea provided the Japanese meet four demands: to release all political prisoners, guarantee food provisions for three months, not interfere with the maintenance of peace or Korean activities for the sake of independence, and not interfere with the training of workers and peasants. The Japanese agreed. Yo Unhyong promptly asked one of his lieutenants to draft a Korean Declaration of Independence.

The CPKI set up headquarters in Kyedong and sent teams to the countryside to spread the word. By the end of August, some 145 CPKI branches existed in north and south Korea. The release of about 16,000 prisoners, most of them with leftist leanings, immediately gave the CPKI a more radical tinge. Within a matter of weeks, the CPKI had succeeded in creating a large number of factory unions and peasant unions. Many sprang up spontaneously without CPKI urging. In many factories workers took over the plant. In other factories workers called strikes and slowdowns (Cumings 1990, 73). With the help of Koreans demobilized from the Japanese army, the CPKI kept its promise to minimize violence against Japanese in Korea.

Individuals judged to be collaborators were not permitted to join the KPR, making it even more left-leaning. Still, Yo Unhyong made an effort to be inclusive. Within the KPR peacekeeping duties were shared by groups that belonged to the left and also some that later allied themselves with the right, such as the Choson Hakpyong Tongmaeng (the Korean student-soldier's league). When, at the end of August, the CPKI took steps to form a government, which it called the Korean People's Republic, it proposed that its chairman be Syngman Rhee (who did not return to Korea until October 1945 and never joined the KPR). Leftists were a comfortable majority in the CPKI/KPR. They could afford to be magnanimous.

Formation of the Korean Democratic Party

By this time, the last week in August, both the Koreans and the Japanese knew that the Soviets had halted their advance and that the south of the country would be in American hands. The news caused an immediate change in the political situation within Korea. Leftists made a greater effort to include conservative elements in their new government to make it more acceptable to the Americans. Right-wing Koreans, who knew how much Americans hated communism, became emboldened and formed their own organization, the Korean Democratic Party (KDP), the main platform of which was opposition to the CPKI, which it accused of being the work of "a tiny clique of running dogs of Japanese imperialism," though in fact it was the KDP that included in its roster of members a significant number of pro-Japanese Koreans, while the KPR did not.

Meanwhile, the colonial government in Korea contacted the Americans and told them that the country was in a state of anarchy. "The condition in northern Korea has taken a sudden turn for the worse since 23 August and the lives and property of the Japanese residents are exposed to imminent danger," went a message from the governor-general to U.S. occupation headquarters in Okinawa. A Japanese lieutenant general in Seoul warned Americans of "communist and independence agitators" and of possible sabotage of the American landing in Korea by "red" labor unions. Adding to the anarchy they described, the Japanese sold their goods in Korean warehouses, printed money for use as bribes, and distributed "imperial gifts" to Korean collaborators (Cumings 1990, 82). The American occupation authorities evidently took the word of their recent enemies. Almost immediately upon their arrival they snubbed the KPR and threw their weight behind the KDP.

In December 1945 another conference of the World War II Allies was held, the first after the surrender of Japan. This one was held in Moscow and attended by the foreign ministers of the United States, Soviet Union, United Kingdom, and China. The Allied powers concluded that an interim government was to rule Korea for up to five years, leading to eventual full independence. To implement the plan Allied representatives set up the U.S.-Soviet Joint Commission, which met at the Toksu Palace in Seoul in January 1946. The commission was to initiate democratic activity in Korea by holding nationwide elections. The trustees were to see to the repatriation of Japanese soldiers, officials, and civilians to Japan and to ensure the return of Korean citizens who had been sent to the far corners of the now-defunct Japanese empire.

U.S. Policy in South Korea

General Douglas MacArthur (1880–1964), supreme commander of American forces in the Pacific, appointed John R. Hodge (1893–1963) to the post of commanding general United States armed forces in

THE MAKING OF YO UNHYONG

Yo Unhyong (or Lyuh Woon-hyung) was born on May 26, 1885, near Seoul. He learned early in life about politics. His uncle was one of the leaders of the Tonghak Rebellion. When Yo was just eight, his family went into hiding in a remote village to avoid government reprisals.

Yo lived by his nationalist and democratic convictions. He quit communications school in 1902 because graduates were obliged to work for the government. In 1903, when he lost his wife, father, and mother, he inherited a sizable estate complete with virtually enslaved tenant farmers; his response was to free them all, giving them enough land to be independent farmers.

Yo believed that Korea needed a strong military, and to that end he studied at Manchuria's new Korean military academy in 1913. He also accepted the ideas of An Changho, who taught that widespread literacy was the way Korea could free itself from the Japanese, and in 1917 Yo earned a degree in English at Nanjing, China. He promoted literacy and taught Korean children in Shanghai.

In 1918 a visit from Charles Crane, special envoy of U.S. president Woodrow Wilson, made a lasting impression on Yo. World War I had just ended, and Crane was publicizing Wilson's "Fourteen Points," which called for the independence of small states. This visit from the American delegate gave Yo and other Koreans great hope for international support for an independence movement. In his optimism Yo met with the Chinese nationalist Sun Yat-sen to plan strategy for both countries at the upcoming Paris Peace Conference (January 1919). His colleague Kim Kyu-sik (1881–1950) attended the conference but was neither seated nor heard because the other nations accepted Japan's claim to sovereignty over Korea.

Korea. Hodge was a blunt, unostentatious "soldier's soldier" with a distinguished record in the Pacific War but no experience with Asian culture or politics. He was chosen for the job because he and the XXVI Corps he commanded were near Korea at the time (Cumings 1990, 122–123).

Arriving with his troops on September 8, 1945, via a 21-ship convoy protected by a flotilla of destroyers, Hodge alienated many Koreans almost immediately. With an apparent indifference to feelings of a people who had endured 40 years of foreign domination, he announced

Undeterred, Yo traveled throughout China, Manchuria, and Russia encouraging Korean communities to continue pressing for Korean independence in coordination with the March First Movement of 1919. He even traveled to Japan to argue for independence directly with the Japanese.

By 1920 Yo had joined the Koryo Communist Party. He attended a 1922 conference in Moscow, where he met the Russian revolutionary leader Vladimir Lenin (1870–1924), and he later met Mao Zedong (1893–1976), leader of China's communist movement. Then Yo returned to Shanghai and worked for Chiang Kai-shek, leader of the Chinese Nationalist Party and Mao's nemesis.

Yo's nationalist activities did not escape the notice of Japanese authorities, and in 1929 the Japanese arrested Yo in Shanghai. He was deported to Korea and convicted of treason for sending Kim Kyu-sik to the 1919 Paris Peace Conference. After his prison term (1930–32) Yo worked as the editor of the *Chungang Daily News*. In this role he again provoked Japanese authorities, this time for his pro-Korean, anti-Japanese coverage of the 1936 Olympics. Yo was again arrested and his newspaper closed down. He was arrested yet again in Japan in 1942 and jailed for a year.

Now in his late 50s, Yo Unhyong stayed out of sight upon his return to Korea, but his role in history was not over. After its defeat in World War II in 1945, Japan turned to the well-known Korean nationalist to lead the interim government of Korea. Yo Unhyong remained on the scene for two years after General Hodge dismissed his interim government and continued to work for a left-right coalition to keep the division of Korea from becoming permanent. He met Kim Il Sung several times in 1946. Yo, trying to pull the left and right together, was attacked by both. He survived several assassination attempts but was shot and killed on July 19, 1947.

that for the present he was keeping the Japanese colonial government in place with all its Japanese and Korean personnel, including Governor-General Abe Nobuyuki (1875–1953). Koreans were outraged. After pressure from the U.S. State Department in Washington, Hodge replaced the Japanese staff with Koreans who had been a part of the colonial government. However, he retained key Japanese figures as unofficial advisers.

Showing an immediate preference for the wealthiest, most privileged, most pro-Japanese, and least popular groups within Korea,

Hodge snubbed the KPR leadership while giving his trust to the KDP, whom he pronounced the "democratic" faction. The conservatives of the KDP, concerned about their collaborationist taint and anxious to be led by men with good anti-Japanese, nationalist credentials, persuaded Hodge to bring back two exiled nationalist leaders, Syngman Rhee and Kim Ku (1876–1949). Though Hodge refused to grant any legitimacy to the Shanghai Provisional Government in Exile, to which both Rhee and Kim had belonged, he and other Americans smoothed the path for their return. Rhee, the favorite of Americans in Washington, was admired as a Christian and a fierce anticommunist. Many who admired him, and also many of those who disliked him, regarded Rhee as the Korean equivalent of Chiang Kai-shek, the anticommunist Chinese nationalist leader who also had America's support. With help from a U.S. intelligence agent, Rhee arrived in October on the personal plane

KIM KU, "THE ASSASSIN"

Born on August 29, 1876, Kim Ku was a resilient and controversial Korean nationalist who could have been the first president of a unified Korea in 1945. His first political activity, at age 18, was as a participant in the Tonghak Rebellion in 1894. The aftermath left him hiding from the authorities for a time, a skill he had to employ at several other times later in life.

The Japanese called him "the assassin," and with good reason, for he had extremely violent propensities. Upon learning of the murder of Queen Min in 1895, he killed the first Japanese he met, strangled the man with his bare hands and left the body in an inn with "Kim Ku" scrawled in blood on the wall. He was jailed in 1895 and sentenced to death, but King Kojong commuted this to a life sentence. In 1898 he escaped from prison. After nearly a decade on the run, Kim was arrested again on charges of complicity in the assassination of Ito Hirobumi, but he was released the next year. Arrested again in 1911 and sentenced to 17 years in prison, he was released early once more in 1914, this time out of sympathy for the death of his daughter.

In 1931 Kim formed the Korean Patriotic League, an organization that sponsored assassins; members of Kim's group twice attempted to assassinate Emperor Hirohito (in Tokyo in 1931 and Shanghai in 1932). Active in military matters, Kim contacted the famed Chinese nationalist leader Chiang Kai-shek in 1933 and acquired permission to send Koreans to the Chinese military academy. Thereafter he founded of Douglas MacArthur. He was introduced to the Korean public by Hodge himself.

With much less enthusiasm Hodge permitted the return of Kim Ku, known as "the assassin," who arrived with his supporters in the American zone in November. Hodge soon had reason to wish he had kept Kim out. In December, in yet another conference of the World War II victors, the United States and the Soviet Union formerly agreed on a five-year "trusteeship" for Korea. When Hodge broke the news to the KDP leaders on December 29, Song Chin-u, the head of the KDP (and the man whom the Japanese had first turned to to lead the interim government), said that he would help to support this policy. Kim Ku thereupon arranged his assassination. Kim Ku organized mass demonstrations against the trusteeship, condemned those Koreans appointed to government office by the Americans, calling them collaborators and

---

the Korean Liberation Army (KLA), the military arm of Korea's Provisional Government in Exile. After the Japanese bombed Pearl Harbor on December 7, 1941, Kim's government declared war on Japan and Germany and dispatched the KLA to fight the Japanese in parts of China and Southeast Asia. When it became clear that World War II was turning against Japan, the army began to mobilize for battle in Korea. But the war ended so abruptly after the atomic bombings of Hiroshima and Nagasaki that the KLA was too late to engage Japanese forces in Korea.

Kim was the last and longest-serving president of Korea's Provisional Government in Exile. His main political rival, Syngman Rhee, had been its first president (1919–25). After a series of four presidents in two years, Kim Ku had become the sixth president in 1927 and remained in office through 1945. Upon Japan's surrender in August 1945, he tried to return to Korea, but the American military delayed him such that he did not arrive until November 23. They also refused to recognize Kim's provisional government, allowing him to return only as a "private citizen," not as president. Once again, Kim had to rely on his own resourcefulness to influence Korean affairs.

When Yo Unhyong was killed in 1947, many assumed it was set up by "the assassin," Kim Ku. With Yo out of the way, there remained only two rivals for power—Kim Ku and Syngman Rhee. After losing power to Rhee, Ku himself was assassinated on June 26, 1949, by a man assumed to be in Rhee's employ. Kim Ku is recalled with fondness today by many South Koreans.

traitors, and rallied other nationalists to form an antitrusteeship movement that pushed for immediate independence.

Probably the most fateful decision made by General Hodge's military government was to retain the existing apparatus of the Japanese colonial government and to staff it with right-wing Koreans. KDP members were put in some of the highest-ranking positions. This intrusive and efficient bureaucracy, created by the Japanese for the totalitarian control of their colony, included the police, which used its power to suppress political opposition to Korea's extreme right wing. By the time Hodge wanted to bring more moderate leaders to power in the American zone, right-wing control of the bureaucracy had made this impossible.

Soviet Policy in North Korea

Meanwhile, north of the 38th parallel the Soviets took steps to establish control of the political forces within their zone. Kim Il Sung arrived in the Soviet occupation zone of Korea in October 1945, the same month that Syngman Rhee arrived in the American occupation zone. The Soviets gave Kim Il Sung the same sort of conspicuous and visible support the Americans gave Syngman Rhee. Kim was first introduced to the top Korean Communist Party leadership, then to Koreans at large in a mass rally attended by tens of thousands of people. Potential rivals for the leadership of the Korean left in the Russian zone were eliminated, either by people working for Kim himself or by the Soviets. Hyon Chun Hyok, a charismatic communist schoolteacher who, according to the military historian Allan Millet, was Kim Il Sung's rival for the position of general secretary of the Communist Party, was assassinated on September 28, 1945. At the time, he was in a truck sitting next to Cho Mansik (1883–1950), another popular Korean activist often called the "Gandhi of Korea," whom the Soviets suspected of being difficult to control, so the assassination also served as a warning to Cho. Cho was eventually arrested and died in prison in mysterious circumstances.

Since the revolutionary platform of the people's committees was not a threat to the Soviets, they were not suppressed, and the Soviets helped them enact their popular program of land redistribution, women's equality, and the complete eradication of the hated colonial bureaucracy, which Hodge in the American zone had decided to keep. All pro-Japanese collaborators were ruthlessly purged, another move popular with everyone except the collaborators. At the same time, Korea's Communists laid the groundwork for the totalitarian state that North Korea would soon become. Freedom of the press was virtually eliminated. By the end of 1946, all newspapers, whether communist or noncommunist, carried the same news. Christians, who were seen as opponents to the regime, were imprisoned, often on trumped-up charges. Churches remained open, but any political activity connected with them was ruthlessly stamped out. All nonleftist political opposition was methodically eliminated; a few noncommunist parties were allowed to exist for a show of pluralism, but with no power. The groundwork was laid for a vast security apparatus of secret police and informers. In a manner oddly reminiscent of the Japanese during the last period of their rule, virtually all North Koreans were bullied into joining organizations and attending meetings—in schools, workplaces, government offices, and villages—at which they received a thorough indoctrination in the views of the regime. In a technique also used by communists in China and Vietnam, the ideologically backward were made to engage in criticism and self-criticism sessions (Cumings 2005, 229–231).

The very thorough eradication of freedom in the Soviet zone was actually associated with less violence than actions taken in the South, perhaps because other aspects of Soviet policy were popular. Still, a lot of people must have disliked it. An estimated 388,000 natives of North Korea fled southward to the American zone. Including those from North Korea, Manchuria, Japan, and China, official records show a total of 2,380,821 Koreans coming to the American occupation zone between October 1945 and December 1947, greatly adding to the chaos in the South and the troubles of the American military regime (Cumings 1990, 60). As the groups and regimes empowered by the Soviets and the Americans within their respective zones were diametrically opposed to each other, it became even more likely that a civil war would immediately follow any attempt at a reunification.

The Anticommunist Purge in the South

In early 1946 Kim Ku joined forces with his rival Syngman Rhee to form the Representative Democratic Council, a right-wing coalition. Its opposition was the Democratic National Front, a left-wing alliance of Yo Unhyong, Pak Hongyong, and Kim Il Sung. By early 1947, however, it was clear that Syngman Rhee was preparing for a separate government in the South; Rhee had accepted the division of Korea, at least for the moment, postponing unification until he had consolidated power in the South. Kim publicly broke with Rhee. In a desperate move he traveled to Pyongyang, hoping to form a left-right coalition and prevent the nation from being permanently divided. It was a gamble that did not pay off: Kim Il Sung was not cooperative, and Kim Ku was left without a strong case for running against Syngman Rhee.

Syngman Rhee and his KDP colleagues, with the help of the American military government, took action against the left in the American zone. Part of the work was done by paramilitary youth organizations modeled on the Black Shirts of fascist Italy and the Brown Shirts that had helped the Nazis come to power in Germany. The most prominent of these youth groups, the Korean National Youth, had U.S. funding and perhaps training. Its members wore blue shirts (Cumings 2005, 206–207). Other parts of the anticommunist purge were conducted by the police as they battled a series of popular uprisings and rebellions in the countryside and strikes in industrial areas. The youth groups confronted, harassed, and at times killed suspected communists, which meant in practice those connected with the KPR, the committees it had organized, and the labor unions and peasant organizations around the country. It meant Koreans demanding the redistribution of land (whose concentration into fewer hands had occurred during the Japanese occupation), demanding lower prices for rice, striking for higher wages, as well as those who attacked landlords and police.

Peasant uprisings and industrial strikes spread across the Kyongsang and Cholla provinces beginning in September 1946 in a series of incidents known in Korea as the Autumn Harvest Uprisings. A general strike by railroad works began in Pusan and spread to Seoul, freezing transport throughout the country. The strike soon spread to printers, electrical workers, the telegraph office, and postal employees. Students joined the strikers; most newspapers supported them. On October 1, 1946, during a demonstration of children marching in support of the strikers, police killed one of the demonstrators. The next morning more than 1,000 demonstrators appeared in the streets bearing the body. When the demonstrators approached the police station, the police fled. On October 3 a group of 10,000 overran the police station in Younchon, killed officials and police, and burned the police station to the ground. As the rebellion spread it was suppressed by a combination of forces: the American military government, the Korean police, a Korean "constabulary" (really the core of a Korean army, called by this name because Hodge had been ordered not to form a Korean army), and the paramilitary youth groups who were made into "temporary police." The methods used were exceptionally savage. In some cases entire villages were destroyed and their inhabitants slaughtered.

Another small war between the people and the authorities occurred on Cheju Island between 1947 and 1949 (and thus continuing while

JAMES HAUSMAN

One of the more colorful characters among the Americans who went to Korea at the end of World War II was a U.S. Army captain named James Hausman (unknown–1996). When the U.S. military withdrew in 1947, he stayed on as an adviser with the Korean Military Advisory Group, KMAG.

As a close confidant of Syngman Rhee, he helped Rhee with military operations, such as quelling the communist movements in Cheju, Yosu, and Sunchon. He shunned the limelight but quietly became a close adviser and frequent visitor to the South Korean presidential mansion (known as the "Blue House" because of its blue-tiled roof).

The political left wing came to view Hausman's role as critical in the elimination of left-wing influence in South Korea. In criticism of that role, they referred to him as the "Ugly American" of Korea. The right wing, on the other hand, gave him credit for exactly the same thing, and these Koreans thank him for saving the country.

After the end of Syngman Rhee's regime in 1960, the U.S. military came to see Hausman as an invaluable resource, a living encyclopedia of tradition and history concerning Korea. This was particularly important in light of the fact that the U.S. military practiced rotating soldiers, including commanding generals, in and out of Korea on a one-year and two-year basis. Hausman became the voice of consistency for the U.S. military in Korea. He served as the head of a small group of Korean experts attached to the headquarters of the Eighth Army, the only American army with such a unit of specialists, for another 20 years, finally retiring and returning to his home in Texas, where he died in 1996.

the military occupation gave way to the establishment of the Republic of Korea, ROK, in the south in 1948). Cheju was controlled by the same people's committees that had been formed by the KPR and that Rhee and the KDP, with the help of the American military government, had been trying to uproot. Fighting on the side of the islanders was conducted by guerrilla groups calling themselves "People's Armies." On the government side at various times were paramilitary youth groups, Korean police, and after 1948 the Korean army. By the time the island had been pummeled into submission, 20,000 homes on the island had been destroyed, and between 15,000 and 30,000 people had been killed. The operation to root out the communists was extremely difficult because they occupied some of the numerous caves that dot the volcanic hills in the middle of the island.

Division

Because Korea's various factions could not agree either on whether to accept trusteeship or when to hold elections, the U.S.-Soviet Joint Commission referred the case to the United Nations (UN) which established the United Nations Temporary Commission on Korea (UNTCOK) on November 14, 1947. Its mission was to help Korea form an elected government. An UNTCOK team arrived in Seoul in January 1948 to lay the groundwork for nationwide elections. Leaders in Pyongyang, however, did not recognize the team and refused them access to the Soviet

UN ORGANIZATIONS IN KOREA

The United Nations played an active role in Korea in the postliberation era and ultimately provided military aid for South Korea in the Korean War. The various UN-sponsored organizations served different purposes as the situation on the peninsula changed.

Before the UN involvement, the U.S.-Soviet Joint Commission set up a trusteeship to guide Korea to its own independent government. Korean factions opposed trusteeship, and the trustees sent the issue to the United Nations. It established UNTCOK, the United Nations Temporary Commission on Korea (November 1947). The following year it dropped the "T" and created UNCOK, the United Nations Commission on Korea. UNCOK representatives, on a mission to prevent hostilities between the North and South, were in Seoul on June 25, 1950, when North Korea invaded. Their testimony convinced the United Nations that North Korea was indeed the aggressor, and thereafter the United Nations sided with South Korea.

The UN General Assembly organized UNCURK, the United Nations Commission on Unification and Rehabilitation of Korea, on October 7, 1950, the same day it authorized UN troops to cross the 38th parallel into North Korea. Like other UN organizations, it was never recognized by North Korea. UNCURK was abolished in 1973 when North and South Korea were both granted "observer" status at the United Nations. Allies of each side blocked the other from gaining member status until 1991, when both sides were finally admitted to the United Nations.

zone. The elections were also widely boycotted in the South, where they were opposed by Kim Ku and Kim Kyusik. UNTCOK went ahead in the South, and legislative elections were held in May 1948 with 30 UN observers. Syngman Rhee became the head of the new assembly, which subsequently adopted a constitution providing for a presidential form of government. On August 15, 1948, the Republic of Korea was proclaimed, with Rhee as its first president. Less than a month later, on September 9, Kim Il Sung proclaimed the Democratic People's Republic of Korea (DPRK).

The Korean War

The Korean War started on a Sunday morning, June 25, 1950. Koreans do not call it the "Korean War." Rather, they refer to it as the "June 25 Incident," the date the sudden invasion of Seoul had penetrated the national consciousness. But the hostilities and preparations for the war predated that June 25 by at least two years.

Increased Hostilities and the "Acheson Line"

By early 1950 Syngman Rhee had largely, though not completely, succeeded in suppressing the communist insurgency in South Korea. A few weeks before the war he met with U.S. secretary of state John Foster Dulles (1888–1959, secretary of state 1953–59) in Seoul; Rhee pleaded with Dulles not only for a commitment to defend Korea but for a go-ahead to attack the North, saying such a move could succeed in a few days (Haliday and Cumings 1988, 65). North Korea, of course, spoke of liberating the South. A low-intensity conflict, which military historian Allan Millett called a "border war," had been going on along the 38th parallel since the end of 1949. According to Millett, the provocation came primarily from North Korea, which used the border war as a way of softening up and testing the mettle of its adversary (Millett 2005, 204–205). This ongoing conflict once left a lot of room for argument concerning the exact beginning of the war. North Korea for years claimed that the South had actually started the war. Some scholars outside of Korea found these claims credible. This view required modification after the fall of the Soviet Union in 1991, when the Kremlin released classified documents showing that Kim Il Sung launched the invasion only when he had received Joseph Stalin's permission to do so. Stalin had withheld this permission until January 1950, when he agreed with the concept that the Korean Peninsula should be unified by force and to supply more

North Korean tanks heading south on June 25, 1950. North Korean tanks and supplies from Russia provided an overwhelming advantage in the early stages of the war. (Academy of Korean Studies)

equipment, including precious petroleum for the North Korean tanks and trucks.

The troops of the Republic of Korea were not prepared for the attack and were taken by surprise, as they would not have been if they had planned an imminent attack of their own. The fact remains, however, that reunification by force was a policy of Syngman Rhee's ROK, as it was of Kim Il Sung's DPRK. Neither side recognized the other's legitimacy. Each side claimed all the territory of the other and asserted the right to reclaim it by force.

Stalin may have changed his mind and permitted the invasion because of the changed security situation. The Chinese Communists completed their takeover of mainland China in October 1949. This development not only gave the North Koreans inspiration, it also gave them soldiers. Many Koreans, high-ranking officers on down to foot soldiers, had fought for Mao and then returned to Korea. Furthermore, in 1949 the Soviet Union tested its first atomic bomb, which may have increased Stalin's confidence.

Another factor in the timing of the invasion seems to have been what appears in retrospect an extremely inept statement by U.S. secretary of state Dean Acheson (1893–1971). As part of his country's search for peace in the post–World War II world, Acheson on January 12, 1950, declared that the U.S. line of defense ran along the western edge of the Pacific, a line that included Japan and the Philippines but excluded Korea and Taiwan. It came to be known as the "Acheson Line." Acheson's declaration gave great hope to Kim Il Sung, Stalin, and Mao that the United States was heading toward a new phase of isolationism and would not intervene in communist Korea or Taiwan. The statement followed the Communist takeover of China by three months and countered the calls from the American right to support Chiang Kaishek in his attempt to retake the Chinese mainland. The Acheson Line declaration may also have helped persuade Stalin to reverse his position on Kim Il Sung's proposed invasion of South Korea.

June 25, 1950

In June 1950 the North Korean army had approximately 100,000 soldiers, a substantial number of whom had just returned from successful support of Mao in China. South Korea's 65,000 soldiers were neither as well trained nor as well equipped as the Communists. Only a small group of American military advisers remained in South Korea at the time.

When the North Korean tanks and soldiers rolled across the 38th parallel toward Seoul, they quickly overpowered an unprepared South Korean army and the few American personnel. The attack was well planned and well coordinated. It opened with an artillery barrage followed closely by armored vehicles and infantry. Four separate Korean People's Army spearheads drove south through gaps in the hills. Topography offered more formidable obstacles to their advance than the Republic of Korea forces. The American advisers withdrew with the South Korean Army, which fled southward in disarray, abandoning equipment as it went. At 9:30 A.M. Kim Il Sung broadcast the DPRK's version of what was happening: "The South Korean puppet clique has rejected all methods for peaceful reunification . . . and dared to commit armed aggression . . . north of the 38th parallel. The Democratic People's Republic of Korea ordered a counterattack to repel the invading troops . . ." (Hastings 1987, 53).

Seoul, which had the misfortune of being quite close to the 38th parallel, was taken in three days. The North Korean Army then paused to consolidate its position and allow its logistical support to catch up. By July 5, when it began moving south again, the United States had shipped troops to stiffen ROK resistance and block the roads southward. The first American units to face the enemy, hastily thrown into action, were composed partly of troops untested by combat and partly of World War II veterans softened by an easy life as occupiers of Japan.

They arrived amid optimistic rumors that the North Koreans would flee when they learned they were going to be facing the U.S. Army and that they would be home in a week. With head-spinning suddenness they found themselves in a desperate losing battle against a better-prepared enemy whose capabilities the United States had greatly underestimated. Facing Soviet-made T-34 tanks and armed with handheld bazooka rocket launchers that did not pierce tank armor, they were quickly overwhelmed, and their retreat was disorderly. The same inglorious pattern was repeated time and again as retreat turned into a desperate holding operation within the Pusan Perimeter, a 150-square-mile corner of Korea that included the port of Pusan, vital for the landing of troops, and the city of Taegu.

The unpopularity of the ROK regime added to its military weakness. Its generals were men who had fought for Imperial Japan and whose later combat experience consisted of operations against communist guerrillas in the South. As soon as the invasion began, the earlier civil war in the South was revived, and ROK forces again fought local guerrillas, who assisted the North Koreans in their successful 14-day siege of Taejon (Deane 1999, 92).

UN Intervention

Within two days of the invasion, the United States took the issue to the United Nations, and between June 27 and July 7 it was able to obtain UN condemnation of North Korea. In a series of resolutions, the United Nations ultimately authorized deployment of armed forces to rescue South Korea. These actions could have been vetoed in the UN Security Council by the Soviet Union. The Soviets, however, were boycotting the United Nations in protest of the body's decision not to recognize the People's Republic of China.

The United States was delegated to lead the armies under the UN flag. President Harry S. Truman (1884–1972) assigned General Douglas MacArthur as commander of the UN forces. MacArthur was then and remains today a controversial figure, celebrated and reviled. He fought in three major American wars (World War I, World War II, and the Korean War) and held enormous personal power as military adviser to the Philippines when it was an American protectorate and as the Supreme Commander of U.S. forces in the Far East during the U.S. occupation of Japan and Korea.

He can be credited with outstanding achievements. Among these are the rebuilding of Japan as a stable and peaceful democracy and his daring amphibious invasion at Inchon during the Korean War. He can also be blamed for some truly catastrophic blunders. One of these occurred during World War II, when with eight hours of warning after the Pearl Harbor attack, MacArthur's forces in the Philippines were caught napping. Three other major errors occurred in the Korean War. Despite reports by the CIA and his own intelligence department that an invasion was imminent, MacArthur did little to train his divisions in Japan for combat. In the fall of 1950, having pursued the enemy almost as far as the Yalu River, he ignored evidence that the Chinese People's Liberation Army had crossed the Yalu into Korea. A third and final error quickly followed. Ignoring the American tradition that generals do not start wars, he wrote a letter to the Republican House minority leader, arguing for the expansion of the war into China. Had he gotten his wish, we might be able to say that MacArthur fought in three world wars, not just two. Instead, he lost his command.

Eventually 16 nations sent combat troops to fight with the United States under the UN flag. Five other nations supported the United Nations by sending noncombatants, mostly hospital units. Some nations sent small units attached to American units; others sent significant numbers that contributed significantly to some of the battles.

The UN forces were ready for action by mid-September. MacArthur sent a diversionary force of ships to bombard the east coast, leading the North Koreans to believe the invasion would be on the east coast. The landing of troops, however, took place near Inchon, on the west coast not far from Seoul. It was at Inchon that the Japanese had invaded Korea in 1904 during the Russo-Japanese War, so the idea was not new, but Inchon with its treacherous tides that could ground a flotilla of ships if the landing was not well timed offered risks for a major amphibious operation such as MacArthur planned. The same mystical faith in his own genius and destiny that led MacArthur to make his worst blunders helped him to persuade the doubters in the American command. The Inchon landing on September 15, 1950, turned out to be a masterstroke. Within days, as U.S. troops, artillery, and armor poured into Korea through two major landings at Inchon, U.S. and ROK troops broke out of Pusan Perimeter and pushed northward. What historians Jon Haliday and Bruce Cumings call "the first Korean War" ended on September 30, 1950, as "ROK Army units crossed into the North, pressing a rollback against rapidly withdrawing Northern forces." The war for the South left 111,000 South Koreans killed, 106,000 wounded, and 57,000 missing; 314,000 homes had been destroyed and 244,000 damaged. American casualties totaled nearly 5,000 dead, 13,659 wounded,

MacArthur's landing at Inchon on September 15, 1950, bisected the line of advancing North Korean soldiers, leading to the capture of 250,000 prisoners of war. They were held on Korea's second-largest island, Koje, just off the coast from Pusan, until the end of the war. The prisoners are gathered in the center of the yard as guards look on. They were housed in tents and enclosed in barbed-wire compounds. (Academy of Korean Studies)

and 3,877 missing in action. North Korean casualties are not known (Haliday and Cumings 1988, 95).

These are large numbers, standing for misery beyond imagining, yet they are small compared to the tragedy to come. Leaders in the U.S. State Department had decided on a rollback—to push the DPRK armies north of the 38th parallel, perhaps to agree on a ceasefire from an improved position or perhaps to keep going until Korea was unified.

In retrospect, knowing how little ground was ultimately gained and at how much cost, the decision seems like a great mistake. Diplomat and State Department adviser George Kennan, the original architect of the U.S. policy of "containment" of the Soviet Union, thought that an attempt to unify Korea under the ROK would be risky while offering little prospect of improved U.S. security, but in 1950 America's anti-communist hysteria was approaching its peak, driven by revelations of widespread spying for the Soviets during the 1930s and 1940s, the communist takeover of Eastern Europe after 1945, the loss of China to Mao Zedong's Communists, and the Soviet explosion of the atomic bomb, both in 1949. Anyone arguing for restraint would have been called an appeaser by the American public, American officials, and Senator Joseph McCarthy (1908–57), who was beginning to make a name for himself by charging that the federal government was riddled with communist agents. In addition, it is never easy to justify the military decision of permitting a fleeing enemy to regroup.

MacArthur was ordered to cross the 38th parallel but avoid any act that would engage the United States and the United Nations in a larger war either with the Soviets or the Chinese. These instructions to MacArthur meant to avoid provoking an attack from China were beside the point. Mao Zedong had already decided to bring China into the war if the Americans crossed the 38th parallel. A North Korean defeat, putting Syngman Rhee's U.S.-friendly regime on China's Manchurian border, would threaten the revolution that Mao was still consolidating and give hope to whatever opposition still remained in China. The United States was a friend of Mao's old foe, Chang Kai-shek (Jiang Jieshi) and the Nationalists, who set up a rival China in the former Japanese colony of Taiwan. Whether or not North Korea won, China could not tolerate its destruction. Shortly after the Inchon landing the Chinese premier, Zhou Enlai, gave a public speech announcing his intention to intervene if the 38th parallel was crossed. Leaders and opinion-makers in the United States dismissed the threat as a bluff. Like MacArthur, they had little respect for China's military capabilities.

The United States obtained a UN resolution to move into North Korea on October 7, and the UN forces captured Pyongyang on October 19. The UN forces then continued north to the hills overlooking the Yalu River, the border with China. McArthur, contravening orders, brought his troops into the counties bordering the Yalu, and in late October the Chinese People's Liberation Army began crossing the river into Korean territory. MacArthur for a while ignored their presence. It is possible that the true state of affairs was hidden from him by his chief intelligence officer, General Charles Willoughby, who knew that MacArthur did not like receiving information that interfered with his plans (Halberstam 2007, 373–374). Speaking of a giant "pincer movement," MacArthur had allowed his troops to be scattered widely among the hills of northern Korea. The Chinese attacks surrounded the poorly deployed troops. In the Battle of Chosin Reservoir 30,000 U.S. troops fought their way out of encirclement at the cost of more than 15,000 casualties.

U.S. officials commonly referred to the Chinese attackers as "hordes" and "human waves," giving the impression that this nation of 600 million was sending vast numbers of expendable Chinese into American and ROK fire, but in fact the forces on each side were deploying roughly equal numbers. The Chinese simply "outgeneraled" MacArthur. He had not taken the trouble to study their methods; they were familiar with his.

The U.S. Air Force, which had been bombing North Korean cities and troops since the beginning of the war, were given an increased role at this point in a move that would have immense long-term effects on North Korea, formerly Korea's industrial heartland. In the words of historians Jon Haliday and Bruce Cumings, "MacArthur ordered that a wasteland be created between the front and the Chinese border, destroying from the air every installation, factory, city and village over thousands of square miles of North Korean territory" (Cumings 1997, p. 293). MacArthur's successors continued this policy and eventually extended it to all of North Korea. Whole cities were reduced to rubble or set aflame with incendiary bombs and napalm. Navy artillery destroyed a major North Korean port city. The air force bombed dams in North Korea, causing hugely destructive floods. With negligible air power of its own, North Korea was helpless against these attacks, which continued until the armistice in 1953. With Chinese help the North Korean army regrouped and moved south, taking Seoul again on January 4, 1951.

Truman Fires MacArthur

In late September 1950, still flush with the glory of his Inchon landing, MacArthur gave a long interview to *Life Magazine* in which he advocated building up Chiang Kai-shek's armies for future use on mainland China (Deane 1999, 117). As the troops under his command suffered reverses he spoke more and more of widening the war and of using the atomic bomb. On December 1, 1950, he told a reporter that the restriction placed on him against attacking Chinese bases beyond the Yalu River were "an enormous handicap without precedent in military history" and sent a transcript of the interview to the United Press. Truman responded with an order (tactfully addressed to all military commanders, not just MacArthur) to clear statements on foreign policy with the U.S. State Department. MacArthur repeatedly defied this directive (Pearlman, 7). While MacArthur was insisting that he could not win under the restrictions placed on him, an 8th U.S. Army commander,

General Matthew Ridgway (1895–1993), stopped the North Korean advance and began pushing it back. As these facts called MacArthur's military skills into question, he went on the offensive politically. He wrote letters to his friends in Congress criticizing the administration's conduct of the war; the letters were made public and debated. On April 11, 1951, Truman dismissed MacArthur and replaced him with General Matthew Ridgway. Chiang Kai-shek and much of the American public were dismayed. America's chief allies in Europe, who had worried that all-out war in Asia would spread to the West, breathed a collective sigh of relief.

Stalemate

UN forces retook Seoul on March 15 and again crossed the 38th parallel, but they were unable to push farther north. For the two years after MacArthur's dismissal in April 1951, little territory was gained or lost. Rather, battles near the 38th parallel moved the line slightly north or slightly south. Some of the greatest battles of the Korean War, such as Heartbreak Ridge (September 13–October 15, 1951) and Pork Chop Hill (March 23–April 16; and again between July 6–11, 1952), took place during this time. (*Pork Chop* is the English rendering of the Korean *pokchap,* meaning "confusion" or "chaos," an apt description of the battle.) Yet none was significant in changing the outcome.

Given the stalemate, the combatants looked for ways to negotiate an end to the conflict. The first attempts at a peace conference were actually made even earlier. On July 10, 1950, negotiators met at Kaesong, North Korea, the old Koryo dynasty capital, just north of the 38th parallel. In August the talks were suspended and the location criticized as unsafe for the southern forces. Thereafter, both sides met at a small village called Panmunjom (meetings are still held there to this day), but the next peace conference was not until October 25, 1951. Finally, in spring 1953 negotiations to end the war made significant progress. Whether Stalin's death in March 1953 helped the talks get started is debated, but exchanges of prisoners in April and May, including some diplomats and civilians held since the outbreak of the war, helped ease tensions. A total of 6,670 North Korean and Chinese prisoners were exchanged for 669 UN personnel in an initial exchange.

During their initial march north the U.S.-UN troops had captured some 130,000 North Korean soldiers. The problem of housing so many prisoners was solved by placing them all on Koje Island, the second-largest island in Korea, not far from Pusan. There, in large barbed-wire complexes, the prisoners were separated into three groups: hard-core Communists, North Korean soldiers who wanted to return to North Korea, and North Korean soldiers who indicated that they would rather defect to the South. Unbeknownst to the United States, its irascible ally Syngman Rhee had already released 25,000 prisoners from the POW camp on Koje Island into the South Korean population. Rhee said he could not condemn so many people who wanted freedom from a life of misery in North Korea. While Rhee's motive may have been sincere, the action infuriated the Americans. They feared—rightly, it turned out—that the North Koreans would similarly "release" South Korean and American prisoners into North Korean society and they would never be heard from again. In the final exchange, 75,823 Communist prisoners were exchanged for 12,773 UN forces, including 3,598 Americans. How many prisoners were kept in the North is unknown.

The Demilitarized Zone (DMZ)

The cease-fire line determined on July 27, 1953, when the armistice was signed, is a line that roughly parallels the 38th parallel; it dips slightly south of the 38th parallel in the west and runs 50 miles north of the parallel to the east. This line and the surrounding area, a buffer zone extending 1.24 miles (2 km) north and 1.24 miles south of the line, form what is called the Demilitarized Zone, or DMZ. Contrary to its name, the zone is one of the most heavily armed areas in the world. The land within the Demilitarized Zone is heavily mined, armed soldiers patrol each side, and behind the lines on both sides are heavy artillery and tanks.

The DMZ continues to be a flash point in the conflict between the two sides. From time to time there have been incidents in the DMZ—shootings, line crossings of defectors, and a propaganda battle in which large loudspeakers encourage the opposing soldiers to enter the paradise on the other side. Sometimes soldiers with debts or family problems on one side have sought "freedom" by crossing over to the other side. Such soldiers have included Americans.

In the western DMZ, not far from Seoul to the south and Kaesong to the north, lies the village Panmunjom, where north and south meet to discuss issues related to the two halves of the peninsula. These meetings are supervised by members of the Neutral Nations Supervisory Commission (NNSC), a team of neutral nation observers established by the Korean Armistice Agreement ending the war. Originally, the neutral nations were Switzerland and Sweden, affiliated with South Korea, and

Poland and Czechoslovakia, affiliated with North Korea. The Czech component of the NNSC was forced out by North Korea in 1993, and the Polish component was forced out in 1995. They were no longer communist and no longer trusted by the DPRK. The negotiators from the South are represented by the United Nations, the United States, and the Republic of Korea (ROK). The other side is represented only by North Korea, a fact it uses for propaganda purposes: Stating that it is independent and not beholden to any other nation, North Korea accuses the South Koreans of being puppets of American imperialists.

Atrocities

One of the more troubling issues of the Korean War has been the atrocities committed by both sides. The U.S. forces have been accused of indiscriminant bombing of cities in the North with napalm, an incendiary jelly meant to stick to its targets. Napalm burned wide swaths of land, and napalm fires could even suck the air out of tunnels and underground bunkers. The widespread use of napalm destroyed many cities in North Korea. Its later use in Vietnam led to a UN ban in 1980.

The Korean War was both a conventional and guerrilla war. North Korean soldiers were known to shed their uniforms, wear civilian clothes, and launch surprise attacks. Civilian partisans, whether devoted to the North Korean cause or threatened into helping, were also said to participate in surprise attacks on UN forces. The suspicion that harmless-looking women and old men might actually be working for the enemy led American soldiers to kill civilians. Charles Grutzner, a war correspondent for the *New York Times,* wrote that "fear of infiltrators led to the slaughter of hundreds of South Korean civilians, women as well as men, by some US troops and police of the Republic." Another American correspondent wrote, "It is not the time to be a Korean, for the Yankees are shooting them all . . . nervous American troops are ready to fire at any Korean" (Haliday and Cumings 1988, 88).

In 1999 the U.S. government issued a formal study on Nogun-ri, a village where American soldiers allegedly killed between 200 and 300 South Korean civilians in the midst of the chaos of the retreat from Seoul in the first month of the war. The study concluded that the American soldiers had killed civilians, probably because they believed that North Korean soldiers had infiltrated the column of refugees. The report concluded that some of the more sensational allegations, such as that the air force strafed the refugee column, were not true.

Refugees fleeing the oncoming Communist North Korean army (Academy of Korean Studies)

Another heart-wrenching case was the demolition of a bridge over the Naktong River, just outside of Taegu. The American military had orders to blow up the bridge after crossing it so that the advancing North Korean army could not use it. The Americans tried three times to close the bridge, but desperate refugees kept on coming. The first two groups of refugees were able to cross safely, but not the third. By that point the soldiers could wait no longer: They destroyed the bridge, killing the refugees who were crossing.

The Korean War created an estimated 5 million refugees as people fled battle zones and cities under siege (Oberdorfer 2001, 10). A great many more lost their homes when the UN forces decided on a systematic program of destroying small villages that were being used as shelter by North Korean guerrillas (Cumings 2005, 294–295). An estimated 10 million Koreans belonged to families that were separated by the line that divides North Korea from South Korea. The war, by making unification a more distant prospect, made that separation permanent.

North Korea as well was responsible for atrocities and war crimes during the conflict. The Korean People's Army killed hundreds of American prisoners of war by outright execution and let thousands more starve to death in prisoner of war camps. There are well-documented accounts of mass murders of South Koreans by North Koreans and disputed cases as well (Haliday and Cumings 1988, 92).

The word *brainwashing* first entered the American lexicon during the Korean War. Brainwashing is an attempt to break down the personalities of prisoners so that they will do anything their captors demand. It is thought to have first been used by the Chinese but probably only upon one group of prisoners. "The notion that the Chinese 'brainwashed' the bulk of their prisoners in Korea is simply unfounded," writes the British military historian Max Hastings. "They appear to have employed the sophisticated techniques generally associated with this term only in one case—that of the American aircrew from whom they extracted confessions of participation in bacteriological warfare, their most notable propaganda achievement" (Hastings 1987, 301). Some historians, the most authoritative being Bruce Cumings, are not sure whether brainwashing was used even in this case; he notes that while 10 of the airmen subsequently retracted their confessions, the other 16 did not. He therefore considers it possible that the confessions were true, and that the United States actually did experiment with bacteriological warfare in the Korean War. Both the brainwashing accusation and the germ warfare accusation are closely linked to the cold war propaganda of the 1950s, and they still await objective study.

Whether or not any UN prisoners were brainwashed, many were subjected to brutal interrogations, sleep deprivation, and physical abuse in the course of a strenuous and rather clumsy effort by the Chinese to convert their prisoners to communism. As part of this program, the prisoners were treated to long lectures on such topics as "The Democratic Reformation and Democratic Structure in North Korea and

the Peaceful Unification Policy of the North Korean Government,"
"The Chinese People's Right to Formosa," and "Corruption of the UN
by the American warmongers" (Hastings 1987, 294–295).

The Korean War was a stalemate. After three years of violence and
death, of relocations and separated families, the two halves of Korea
returned to where they had been before the war, with injured, maimed,
and wounded on both sides. Neither side gained anything; both sides
lost much in the way of life and property.

The Korean War was both a civil war and a product of the confrontation between international superpowers in the cold war. There were
millions of victims. They include not just the millions of people killed
and not just the millions who were wounded. They encompass not just
the millions of refugees and not just the 10 million who were separated
from family members, but all 40 million Koreans affected by the war at
the time, and even more counting those born after the war. The effects
of the war continue. The peninsula is still divided. In both countries
the near presence of a feared enemy has been used to justify political
repression and the maintenance of huge armed forces, absurdly disproportionate to the size of these two small countries. Both sides waste a
huge percentage of their gross national product on armaments; both
have been molded in obvious ways and subtle ways by the memory of
a terrible war that technically has never ended.

7

SOUTH KOREA'S LONG ROAD
TO DEMOCRACY
(1953–2009)

L ooking at the two Koreas today, outsiders see a simple moral: Capitalism works, communism does not. The people of South Korea enjoy both democracy and prosperity; the people of North Korea are poor and live in a police state. For the first three decades following the Korean War, this moral would have seemed less obvious. For much of that time, and especially the first two decades, a case could have been made that North Korea was the better off country. Though poorer, its people enjoyed greater personal security and a fairer distribution of goods. If they depended on Soviet aid, they depended on it less than South Korea depended on American aid. Restrictions on personal and political freedom were greater in North Korea than in South Korea, but in both countries the outward forms of democracy were hollow.

For nearly half a century South Korea was ruled by a series of strongmen: Syngman Rhee (president 1948–60), Park Chung Hee (1917–79, president 1961–79), and Chun Doo Hwan (b. 1931, president 1980–88). Their rule was punctuated by brief periods of democratic reform, when opposition leaders won electoral victories, the Korean people flowed into the streets to demand real democracy, or when the strongmen themselves promised democratic reform and it seemed that the end of autocratic rule had come at last. Time and again this hope was thwarted. By the 1990s South Korea's "economic miracle"—really achieved over the course of a century at an incredibly high human cost—was well advanced, but its democratic miracle was still new.

In the modern world democracy enjoys such international prestige that most tyrannical governments clothe themselves in its trappings. They hold elections and permit limited amounts of free speech, while the police arrests dangerous political opponents and the army stands by to declare a national emergency and restore order whenever real change threatens to occur. It is useful to bear this pattern in mind when examining the evolution of the state and the constitution of South Korea under Syngman Rhee and his successors. The United States, which guaranteed South Korea's security and supported it with billions of dollars of foreign aid—sometimes amounting to more than half of its national budget and two-thirds of its defense expenditures—wanted South Korea to be a democracy, and so did the majority of the South Korean people. For this reason South Korea's despots could not rule simply as military dictators. Instead, with the help of special powers and in the name of combating communist subversion and with the rewards they could dole out to key supporters, they manipulated an outwardly democratic system to stifle opposition and retain power. Even so, the hypocritical concessions Korea's strongmen made toward democracy were not without effect. They were the openings that allowed opposition to survive and through which the majority was ultimately able to express its will.

The Presidency of Syngman Rhee (1954–1960)

Syngman Rhee, whom the United States had supported as an anticommunist democrat, seems to have had few democratic instincts; 73 years old at the time he officially took power, he was a product of the previous century, a liberal and modernizer by the standards of the late years of the Choson dynasty. In 1898 he had gone to prison for his share in the Independence Club's demand for a national assembly, which would have been an advisory body that left ultimate power in the hands of the king. Virtually all his actions as head of state tended to concentrate decision-making power into his own hands, and he seemed to hang on to it by any means necessary. In a true democracy he could not have held on to power, because his base of support was too narrow. Rhee commanded the loyalty of a small group of highly conservative large landowners and businessmen, former collaborators with the Japanese, former Korean members of the Japanese colonial bureaucracy (which continued to exist and served the new Korean state), the police, paramilitary youth groups, the army, and the United States.

The threat of communist subversion served Rhee's purposes from the start. The Republic of Korea's 1948 constitution prohibited any restrictions on freedom of speech, press, assembly, or association, with an important loophole, "except as specified by law" (Eckert 1990, 349). The exception was not long in coming. In 1948, following allegedly com-

210

munist-led insurrections in Yosu and Sunchon, the National Assembly passed a vaguely worded National Security Law (NSL) that gave Rhee broad powers to round up those he considered dangerous to the state. Under the NSL Rhee purged his potential opponents in the army, the press, and educational institutions in the name of anticommunism. By the spring of 1950, South Korea's prisons held more than 60,000 people, the majority of them charged with violation of the NSL.

Rhee also used the NSL to beat the National Assembly into obedience. In early 1949 the National Assembly began to investigate, arrest, and try Japanese collaborators, a series of actions that threatened Rhee's power base but that he could not at first openly oppose. The National Assembly continued to assert itself, promoting land reform and demanding the resignation of Rhee's entire cabinet. Rhee struck back using the NSL to put 16 assemblymen in jail. As a result the trials of the collaborators and the land reformers and the attack on the cabinet essentially went nowhere.

In 1951 Rhee established the Liberal Party, which Carter J. Eckert describes as "a motley assortment of opportunists held together by a desire for power and loyalty to Rhee" that had at its core Koreans who had served in the colonial bureaucracy during the Japanese period (Eckert 1990, 350). Liberal Party victories at the polls were assured by a combination of electoral fraud, police surveillance, strong-arm tactics by paramilitary groups, and the NSL. In 1952, during the Korean War, when it appeared that he would lose the election in the National Assembly, which under the Korean constitution elected the president, he changed the constitution, to provide for direct election by the populace. In 1953 he instituted a midnight to 6:00 A.M. curfew in the cities. In 1956 he changed the constitution again, this time removing the provision limiting him to two terms, and ran for a third term as president. Though the 1956 balloting saw numerous charges of election fraud and ballot stuffing, Rhee still won his third term. The Rhee administration unraveled as a result of the 1960 elections, however. Oddly, the election for president was not the issue; the vice-presidential ballots were the center of the controversy.

The April Revolution

While the aging Syngman Rhee took steps to tighten his grip on the reigns of power, the society over which he ruled did not stand still, and the changes led to an erosion of support even among the narrow groups that had acquiesced to Rhee's rule. Partly through the brutal

LIVING WITH A CURFEW

Life in Korea from 1953 to 1980 was influenced by the midnight to 6:00 A.M. curfew. All social events, all outside activities, all traffic—everything came to a halt before midnight. The situation was like that of Cinderella leaving the ball, except that the risks were more serious, including jail time.

The rush to get home started around 11:00 P.M., when dinner guests, revelers, businesspeople at dinner meetings, and the like had to make their ways home. The buses ran only until 11:00, and taxis then began their last round, looking for a fare or two that headed them in the direction of the garage. Few private citizens had cars.

The chaos in the streets peaked between 11:00 and 11:30. Then sheer panic set in for the poor fellow who had stayed a little too long at a social engagement. He would hold up two fingers—indicating he would pay double the taxi fare—or three fingers, or even five fingers. Sometimes a person could not catch a cab, and that meant staying overnight at a friend's house or at one of the cheap hotels once found in every neighborhood. Once the clock struck 12:00, all activity on the streets ceased. The only activity was the occasional military patrol.

Today's Seoul is a city that never sleeps, a sea of neon lights with markets and nightclubs that are open well into the night. Seeing this, one can hardly imagine that there was ever a curfew, but curfew there was, strictly enforced from the end of the Korean War until the start of the Chun Doo Hwan government.

repression early in his regime and partly through a program of land reform after the Korean War, Rhee had largely succeeded in quelling political activity in the countryside. In fact, the landowning peasantry had become rather conservative and was the only really popular base of Rhee's support, but the cities were another matter. By 1960 nearly 30 percent of Koreans lived in cities of 50,000 or more, double the number that had in 1945. Partly with American assistance, school enrollments had increased, literacy rates had more than tripled, and more than 70 percent of the population could read and write. The readership for newspapers and magazines had expanded enormously—the circulation of *Tong a Ilbo*, the nation's leading newspaper, went from 20,000 to about 400,000 between the end of the war and 1960. The press was increasingly hostile to the government.

South Korea's enormously expanded population of students was a particularly destabilizing element for the regime of Rhee and his successors. There were far too many of them to find employment appropriate to their skills, especially university graduates, whose number increased twelvefold between 1948 and 1960. Thus, they were a discontented class, with time on their hands. Furthermore, they had inherited from Korea's Confucian past a belief that it is a scholar's duty to keep watch on the virtue of the state.

The constitution provided for an independent vice president, and Rhee's vice president from 1956 to 1960 was Chang Myon (1899–1966), who had served as ambassador to the United States at the outbreak of the Korean War. Chang was a New Faction Democrat and a proponent of reform, a potential rival for the presidency. Rhee determined that he would see his candidate, Yi Kibung, elected vice president in 1960. Yi Kibung was a distant relative, and the childless Rhee had adopted Yi as his son. Yi, however, was perceived not only as abrasive but as the core of the growing corruption of the Rhee administration. His popularity fell in the campaign, yet in the March 15 elections Yi won by a wide margin. Clearly, the ballot boxes had been compromised. Chang Myon resigned in protest. Students began demonstrating, and demonstrations spread and grew larger each day.

On April 11 the body of a 17-year-old boy was discovered in the bay around Masan, a port city in South Kyongsang that had been the site of demonstrations against the elections in March. The boy had apparently been struck and killed by a tear gas canister and dumped into the bay by the police. The citizens of Masan immediately thronged the streets in renewed protest, while Rhee laid the blame on his favorite boogeyman, "communist infiltrators," who, he said, had caused the trouble by organizing the demonstrations in Masan. As the student protest spread, Rhee's attempts at suppression became increasingly savage. On April 18 Rhee's Anticommunist Youth Corps attacked a demonstration of students at Korea University in Seoul. The following day students from Korea University, about three miles east of the Blue House (the presidential mansion), began to march in protest against Rhee. As their column made its way toward the Blue House, protesters' courage and numbers mounted—to an estimated 30,000. They marched past Sungkyunkwan University and Seoul National University, picking up more students. Soldiers blocked their final approach to the Blue House. It appeared that the demonstrators could overwhelm them, and the soldiers were ordered to shoot if necessary. When the protesters kept coming, shouting for Rhee to go and confronting the soldiers, the soldiers opened fire. Students fell, but others pressed forward. The soldiers continued to fire until about 125 students were dead and 1,000 more were wounded. Then, in sympathy with the protesters, the soldiers decided to stop protecting a corrupt government. They laid down their weapons and went home. The students were now in control.

In most contexts the term *student government* refers to student involvement in school and student body activities. In Korea in 1960, however, *student government* meant students running the government, literally. Students manned police stations, city hall, and central government offices. After a time government officials returned to service and society returned, somewhat, to normal.

Rhee remained in Korea for one more week, hoping that the demonstrators would blame those around him and not him. On April 28 Yi Kibung's eldest son shot his father, his mother, his younger brother, and himself in a suicide pact. Rhee's life was in danger, and he finally saw that he had better leave Korea. He resigned on April 27, leaving his foreign minister, Ho Chong, as the head of the government, but he still had trouble letting go. On the way out of town, the aged president made one last suggestion for saving the situation: that he leave the Blue House by walking away alone. The people, he reasoned, would be saddened at such a pitiful sight and would rally around him and beg him to stay. His advisers got him into the car and off to the airport. Rhee spent the next five years in exile in Hawaii, where he died at the age of 90.

Democratic Interlude and Coup d'État

After Syngman Rhee's resignation in April 1960, Koreans enjoyed a brief and exciting, if also chaotic, period of freedom. With restrictions on the press and on political activity removed, new newspapers, magazines, and political groups flourished. A new constitution was drafted, creating a bicameral parliamentary government, with a prime minister and cabinet responsible to the National Assembly, who would also elect the president (as in the Republic of Korea's first [1948] constitution). In free elections held on July 29, the Democratic Party won a large majority and selected Yun Poson (1897–1990) as president and Chang Myon as prime minister. While Yun later achieved prominence running for president against Park Chung Hee, at this point power was in the hands of the prime minister, and the president was largely a figurehead.

It was a rebirth of democracy, and many individuals and parties vied for power. Some Koreans look back on those days nostalgically, but others shake their heads at some of the excesses of the times. The National

SYNGMAN RHEE: METAPHOR FOR KOREA

The political events of the first half of the 20th century are embodied in the life of Syngman Rhee. Born in 1875 when the Choson dynasty was 483 years old, Rhee was 35 when the dynasty came to an end. He was educated in mission schools—the schools that had such great impact on much of the leadership of the early 20th century. He was arrested by the Japanese in 1898 as a member of the Independence Club, and upon his release in 1904 he left for the United States. When he received word of the protest against Japan in 1919, he left the United States for China and became the first president of the Provisional Government of Korea, headquartered in Shanghai. He did not stay in China long, however, opting to return to the United States in 1922, where he thought he could be more effective in gaining support for the Korean cause. It took years, but his decision to go to the United States paid dividends because that nation was eventually to be his greatest ally.

After Korea was liberated from Japan in 1945, Rhee returned, like many others of the Korean diaspora. The migration out of Korea, started during the deprivations of the Japanese colonial period, was beginning to be reversed. However, emigration resumed with the Korean War and subsequent economic desperation, and a new Korean diaspora was established. Eventually, some 2 million Koreans emigrated to the United States, and in the end Rhee was among their numbers.

The geographical divide between North and South Korea mirrors an ideological divide in the minds and hearts of the people. Rhee is representative of Koreans in this respect as well. He had no regard for the Communists, or, for that matter, anyone espousing leftist ideas. What was true of Rhee and others on the right was also true of the many hard-liners on the left: There was only one way, "my way." In this way as in many others, Rhee, the hard-liner, was an embodiment of the Korea of his age.

Assembly was contentious, and fistfights were known to break out on the floor during legislative sessions. Critics often cite this as an example of how troubled the Korean experiment in democracy had become. In reality, however, the situation was not all that bad—any growing democracy has its less-than-perfect moments—but such bad examples were all the excuse the military needed to take control.

General Park Chung Hee (center) took over the government on May 16, 1961, 11 months after student-led protests drove Syngman Rhee from power. Park, a two-star general, later led Korea to the first stage of a remarkable economic development. (Academy of Korean Studies)

On the morning of May 16, 1961, the military rolled into the streets of Seoul. After commandeering the radio stations they proclaimed martial law and announced that the military was assuming control of the government for the good of the nation. Although Kim Jong Pil (b. 1926) led the group of colonels who planned the coup d'état, a major general, Park Chung Hee (1917–79) soon emerged as the most important member of the military cabal that had taken over the country.

Park asserted that the military was cleaning up the corruption for the sake of national security: North Korea could read the political and social chaos in South Korea as an opportunity to step in, so the military would stabilize the situation temporarily. "Temporarily" for Park Chung Hee turned out to be the next 18 years, during which he invoked national security to justify suspension of basic rights. Standing firm against a possible invasion from the North was a recurring theme throughout Park's administration.

Besides declaring martial law and controlling all mass media, the military takeover of May 16 involved the systematic arrest of all politicians, reporters, and professors who were deemed problems to the military. With the help of a special military tribunal, Park also purged the military—his ultimate source of power—of anyone who opposed his rule. Park dissolved the National Assembly, forbade all political activity, and severely censored the press. In what would prove to be a temporary effort to appeal to conservative morality, the military government also broke up prostitution rings and closed down bars and dance halls. In 1961 Park made Kim Jong Pil the head of a new secret police organization, the Korean Central Intelligence Agency (KCIA), which established a vast network of agents who would help to repress Park's political opposition throughout his rule. For two years Park saw to the restructuring of the government to his liking. Then in 1963, under strong pressure from the United States to end military rule, he retired from the military and ran for president as a civilian. The most oppressive and obvious bans on free speech and political activity were lifted, and with the help of the KCIA and what Carter Eckert calls "a large reservoir of funds whose precise sources have never been conclusively identified" (Eckert 1990, 362), Park created the Democratic Republic Party (DRP), which became the vehicle for his forays into electoral politics. To weigh the elections in the DRP's favor, the military junta excluded many of Park's strongest rivals from participation. Though it is unlikely that Park would have won a truly free election, many Koreans who longed for stability supported him; his base of support included not only right-wing business and military figures but also many poor Koreans who regarded Park's rivals as an elite group out of touch with problems of the common man. The DRP won 32 percent of the popular vote but a majority of seats, thanks to a system that gave great advantages to the party winning a plurality of votes. Yun Poson, probably judging that a step toward democracy had been made, publicly congratulated Park on his victory. In the years to come, Park would continue to rig the system to maintain the maximum appearance of democracy with the minimum of interference with his power. The period would see vocal protests and demonstrations in opposition to Park's policies, in strong contrast to the total muzzling and fake unanimity of opinion in Kim Il Sung's North Korea, but whenever the civilian electoral machinery threatened to unseat him, Park would take steps to see that he stayed in power. Still, while showing himself to be at least as authoritarian as Syngman Rhee, he would prove to be a more competent leader, and his plans for the economic revitalization of South Korea won enthusiastic support from development experts in the United States and from a growing class of Korean technocrats.

The Park Chung Hee Years (1961–1979)

Park had begun his career as a cadet in the Japanese Imperial Military Academy and upon his graduation in 1944 he served the Japanese as an officer in Manchuria, where some allege that he helped pursue anti-Japanese Korean guerrillas. Thus, Park developed much of his world-view by watching Japan at the height of its imperial expansion. Having seen the might of the Japanese economy during the war years and the rebound of the economy after World War II, he wanted nothing more than to turn Korea into an economically powerful country. Economic development, and little else, was the goal of the Park administration, and his foreign policy supported those efforts.

After Japan fell from power at the end of World War II, Korea had no diplomatic relationship with its former colonizer. The diplomatic standoff continued through the early 1960s, but Park needed Japan for economic assistance, investments, and loans. It took him four years to prepare for diplomatic recognition. Finally, in 1965 he was able to move Korean sentiment sufficiently to exchange diplomats and set up embassies in opposite capitals. As part of the treaty, South Korea received $300 million in grants, $2 billion in public loans, and $300 million in commercial credits (later raised to $500 million) over a 10-year period. Even then, however, Koreans launched huge demonstrations against the establishment of diplomatic ties with Japan.

Park's economic plan worked. Korea received a tremendous boost in development from Japan. Prior to 1965 the United States was Korea's biggest trading partner; within a year after the signing of the normalization agreement, Japan enjoyed this distinction, a situation that continued throughout the 1960s and 1970s. Japan led all other countries in foreign investment in Korea, and later, as postwar Japan rose to become a world competitor in the electronics and automotive industry and subcontracted work to nearby Asian countries, Korea's economy boomed in tandem with Japan's. Even so, the political costs for Park were great. Many critics emphasized his pro-Japanese past and called him *sakura*, a Japanese word literally meaning "cherry blossoms," implying that Park was pro-Japanese at best and a collaborator at worst.

Both to counter his critics and to foster nationalism, Park went on a monument-building campaign, commemorating heroes of Korea's 16th- and 20th-century struggles with Japan. The chief beneficiary of the hagiography was the 16th-century naval commander Yi Sunsin. When Toyotomi Hideyoshi's navy invaded Korea in the 1590s, Yi led the attack on Japanese supply ships, the only bright spot in that dark period. The late 1960s saw huge monuments built along the southern coast, in Yi's hometown just south of Seoul, and in Seoul. The most noteworthy of these is the impressive statue of Yi Sunsin overlooking the busy Kwanghwamun intersection in the heart of Seoul. In effect, Park was demonstrating that if he had to seek assistance from the Japanese with one hand, he could still thumb his nose at them with the other.

Park's economic strategy was central planning, a strategy modeled on Japan's and making use of an Economic Planning Board similar to Japan's Ministry of Trade and Industry. As in Japan, direct government investment encouraged the growth of giant industrial conglomerates (in Japan called *zaibatzu*, in Korea *chaebol*). This basic model of growth and investment was typical of countries lying within Japan's sphere of influence—and, in fact, the roots of the South Korean economic system lay in the period of Japan's colonial rule in Korea, when much of Korea's development was led by subsidiaries of Japanese *zaibatzu*, such as Mitsui and Mitsubishi (Han Woo-keun 1970, 482). It was continued past the time of Park and his authoritarian successors and into the era of democratic South Korea.

There were and are about two dozen *chaebol* in the Republic of Korea; the ones whose names are most familiar to Americans are the automaker Hyundai and the electronics firm Samsung. The most significant difference between Japan's *zaibatzu* and South Korea's *chaebol* were that *chaebol* could not own banks. Both were family owned and benefited from close ties between its members and members of the government.

A 1998 report by Dick Nanto, a trade analyst for the U.S. Congressional Research Service (CRS), summed up this model and its contrast to European and American capitalism. "Companies in Asia tend to rely more on bank borrowing to raise capital than on issuing bonds or stock," said Nanto, noting that this system gives government more control over who has access to loans when funds are scarce. The government directs funds toward favored industries at low rates of interest, while consumers pay higher rates for purchasing products that the government has considered to be undesirable (such as foreign cars). While this capitalist model, which strongly favors production over consumption, proved its success in lifting Asians from poverty in the postwar period, its use also helps explain the corruption scandals that rocked the ROK as soon as its government became democratic enough and transparent enough for corruption to become visible. As the CRS report observed:

219

> *A weakness of this system is that the business culture in Asia relies heavily on personal relationships. The businesses which are well-connected (both with banks and with the government bureaucracy) tend to have the best access to financing. This leads to excess lending to the companies that are well-connected and who may have bought influence with government officials. . . . [South] Korean banks and large businesses borrow in international markets at sovereign (national) rates and re-lend the funds to domestic businesses. The government bureaucrats often can direct the lending to favored and well-connected companies. The bureaucrats also write laws regulating businesses, receive approval from the parliament, write the implementing regulations, and then enforce those regulations. They have had great authority in the Korean economic system. The politicians receive legal (and sometimes illegal) contributions from businesses. They approve legislation and use their influence with the bureaucrats to direct scarce capital toward favored companies. (Nanto 1998)*

Within this central planning model Park launched a series of five-year plans, each loaded with goals that would lift South Korea to the next level of development. In the first five-year plan, 1962–66, he laid the groundwork by providing sufficient electricity, fertilizer, petroleum, and cement. In the second five-year plan, 1967–71, the emphasis was on steel, chemicals, and machinery. In the third five-year plan, 1972–76, machinery and chemicals to help factories produce exports were fostered, as well as shipbuilding, transportation, and household electronics. Park's fourth and last five-year plan, 1977–81, was also the last to emphasize heavy industry. In the end Park achieved his dream—Korea became an industrial powerhouse.

Korea's growth in this period exacted a high price from its industrial workers, thanks in part to the suppression of free labor unions by every South Korean regime since the colonial period. From the early 1960s American companies were lured to establish factories in Korea by a savings in labor costs that sound almost impossible: Korean workers earned one-10th the wage of American workers but were two and a half times as productive. Before 1971 Park's economic development plans were aimed mostly at large industries in the Seoul area and in his home province, North Kyongsang. This changed after the presidential election of 1971. Because the vote was so much closer than expected, many people spoke of it as a "near defeat" for Park. The surprising opposition candidate was Kim Dae Jung (1924–2009), who had the solid support of his home province of Cholla, an underdeveloped agricultural region in the southwest of the peninsula. Kim also received support from other rural areas in a vote described as split between the urban "haves" and the rural "have-nots."

The outcome hit Park hard. The president's roots were in the countryside, and he regarded himself as a son of the soil, a farmer's son. For pragmatic as well as personal reasons, he launched a series of reforms to improve the rural economy. Like many of Park's programs, his new rural program, called the "New Village Movement" or "New Community Movement" (Saemaeul Undong), was loved and hated for what it did and the heavy-handed manner in which it did it. Rural villages that cooperated with the new program were rewarded with free surplus cement that could be used to pave village roads and build walls and community buildings.

A typical loved-but-hated policy of the New Village Movement called for removing the straw-thatched roofs of village homes. Park decreed that there would be no more thatched roofs—he disliked the underdeveloped appearance of the "little grass shacks." Some poor farmers found it a financial burden to remove a perfectly good thatched roof and install a metal or corrugated-fiber roof that provided no insulation. The appearance of the rural village changed almost overnight. Gradually, even those farmers who were not prepared to change and who opposed the Park policies found their standard of living improving as Park brought electricity and running water to farm homes, and new local industry boosted rural incomes.

Vietnam War and "Reform"

Park's next major challenge came from Southeast Asia. The Vietnam War had been raging since 1956; in 1964 the United States formally entered the conflict. It was a conflict with both open and unacknowledged similarities to the war that Koreans themselves had endured. The similarities were even geographical, for the Communists (who, as in Korea, had the best nationalist credentials and the support of the Soviet Union) were based in the North, while the anti-Communists (as in Korea, a group dominated by big landowners and former collaborators and supported by the United States) were in the South. Guerrilla warfare and a confusion between combatant and noncombatant would lead to widespread slaughter of civilians and the systematic burning of villages. Plus, the United States would conduct a massive bombing campaign in an attempt to break the enemy's will. A loyal ally of the United States, Park sent soldiers to Vietnam in fall 1965, the Tiger and the Blue Dragon Divisions. The next year South Korea sent a third combat division, the White Horse, and a logistics division, the Peace Dove.

In all, South Korea sent a total of around 300,000 troops to Vietnam between 1965 and 1973.

The Vietnam War provided an economic boost for South Korea in the late 1960s. In exchange for South Korea's support, the United States purchased much of its supplies, services, and equipment from South Korea. South Korean contractors were favored for participation in South Korean construction projects. In 1966 the Vietnam War accounted for 40 percent of Korea's foreign exchange.

As the Korean War had jump-started the Japanese economy of the early 1950s—for the boost it gave the economy, Japanese prime minister Yoshida Shigeru called the Korean War a "gift from the gods"—so the Vietnam War jump-started Korea's economy in the late 1960s. Koreans' construction experience in Vietnam became the springboard for the next phase of economic development for South Korea, construction work in the oil-rich countries of the Middle East and Southeast Asia. As a result of this development, many cities have major landmarks built by Koreans. Among these are the world's tallest buildings from 1996 to 2003, the Petronas Twin Towers in Kuala Lampur: One of the towers was built by a Korean construction company, the other by a Japanese company. However, the Vietnam War would have other consequences for South Korea as well.

South Korea's participation in the Vietnam War helped keep Park Chung Hee in power. It put an end to criticism of his regime from the United States. While South Korea was a key U.S. ally in Vietnam, there was no chance that the United States would draw down its foreign aid to Park Chung Hee's regime or make serious demands for reform. The boost the war gave to the South Korean economy helped make the regime almost popular, and it gave Park powerful incentives to distribute to important supporters. Those South Koreans who looked to the United States as a friendly older brother were proud to be on the winning side of the cold war, participating in a victory over communism, which would have strong resonance for South Korean's who remembered their own war with the North and continued to fear attack from Kim Il Sung's DPRK.

Resistance to the Park Regime

At the beginning of the 1970s, however, as Park's first decade of power came to an end, his party began to face a strengthened democratic opposition in the New Democratic Party (NDP), led by a younger generation of political leaders, including Kim Young Sam (b. 1927) and

Kim Dae Jung. Both were moderate democrats, not leftists, and both were outspoken critics of the Park regime and were gathering strong support. In 1971 Kim Dae Jung as a presidential candidate of the NDP won 45 percent of the vote, including more than half of the urban vote. The DRP was still in power, but it may have seemed to Park that its time was limited unless he took action while he could. To assure that no change of regime occurred, Park rewrote the constitution in 1972.

The new constitution was called the Yushin Constitution; the term *Yushin* was officially translated as "revitalizing reforms." While it sounded good, in reality the new constitution was a tool that gave Park greater authoritarian power to arrest those he wanted to. He cracked down on newspapers, arresting some reporters and having others dismissed from their newspapers. He went after other "impure" elements as well, including some professors who had criticized him. He had already pressured the National Assembly in 1969 to eliminate the two-term limit on his office, allowing him to remain president indefinitely. Park saw Kim Dae Jung as a particularly dangerous opponent and was likely behind an assassination attempt (disguised as a car accident). Kim, left with a permanent hip injury, fled to Japan, where he spoke out against Park and the Yushin Constitution. In 1973 South Korea's spy agency, the KCIA, kidnapped Kim from a Tokyo hotel and brought him back to Korea, where he remained under house arrest from 1973 to 1979.

On August 15, 1974, at a public meeting at the Citizen's Hall in downtown Seoul, a young Korean, a pro-DPRK resident of Japan named Mun Se-gwang (1951–74), made an attempt on Park's life. Despite rigorous security measures, he somehow had a handgun. He rose from his seat near the front of the hall and started shooting at Park. He missed Park but fatally wounded Park's wife, Yook Youngsoo, known as Madame Park (1926–74). Unlike her unsmiling and dour husband, Madame Park was well loved by the people and lent great dignity to public occasions. Her death was a blow to Park and to the nation. After her death Park became more austere in his own life and even more severe on his perceived enemies.

Yet, before the Yushin Constitution and after it, even as the South Korean economy boomed in an atmosphere of political repression, dissent grew. Disaffection spread to many sectors of society, including labor, which had been harshly repressed under the Park Chung Hee regime even before the Yushin Constitution. Keeping wages in South Korea cheap was a way of luring business to the country and keeping the heads of the great South Korean business conglomerates happy. From its beginnings the government developed sophisticated methods for repressing labor, some of them evidently borrowed from Korea's colonial period. Syngman Rhee had created a national, state controlled company union, which represented the interests of management and helped to break strikes and prevent the rise of independent unions. In 1961 the KCIA created unions for each industrial sector and founded a new national labor federation whose leaders pledged their loyalty to Park's program; two years later the government outlawed political activity by labor (unless it was activity that favored the ruling party). Labor's bargaining power was further weakened by an influx of young women and displaced peasants into the industrial labor market, and a generation of workers suffered for South Korea's economic boom.

South Korea's export companies and American manufacturers that relocated jobs to Korea thrived on the low-skilled labor in sweatshop conditions; many lived in company dormitories that were stiflingly hot in the summer and under-heated in winter, ate company food, and had one or two days off a month. Conditions like these at last spawned a real labor movement, arising from the shop floor without help from any existing political party. The late 1960s and early 1970s saw a series of strikes at the firms of American and Korean companies, by electronics workers, metalworkers, chemical workers, and autoworkers. In a vast warren of small sweatshops known as Seoul's Peace Market, 20,000 workers, the majority of them young women, toiled in unhealthy conditions for wages that, in the words of a study by the American Friends Service Committee, amounted to "the price of a cup of coffee at a tea room" (Cumings 2005, 574). In 1970 a textile worker named Chon Taeil immolated himself at Seoul's Peace Market, shouting, as he burned, "Obey the labor standards act" and "Don't mistreat young girls." The suicide shocked the nation, brought student demonstrators into the streets, and resulted in the formation of the Chonggye Garment Worker's Union, founded within a month of Chon Taeil's death by his mother, Yi Sosun. Park's regime promptly passed a law that gave the president power to restrict civil liberties, set wages and prices, and stamp out industrial strikes and independent labor unions. Despite these measures, workers kept organizing.

Korea's churches became centers of resistance to the regime, as they had during the Japanese colonial period at the time of the 1919 March First Movement. Korea's Catholics, influenced by Latin American liberation theology, began Korea's Minjung ("masses" or "common people") Movement. The Urban Industrial Mission (UIM), run by Christians, sought to make workers aware of their rights. In 1974 George Ogle, a

Methodist missionary associated with the UIM, was deported by Park for defending eight men who had been tortured into confessing they were part of a Communist conspiracy. The Reverend Cho Hwasun, a female Methodist minister who worked at the Dongil Textile Company in Seoul, helped to found an independent women's union. Throughout the 1970s the members of this union bravely confronted the company and the government, steadfast in the face of persecution by the hired thugs, the police, and the KCIA.

Though unskilled laborers in South Korea worked for next to nothing, wages among skilled laborers rose in the late 1970s because the use of skilled South Korean workers for construction projects in the Middle East left a shortage of them at home. In 1979 Korea's economy suffered a severe downturn, caused partly by high levels of debt, by the second of the 1970s great oil shocks, and by rising labor costs. Park's regime became less popular than ever, and severe labor disputes erupted in several sectors. First the miners at the Sabuk coal mines in the central mountain region went on strike. Miners demanded improved safety and wages as well as the right to organize. Park summoned riot police to break up the demonstrations by force, and the severity of the fighting between miners and riot police made the news. Then, in an incident at the YH Trading Company, the government took an action that helped to lead to Park's abrupt and bloody end.

The YH Trading Company was essentially a large sweatshop in which Korean women manufactured wigs for export made from other Korean women's hair and did simple needlework, for which they were paid next to nothing plus room and board at the company dormitories. In early August 1979 workers at the company were holding a sit-down strike. On August 7 the owner shut the factory, fired all its employees, closed the dormitories and mess halls, and had the police evict the workers. Many were severely beaten. Kim Young Sam, then chairman of the New Democratic Party, agreed to let them use the party headquarters. On August 9 about 1,000 police stormed the building, in the process killing a woman worker. Park Chung Hee called for "a thorough investigation into the true activities of certain impure forces which, under the pretense of religion, infiltrate factories and labor unions to agitate labor disputes and social disorder." Park's attacks were aimed particularly at the UIM, which the government-controlled media accused of Communist connections. In the United States the administration of President Jimmy Carter called Park's actions "brutal and excessive." Hearing this, the opposition parties stepped up support of the workers.

On October 4 the DRP, the ruling party, voted to expel Kim Young Sam from the National Assembly. Workers and students demonstrated in the streets of Masan and Pusan, ordinarily a privileged and relatively content area where Park had usually enjoyed support. Demonstrators demanded Kim's reinstatement, Park's resignation, and an end to the Yusin system. The political moment obviously resembled the democratic ferment that had led to the end of the Syngman Rhee regime, and Park and his advisers debated whether the response should be liberalization or stepped-up repression.

On October 26, 1979, Park met to discuss the situation over dinner at a KCIA safe house with Kim Chaegyu, head of the KCIA along with Cha Chichol, Park's ever-present bodyguard and confidant, a short, squat man known for his toughness and also said to be a strong influence on Park. Partway through the meal Kim excused himself and went outside, where his coconspirators were waiting. He got a revolver from one of them and returned to his place at the table. Looking at Park's armed bodyguard, Cha Chichol, he exclaimed, "How can we conduct our policies with an insect like this!" and shot him (Cumings 2005, 379). Park was not armed, and Kim shot him next. Kim then attempted to shoot Cha again to make sure he was dead, but his gun jammed and he ran from the room. After acquiring a pistol from one of his aides, Kim shot Cha again several times, and then shot Park again. Then he left the house and went to the waiting jeep of the chairman of the Joint Chiefs of Staff, Army General Chong Sunghwa. The president had been shot, Kim told Chong, not revealing that he had done the shooting. Kim suggested that they go to KCIA headquarters to monitor events and decide what to do. On the way Chong recommended that they change course and go to his headquarters, the Ministry of Defense. When they arrived Chong ordered Kim's arrest; he had concluded that Kim was behind the shootings. The prime minister, Choi Kyu Ha, was an uncharismatic bureaucrat who had been picked by Park Chung Hee specifically for his mediocrity; Park had regarded him as an unthreatening number two. Choi became acting president and declared martial law. In February, after a brief period during which younger officers of the Korean military purged their ranks of the older generation, the interim government launched a general liberalization. It restored the political rights of Kim Dae Jung and other politicians and allowed the rehiring of university professors who had been fired for political reasons. Expelled students returned to the universities. Koreans around the country met to discuss rewriting the constitution and to prepare for a new election.

Chun Doo Hwan (1980–1988)

Sadly, South Korean's democratic impulses were thwarted again, as they had been at the close of Syngman Rhee's reign. Once again the ROK's powerful military establishment was the culprit. The new military strongman was Major General Chun Doo Hwan, chief of the Defense Security Command and a Park loyalist. Chun had headed the investigation into Park's assassination and together with an ally and friend, General Roh Tae Woo (b. 1932), had conducted the purge of the South Korean military in the immediate aftermath of Park's death. In April 1980 Chun made himself head of the KCIA while keeping his post as commander of the Defense Security Command. At this moment, when a strong show of American support for democracy might have given pause to the ROK's military, the American commander appeared to approve the coup that was in the making. Protestors took to the streets. There were demonstrations of 50,000 in Seoul each day. On May 17, 1980, Chun declared martial law, closed the universities, dissolved the legislature, and banned all political activity. Thousands of political leaders and dissidents were arrested overnight on May 17–18, among them the three Kims—Kim Young Sam, Kim Dae Jung, and Kim Jong Pil.

The Kwangju Uprising

In the early morning of Sunday, May 18, 1980, soldiers seized Seoul and the provincial cities, setting up camps on the soccer fields of the various universities. The show of force and the effectiveness of military control quelled all resistance with relatively little bloodshed, except in the southwestern city of Kwangju, the center of South Cholla Province, a stronghold of the presidential candidate Kim Dae Jung. On the second day of Chun's coup d'état, an elite team of paratroopers launched a savage attack in Kwangju that unleashed a small-scale rebellion. On May 18 the paratroopers attacked a demonstration of about 500 Kwangju residents who were demanding the lifting of martial law. In another country—even another dictatorship—this situation might have been met with bulletproof riot shields and tear gas. Instead, the paratroopers attacked with nightsticks and then bayonets, killing 200 people. Over the next week hundreds of thousands of Kwangju residents poured into the streets. Seizing weapons from local armories, they drove the paratroopers from the city, formed citizens' councils, and appealed to the American embassy for intervention to negotiate an end to the crisis. Not only did the Americans not respond, they permitted the release of ROK frontline troops from their duties along the DMZ to help suppress the rebellion, a move still remembered with bitterness in South Korea. Loudspeakers from helicopters told people to disarm and return to their homes. Shortly before dawn on May 27 soldiers entered the city, shooting at those who refused to disarm. The paratroopers and regular solders quickly managed to secure the city. About 30 civilians died defending the provincial capitol, which the Kwangju resistance fighters had taken over as their headquarters. Altogether more than 200 were killed and several hundred more injured.

Chun arrested Kim Dae Jung on May 18, blaming him for the rebellion that started after his arrest. Kim was found guilty in a show trial and but for American pressure would have been executed; he was sentenced instead to life in prison. By September 1980 Chun compelled Interim President Choi Kyu Ha to resign, and Chun assumed the office of interim president of the Republic of Korea. Subsequently, he was elected to a five-year term under a new constitution in February 1981. The new constitution provided for an electoral college that would elect the president, many of the electors being appointees of Chun.

Soon after Ronald Reagan's inauguration in January 1981, the new U.S. president invited the new ROK president to visit, the first head of state to be invited as an official visitor. Just before his visit to the United States, Chun broke up the Chonggye Garmet Workers Union, the union that had begun with the suicide of Chon Taeil. Adding to the previous regime's arsenal of antilabor tools, Chun created a special force of strike-breakers, the "white skulls" (paekkol). The white skulls were skilled in Asian martial arts and equipped with protective padding, shields, and motorcycles. Within a few years workers arrested under South Korea's National Security Law constituted a third of all political prisoners.

The Chun Government

Chun was the least popular of the autocratic leaders who ruled South Korea for its first four decades. His aim was evidently to continue Park's policies and methods, but the effect was rather different since South Korea was a less compliant subject for autocracy by 1980, and also because Chun was a man of less ability than Park. If there was another major difference between the governing style of Park and Chun, it was that Chun evinced a distinct propensity for totalitarian tactics, akin to those used by Kim Il Sung in the DPRK. He created a group of "purification camps" in remote mountain areas and filled them with 37,000 journalists, students, teachers, labor organizers, and civil servants, where, in classic Red Chinese, North Korean, and Vietnamese style, they were reeducated in an atmosphere of beatings, forced marathon runs, near-starvation, group criticism, and verbal indoctrination. The KCIA, renamed the Agency for National Security Planning (ANSP, also abbreviated NSP), issued a decree commanding newspapers to print Chun's photograph in every issue. A comedian who had the misfortune of resembling Chun Doo Hwan was banned from television (Cumings 2005, 384).

With a narrow base of support even among Korea's elites, Chun relied heavily on the loyalty of military officers in North Kyongsang province and Taegu, its capital. They were collectively known as the "T-K" group or the Hanahoe ("Club of One Mind"), and Chun put them in positions of power. George E. Ogle, author of *South Korea: Dissent within the Economic Miracle*, notes: "Under Chun's regime, *Hanahoe* members virtually monopolized politically sensitive positions . . . the Army Security Command, the Special Forces Command, the Joint Chiefs of Staff, and the Ministry of National Defense" (Ogle 1990, 99).

The Chun government was able to make the economy function, and after a rocky first year the economy rebounded and flourished again. Chun dubbed the fifth five-year plan (1982–86) "The Five-Year Economic and Social Development Plan." This plan shifted away from Park's emphasis on heavy industries and toward technology, precision machinery, and electronics, including televisions, VCRs, and computer products. As the new title implied, plans included the goal of improving social welfare.

To counter his unpopularity Chun lifted the midnight to dawn curfew that had been a part of Korean life since the Korean War nearly 30 years earlier, and he rescinded the requirement that students in middle and high school wear uniforms, one of the last remnants of Japanese colonial influence in Korea. On the other hand, overwhelmingly heavy-handed repression of the press and suppression of the universities continued. These moves by Chun, repressive on the one hand and liberalizing on the other, split the populace. A portion of Korea's expanding middle class disliked Chun. Much of it was more interested in making money, and he, like Park before him, was able to exploit fear of North Korea. Ultimately, what delayed South Korea's full democratization was factional division among Chun's opponents.

Soon after taking office President Chun Doo Hwan publicly announced that he intended to step down after one term. Journalists and historians are divided in their assessments of Chun's motives. Don Oberdorfer, author of *The Two Koreas*, who interviewed Chun during his presidency, believes that Chun was sincere and wanted to avoid the bloody end met by his predecessor (Oberdorfer 2001, 162). Chun

THE DESTRUCTION OF KAL FLIGHT 007

On August 31, 1983, a Korean airliner loaded with 269 people was shot out of the sky as it left the airspace over Kamchatka. The Kamchatka Peninsula is the easternmost part of the former Soviet Union, and it was a Soviet jet that shot down KAL Flight 007. There was some controversy about whether the Soviets knew it was a passenger airliner or believed instead that they were calling the South Koreans' bluff—that South Korea, in league with the United States, was using a passenger plane filled with intelligence-gathering equipment. The airliner did, after all, go by the number 007, like the fictional British spy James Bond.

Whatever the calculations of the Soviets, 269 people met a horrific death. The plane was disabled at 35,000 feet and took an agonizing 10 minutes to fall from the sky to the water. The passengers were mostly Koreans, but there were a number of other nationalities, including Americans. Among them was a member of Congress, Larry McDonald of Georgia.

Ronald Reagan, then president of the United States, called this incident "the Korean Airline massacre" and described it as "one of the most infamous and reprehensible acts of history" (Entman 1991). He cited the incident when he withdrew from arms control negotiations with the Soviet Union and began a massive nuclear military buildup the Soviets could not match and that eventually, some say, helped to precipitate the fall of the Soviet Union.

planned to support Roh Tae Woo, his co-conspirator in the 1979 military coup, as the next president by means of the rigged electoral college by which he himself had come to power; the constitution Chun had established did not provide for a direct election to the presidency. For Chun, even if he sincerely wanted to push South Korea down the road to democracy, retiring was bound to be difficult. He had acquired the presidency by violence and illegality, and once out of power he might face the vengeance of his surviving enemies.

His plans were complicated by the approach of the 1988 Olympics, which were to be held in Seoul. Though the selection of his country as the host of Olympics was a triumph for Chun, testifying to South Korea's growing prosperity and lending an aura of legitimacy and international recognition to his presidency, it also emboldened the opposition. They judged, correctly, that Chun would find it harder to practice his usual methods of intimidation and repression when the eyes of the world were focused on Seoul. Many Koreans, hoping that Chun's promise would translate at last into a truly democratic Korea, were furious when Chun announced that Roh Tae Woo would be "elected" president under the existing system. In June 1987 the discovery that a student had been tortured to death by the police led to nationwide demonstrations against the regime. The protesters' demands included direct election of the president and freedom of the press. More vocal and widespread than any since 1980, and subject to brutal suppression by riot police, the protest made some in the Reagan administration wonder if South Korea might be on the verge of a revolution, and the Americans put Chun under intense pressure to prepare for a more democratic transition.

On June 19 Roh Tae Woo announced that he would be the next ruling party candidate for president and he would welcome a change in the constitution so that direct election of the president would be possible. Elections were announced to be held on December 27, together with amnesty for political prisoners, including Kim Dae Jung, and abolishment of the existing law restricting the press. The constitution was quickly amended, and Roh, with a suddenly impressive record of giving Koreans what they wanted, ran an open and fair campaign for the presidency. Three major parties opposed Roh, each headed by a Kim—the same "three Kims" Chun had arrested in May 1980. Kim Jong Pil (b. 1926), often distinguished from the other Kims by his initials, J. P., had at one time been Park Chung Hee's closest adviser. A colonel when Park took over in 1961, Kim Jong Pil had advanced to KCIA director and prime minister under Park. So close that he had married Park's niece, he nonetheless fell into disfavor and even left the country for a time. Kim Young Sam (b. 1927), or Y. S. Kim, was a strong opposition leader. Once the youngest member ever of the National Assembly, he became a key leader in the fight for democracy during Park's and Chun's administrations. The third Kim was Kim Dae Jung, or D. J. Kim, the candidate who had surprised Park Chung Hee with a strong showing in 1971, who had been kidnapped, tortured, and imprisoned by Park, and who had barely escaped execution by Chun. His native Cholla region had lagged in economic development and remained bitter over the government's suppression of the Kwangju uprising of 1980.

None of the three Kims would either step aside or form an alliance to create a united opposition ticket. As the vote count would reflect, their constituencies were strongly rooted in rivalries between different Korean regions. A Korean-American professor, Manwoo Lee, has commented that "each candidate was like a Chinese warlord, occupying his own solid territory" (Manwoo Lee 1990, 49–51). Together, they received a high enough share of the electorate to represent a decisive rejection of the Chun years and Roh's party, yet the surprising result was that Roh won the December 1987 election with a 37 percent plurality. In a messy and unsatisfying way, a step toward genuine democracy had been taken.

The Administration of Roh Tae Woo (1988–1993)

Roh Tae Woo was inaugurated in February 1988 under a new constitution that was the most liberal in Korean history. The military was forbidden to engage in political activity. The president could stay in office for only one five-year term, and his powers were reduced—he could not dissolve the National Assembly, while the assembly had the power to investigate affairs of state and approve the president's choices for the Supreme Court. The National Security Law, which gave the government broad powers to arrest dissidents and labor leaders, was retained, but in theory the National Assembly's new powers could act as a break on the ruling party's abuse of this law. The ANSP, which essentially functioned as South Korea's secret police, was not dismantled, and there remained suspicions whether the military would accept its new nonpolitical role.

The first test of whether Roh would actually let this new constitution work, even when it thwarted his will, came in April 1988 when for the first time in its history the ruling party failed to win a legislative majority. The opposition proceeded to use its newfound power. It rejected Roh's nominee for chief justice, the first such rejection in Korean history, and launched an investigation into corruption and human rights abuses by Chun Doo Hwan. An investigation of Chun could be awkward for Roh. Not only were the two close friends who had risen in the ranks together, not only were they leaders from the same party, but Roh owed his position to Chun and Chun's first crime—the 1979 coup—had been enacted in partnership with Roh.

The hearings, which ran for months, were covered by South Korean radio and television. The *New York Times* called them "South Korea's version of the Watergate hearings": "People crowd around television sets in coffee shops. Taxi drivers keep the radio on all day. Janitors stop work to listen. . . . Two men on the street get into a shouting match, with one denouncing what he sees as conclusive evidence of corruption and the other criticizing the poor quality of the legislator's questioning" (Chira 1988). Roh pleaded on Chun's behalf for clemency, stopped short of pardoning him, and took steps to distance himself from the previous regime by firing members of Chun's cabinet. He suggested that Chun leave his home and return his embezzled property in exchange for avoiding prosecution.

Chun duly appeared on television on November 23, 1988, apologized to the nation, and said that he would fulfill these conditions. Many, perhaps most, South Koreans wanted retribution from Chun, but the majority in the National Assembly hesitated. Chun Doo Hwan still had powerful friends in the ROK's military forces. South Korea's experiment in freedom was still new. A coup was not out of the question.

As the hearings continued Chun took refuge in a Buddhist monastery in the mountains east of Seoul. When the investigation ended on February 1, 1989, 47 people had been arrested on charges of corruption or abuse of power, including the former mayor of Seoul, the former construction and transportation ministers, Chang Sedong (who had run the ANSP), and several of Chun's relatives. Chun, though disgraced, remained safe in his Buddhist monastery, and Roh Tae Woo had yet to be called to account for his own part in the misdeeds of Chun's regime.

By early 1988 the newspapers that had been closed by the Chun administration in 1980 reopened, and several new papers had begun circulation. The most notable of the new newspapers in Seoul was the left-leaning *Hangyoreh Shinmun.* Its name was pure Korean, unlike those of other newspapers, which had Sino-Korean names. The *Hangyoreh* was also different in format. Rather than a title block of Chinese characters that ran vertically, like all other South Korean newspapers except the *Seoul Daily, Hangyoreh* ran its title horizontally across the top of the page. In later years all the newspapers changed their formats to follow that of *Hangyoreh.*

Another measure of the recovered strength of the South Korean press was the flowering of the provincial newspapers. Before 1980 each provincial capital had two newspapers; between 1980 and 1987 each had only one. After 1987 each provincial capital had three daily newspapers. Similarly, the broadcast media began to flourish after 1987. Although TBC, the television station that Chun had closed, did not revive, a new national station, private and independent, was established, the Seoul Broadcasting System (SBS). A cable television industry has since developed.

The 1988 Olympic Games went smoothly, showcasing South Korea to the world as an example not just of economic development but also of peaceful transition from military to elected government. The Seoul Olympics also stimulated South Korea's economy, more than paying for themselves.

Roh's five-year plan (1987–91), the sixth in the series of plans inaugurated by Park in 1962, pursued many of the same goals of the Chun government, but the international trade climate dictated some domestic changes. Industries once subsidized by the government were no longer subsidized, and import tariffs that had protected domestic industries were lifted. This exposed domestic products to foreign competition. In return foreign trading partners lifted their own tariffs on imports from South Korea.

The Roh administration enjoyed historic success in the area of diplomacy. In 1990, before the fall of Communism in the Soviet Union and Eastern Europe, Roh made history by meeting with Soviet premier Mikhail Gorbachev. Setting aside their cold war and Korean War differences, South Korea and the Soviet Union decided to exchange diplomats and normalize relations. This was a great blow to North Korea. Soviet and South Korean ties developed rapidly, leading to large-scale trade between the former enemies.

South Korea also gained UN recognition under the Roh administration. This development was a product of the end of the cold war, which ended with the gradual liberalization of the Soviet Union under Mikhail Gorbachev in the late 1980s. Both Koreas had been kept out of the United Nations for four decades by the Security Council vetoes of the Soviet Union (blocking the ROK) and the United States (blocking the DPRK) as well as their irreconcilable claims on one another's territory. In 1991 South Korea dropped its claim over the North; North Korea, under pressure from China (now its sole ally), announced that it had "no choice" but to apply for UN membership as well, even though dual membership would be an obstacle to unification. Both countries joined the United Nations that year.

There is no question that the administration of Roh Tae Woo was more democratic than any that Korea had experienced in its history. South Koreans still did not enjoy the freedom of people in a Western democracy, however. The repressive state structures such as the ANSP and repressive laws such as the National Security Law still existed to hem in ROK citizens who might be a threat to the state. Before he was out of office Roh used them to break up strikes that, Roh said, were threatening to make Korean labor too expensive for the world market.

The ROK (like the United States and Japan) was in recession at the time, but Roh, who would later be found to have taken extensive bribes and kickbacks from Korea's business leaders, blamed his country's labor movement for South Korea's slowing growth.

On January 23, 1990, Roh Tae Woo suddenly announced that he had made an alliance with longtime opposition leaders Kim Young Sam and Kim Jong Pil, accomplishing a three-party merger that would create a strong single conservative party similar to the one that had dominated Japan since the end of American occupation. Even the names were similar: The Japanese governing party was the Liberal Democratic Party; the new Korean coalition was the Democratic Liberal Party. For Roh it was a way to break a deadlock in the National Assembly, which had been dominated by his opposition since shortly after his election. For Kim Young Sam it was a way to leapfrog to the presidency over his rival, Kim Dae Jong of Cholla. Kim joined the government party, and Roh supported his run for president.

The Administration of Kim Young Sam (1993–1998)

The partnership was successful: Kim Young Sam was elected in late 1992 with slightly more than 40 percent of the vote and took office in February 1993. He was the second president in South Korea's history to come to office in what is generally regarded as a free and fair election and the first person without a military background to be so elected. Almost immediately he removed from key security positions several members of Chun's old Hanahoe ("Club of One") group that Roh had retained in office.

Loyal to his alliance, Kim resisted pressure to prosecute Chun and Roh for corruption, abuse of power, and their joint participation in the illegal coup that that brought Chun to power after Park's assassination. He argued that history would be their judge. In 1995, however, evidence surfaced that both former presidents had secret bank accounts worth hundreds of millions of dollars. Kim Young Sam arrested them for their bribe-taking and financial corruption. While the men were in custody, activists pressed the government to bring charges of mutiny for the military revolt of December 12, 1979, and sedition for taking over the government by military force on May 18, 1980. Both men were tried on charges of corruption and murder in 1996. Chun was found guilty on all charges and sentenced to death. Roh was found guilty and sentenced to life in prison. After appeals the sentences were reduced to life for Chun and 17 years for Roh. In early 1998 they were both pardoned and released by the next president, Kim Dae Jung.

Students shout death to former presidents Chun Doo Hwan and Roh Tae Woo during a trial at the courthouse in Seoul on Monday, August 5, 1996. The prosecution demanded the death sentence for Chun Doo Hwan and life imprisonment for Roh Tae Woo. (AP Photo/ Ahn Young-Joon)

Apart from the trial of Chun and Roh, Kim Young Sam's administration was outwardly uneventful until his last months in office. Prosperity and continued economic growth were the order of the day. Kim's five-year plan (1992–96) focused on high-tech fields, and its greatest concern was to transform the economy from one reliant on low wages to one based on innovative technology. Growth in South Korea, one of Asia's mighty economic "tigers" in the parlance of the 1990s, continued to be strong, assisted by an enormous flow of funds by investors searching for the high rates of return that emerging markets offered.

However, as U.S. Federal Reserve Chairman Alan Greenspan would observe, "In retrospect, it is clear that more investment monies flowed into these economies than could be profitably employed at modest risk" (Nanto 1998). In 1997 South Korea, closely linked to the Asian regional economy and the worldwide financial system, fell prey to the financial contagion that began in Thailand in July 1997 and by November had spread to Indonesia, South Korea, and Japan. Foreign investors began pulling their money out of Korea, lenders called in debts, and the financial sector threatened collapse. To keep the economy afloat, South Korea needed bailout loans from the International Monetary Fund (IMF) totaling $57 billion, the largest loan the IMF had ever given. Usual IMF policy is that a member state can borrow five times the amount it pays into the fund. South Korea, however, needed to borrow 19 times this amount. Under the terms of the loans, several South Korean banks with high debts collapsed, as did several highly leveraged companies.

The financial crisis nearly bankrupted South Korea. One indicator of its severity was the won-to-dollar exchange rate. Before the crisis one U.S. dollar exchanged for about 800 South Korean won; after the collapse the exchange rate went as high as 2,000 won to the dollar before settling at around 1,200 won. Another indicator was gross national product (GNP) per capita. In 1994 South Korea had just crossed the $10,000 threshold, a sign of prosperity in a developing nation. After the crash that figure fell to the $6,000 range. South Koreans blamed Kim Young Sam for failing to observe the critical foreign reserves and other economic indicators, and his administration left under a cloud of embarrassment: He had presided over one of the largest economic collapses in recent history.

The 1997 Election

In the presidential election held in December 1997, the major candidates were Kim Dae Jung, Kim Jong Pil, and the newcomer Lee Hoi Chang (b. 1935). Lee, a former judge and the head of the government's audit bureau, was widely regarded as "Mr. Clean"—a man with a perfect record. A scandal surrounded him anyway: He had two sons, and somehow neither had served in the military. Both, though otherwise healthy, had been exempted from service on the basis of low body weight. In a country where the draft is universal, this smacked of privilege, if not abuse of power. Then, in a surprise move Kim Dae Jung made an alliance with Kim Jong Pil, his longtime rival. The unexpected move and Lee's sudden embarrassment netted Kim Dae Jung the votes he needed.

Kim Dae Jung's election in 1997 was a real milestone in South Korea's democratic development. Syngman Rhee's elections were tainted by American support and then by his own manipulation of the polls. Park Chung Hee and Chun Doo Hwan came to power by force. Roh Tae Woo, though popularly elected, built his political base on his association with Chun and their common military exploits. Kim Young Sam had been a longtime opposition leader, but he was elected by defecting

Two main opposition leaders, Kim Dae Jung, left, and Kim Jong Pil, right, raise their hands before a joint rally to denounce the ruling party's recruitment of lawmakers-elect at Boraemae Park in Seoul on Sunday, May 26, 1996. About 40,000 supporters attended this rally. (AP Photo/Yonhap)

to the majority party, the party of the military. The election of Kim Dae Jung was the first peaceful transfer of power to the opposition party in South Korea's history.

The Kim Dae Jung Administration (1998–2002)

Kim Dae Jung was elected on a pledge to work for democratic reform, attack corruption in government and business, curb the power of *chaebols*, and change policies that promoted economic growth at the expense of democracy. He promised, in addition, to take steps toward reconciliation with North Korea that might lead one day to a reunification of the two countries. Though his tenure in office would not be without its scandals and disappointments, it marked a decisive shift in the politics of the Republic of Korea.

Even in the midst of a financial crisis, the new president made the further democratization of South Korea an immediate priority. Whereas Kim Young Sam had put his allies in charge of the ANSP, Kim Dae Jung took steps to reduce its power, its funding, and its staff. He turned the

ANSP's focus away from domestic spying toward the more legitimate function of gathering intelligence about North Korea and sponsored an investigation that revealed its structure and its past activities to the people of South Korea. In his first year in office, Kim's government passed an amnesty for all those political prisoners who had renounced their antigovernment views. He then broadened the amnesty to include those who remained obdurate (or steadfast, depending on one's point of view). Among those released was Woo Yong Gak, who had spent almost 40 years in prison for refusing to renounce his loyalty to North Korea. After decades when workers had organized bravely in the face of government repression, Kim Dae Jung facilitated a remarkable change in labor's position in the system, bringing labor leaders together with business and government in an attempt to fairly spread the sacrifice demanded by the International Monetary Fund (IMF) in exchange for its assistance to South Korea.

Upon taking office in February 1998, Kim had to deal with an ailing economy. The crash had struck South Korea just three months before, and Kim found it necessary to seek help from the IMF, which meant giving in to the IMF's free trade policies, policies that often make the leaders who must help to implement them extremely unpopular. As it happened, however, the IMF requirements for South Korea were not so different from the economic reforms that Kim had been calling for throughout South Korea. They included greater transparency in exchange for their loans and an improved debt-to-equity ratio. These demands as well the financial crisis itself put pressure on the *chaebol*, the largest of which, Daewoo, went bankrupt. By 1999 South Korea had returned to its previous high growth rates—11 percent in 1999 and 9 percent in 2000. The U.S. recession in 2001 slowed South Korean growth to 6 percent.

The most ambitious of Kim Dae Jung's initiatives was his Sunshine Policy of gradual engagement and reconciliation with North Korea. Kim Dae Jung was not the first ROK president to make moves in that direction, but he was by far the most serious and persistent. His rather one-sided efforts to woo a secretive and troubled DPRK—one in the midst of a far more serious economic crisis than South Korea's—brought him a mixed response from North Korea's leader, Kim Jong Il, hostility from the United States, and ultimately reduced his popularity in his own country.

The thankless campaign began as soon as Kim Dae Jung took office. He mentioned it in his inaugural address, reminding his audience of a need to respect the pride of North Koreans and suggesting a multistage process under which the DPRK and the ROK would be linked in a federal system. Kim laid down three general principles he said should guide the process: "First, we will never tolerate armed provocation of any kind. Secondly, we do not have any intention to undermine or absorb North Korea. Third, we will actively push reconciliation and

South Korean students and jobless people fill out application forms during the 2001 "job fairs" at Hanyang University in Seoul on April 20, 2001. The unemployment rate was 4.8 percent for March according to the National Statistical Office. (AP Photo/Ahn Young Joon)

cooperation between the South and North beginning with those areas which can be most easily agreed upon" (Oberdorfer 2001, 407). He lowered barriers to trade with North Korea and met with Western leaders to win cooperation for the policy.

North Korea itself, for whatever motives, repeatedly put obstacles in the path of Kim's attempts at engagement. In June 1998 a North Korean submarine was found caught in South Korean fishing nets, and its crew was captured. The sub was of a special Yugo class of small subs the DPRK used to drop off spies and commandos (as it had attempted to do in a similar incident in 1996), and three weeks later the body of a dead North Korean commando was discovered off the South Korean coast. Kim Dae Jong, at some risk to his political reputation, chose to take the incident as an attempt by hard-liners within the DPRK to derail a process that others in the country favored, and after appropriate measures to step up ROK alertness, he continued to pursue engagement. In 2000 Kim Dae Jong and Kim Jong Il met in the DPRK capital of Pyongyang, where the two leaders posed for cameras, representatives from the North and South established joint business ventures, and separated Korean families were tearfully united. Kim Dae Jung was awarded the Nobel Peace Prize for his efforts on behalf of unification.

Unfortunately, the shadow of scandal later fell over these efforts. After he left office evidence came to light that Kim Dae Jung had bribed the DPRK to participate, with payments of at least $150 million. Long before this "cash-for-summit" scandal broke, however, the Sunshine Policy had fallen victim to North Korea's apparent ambitions to become a nuclear weapons state and to U.S. president George W. Bush's decision to label North Korea a member of the "axis of evil" in his January 29, 2002, State of the Union speech. Another unrelated scandal helped dampen enthusiasm for Kim Dae Jung's presidency: In 2002 his son Kim Hong Up was found guilty of bribery, fined more than $400,000, and sentenced to three and a half years in prison. His two other sons also were convicted on corruption charges.

Despite Kim Hong Up's conviction for bribery and despite an economy that was falling again, Kim successfully promoted his pick for a successor, a relatively obscure former human rights lawyer and minister of Maritime Affairs and Fisheries named Roh Moo Hyun (1946–2009). After a campaign in which he emphasized his willingness to stand up to the United States—even saying that Korea might remain "neutral" in a war between the United States and the DPRK—Roh won a narrow victory over his rival, Lee Hoi Chang (b. 1935) who had previously been defeated by Kim Dae Jung.

Roh Moo Hyun's Administration (2003–2008)

No less idealistic and ambitious than Kim Dae Jung, Roh proved to be a less skillful politician. His term of office was troubled almost from the outset, and Roh had to expend much of his energy on a struggle for political survival. When Roh took office South Korea's conservative, right-leaning Grand National Party (GNP) held a plurality of seats and effective control of the National Assembly. In a way, the GNP was the same conservative party that, under different names, had been in control of the National Assembly for more than four decades. In an attempt to alter this pattern, Roh and his supporters formed the Yeollin Uri Party ("Our Open Party," often called the Uri Party), a center-left, social-democratic party made up of defectors from the minority Millennium Party and several members of the Grand National Party. The party stood for increased assistance to low-income Koreans, decreased emphasis on economic growth at any cost, engagement with North Korea, and opposition to the U.S. hard-line approach to North Korea.

Roh, while not joining the Uri Party, openly supported it in the run-up to National Assembly elections. If the Uri Party won enough seats, the power of the conservatives would be broken and he would have an ally for his legislative program. His open endorsement of the party was a technical breech of the rules, and his opponents in the National Assembly promptly seized on it to impeach him. Past presidents of the Republic of Korea had done some terrible things, but none of them had ever been impeached. By a two-thirds majority Roh was stripped of his powers, and the prime minister assumed his powers. Once again the streets of Seoul filled with angry protesters, many wearing yellow scarves that identified them as supporters of the Uri Party and others supporting his impeachment. One Roh supporter set himself on fire.

While South Korea's Constitutional Court prepared to deliberate the legality of Roh's impeachment, the people went to the polls again, and they delivered a sharp rebuke to the GNP. The Uri Party won 152 seats, giving it a slender majority in the 299-seat National Assembly. With other center and left-leaning parties winning a handful of votes, the conservative party was now in the minority. Soon afterward the Constitutional Court overturned Roh's impeachment, declaring that while Roh had violated a law, his error was not serious enough to warrant his removal from office.

Despite this victory, Roh had a hard time pleasing the South Korean public and often seemed to be caught between the expectations of the right and left. Having run for president by campaigning against U.S. policy, he nevertheless made South Korea a part of U.S. president

Bush's small coalition in the second Gulf War and sent 3,000 ROK troops to fight in Iraq. With the United States still defending the DMZ between North and South Korea, Roh could hardly refuse, but the move angered many South Koreans who had voted for Roh. U.S. president Bush showed himself visibly cool to Roh because of their differences over North Korea and perhaps also because of their differences of ideology, so South Koreans who favored warm relations with the United States were not pleased with Roh either. His attempts to continue Kim Dae Jong's Sunshine Policy began to look more and more misguided as North Korea made increasingly aggressive moves in its showdown with the United States, including withdrawing from the Nuclear Nonproliferation Treaty in 2003, test-firing long-range missiles, and detonating a nuclear weapon in 2006.

By the time of South Korea's next presidential election, none of these issues mattered much, as the country's economic growth had slowed considerably. Unemployment was high among the young, housing prices were high, and rising labor costs (an unfortunate side effect of a fair distribution of wealth) were making it hard for small and medium-sized businesses to compete with their counterparts in poorer countries.

The economic malaise that marked the end of Roh's term made it a foregone conclusion that conservatives would win back control of the National Assembly and that a conservative candidate would win the presidency. Lee Myung Bak, the former mayor of Seoul, was a pragmatic politician who promised stronger ties with the United States and a slower journey toward rapprochement with North Korea. As election time approached Lee had an enormous lead in the polls, so much so that there was not much excitement attached to the election.

As voters in democratic countries often do, South Koreans blamed the majority party for the condition of the economy and threw it out of office. Voter turnout was low for South Korea, as if its people had begun to take the franchise for granted. That, too, was their right. It is hard to think of any nation whose people have paid a higher cost for it.

Lee Myung Bak's Administration (2008–present)

Lee Myung Bak was elected on a conservative platform and inaugurated in February 2008. He promised to improve the economy and take a hard line against North Korea. Although North Korea had welcomed two summit meetings, established a trade zone along its border with South Korea, and opened two tourist sites to South Koreans (first the Diamond Mountains on the east coast and later the old capital of

243

Kaesong just north of the DMZ), it continued to provoke international concerns by exploding a nuclear device and launching missiles into the North Pacific.

Excursions to the Diamond Mountains, which had provided significant foreign exchange to North Korea, were suspended indefinitely when a woman in her early 50s wandered off the path and was shot and killed by a North Korean guard in July 2008. South Korea demanded on apology, but North Korea refused, saying its guard was only obeying standing orders.

One of the successes that Lee rode into the Blue House was his transformation of a section of Seoul by restoring a once-polluted stream into a showpiece of nature in the middle of the city. Initially opposed by taxi and bus drivers, once the stream was completed its beauty swept the population of Seoul off its feet. However, Lee's administration thus far has been less successful. Once nicknamed the "bulldozer" because of his style of pushing his agenda through all opposition, as president Lee was no longer able to bulldoze his programs past the opposition. Hampered by the economic slowdown that spilled over from the U.S. recession in 2008–09, Lee has not been able to deliver on his promise of an economic recovery.

In early 2009 Lee vigorously pursued corruption charges against his predecessor, Roh Moo Hyun. Roh denied the charges at first, but then admitted to having taken money. On the eve of turning himself in for arrest, he requested to visit his home in the countryside. While hiking up a small mountain overlooking his home, he plunged off a sharp precipice. The nation turned on President Lee for having pushed the investigation when the alleged bribery was relatively small. By mid-2009 Lee's approval ratings had fallen very low.

8

NORTH KOREA
(1945–2009)

Officially named the Democratic People's Republic of Korea (DPRK), North Korea is neither democratic nor a republic. Rather, it is a dictatorship. The country has had just two leaders in the more than half-century of its existence: Kim Il Sung (1912–94) from 1948 to 1994 and his son Kim Jong Il (b. 1943), who has been in control since 1994.

North Korea is a communist country. Its institutions are closely modeled on those of the Soviet Union, and its methods of leadership resemble those used by the Soviet dictator Joseph Stalin during the 1930s and 1940s. The resemblance has many facets, including North Korea's command economy, the cult of personality that surrounds its leader, the abusive style of its propaganda, and the government's intrusions into the personal and mental lives of its citizens, who suffer from malnutrition yet are required to shout that they live in a utopia. Yet some important aspects of the DPRK's governing style and ideology are entirely its own and unique in the communist world. One special feature of North Korea is its extremely secluded, isolationist nature, harkening back to the isolation of the Choson era, so that it seems more appropriate than ever to call this half of Korea a "hermit state." It and Cuba are the only communist states ever to have a hereditary succession, and it has carried the public adulation of its leader to religious extremes that might have embarrassed even Stalin. North Koreans, expressing the thoughts of their leader, describe their state as independent and self-reliant. They have a unique word for this stance, *juche,* a philosophy supposedly originated by Kim Il Sung, who DPRK propaganda insists was a genius, and best interpreted by his son Kim Jong Il, also described as a genius in official pronouncements. To judge by their speech and behavior (strictly controlled, so their actual feelings are a mystery) North Koreans are fiercely proud of the concept. They insist that it is a model for the world to emulate.

North Korean leaders have limited their diplomatic and trade contacts even within the communist world. The collapse of international communism in the late 1980s left the DPRK friendless and unable or unwilling to make the reforms that were bringing a better life to the people of China, Russia, Eastern Europe, and Vietnam. The country's only bargaining tools were its ability to produce a nuclear weapon and a history of unpredictable behavior that made outsiders wonder if North Korea would use the weapon even if it meant suicide.

Rival Communist Factions

After the Japanese withdrew from Korea on August 15, 1945, four factions of Korean communists vied for power: the guerrilla faction, the Russian faction, the Chinese faction, and the South Korean faction. Each faction struggled for supremacy while supposedly working together for the achievement of common goals within the Korean Workers' Party (KWP), the DPRK's Communist Party, which thoroughly controlled the state by the time the DPRK was founded. Each faction had its own claim as the legitimate leader of Korea after World War II. Kim Il Sung, who led the KWP and thus the DPRK at the country's founding on September 9, 1948, was head of the faction that ultimately bested all the others. But his task was not easy.

Kim Il Sung led the guerrilla faction, a group of freedom fighters who had battled the Japanese in Manchuria during the Japanese occupation. Despite their exile the guerrilla faction claimed the right to govern because of its activity against the Japanese. Kim, a senior officer in the Red Army, had won the trust of Soviet leaders and had the backing of the Soviet Union. In *The Guerrilla Dynasty*, a 1999 study of North Korea's leadership, Adrian Buzo advances the idea that the views of this group were strongly influenced by their intense but rather narrow experiences as guerrilla fighters with a limited exposure to the outside world or even to the Korean communist movement, creating a collective personality like that of Kim Il Sung: "Rural, patchily educated, ideologically unsophisticated, suspicious of outside linkages, rigidly disciplined, and inured to hardship" (Buzo 2008, 25). The Soviet Union favored Kim because he had no political base of his own in Korea and therefore seemed dependent on them and controllable. Thanks to Kim's political skills, ruthlessness, the patronage of the Soviet Union, and a certain amount of luck, this group came to dominate the DPRK's communist oligarchy in its early years, and after the Korean War it gradually won a complete monopoly of power. As it did so, the North Korean government became increasingly rigid and hostile to divergent views.

What distinguished the Russian faction from Kim Il Sung's guerrilla faction, which was also based in Russia, was that its members had been in Russia for a generation or two. Most of the Koreans who had come to Russia more recently, in the 1930s, had been killed in 1937 under suspicions of being Japanese spies in one of the periodic purges during which Stalin eliminated entire categories of people. Thus, the members of the Russian faction had little knowledge of Korean life and little connection to Korea's native communist movement either in Korea or Shanghai. However, they were well educated, had a good understanding of life outside Korea, and were thoroughly grounded in Soviet institutions and the Soviet version of communist ideology. Their claim to legitimacy was based on their pedigree as communists: They had lived through the Russian Revolution of 1917 and had served in the Red Army. Following the liberation, in which they were not allowed to participate, these Russian Koreans came into Korea with the Red Army, serving as translators and power brokers. Their leader was a Korean Russian named Alexei Ivanovich Hagai (Ho Ka'ae in Korean; 1908–53).

At the time of the Korean War, Kim Il Sung, though the dominant figure and the head of state, did not yet have complete control over the DPRK or its policies and might theoretically have been outmaneuvered and replaced by some abler individual. With tactics similar to those that brought Stalin virtually absolute power following the death of Lenin, Kim Il Sung played other men and factions against each other within the Korean Workers' Party bureaucracy. He made temporary alliances to eliminate his rivals, then turned against his former allies. To solidify his leadership position Kim Il Sung set out to first discredit the Russian faction. In 1951, when Hagai was the number-two man in the DPRK, Kim Il Sung demoted him over a conflict about the rules for party membership. However, Hagai was too important and had too many supporters to simply be eliminated. In what some analysts plausibly regard as a plot to eliminate him, Hagai was put in charge of agriculture and the water reservoirs, which were a frequent target of U.S. bombing. When, inevitably, the reservoirs were bombed on Hagai's watch, Kim Il Sung accused him of mismanagement and neglect of his duties. Following this accusation in 1953, Hagai reportedly committed suicide. It is possible that he was actually murdered (Lankov 2002, 150). Kim could conveniently blame the Soviet Koreans for wartime setbacks in

1953, because Soviet assistance, which had been key to North Korean advances early in the Korean War, had by then been eclipsed by Chinese support. In fact, North Korea's changing alliances between the Soviets and the Chinese dominate much of its history. Kim Il Sung was adroit at playing one against the other to the advantage of North Korean independence—and his own position.

Kim Il Sung next saw to the weakening of the Chinese faction. The first scapegoat was Mu Chong (1904–51), its leader. Mu had spent much of the previous decade with Mao Zedong in Yenan and was a veteran of the Long March of 1934–35, a retreat that has a place in Chinese communist history roughly equivalent to the place that Valley Forge has in American history. In that campaign the Chinese communists formed the alliances and strategies that would eventually lead to their conquest of China. Though Mu took part in these seminal events, his fortunes in Korea were not the same as Mao's in China. In October 1950 following MacArthur's Inchon landing, U.S. forces pushed all the way to the Chinese border. A few months later Mu Chong was among several generals blamed for these military reverses at a Korean Workers' Party Congress in December; he fled to China and died soon afterwards. In 1953 Kim saw to it that a second Korean communist leader from China, Pak Il-u (1911–?), who had been serving as both Kim's minister of the interior and Mao's representative to Korea, was removed from his posts; in 1955 Pak Il-u was expelled from the Korean Workers' Party on the charge of "factionalist and anti-party activities" (Nam 1974, 108). (The minister of the interior was in charge of internal security, not parks and farmland, as in some countries.) Others in the Chinese faction remained in positions of leadership during the Korean War, permitting Kim to continue appealing to the Chinese for support, but after the war many of these holdouts were purged as well.

The South Korean faction of communists should have had the strongest claim to power because its members had fought the Japanese on Korean soil. Most had been jailed at least once by the Japanese police, yet they stayed to lead the struggle within the borders of Korea. Their leader, Pak Honyong (d. 1955), was the most powerful man in the communist movement in Korea during the late colonial period. Before and during the war, thousands of South Korean communists were trained in North Korea for guerilla activities (Nam 1974, 95) that were meant to spark a revolution in the south, and prior to the Korean War Pak Honyong had led Kim Il Sung to expect a massive uprising of communists in South Korea that would assist in the conquest and reunification of the country. However, while uprisings and guerrilla actions took place during the war, they did not do so on the scale that Pak had promised, which made Pak vulnerable. Unlike the Chinese and Russian factions, which had the support of outside groups, the domestic faction of communists had no outside backer. Kim Il Sung needed Chinese and Soviet aid to rebuild from the war's destruction; he lost no such assistance by dismissing the domestic faction.

Kim's official view of the Korean War held the southern communists responsible for the loss of the south. Before the war formally ended, in a meeting of the central committee in December 1952, Kim and his group attacked those who had been members of the South Korean Workers' Party. In early 1953 rumors were spread that the southerners were planning a coup. On August 3, 1953, posters appeared on the streets of Pyongyang announcing the trial of 12 former leading members of the South Korean Workers' Party for acting as spies for the "American imperialists" and having come to the north "on orders from American masters" in order to "establish capitalist domination of the country" (Nam 1974, 94). Pak Honyong, then minister of foreign affairs, was arrested and charged with treason. Found guilty in 1953 after a four-day trial, he was not executed until 1955. The delay may be evidence that Kim was at first uncertain of his control but eventually became so confident in his mastery that he could execute a once-prominent colleague.

Of the remaining leaders who had roots in the southern half of the peninsula, many were likewise arrested, charged with crimes, and either executed or sent to reeducation camps. For instance, Yi Sungyop (1905–53), the minister of state control, was one of the 12 arrested on August 3. He was eliminated after being charged with spying for the United States. Other prominent southerners remained loyal to Kim, however, and held significant positions for the next 20 years.

Kim Il Sung's Stalinist Style

In virtually every political move Kim Il Sung had so far made and in most of his future behavior, he showed himself to be a thoroughgoing Stalinist. Like Stalin, he established a cult of personality in which he, the leader, came to embody the state. Praise of the leader equaled praise of the state; criticism of the leader was treason, and under both Stalin and Kim dissent was crushed. Kim also took his cue from the career of Stalin in his tactics when he formed temporary alliances and eliminated rivals within the party bureaucracy. He was Stalinist in his control of information and use of propaganda inside and outside the state, in his insistence that the country was threatened by a capitalist world that wished to destroy its revolution, and in his tendency to attribute setbacks to conspiracies by spies and saboteurs (until he had eliminated his rivals, after which the accusations of treason ended).

Kim was Stalinist as well in his economic development policy, which was consistently driven by a rigid and simplistic communist ideology and a belief that the primary purpose of economic development should be to ready the state for war. Though Kim and many of the men closest to him came originally from a peasant background, he seems to have been little interested in the lives of peasants. He saw agriculture's job as the feeding of soldiers and factory workers, and he forced Korea's farmers to join huge communist collectives, with the ultimate goal (never quite achieved) of turning farmers into wage earners. Like Stalin, he consistently allocated a disproportionate share of state resources to heavy industry—industry of the kind that was important to warfare.

The Soviet Union's development of heavy industry in the 1930s, achieved by forcing great sacrifices on the Russian people, was widely credited with its defeat of the Nazis. If the forced development of heavy industry at the expense of all other sectors of the economy had worked for the Soviet Union, then the same methods would work for the DPRK—or so its leader appeared to believe. The war that Kim Il Sung was preparing his country for was not World War III, however, but a second round of the Korean War, which would once and for all unify Korea as a communist state. To build socialism as he understood it, to unify Korea, and to retain power were Kim Il Sung's three primary aims as the leader of the DPRK. He pursued them unwaveringly from the time he took power until his death, after which his son Kim Jong Il has pursued them just as unwaveringly.

As in Stalin's Russia (and also as in Park Chung Hee's South Korea), goals for the whole country's economic growth were set in a series of multiyear plans. In contrast to South Korea, the economy was micromanaged from the top. Each factory and collective was given highly specific objectives, and workers and peasants were mobilized by ideological and nationalistic exhortations and encouraged to meet or beat preset numerical goals of production. Teams of workers were encouraged to compete with each other in "speed battles." Since ideology (rather than individual self-interest) was the driver of both workers' and managers' efforts, a Korean Workers' Party committee was put in charge of production both at agricultural cooperatives and factories. In agriculture this method was named the "Chongsan-ni" model (after a cooperative where this system was supposed to have produced wonderful results), and in industry it was named the "Taean Work System," after the factory where it was first used (Oh and Hassig 2000, 63).

In the 1950s and the early 1960s, as the DPRK recovered from the ravages of the Korean War, Kim Il Sung's methods resulted in rapid growth for the North Korean economy and perhaps in an improved life for most of its people. For those under the top level (where party bigwigs enjoyed special privi-

Kim Il Sung, chairman of the Central Committee of the Workers' Party of Korea and premier of the cabinet of the DPRK, in April 1962 (AP Photo)

leges and material benefits, as they did in the Soviet Union), life was hard. Meat and fish were rare luxuries, but the distribution of goods was fairer than it had previously been. Education was more widely available. Every citizen not deemed an enemy of the state was assured a job and the bare means of subsistence. During this period the economy of the DPRK grew rapidly and on a per capita basis was well ahead of the ROK.

As the experience of the Soviet Union, the People's Republic of China, and the DPRK all show, however, micromanaged, top-down economic planning has severe limits. There is initial fast growth based on the building of infrastructure and the mobilization of previously underutilized manpower and industrial capacity. Then there is stagnation. The absence of feedback between different sectors of the economy leads to bottlenecks in the system or the overproduction of goods for which there is no immediate use. Mistakes like these could apply to entire factories: In the 1980s the Soviet Union helped North Korea build a factory capable of producing 10 million ball bearings every year; the factory was successfully completed, but there was no demand either in Korea or outside for the bearings (Buzo 1999, 169–170).

In the DPRK central planning was more than usually inept, since Kim Il Sung had a mistrust of professional expertise and made a point of putting undereducated but loyal Communist bureaucrats from his guerrilla faction in charge of the economy. Party bureaucrats and managers with political pull would get the resources they needed for their projects so that they would meet their goals under the multiyear plan, while those without such pull would not, regardless of which projects were really essential.

Kim Il Sung's management of the North Korean economy was also misguided in one of its core principles—autarky, the goal of making North Korea economically self-sufficient with a minimum reliance on imports from and exports to other countries. Autarky had been the economic goal of Japan and to a degree of the Soviet Union in the 1930s; it was in part a reaction to the international depression of that period, when a sharp decline in world trade made self-sufficiency seem necessary. This goal was less appropriate to the postwar era, when world trade expanded, and less practical for relatively small North Korea than for the vast Soviet Union or imperial Japan (which had conquered Korea and Manchuria in pursuit of autarky). Though the word *juche* is sometimes translated as "self-reliance," and economic self-sufficiency was one of its principle goals, the DPRK has always depended on foreign aid; only the sources of the aid have changed over the years.

The De-Stalinization Struggle

Joseph Stalin died in 1953. In 1956 Nikita Khrushchev (1894–1971), first secretary of the Soviet Communist Party, began to implement a policy of "de-Stalinization" that called for an end to cults of personality, such as those built up by Stalin, Mao, and Kim Il Sung. Stalinists were deposed throughout Eastern Europe at Khrushchev's bidding. In summer 1956 Khrushchev summoned Kim to Moscow for six weeks of training in the new Soviet leadership style. It must have been a bitter pill for Kim to swallow.

In the meantime Kim's rivals at home were adjusting to the new communist world order radiating from Moscow. Pak Changok (d. 1956), the leader of the Russian faction, and Choe Changik (1896–1957), the leader of the Chinese faction, prepared a plan to discredit Kim Il Sung as a Stalinist. At the next general meeting of the Central Committee, scheduled soon after Kim's return from Moscow, they were going to denounce Kim on the same grounds that Khrushchev had censured Stalin.

Kim struck first by postponing the meeting for one month. This gave him time to line up his allies. When the Central Committee met and Pak and Choe launched their attack on Kim's old-fashioned Stalinist methods, Kim and his side were ready to respond. The speeches of Pak, Choe, and other critics met with such boos and heckling that they could hardly be heard. Kim won the day, and his opponents were expelled from the party. Kim's critics at the 1956 meeting accused him of ignoring the needs of his people for the sake of developing industry, of creating a police state, and of fostering a cult of personality.

The Soviets and the Chinese did not stand idly by as their Korean allies were dismissed. In September 1956 they sent a combined delegation to correct the abuses in North Korea. Kim was told to stop the purges and reinstate the leaders of the Chinese and Soviet factions. A second meeting of the Central Committee was held on September 23, at which the expelled leaders were welcomed back into the party with full privileges.

Still, Kim was determined to have his way, and in 1957 he unleashed another series of purges against members of the Chinese and Soviet factions. He kept some members of the discredited factions in leadership positions while removing other, stronger ones. From 1957 to 1961 many of the Chinese faction returned to China, and many of the Russian faction returned to the Soviet Union. Kim and his faction were in complete control. Nor did the token survivors of the purges last long. Once they had served their purpose, they, too, were dismissed.

Owing to the repeated purges of the 1950s and 1960s, the ruling elite of North Korea is a very tight-knit group. It consists of the old guerrilla faction who served Kim Il Sung and over the years intermarried with the new leadership, and its members are now related through ties of kinship and marriage. The core leaders in charge of North Korea today are virtually one extended family.

One reason Kim Il Sung was successful in purging the Chinese and Russian factions was that he justified the purges as essential measures for national independence. Kim claimed to be untainted by foreign influence, and he called into question the motivations and loyalties of those supporting the Soviet and Chinese factions. Kim loyalists argue that although communism itself originated outside Korea, Kim tailored the doctrine to fit Korean needs.

TYRANNY

It is difficult to exaggerate the daily violation of personal liberty that is the norm in Kim Il Sung and Kim Jong Il's North Korea. Despite a written constitution that provides guarantees of freedom of speech, assembly, residence, and association, people live highly regimented lives. Their work is outlined in detail at the beginning of each day, and they are required to attend political study sessions after their day's work is done. In apartments, houses, and public buildings a public address speaker wired to a local transmitter blares out official local news, and sound trucks in the streets broadcast local announcements—for example, that a group of foreigners is about to come to town, and residents should either stay indoors or if they leave the house wear their best clothes. Radios are permanently set to receive only the official radio station, and the possessor of a radio can expect to receive unannounced visits from security officials to make sure that the radio has not been tampered with. If North Koreans wish to travel to another town, they must obtain a permit and report to the police station at their destination. They are told that if they defect to South Korea they will be tortured and executed by the South Koreans. Every aspect of life is closely monitored by a group of overlapping military and paramilitary security organizations such as the Ministry of People's Security and the State Security Department, which employ hundreds of thousands of officials and agents and operate in every region, plus a large network of informers. Those suspected of

The Sino-Soviet Split

In the mid 1950s the Soviet Union and China began to differ on fundamental issues. While Khrushchev embarked on his de-Stalinization campaign, talked about loosening control of civil society, and initiated arms control talks with the West, China was headed in a more militant direction. Following a rapid program of industrialization and socialization that had been aided by the Soviet Union, Mao from 1958 to 1961 initiated the Great Leap Forward, an ambitious program of economic development. However, the program ended in disaster, and three bitter years of economic crisis and famine followed in 1960 to 1962.

The split between the two great communist powers worked well for North Korea. Kim Il Sung first sided with China and signed a special agreement with Premier Zhou Enlai (1898–1976) that provided more crimes may disappear in the middle of the night, never to be heard from again. Individuals are deterred from crimes by the knowledge that their whole family will be punished, perhaps by imprisonment or banishment and at the very least by having the crime entered in their personal records. Citizens are expected to inform on each other, even children on parents—if they do not, they are implicated in the crime (which may be some casual remark not considered a crime in most other countries). North Koreans who travel abroad—for example, diplomats—must undergo months of reeducation, a program of hard work in the countryside accompanied by lectures and study sessions.

While the DPRK claims to be a classless society, it has created an elaborate new caste system based on loyalty to the state. Citizens are broadly divided into three basic loyalty groups: the core class (Koreans considered firmly loyal), the wavering class (suspect but capable of being won over by intensive political education), and the hostile class. In each class there are many subgroups, and each one consists of a large part of the Korean population—there are usually more people in the hostile class than the core class, and the wavering class, the largest, may be less than half the population. Each group receives a different kind of attention. Members of the hostile class, so called because once in their lives they expressed dissatisfaction with the regime or because before liberation their family were landlords, merchants, or members of religious organizations, can expect to have a harder-than-average life subject to very close scrutiny by the state security forces (Oh and Hassig 2000, 127–147).

aid to North Korea. Then Kim signed a Soviet agreement that gave the country even more aid.

At their 1962 party congress Soviet leaders began to criticize the Chinese openly. North Korea, after splitting loyalties in order to obtain aid packages from both sides, ended up siding with the Chinese and even criticized the Soviet Union for backing down during the Cuban Missile Crisis (1962). The Soviets cut off aid to Korea, but then North Korean relations with the Chinese soured. By 1966 China was in the throes of the Cultural Revolution, a purge of perceived capitalist and revisionist elements in China. First Mao's wife and then the Red Guards criticized Kim as a "fat revisionist." The Sino-Soviet split, which had helped Kim Il Sung to assert his independence while receiving substantial amounts of aid from both the Soviet Union and the People's Republic of China, now increased North Korea's isolation. The situation was not permanent, however, since both China and the Soviet Union viewed North Korea as a buffer state whose continued existence as a communist country was strategically important. They would not abandon it entirely until the end of the cold war. Even now China has a vested interest in preventing the total collapse of the DPRK, since such a collapse would create instability and refugee problem on China's borders.

North Korea Stands Alone

When the Sino-Soviet split left Korea to its own devices in the early 1960s, unique aspects of Korean Communism became more apparent. "Kim Il Sungism," which already pushed the cult of personality, took on new life. *Juche* gradually came to replace the established models of 20th-century communism, Marxist-Leninism and Maoism. At this time Kim Il Sung also came to be called "The Great Leader." Such significance was attached to this title that his son did not dare to take it when he succeeded in power but rather created his own, "The Dear Leader."

After losing the backing of the two superpowers, Korea began a series of audacious moves on its own. In early 1968 it sent a highly trained suicide squad into Seoul to assassinate the South Korean president, Park Chung Hee (1917–79). The squad was trained in long-distance running with heavy backpacks loaded with arms and ammunition. South Korean soldiers monitoring the DMZ knew something or someone had come through, but they did not know how many nor did they imagine that men on foot could get out of the area so quickly. The commandos, wearing South Korean army uniforms, passed by genuine South Korean soldiers without incident. Finally, on the outskirts of the old city walls of Seoul, a soldier met the disguised commandos and asked them to declare their unit and their mission. He was shot. The confrontation had taken place within a few hundred yards of the presidential mansion, the Blue House, and the sound of gunfire alerted surrounding guard units. The North Koreans fought to the death, and all but one died.

Later in 1968 North Korea captured the USS *Pueblo*. The *Pueblo* was a spy ship of the U.S. Navy, but its crew claimed that the vessel had been in international waters. Their North Korean captors accused the crew of trespassing in North Korean waters and threatened to kill them all as spies. In the end North Korea held the U.S. seamen captive for one year then released them. The ship is still held in North Korea, where it serves as a museum attesting to "the people's valiant struggle against American imperialism."

North Korea in the Era of Détente

In words and actions, Kim Il Sung exhibited a belief that his nation was in the vanguard of a worldwide revolutionary struggle between communism and capitalism. He rejected Nikita Khrushchev's vision of "peaceful coexistence" between the two kinds of societies. The future belonged to communism. The capitalists, who according to Marxist-Leninist theory were doomed to expire due to their system's internal contradictions, would do anything in their power to eradicate communism.

Certain events of the 1970s seemed to confirm this view and gave Kim Il Sung cause for optimism: The United States, which Kim Il Sung regarded as North Korea's chief enemy, continued to pursue a highly unpopular war against Communists in Vietnam, a war it finally lost in 1976. In the early 1970s the capitalist economies of the West suffered a recession linked to the Arab oil embargo of 1973, and the American economy battled slow growth and inflation throughout the decade. The United Nations was no longer subservient to the United States as it had been at the time of the Korean War. Communist or leftist insurgencies were gaining ground in Southeast Asia, Africa, and Latin America. Later on in the decade the 1979 Iranian revolution (which, though led by a Shii Muslim cleric, received enthusiastic support from left-leaning Iranian students) gave further evidence of the erosion of Western power.

Other trends should have given Kim pause. The most serious was the decline of his nation's economy relative to the economy of the country he hoped to master by force of arms. In 1970 the GNP of the Democratic People's Republic of Korea was $3.98 billion, roughly half the size of the GNP of the Republic of Korea, which was $7.99 billion. In terms of per capita GNP this made the two countries roughly equal, since there were about half as many people in North Korea as in South Korea. The economies of both countries had grown during the 1960s, but South Korea's economy had grown faster. This trend continued throughout the 1970s. By 1980 South Korea's GNP was four and a half times larger than North Korea's GNP (Buzo 1999, 91).

Between 1972 and 1974, in a sign that North Korea recognized the need to modernize its equipment if not its economic model, the DPRK spent millions of dollars on machinery and infrastructure from the West. The purchases were all on a gigantic scale. They included a French petrochemical factory, a Swiss watch factory, Japanese textile factories and steel-making equipment, a Finnish pulp and paper mill, a cement plant, and Swedish mining and smelting equipment. All were bought on credit in the expectation they would pay for themselves in increased exports. They failed to generate the expected income because the DPRK's managers (chosen by Kim Il Sung for their political reliability) lacked the managerial skills to make good use of the new equipment and because there proved to be little international demand for the products of these plants. The DPRK amassed a large foreign debt, and since it ultimately defaulted on those debts, it acquired a bad credit rating and found it very difficult to make future purchases.

The DPRK's interests were also threatened by a series of foreign policy initiatives that U.S. president Richard Nixon launched at the decade's outset aimed at lowering tensions between the United States and the communist world. Exploiting the divisions between the Soviet Union and the People's Republic of China, Nixon began making overtures to China in the early 1970s. The United States withdrew its opposition to China's entry to the United Nations, Nixon visited China, and diplomacy was normalized between the two countries, leading to trade links between the United States and China and a widening of the Sino-Soviet split. With somewhat less success, the United States pursued a policy of reduced confrontation, or "détente," with the Soviet Union. Highlights of détente included a series of nuclear arms agreements (SALT 1 in 1972 and the Threshold Test Ban Treaty in 1974) and the Helsinki Accords, in which West Germany officially recognized East Germany and the Soviet Union agreed to buy U.S. wheat and sell the United States Soviet oil. U.S.-Soviet détente reached a symbolic climax with cooperation in space when in 1975 an Apollo spacecraft docked in orbit with the Soviet's Soyuz space station.

Kim Il Sung's public view of the events was that the United States was losing its grip; he called Nixon's visit to China, "a trip of the defeated that fully reflects the declining fate of US imperialism" (Buzo 1999, 93). Privately, he seems to have felt that the Soviet Union and China were proving unreliable, and he pursued his foreign policy aims of isolation and weakening of the ROK through the Non-Aligned Movement (NAM), a loose organization of countries that asserted their independence from both the Soviet bloc and the West. In 1975 the NAM passed a resolution endorsing the DPRK's position on reunification—among other points the first condition was withdrawal of U.S. troops from the peninsula. However, the DPRK's methods for achieving this result—threats and bribery—ultimately made it unpopular within the movement, which was in any case a much less influential force in world affairs than Kim Il Sung appeared to believe.

Two events in the late 1970s threw the DPRK a pair of lifelines. First, the administration of U.S. president Jimmy Carter (b. 1924), basing its foreign policy on a commitment to human rights, was very cool to South Korean president Park Chung Hee, whom Carter saw as a dictator. Carter came into office with the intention of downsizing the American troop presence along the DMZ. Recognizing an opportunity, the DPRK immediately stopped referring to the "American imperialist aggressor" and spoke simply of the "American forces." In 1977 North Korea proposed direct U.S.-DPRK peace talks; the United States countered with a proposal of three-way talks between the United States, the ROK, and the DPRK. The DPRK, sticking to long-standing policy, refused. Though occasionally North Korea engaged in informal and usually fruitless talks with South Korean representatives regarding reunification, it refused to do anything that implied recognition of the legitimacy of the ROK. Ultimately, Carter was unable to persuade Congress and his own State Department to downsize U.S. forces in South Korea (Oberdorfer 2001, 84–94, 101). The DPRK's diplomatic intransigence and aggressive military stance made it difficult if not impossible for Carter to follow through with his plans, much as he disliked Park Chung Hee and his successor, Chun Doo Hwan.

Then, in 1979 the Soviet Union invaded Afghanistan. Ultimately, this move would turn out to be a disaster for North Korea. The political stresses and economic cost of this adventure (often compared to America's involvement in Vietnam) would contribute to the collapse of the Soviet Union and thus North Korea's complete diplomatic and economic isolation. In the meantime, however, the Soviet Union needed an ally. U.S.-Soviet détente was at an end. To counterbalance the rising power of Japan and the ROK, the Soviet Union appears to have gradually decided to strengthen North Korea. Closer ties were slowly renewed during the early 1980s; by the middle of the decade, the Soviet Union was the DPRK's main trading partner and source of aid (Buzo 1999, 127–129).

Rogue State

In the 1980s two incidents severely damaged North Korea's standing in diplomatic circles. Burma had been a North Korean ally, but its government admired South Korea's economic success in the early 1980s and gradually extended diplomatic recognition, a major setback for the North Korean strategy.

In 1983 President Chun Doo Hwan visited Burma (now Myanmar), the first South Korean president to do so. Chun's itinerary included a visit to Burma's national cemetery in the capital, Rangoon (Yangôn), on October 9. A bomb hidden in the rafters of a pavilion at the cemetery went off,

259

killing 21 people. Among the dead were 17 South Koreans, including the foreign minister and three other members of the cabinet. Only a delay in his motorcade had saved the president. The Burmese police later arrested two North Koreans and charged them with the murders. Those arrested were widely suspected of being agents of the North Korean government, and Burma broke off diplomatic ties with North Korea.

On November 19, 1987, Korean Airlines flight 858 disappeared over the Andaman Sea, off the coast of Burma, on its way from Baghdad to Seoul. The flight had originated in Europe and stopped briefly in Iraq, where two passengers had disembarked. Authorities were able to track down the two passengers—an older man and a woman in her early 20s traveling together. When they were approached for questioning, each attempted suicide. The man succeeded, but the woman survived. Under questioning she admitted that she and her companion were North Korean spies who had left a bomb on the plane set to detonate once the plane was in the air again. Everyone on the plane—115 people, including the crew—was killed.

Apart from what episodes like these say about the morality of North Korea's leaders, they obviously call their judgment into question. Why did North Korea commit international crimes that did so little to improve the country's security? The answer seems to be that North Korea believed its own propaganda. North Korea had always maintained that the Republic of Korea was a puppet of the United States and retained power solely by the use of force; its people would embrace communism if they were left to their own devices. Historically, North Korea had interpreted every sign of discontent in South Korea (such as student demonstrations against the Yushin Constitution, the National Security Law, and the KCIA) as a sign of collapse of the South Korean system. Under these premises South Korea needed only a little push to fall apart, and the confusion sowed by actions such as the assassination of a president or the blowing up of an airliner had a serious chance of hastening that outcome.

Instead, they have increased the world's mistrust of North Korea. The Burma incident, occurring as North Korea was attempting to shape the Non-Aligned Movement to its ends, increased the suspicion of the other members. The murder of the KAL passengers may have been intended to scare people away from participation at the 1988 Seoul Olympics (French 2005, 144). It did not have this effect, but it occurred as Soviet premier Mikhail Gorbachev was taking steps to liberalize the Soviet Union and helped to hasten the Soviet Union's disengagement with North Korea. Counterproductive in the short term, the cumulative effect of these actions has been to enhance North Korea's reputation as a rogue state, a country that flouts international norms of behavior.

Tentative Diplomatic Overtures

In the late 1980s and early 1990s Kim Il Sung lived to see the end of the cold war, the democratization of Eastern Europe, the transformation of China into a nation that was Communist in name only, and the collapse of the Soviet Union. He and his son Kim Jong Il, who by this time may have been making a large share of the decisions in Pyongyang, had many opportunities to adapt to the changing circumstances. They occasionally showed signs that they were making rational adjustments—to normalize relations with Japan or to launch a Chinese-style free-market economic experiment. In the end their ultimate choice seems to always have been a continuation of old policies.

By means of very favorable trade agreements and loans that were not expected to be paid back, by 1988 the Soviet Union was giving North Korea the equivalent of $1 billion a year—a large fraction of the DPRK's relatively small GNP. The Soviet Union was in serious economic trouble itself. Gorbachev had decided by 1988 to seek expanded trade with South Korea, and he sent his foreign minister, Eduard Schevardnadze, to break the news to North Korea. Schevardnadze's DPRK counterpart accused the Soviets of betraying socialism for money, but these sharp words did not change the Soviet decision. In 1989 the Soviet Union officially recognized the Republic of Korea. In 1990 the Soviet Union's military aid, investment, and trade with North Korea were sharply curtailed, and it announced that all future business would have to be conducted in hard currency. From this point onward the economy of the DPRK began to shrink (Bluth 2008, 38). In response North Korea made a series of tentative and for the most part inadequate diplomatic gestures beyond the communist world.

In 1988, already frustrated and furious at its abandonment by the Soviet Union, the DPRK took steps to normalize its relations with Japan. An important motivator for these moves seems to have been a desire for an immediate cash infusion in the shape of war reparations: Japan had earlier paid reparations to South Korea after normalizing relations with the ROK in 1965. North Korea's representatives insisted that Japan apologize both for its occupation of Korea and for the 45 years of abnormal relations after World War II; ultimately, the negotiations went nowhere. Around the same time North Korea took steps to establish a dialogue with South Korea. These meetings, too, went

THE CULT OF PERSONALITY

In the late 1980s North Korea offered to return the bodies of American servicemen who had served in the Korean War. A few American officers visited Pyongyang to arrange the returns. One such officer found himself in trouble for discarding a newspaper.

Returning to his hotel after the day's activities, he found the cleaning lady and a group of policemen waiting for him. They accused him of defaming the "Great Leader." How? By throwing away his newspaper, which bore a picture of Kim Il Sung. The American officer admitted having put the newspaper in the trash but protested that he was only being neat. He had made a terrible mistake, the North Koreans informed him; it was not acceptable to throw a picture of the "Great Leader" into a garbage can. After the officer apologized and promised never to repeat his offense, the North Koreans allowed him to continue his stay.

Like Mao and Stalin, who built monuments to themselves and otherwise took credit as the providers of the good things that everyone enjoyed, Kim Il Sung employed self-aggrandizement, putting his face on all the money and setting up statues of himself in every town, in one case a 60-foot-tall figure with one hand on its hip and the other pointing into the distance. As the American visitor discovered, the Great Leader's propaganda has been very successful in shaping North Korean culture.

The extreme nature of the cult of personality surrounding Kim Il Sung (always called the Great Leader) and Kim Jong Il (always referred to as Dear Leader) must be seen to be believed. Films made in the DPRK (available on the Internet in clips with titles such as "Dear Leader Kim Jong Il the Great Brilliant Commander" and "Kim Sung Il Dies") feature Orwellian imagery of abject crowds adoring godlike leaders, soldiers goose-stepping with mechanical precision, tanks and artillery assaulting an unseen enemy, and commentary asserting Kim Jong Il's genius and international stature. The resemblance to Nazi and Soviet propaganda films of the 1930s is very striking and gives the impression of a country that has made itself into a museum of totalitarianism.

nowhere, largely due to North Korea's unwillingness to compromise (Oberdorfer 2001, 223).

In 1990 Kim Il Sung announced a change in his position toward U.S. withdrawal of troops from South Korea, which he had always insisted

North Koreans pay homage to a bronze statue of Kim Il Sung that measures some 60 feet tall in central Pyongyang, North Korea. (AP Photo/John Leicester)

should be immediate. As a further sign of a softening of its position toward the United States, North Korea responded to long-standing U.S. requests for the return of Korean War remains. In the view of Don Oberdorfer, this would have been a good time for vigorous engagement with North Korea, in particular with respect to the country's nuclear weapons program, but the United States was distracted by the buildup to the first Gulf War. Once again North Korea's ambivalent diplomatic efforts bore little fruit.

In 1991, as an unexpected dividend of the end of the cold war, both the ROK and the DPRK were able to join the United Nations—their entry would earlier have been blocked by a veto. That same year the two countries signed a Joint Declaration on the denuclearization of the peninsula, an agreement that forbade both sides from testing, manufacturing, producing, receiving, possessing, storing, deploying, or using nuclear weapons and forbade the possession of nuclear reprocessing and uranium enrichment facilities. In what seemed like a further step toward good world citizenship, in 1992 the DPRK signed a nuclear safeguards agreement with the International Atomic Energy Agency (IAEA), as it was obliged to do as a signatory of the Nuclear Non-Proliferation Treaty (NPT). Then, in 1993 North Korea refused the IAEA access to two suspected nuclear waste sites and announced its intention to withdraw from the NPT. Whatever the motivation for this move, it got the attention of the United States. The confrontation between the United States and North Korea escalated; the rhetoric from Pyongyang included a phrase about turning Seoul into a "sea of fire" and the United States sent an aircraft carrier and a navy flotilla toward Korean waters. There were calls within the United States to bomb the nuclear development site in Yonbyon.

The defusing of the conflict came from a most unlikely source. Former U.S. president Jimmy Carter had years earlier received a message from Kim Il Sung, inviting Carter to Pyongyang. Now was the time to take the North Korean leader up on his offer. Carter was able to obtain promises from North Korea to decommission the nuclear site and rejoin the nonproliferation treaty if the United States led a coalition including South Korea and Japan in providing less dangerous light-water reactors and fuel oil supplies. The Clinton administration, after grousing about Carter going off on his own, accepted the agreement and negotiations began in earnest between North Korea and the United States. Over the next two years the United States held direct talks with the DPRK and reached a series of agreements on nuclear matters, including the 1994 Agreed Framework. Under the Agreed Framework the United States would ease economic sanctions against North Korea, the two would move toward full normalization of political and economic relations, North Korea would freeze its nuclear program and permit monitoring by the IAEA, the United States would help replace the DPRK's graphite-moderated reactors with light-water reactor plants (less useful for weapons production), and until the new reactors were online the United States would provide North Korea with heavy fuel oil.

The Korean Electric Development Organization (KEDO) was established in 1994 to develop the new nuclear power generating facilities, and work began on the new site. The old site was closed down, the "hot" nuclear rods were removed and stored, and cameras were set up so that IAEA officials could monitor activities. The administration of U.S. president Bill Clinton (b. 1946), which faced an American congress reluctant to reward North Korea for good behavior, managed to push most of the cost of KEDO onto other countries. South Korea promised to pay for 70 percent of the cost and Japan for 20 percent.

The 1994 Agreed Framework broke down in the early 2000s during the administration of U.S. president George W. Bush, but the seeds of the problem were sown in the 1990s. Perhaps, with so many parties to the agreement and such mistrust between them, trouble was inevitable. As long as the North Korean government remained secretive, it was difficult to be sure if it was fulfilling its commitments. As long as the North Korean government was in dire economic straits, other governments would be tempted to withhold funds—as Japan and the United States eventually did—in order to extract further concessions or merely in the hope that North Korea would collapse.

In the early 1990s and since then, it has sometimes seemed that North Korea wishes to imitate the success of China's forbidden forays into capitalism but is unable to. China had conducted a series of free-market experiments in the 1980s by creating Special Economic Zones (SPZs). In 1991, in the hope of attracting foreign investment, North Korea declared Rajin City and Sonbong County—an area on North Korea's shared border with Russia and China—to be a Free Economic and Trade Zone (FETZ). This free trade experiment still exists, and others have been added to it without causing any substantial changes either in the structure or the growth of the North Korean economy. Paul French, a journalist specializing in East Asian economic development, attributes the relative failures of such experiments to a fundamental lack of commitment and understanding by the DPRK leadership.

> *The DPRK authorities built virtually nothing; those who invested in Rajin-Sonbong found totally inadequate, or even non-existent, facilities in terms of water, power and other utilities to support their inward investments, while little or no official encouragement was given. Pyongyang's history of defaulting on Western*

> *creditors since the 1970s did not offer foreign investors much incentive to trust the government either. Rajin-Sonbong, like Sinjui (another FETZ created more than a decade later) . . . was too little, too late. (French 2005, 87)*

Additionally, while North Koreans would have benefited greatly from the employment opportunity Rajin-Sonbong might have provided, the DPRK consistently limits access to local labor out of fear that workers will be influenced by the West. The DPRK's commitment to thought control takes precedence over economic development.

Kim Jong Il's Rise to Power

Kim Il Sung's son Kim Jong Il was born in 1943, probably on the Russian coast near the border with Korea, but his official biography claims he was born on the slopes of Mount Paektu, the tallest mountain in Korea and the spiritual headwater of Korean culture. Under the principles of geomancy, or feng shui, Mount Paektu is the home of all the spiritual forces—the forces that flow within the Earth and up and down mountain ranges and affect humankind for good or for ill.

Factual as opposed to mythological information on the early life of Kim Jong Il is sparse. The son of Kim Il Sung and his first wife, who died in 1949, he graduated from Kimilsung University in 1946. As early as 1974, Korea-watchers began to suspect that he was being groomed as a successor to his father. Although before 1980 he was little mentioned in the state-controlled North Korean media and made no official public appearances or official pronouncements, analysts such as Adrian Buzo believe that Kim Jong Il began to have a significant influence on North Korean policy in the 1970s. To observers of North Korea and probably to many Koreans, newspaper, radio and television allusions to the activities of the Party Center were understood to be allusions to Kim Jong Il (Buzo 1999, 87–88).

After 1980 Kim was given prominence as the best interpreter of his father's *juche* ideology. In 1982 two books on the subject were published under his name: *On the Juche Idea* and *The Workers Party of Korea Is a Juche-type Revolutionary Party Which Inherited the Glorious Tradition of the Down-with-Imperialism Union.* Needless to say, these works received a highly favorable critical reception. One reviewer described *On the Juche Idea* as "an everlasting ideological exploit which clarified like a beacon light important philosophical tasks that had not been raised or solved in the history of human thought and the pressing theoretical and practical problems of our age" (Buzo 1999, 117).

By taking the step, unique in a communist country, of grooming his own son as a successor, Kim Il Sung evidently hoped to avoid the posthumous fate of Joseph Stalin, who had been denounced as a mass murderer by Nikita Khrushchev in 1956. He hoped to ensure that even after his death he would be regarded as infallible and that the direction of the country would not change. If this was his intention, then he seems to have been successful. When the "Great Leader," Kim Il Sung, died in 1994, outsiders wondered if his son Kim Jong Il, the "Dear Leader," would at last open up the country to reforms. These expectations were disappointed, because Kim Jong Il had already been in power for years. North Korea was by this time in a severe economic crisis, but the policies that had failed to avert the crisis were Kim Jong Il's policies. Even if he had possessed the exceptional talents that would have been required to accomplish the reformation of a deeply troubled, impoverished, and traumatized state, he showed little inclination to make basic changes.

It may be that Kim Jong Il was in a bind. A less tightly controlled state might have collapsed under the economic pressures that North Korea faced, and a less autocratic government would have been driven from power. But in order to make fundamental changes in North Korea, Kim Jong Il would have had to relax his grip on the Korean people and admit to essential flaws in the ideology that justified his rule. Deng Xiaopeng (1904–97) in the People's Republic of China managed a feat like this with remarkable finesse, to the world's astonishment. Mikhail Gorbachev had attempted a similar deed in the Soviet Union and failed (the Soviet Union collapsed). It is not surprising that Kim Jong Il, ruling a country with fewer resources and in far more desperate circumstances, found the task beyond his powers.

Floods and Famine

One of the major challenges to face Kim Jong Il was a series of bad harvests leading to a collapse of North Korean agriculture. Though Kim Jong Il later blamed these reverses on climatic disasters, the problem seems to have been rooted in government policy. North Korea, in a desperate effort to replace the food aid it had once received from communist allies with domestically grown crops, had begun to reclaim hillsides for the cultivation of new crops. Rice must be grown in flooded paddies, so it can exist only in flat lowland fields, but corn and potatoes can be grown on hillsides.

The result was disastrous. Korea's climate is dominated by summer monsoon rains, and when the rains came they washed away the newly

THE NAMES OF NORTH KOREA'S TWO LEADERS

Korean names pose many problems for readers of English, and the names of the two North Korean leaders, Kim Il Sung and Kim Jong Il, are no exception. English representations of the names (pronunciation and spelling) frequently differ from the Korean. Much of the difference is an error that can be attributed to the vast differences between Korean and English; phonologically, no two languages could be more dissimilar.

The first part of the name *Kim Il Sung* is pronounced "kim." Although the Korean *k* is a little softer than an English *k*, it is not quite a *g*. *Il* is pronounced "ill." *Sung* is pronounced as it is in English. Sometimes radio or television reporters use a long *u* sound and pronounce it "soong," but this is incorrect.

Two parts of the name *Kim Jong Il* are the same, *Kim* and *Il*. The other part, *Jong,* is correctly pronounced "jung," though its spelling might cue speakers of English to mispronounce it "jahng." If *Jong* and *Sung* rhyme, why the difference in spelling? It simply comes from inconsistent transcription into English. In Korean, there are two *o* sounds—a long *o* as in "yoyo," and a short *o* as in "onion." The Korean spelling uses the same vowel in both names, Sung and Jong.

These phonological issues are representative of the problems that arise in Korean-to-English and English-to-Korean transcription in general. Other usage matters relate more narrowly to the names of North Korea's two leaders. For instance, a common mistake is to replace the word *Il* with the Roman numeral II. Thus, Kim Jong Il has been called "Kim Jong the Second." Though in an odd way it makes some sense (Kim Jong Il is the second-generation ruler in the family), it is an error.

Even careful transcribers, however, are likely to preserve certain differences between English and North Korean usage. In all North Korean publications, whether written in English or Korean, the names of these two leaders are printed in full capital letters or in boldface type or both. Further, most books, magazine articles, and even articles in academic journals are dedicated to one or both men. The dedication often includes a short statement of gratitude for all that the leaders have done for the nation, the "workers' paradise." This usage quirk applies to these names in North Korea only.

developed crops and the hillsides with them. The root systems of corn and potatoes could not hold on to the hillsides the way native shrubs and trees had done. When the upland crops were ruined, the rice crops in many areas were also ruined by the landslides and mudslides that washed into the fertile paddy land.

Famine appeared first in the mountainous northeastern regions and then spread to the fertile western plains, eventually causing shortages in Pyongyang, whose residents usually enjoy a higher standard of living than other North Koreans. North Korea's first reaction was to hide the development from the outside world, which learned of it first by rumor. Spring and summer flooding damaged crops several years in a row in the mid-1990s, making the problem worse. North Koreans turned to "substitute foods," such as grass, rice roots, acorns, seaweed, berries, tree bark, and soups made with wild plants and weeds, and began to barter their possessions for food. Domesticated animals disappeared as people in rural communities began to eat their farm animals. In 1996 the DPRK grudgingly accepted international aid, a move that gave the world a glimpse of a crisis that had already been permitted to continue for years (French 2005, 129–131). Reporters not normally allowed into North Korea were permitted to photograph obviously starving children and other scenes that helped foreign agencies to see and understand the breadth of the disaster. Photographs of the landscape showed few trees, probably because they had been denuded of their bark. Human rights organizations reported that by the late 1990s gangs of malnourished and orphaned or abandoned children were roaming the country, stealing what food they could. The government put many of these children—some of them eight or nine years old—to work on construction projects, including a 10-lane Youth Hero Highway extending 42 kilometers from Nampo to Pyongyang. Between 100,000 and 300,000 North Koreans fled to China.

Food aid to North Korea, in the form of tons of shipments of rice, wheat, corn, and other commodities, reached unprecedented levels, but not in time to prevent a humanitarian disaster. North Korea's secrecy, which certainly worsened the effects of the famine, also makes it very difficult to estimate the numbers of deaths famine caused. Estimates of the number who died in the late 1990s range from 220,000 (the official DPRK estimate) to as high as 3.5 million (French 2005, 130).

The DPRK's commitment to secrecy and rigid control of the movements of all visitors creates an immense problem for the humanitarian

Red Cross officials distribute food and clothing supplies to the victims of flooding in Unpa County, 94 miles south of Pyongyang, on May 26, 1996. The previous year's summer floods devastated large areas of the country, damaging 145 of 250 counties, affecting 5.2 million people, and leaving 500,000 homeless. (AP Photo/Red Cross International)

nongovernmental organizations (NGOs) attempting to help the North Korean people. They are unable to monitor the distribution of food to see that it is fairly distributed. Further, they can be almost certain that it is *not* fairly distributed, since North Korea uses food as a method of social control and is committed, for example, to feeding its bureaucrats and soldiers first, even while others starve.

Sadly, humanitarian aid to North Korea has also fluctuated in response to political relations between the DPRK and the donor countries. Japan provided 500,000 tons of food aid in 2001 but sent no food aid in 2002 after Kim Jong Il admitted that North Korea had kidnapped 13 Japanese citizens between 1977 and 1983. As the DPRK and the United States traded accusations regarding North Korea's nuclear program, U.S. food aid to North Korea declined from 340,000 tons in 2001 to 40,000 tons in the first half of 2003 (French 2005, 131).

Nuclear Showdown

In early 2000, even as NGOs and national governments shipped food to the starving people of North Korea, leaders in the United States fretted about its nuclear program. The 1994 Agreed Framework, a patchwork of quid pro quos intended to persuade North Korea to refrain from producing a nuclear weapon, was never implemented as planned but limped along until a new, conservative U.S. administration arrived in Washington in 2001 determined to get tough with North Korea.

From the time the Clinton administration signed the Agreed Framework in October 1994, conservatives in the United States had denounced it as an unacceptable appeasement with an untrustworthy enemy. In 2001 many of those critics became officials in the State Department and Defense Department of the new administration, and they set about dismantling the agreement. Soon after his inauguration President Bush announced that all agreements and discussions with North Korea were "under review." North Korea understood this as a clear signal that the agreement was canceled.

Later U.S. statements further antagonized North Korea. In his January 2002 State of the Union address, Bush referred to North Korea as part of an "axis of evil" with Iraq and Iran. In early 2003, as the United States prepared for the Iraq War, Secretary of Defense Donald Rumsfeld said U.S. forces were strong and organized enough to be able to fight on two fronts. North Koreans took this as an assertion that the United States could fight Iraq and Iran on one front and North Korea on another.

That August a State Department official visiting Pyongyang confronted North Korean officials with U.S. intelligence reports that North Korea was again developing a nuclear program. The United States accused North Korea of cheating on the Agreed Framework. North Korea faulted the Bush administration for reneging on the agreement. North Korean officials further claimed the right to develop systems outside the Agreed Framework since its new nuclear program was based not on plutonium, which the agreement prohibited, but enriched uranium.

Secretary of State Colin Powell tried to set up a meeting between the two countries, but the North Koreans brushed aside his efforts as insincere and inadequate. In 2002 President Bush had referred to Kim Jong Il as a "pygmy" and spoken of "loathing" the North Korean style of government, and North Koreans began to fear that nothing short of regime change would satisfy the Americans. In the second Bush administration Secretary of State Condoleezza Rice finally tried to dispel such fears; she repeatedly stated that regime change was not the U.S. objective and that the United States was not considering military intervention in North Korea, but to North Koreans it seemed that the United States was trying to unring the bell. The damage had already been done.

Six-Party Talks

Once the Agreed Framework unraveled North Korea proceeded to equip itself with a "nuclear deterrent." In December 2002 the North Koreans turned off the monitoring cameras and expelled the UN observers. By October 2003 North Korea claimed to have enough nuclear fuel to make up to six bombs.

North Korean officials claimed they had kept their part of the agreement from 1992 to 2000 and deserved compensation for these efforts. The North Korean position was that the country would willingly give up its nuclear warheads and two-stage missiles in exchange for a formal peace treaty ending the Korean War, recognition as a sovereign state, removal of all embargoes, and financial compensation for actual and potential losses to their electric generating capacity.

What emerged as the best way to deal with the crisis were the so-called six-party talks, in which representatives from North Korea, South Korea, the United States, China, Japan, and Russia met to seek a solution. The talks took place irregularly between August 2003 and September 2005 in Beijing.

Japan was of two minds about the negotiations. On one hand Japan felt threatened by North Korea from the moment North Korea had fired a missile over Japan into the North Pacific Ocean in February 2003. On the other hand a far worse impediment to Japanese–North Korean relations had surfaced in September 2002: Kim Jong Il admitted that North Korea had kidnapped Japanese citizens from coastal cities in Japan in the 1970s and 1980s to serve as Japanese language instructors. Some of the captives had married and had families, and thus only a few were repatriated back to Japan in 2002. The admission and apology, which followed years of denial, sparked a more negative response than North Korea had anticipated. Rather than forgiving North Korea, Japan broke off its limited ties with North Korea. For years afterward the kidnapping scandal damaged relations between the two countries. Nonetheless, Japan continued to take part in the labored six-party talks.

It was China, however, that brought North Korea back to the negotiating table. Long North Korea's largest trading partner, China continues to be its principal supplier of basic commodities, such as fuel and food. The Chinese at times threatened to withhold supplies of petroleum and other goods if North Korea continued to hold out. Between 2002, when North Korea admitted it had been developing enriched uranium, and 2004, when George W. Bush was elected to a second term as U.S. president, no progress was made in deterring nuclear proliferation in North

Korea. Then the discussions bore fruit. Although questions of implementation remained, by the end of 2005 the six-party talks brought the North Koreans to an agreement that was much like that negotiated by the Clinton administration in 1994. But North Korea again provoked concern in the United States and Japan by firing long-range missiles and detonating its second nuclear warhead in early 2009. In addition, in March two young American journalists were arrested for illegally crossing into North Korea. They were tried and sentenced to 12 years of hard labor but were released by Kim Jong Il when former president Bill Clinton visited Pyongyang in August. The relaxing of tensions with the release of the journalists gave some hope for improved relations between the United States and North Korea.

The Question of Succession

The only succession to the highest office in North Korea has been from father to son, and it appears that the next succession will also be from father to son. For a long time speculation revolved around two candidates, Kim Jong Nam (b. 1971) and Kim Jong Chul (b. 1981). In January 2009, amid rumors that Kim Jong Il had suffered a stroke, news agencies in South Korea reported that Kim Jong Il had named Kim Jong Un (b. 1985), his youngest son by his third wife to be his successor. The 24-year-old Jong Un was educated in Switzerland under a pseudonym and is said to be Kim's favorite. He returned to North Korea in his late teens, and since then there had been no publicity about him in North Korea's completely state-controlled media.

North Korea Today

North Korea in 2009 remained a closed, secretive state, the last country still shut behind the "iron curtain" once said to have hidden the communist world from the West. In the 1950s and 1960s sinologists and Kremlinologists in the United States used to sift through government news releases, photographs of wall posters, and the published lists of participants in Communist Party congresses for hints of what was really going on in Red China and Red Russia. So, today, observers of North Korea study reports of the refugees streaming across the border to China, analyze the shadows in photographs of Kim Jong Il for telltale clues that the pictures have been manipulated (signifying that Kim is sick or even dead), and wonder if a show of greater-than-average intransigence in ongoing nuclear talks means that hard-liners are now in control of the DPRK.

Thanks to its desperate economic straits and in particular to the persistent efforts of South Korean presidents Kim Dae Jung and Roh Moo Hyun, the door to North Korea was opened just a crack. It is still quite a narrow opening. Two decades after the end of the cold war and the liberalization of the Chinese, Russian, and eastern European economies, the amount of serious change in North Korea is astonishingly small.

The South Korean government, in an effort that is surely more political than economic, has encouraged investment in its "lost other half" despite enormous obstacles routinely put in its path by the DPRK and by the U.S. habit of placing restrictions on exports from North Korea. Bilateral trade between the two Koreas was $220 million in 1998 and reached $700 million by 2004. That year initial construction was completed on the Kaesong Industrial Region, a "special administrative industrial region" built by and run by a South Korean committee, with prominent help from the South Korean *chaebol* Hyundai Asan. With South Korean expertise and financing and extremely cheap North Korean labor supplied by the Korean Workers' Party, factories in the Kaesong Industrial Region are producing inexpensive goods such as shoes, clothes, and watches.

Joint ventures like these are a high-risk business for South Korean investors. It is unlikely that the investors would make such efforts in a country farther away or less linked by bonds of history. In 2005, when Hyundai wanted to fire an executive accused of embezzling money, North Korea demanded that this man be reinstated and remain Hyundai's point man in North Korea. The reason: He had had the rare privilege of meeting Kim Jong Il on several occasions. When Hyundai held its ground, North Korea accused the company of "deception and hypocrisy" and said it was reconsidering all its business deals with Hyundai. South Korean business analysts questioned by the *International Herald Tribune* in October 2005 voiced the opinion that the DPRK, unable to borrow money and desperate for hard currency, just wanted to keep the 1.5 billion that Hyundai had invested.

Four years later the Kaesong Industrial Region still exists, but North Korea has not become a better business partner. Another joint venture between the two countries, the Kumgang Mountain resort on the southeastern tip of North Korea, opened in 1998. It ran into trouble on July 11, 2008, when North Korean soldiers shot and killed a South Korean housewife, a tourist, who wandered into a restricted zone. South Korea's new president, Lee Myung Bak, banned trips to the resort until the incident had been investigated.

While campaigning for president, Lee had promised to get tougher on North Korea, and this incident was an opportunity to show it—but

274

A train made a symbolic crossing of the DMZ, the border between North and South Korea, on May 17, 2007. Train service between the two countries was not initiated, but in a symbolic move the two sides agreed to reconnect the train line that had been severed in the Korean War 57 years earlier. (Academy of Korean Studies)

in any case his demand for an investigation seemed a reasonable move considering a tourist had been slain. Any normal country would have asked for an investigation; any normal country would have provided one. The North Korean response was to threaten to expel all South Korean businesspeople from the resort. North Korea is still an extremely difficult place in which to do business, and its leaders give little impression of a serious desire for change. They seem rather to be hanging on from day to day and year to year.

9

CONCLUSION

More than 60 years have passed since Korea's division along the 38th parallel in 1945. Three generations, closely related by ties of family and culture, speaking the same language, with a shared history that goes back nearly 2,000 years have grown up on either side of this line. They have been changed by their different experiences perhaps more than they realize. They live almost in different realities. They have sharply different pictures of themselves and their brothers and sisters on the other side of the line. There is misinformation on both sides. However, in the view of most outsiders it is the North Koreans, told that their repressive, impoverished country is the wonder of the world, who have the most learning to do.

In 1989 the former German chancellor Willy Brandt visited Korea's DMZ and said that the North Koreans were going to have to do a lot of adjusting when their country was finally reunited—more than East Germans would when the Berlin Wall finally came down. Asked when German reunification would occur, Brandt replied "not in my lifetime." It was only 60 days later that the Berlin Wall fell (Young 2001, xvii). Perhaps a surprise like that awaits the two Koreas, still officially in a state of war, still confronting each other along a border that U.S. president Bill Clinton called "the most dangerous place on earth." Right now the prospect of reunification is only a little nearer than it was in 1989 and maybe even a little less likely than it was in 2000.

That year saw an exciting highlight of the Sunshine Policy. On August 15, the 55th anniversary of Korea's liberation from Japan, 100 Koreans who had been separated by the 1950–53 war met in Seoul and then flew to Pyongyang in a tearful, dramatic reunion documented by journalists and photographers. "We will do our best to make the exchange of visiting groups become a wonderful opportunity to achieve national unity and reunification," read a statement issued jointly by the North Korean and South Korean delegations. "The frozen barrier of

The Hyundai shipyard in Ulsan is the world's largest shipyard and a symbol of South Korea's economic development in the late 20th and early 21st centuries. In 2008 it produced a completed ship every three days. (Academy of Korean Studies)

confrontation and division has just begun to tear apart" (*Bnet Business Network* 2000). The next month the two governments convened a historic summit meeting in Pyongyang. South Korean businesses, led by the giant Hyundai *chaebol*, announced plans to invest in a series of ambitious joint ventures with North Korea.

It was understood, as a background to these events, that things had changed in both countries. South Korea had its first center-left government; the leader who had been jailed and targeted for execution by the country's dictators was now the head of state. South Korea could claim more legitimately than ever before to have a government that expressed the will of its people. As for North Korea, it obviously stood in need of rescue. It was shattered economically, a country on the point of collapse. Its people were starving and dependent on massive doses of foreign aid for their survival. The circumstances of each country had changed drastically since the end of the cold war. Why shouldn't their relationship change? Why shouldn't North Korea do what other communist countries had done and come in from the cold, with the reward of economic growth and diplomatic reengagement with the rest of the world?

For a while it looked as if this were going to happen. In 2000 Kim Dae Jung was awarded a Nobel Peace Prize for his efforts on behalf of improved relations between the two Koreas. Sadly, the 2000 initiatives

277

look much less encouraging in retrospect. In 2003 a South Korean government investigation revealed that through the Hyundai corporation, Kim Dae Jung's administration had arranged for hundreds of millions of dollars, perhaps as much as half a billion, to be paid to North Korea apparently in exchange for agreeing to the summit.

The various joint ventures that Kim Jong Il has permitted in North Korea seem to have the purpose of raising money for projects no outside aid agency would ever support. In the eyes of South Korea, they are seeds of transformation, but it is all too possible that in the eyes of North Korea, they are just a source of ready cash. Hard currency is also needed for the luxuries that Kim Jong Il and other favored people in North Korea enjoy, luxuries that cannot be manufactured in North Korea—even the suits of top DPRK officials come from outside the country.

In 1998 Kim Jong Il said, "The market economy is one of the fishing rods of temptation. Hanging from the fishhook are two specious baits called 'economic cooperation' and 'aid'" (French 2005, 157). He was essentially right. South Korea, with its Sunshine Policy, hopes to tempt North Korea to change itself. North Korea, for its part, seems intent on eating the bait without being hooked.

In early 2009 South Korea's conservative president Lee Myung Bak said that further progress between the two states depended on North Korea's abandoning its nuclear program. Kim Jong Il apparently found this condition outrageous. It was essentially a demand that North Korea live up to the international commitments it had agreed to in the Six-Party talks. The extreme nature of the DPRK's response to this request calls into question both North Korea's willingness to abandon its nuclear program and its desire for reunification.

The governments of both Koreas insist that reunification is their ultimate goal. The world's great Asian powers, which include China, Japan, and Russia, also say whenever the subject comes up they are in favor of Korean reunification, yet as the years go by and so little progress is made it is difficult not to wonder if these statements are sincere.

Does North Korea want reunification? It claims to. For decades it was a staple of North Korean propaganda that the division of Korea was a crime perpetrated by the United States and its puppet regime to the south, yet although Korean reunification might ultimately benefit the North Korean people, it would not benefit the North Korean leadership, who are aware that South Korea is not about to embrace communism and the rule of Kim Jong Il or any of his successors. Now and for the foreseeable future serious moves toward reunification would mean admitting that the ideology and leadership of North Korea are discredited. It would probably result in the loss of power and privilege for North Korea's bureaucrats and generals. For North Korea to sincerely work for reunification would require wisdom and a capacity for self-sacrifice that the country's leadership has not shown so far.

What about the outsiders, China, Japan, Russia, and the United States? They, too, have reasons to prefer a mild alteration of the status quo—a stabilized, nonnuclear North Korea not on the brink of starvation—rather than a unified Korea. In the coming decades China's interests are expected to collide with those of the United States as the two nations compete for world resources. If Korea were unified as East and West Germany were unified—unified, as seems likely, on the terms of the U.S.-friendly half of the country—this would put a close U.S. ally on China's border. Though still a small nation, it would be an economic powerhouse and have one of the world's largest armed forces, and it would have its own grounds for dispute with China. For example, it might have claims on the many ethnic Koreans who are Chinese citizens. It is even possible that China does not really mind if every now and then North Korea does something worrisome in connection with its nuclear program and distracts the United States from other concerns, such as the rising power of China.

Japan has to regard North Korea's missile and weapons programs as a threat. It would very much like to see a Korea that has no nuclear weapons, but it would not necessarily get that with Korean reunification. A unified Korea might decide to keep and build on the North's nuclear program. U.S. forces, no longer needed to prevent a second Korean War, might leave the peninsula; they might have to at the new Korea's request. These forces have contributed to the stabilization of East Asia. When they are gone Japan might have to consider rearming. There might even be a three-way nuclear arms race with Japan, China, and Korea. These outcomes are not certain, but they are genuine risks. For Japan a united Korea could be worse than a divided Korea, even if one of the Koreas is an unpredictable rogue state.

For Russia, as for China, North Korea is a buffer state. Russia since the early 2000s has been increasingly at odds with the United States and would probably not like to have a U.S.-friendly regime (possibly with the U.S. bases still in place) on its border. While North Korea remains an international hot spot, Russia gains prestige as a mediator in the international crises that the DPRK periodically generates.

The United States has more of a genuine interest in reunification than China, Japan, or Russia, but even for the United States change poses risks. The new Korea might decide to stay nuclear and start an arms race in East Asia.

That leaves South Korea as the country most seriously committed to reunification: Reunification would mean that a historic wound would be on the way to healing, Korean families would be reunited, and the South Korean politicians who would accomplish the feat would win the gratitude of their people and a great place in history, but even for South Korea the challenges are daunting. North Korea's economic collapse has turned reunification into a humanitarian goal. Its people need saving, and who better to save them than their own relations to the south? However, it has further difficulties. Even were the DPRK's government and its bureaucrats and military forces to admit their failure, give up their privileges, and ask for reunification on the Republic of Korea's terms, the challenges would be enormous. South Korea, a country of 48 million people, would have to absorb 23 million more. South Korean workers, with their decent wages and their real labor unions, would face a vast influx of millions of workers who are used to living on next to nothing, who have skills that are at best half a century out of date, whose education has been diluted by hours each day devoted to indoctrination into the cult of *juche* and Dear Leader Kim Jong Il, and who have never known what it is like to make their own decisions.

The nearest thing to a precedent for Korean reunification is obviously the German reunification of the 1990s. In broad outline the situations are similar. East Germany, too, was a repressive state shaped by the cold war with a planned economy lagging behind its neighbor, which had benefited from an economic miracle. Germany was successfully and gradually reunited, but the case of North and South Korea is by every measure more extreme. The problems, though similar in shape, are much larger in scale.

If these challenges can be overcome, a unified Korea, a healed Korea, would be a stronger country. With its vibrant economy linked to the whole world, the north would certainly be a hermit kingdom no longer. While it would still be small relative to the great neighboring powers of China, Russia, and Japan, it would have the strength to conduct its own diplomacy. It would have less need to rely on the protection of a single patron than at any time in its previous history. This happy ending may be decades away, but the rewards are great enough to assure that some Koreans on both sides of the 38th parallel will keep dreaming of it and planning for it.

APPENDIX 1
BASIC FACTS: NORTH KOREA

Official Name
Democratic People's Republic of Korea (DPRK; Choson Minjujuui Inmin Konghwaguk) [(Short Form: North Korea (Choson)]

Geography

Area	46,540 sq. mi. (120,538 sq. km). Slightly smaller than Mississippi
Land Borders	China, South Korea, and Russia
Elevations	
Highest:	9,006 ft. (2,744 m) (Paektu-san)
Lowest:	East Sea and Yellow Sea
Terrain	mostly hills and mountains separated by deep, narrow valleys; coastal plains wide in west, discontinuous in east

Government
Communist state one-man dictatorship

Political Divisions

Capital	Pyongyang
Other Cities	Nampo, Hamhung, Chongjin, Kaesong, Sinuijn, and Wonsan
Subdivisions	Nine provinces (*do*, singular and plural): Chagang-do (Chagang), Hamgyong-bukto (North Hamgyong), Hamgyong-namdo (South Hamgyong), Hwanghae-bukto (North Hwanghae), Hwanghae-namdo (South Hwanghae),

Kangwon-do (Kangwon), Pyongan-bukto (North Pyongan), Pyongan-namdo (South Pyongan),Yanggang-do (Yanggang)

Four municipalities (si, singular and plural): Kaesong-si (Kaesong), Najin Sonbong-si (Najin-Sonbong), Nampo-si (Nampo), Pyongyang-si (Pyongyang)

Demographics

Population	22,665,345 (July 2009 est.)
Growth Rate	.42% (2009 est.)
Ethnic Groups	racially homogeneous; there is a small Chinese community and few ethnic Japanese
Languages	Korean
Religions	Traditionally Buddhist and Confucianist, some Christian and syncretic Chondogyo (Religion of the Heavenly Way)

Literacy (ability to write or read by age 15)
  Total Population: 99%
  Male: 99%
  Female: 99%
Age Structure
  0–14 years: 21.3% (male 2,440,439/female 2,376,557)
  15–64 years: 69% (male 7,776,889/female 7,945,399)
  65 years and over: 9.4% (male 820,504/female 1,305,557) (2009 est.)
Median Age
  Total: 33.5 years
  Male: 32.1 years
  Female: 34.9 years (2009 est.)
Birth Rate   14.82 births/1,000 population (2009 est.)
Death Rate   10.52 deaths/1,000 population (July 2009 est.)
Infant Mortality
  Total: 51,34 deaths/1,000 live births
  Male: 58.64 deaths/1,000 live births
  Female: 43.6 deaths/1,000 live births (2009 est.)
Life Expectancy
  Total Population: 63.81 years
  Male: 61.23 years
  Female: 66.53 years (2009 est.)
Total Fertility Rate   1.96 children born/woman (2009 est.)

Economy

Gross Domestic Product (purchasing power parity)	$40 billion (2008 est.)
Natural Resources	coal, lead, tungsten, zinc, graphite, magnesite, iron ore, copper, gold, pyrites, salt, fluorspar, hydropower

Economic Sectors
  Agriculture: 23.3%
  Industry: 43.1%
  Services: 33.6% (2002 est.)

Agricultural Products	rice, corn, potatoes, soybeans, pulses; cattle, pigs, eggs
Industries	military products; machine building, electric Power, chemicals, mining (coal, iron ore, limestone, magnesite, graphite, copper, zinc, lead, and precious metals), metallurgy; textiles, food processing; tourism

Labor Force
  Agriculture: 37%
  Industry and Services: 63% (2004 est.)

Environment

Land Use
  Arable Land: 22.4%
  Permanent Crops: 1.66%
  Other: 75.94% (2005)

Irrigated Land	5,637 sq. mi. (14,600 sq. km) (2003)
Current Issues	water pollution, inadequate supplies of potable water; waterborne disease; deforestation; soil erosion and degradation

International Environmental Agreements

Party to:	Antarctic Treaty, Biodiversity, Climate Change, Climate Change–Kyoto Protocol, Desertification, Environmental Modification, Hazardous Wastes, Ozone Layer Protection, Ship Pollution

Signed, but Not Ratified: Law of the Sea

Appendix 2

Basic Facts: South Korea

Official Name
Republic of Korea

Geography

Area	38,502 sq. mi. (99,720 sq. km). Slightly larger than Indiana
Land Borders	North Korea
Elevations	
Highest:	6,398 ft. (1,950m) (Halla-san)
Lowest:	Sea of Japan
Terrain	mostly hills and mountains; wide coastal plains in west and south

Government
Republic governed by a directly elected president and a unicameral legislature, the National Assembly

Political Divisions

Capital	Seoul
Other Cities	Pusan, Taegu, Inchon, Kwangju, Taejon, and Ulsan
Subdivisions	Nine provinces (*do,* singular and plural): Kangwon, Kyonggi, North Chungchong, South Chungchong, North Cholla, South Cholla, North Kyongsang, South Kyongsang, and Cheju

Demographics

Population	48,508,972 (July 2009 est.)

Growth Rate	.266% (2009 est.)
Ethnic Groups	homogeneous (except for about 20,000 Chinese)
Languages	Korean, English widely taught in junior high and high school
Religions	Christian 26% (Protestant 19.7%, Roman Catholic 6.6%), Buddhist 23.2%, other or unknown 1.3%, none 49.3% (1995 census)

Literacy (ability to write or read by age 15)
  Total Population: 97.9%
  Male: 99.2%
  Female: 96.6%

Age Structure
  0–14 years: 16.8% (male 4,278,581/female 3,887,516)
  15–64 years: 72.3% (male 17,897,053/female 17,196,840)
  65 years and over: 9.4% (male 2,104,589/female 3,144,393) (2009 est.)

Median Age
  Total: 37.3 years
  Male: 36 years
  Female: 38.5 years (2009 est.)

Birth Rate	8.93 births/1,000 population (2009 est.)
Death Rate	5.94 deaths/1,000 population (July 2009 est.)

Infant Mortality
  Total: 4.28 deaths/1,000 live births
  Male: 4.49 deaths/1,000 live births
  Female: 4.02 deaths/1,000 live births (2009 est.)

Life Expectancy
  Total Population: 78.72 years
  Male: 75.45 years
  Female: 82.22 years (2009 est.)

Total Fertility Rate	1.21 children born/woman (2009 est.)

Economy

Gross Domestic Product	(purchasing power parity) $1.278 trillion (2008 est.)
Natural Resources	coal, tungsten, graphite, molybdenum, lead, hydropower potential

Economic Sectors
  Agriculture: 7.2 %
  Industry: 25.1%
  Services: 67.7% (2007 est.)

| Agricultural Products | rice, root crops, barley, vegetables, fruit; cattle, pigs, chickens, milk, eggs; fish |
| Industries | electronics, telecommunications, automobile production, chemicals, shipbuilding, steel |

Labor Force
  Agriculture: 3%
  Industry: 39.5%
  Services: 57.6% (2008 est.)

Environment

Land Use
  Arable Land: 16.58%
  Permanent Crops: 2.01%
  Other: 81.41% (2005 est.)

| Irrigated Land | 3,390 sq. mi. (8,780 sq. km) (2003) |
| Current Issues | air pollution in large cities; acid rain; water pollution from the discharge of sewage and industrial effluents; drift net fishing |

International Environmental Agreements

| Party to: | Antarctic-Environmental Protocol, Antarctic-Marine Living Resources, Antarctic Treaty, Biodiversity, Climate Change, Climate Change–Kyoto Protocol, Desertification, Endangered Species, Environmental Modification, Hazardous Wastes, Law of the Sea, Marine Dumping, Ozone Layer Protection, Ship Pollution, Tropical Timber 83, Tropical Timber 94, Wetlands, Whaling |

Signed, but Not Ratified: None of the selected agreements

Appendix 3

Chronology

From Early Settlements to the Silla Unification of Korea (Prehistory–668)

50,000–20,0000 B.C.E.	Korean Peninsula inhabited by stone-age people probably unrelated to present-day Koreans.
10,000 B.C.E. to 1 C.E.	Ancestors of present-day Koreans migrate into the Korean Peninsula.
2333 B.C.E.	Legendary date of the birth of Tangun, founder of Korea.
700 B.C.E.	Chinese records mention Old Choson, a name later applied to Korean states.
108 B.C.E.	China's Han dynasty sets up four military outposts, including Lolong, in Korea.
100 B.C.E.	Chinese records mention two Korean states, Puyo and Koguryo.
220 C.E.	Fall of China's Han dynasty leaves influential Lolong outpost in Korea, spreading Chinese culture in Korea.
244	Alliance of China's Wei dynasty; Puyo defeat Koguryo.
285	Xianbei armies defeat Puyo; Chinese prop up the Puyo kingdom.
Third Century to 688	Three Kingdoms Period.
382	Buddhist temple is built in Paekche.
371–384	Reign of King Sosirum of Koguryo, who establishes a Bhuddhist temple and a Confucian academy; Koguryo models its bureaucracy and laws on Chinese institutions.
414	Monument to Koguryo's King Kwanggaeto (r. 391–413) declares he has conquered 64 for-

	tresses and 1,400 villages; his domain extends south along Korea's east coast.
554	Paekche and Silla form alliance and drive Koguryo from the Han River valley. Immediately afterward, Silla attacks Paekche and drives Paekche farther south.
532–562	Silla conquers Kaya, royal line of Kaya is incorporated into the Silla aristocracy; Silla captures Han River valley.

Unified Silla (668–935) and Koryo (918–1392)

617–686	Life of Wonhyo, father of Korean Buddhism.
660	Silla, helped by an alliance with Tang China, begins conquest of Paekche and Koguryo.
660–730	Life of Sol Chong, son of Wonhyo, and one of Korea's first Confucian scholars.
892	Silla begins to lose control of parts of the peninsula as the brief Later Three Kingdoms period begins.
918	Wang Kon becomes king of Later Koguryo and changes its name to Koryo, establishing the capital of his new dynasty in present-day Kaesong.
935	Last king of Silla surrenders to Wang Kon of Koryo; the aristocracies of the two kingdoms merge.
949–975	Reign of Kwangjong, fourth king of Koryo. He strengthens Koryo's ties with China and introduces a Chinese-style civil service exam.
1145	Kim Pusik compiles the *Samguk sagi,* Korea's oldest extant history text.
1230	Carving of Tripitaka Koreana on 80,000 wood blocks.
1231	The Mongol invasions of Korea begin.
1234	World's first metal-block printed text is published in Korea.
1274	Mongols force Koreans to build armada to attack Japan; a typhoon prevents the invasion.
1281	Second Mongol attack of Japan; again failed by typhoon or kamikaze, winds of the gods.

1285	Iryon compiles the *Samguk yusa* ("Remnants and reminiscences of the Three Kingdoms").
1259	Korea's King Kojong makes treaty with the Mongol rulers of China (the Yuan dynasty).
1368	The Mongols are driven out of China.

The Early and Middle Choson (1392–1636)

1392	Yi Songgye is crowned king, officially beginning the Choson dynasty.
1396	Capital moved to Hanyang (modern day Seoul).
1408	High military service examination system created.
1437	Sundial and water clock invented.
1446	The Hangul alphabet is promulgated by King Sejong the Great.
1455	Sejo the Usurper seizes throne in a palace coup.
1494–1506	Reign of Yonsangun, who after committing many crimes is exiled.
1501–1570	Life of Neo-Confucian scholar Yi Hwang (pen-name Toegye).
1536–1585	Life of Neo-Confucian scholar Yi I (penname Yulgok).
1592–1598	Japanese invade Korea. Admiral Yi Sunsin employs the Turtle boats to repel Japanese forces.
1627	The first Manchu invasion.
1636	The second Manchu invasion.

Late Choson (1636–1910)

1681–1763	Life of Sirhak ("Practical Learning") thinker Yi Ik.
1724–1776	Reign of King Yongjo, who reformed the law code and the tax system.
1767	Crown Prince Sado (son of King Yongjo) is killed by suffocation in a rice chest.
1784	Catholicism is introduced.
1791	Persecution of Catholicism begins.
1796	King Chongjo builds Hwasong fortress.
1839–1842	Opium War between Great Britain and China.

1854	Japan is "opened" to Western trade by Commodore Matthew Perry of the United States.
1864	Choe Cheu creates movement called Tonghak (Eastern Learning).
1865	More than 23,000 Catholics in Korea.
1864	Beginning of regency of the Taewongun.
1876	Kanghwa Treaty opens Korea to Japanese trade on unequal terms.
1882	Military uprising against Japanese faction leads to stationing of Chinese troops in Korea and extensive Chinese control of Korean diplomacy.
1884	Failure of attempted coup to depose the pro-Chinese Queen Min faction.
1894	Beginning of Tonghak Rebellion; China and Japan intervene, initiating Sino-Japanese War.
1905	Russo-Japanese War leads to Japanese protectorate of Korea.
1907	King Kojong is forced to abdicate.
1909	Ito Hirobumi, former Japanese prime minister and governor-general of Korea, is shot and killed by a Korean assassin.
August 22, 1910	Japan officially annexes Korea.

The Japanese Colony (1910–1945)

1910	Start of Military Period, Japanese annexation of Korea.
1910–1916	Terauchi Masatake is governor-general; ruthless military rule is imposed, while some top Korean aristocrats and officials are bribed into cooperation.
January 22, 1919	Death of King Kojong.
March 1, 1919	Nationalists sign Korean declaration of independence amid widespread demonstrations in March First Movement; Japanese try to suppress movement with force.
April 1919	Formation of Provisional Government of Korea in Shanghai.
1919	Start of Cultural Policy Period.
1923	Japanese mobs attack Korean residents in Tokyo after earthquake.

1927	Yo Un-hyong is imprisoned by the Japanese.
1929	Anti-Japanese student uprising in Kwangju.
September 18, 1931	The Mukden Incident begins Japanese occupation of Manchuria.
1931	Start of Assimilation Period.
1932	Japan establishes puppet state of Manchukuo in Manchuria; many Korean workers move into Manchuria with Japanese encouragement and coercion.
1934	Governor General Ugaki Kazushige introduces new curriculum in Korean schools with increased instruction in Japanese language, ethics, and history.
1935	Korean students and government employees are required to attend Shinto ceremonies.
1937	Japanese authorities shut down Korean-oriented organizations and force Koreans to join groups that indoctrinate them in Japanese nationalism.
1939	Koreans are required to take Japanese names.
1941	Kim Il Sung, future premier of North Korea, moves to Russia; Japanese attack Pearl Harbor, and United States declares war on Japan.

Liberation, Division, and the Korean War (1945–1953)

1945	After the surrender of Japan, the Korean Peninsula is divided between Soviet and American occupation forces at the 38th parallel.
1946	US-USSR Joint-Commission on the formation of a Korean government reaches an impasse.
September 1946	The Autumn Harvest Uprisings.
May 10, 1948	UN-sponsored elections are held in South Korea.
August 15, 1948	Establishment of the Republic of Korea with Syngman Rhee as president.
September 9, 1948	Establishment of the Democratic People's Republic of Korea with Kim Il Sung as premier.
June 25, 1950	North Korea launches all-out invasion of South Korea in attempt to unify the country as a Communist state.
June 27–July 7, 1950	UN condemns North Korea and issues a series of resolutions authorizing international

	intervention to assist South Korea; U.S. general Douglas MacArthur becomes commander of the UN forces.
August 1950	UN forces are driven to the southeast corner of the Korean Peninsula (the Pusan Perimeter).
September 15, 1950	Amphibious landing of troops at Inchon begins successful counterattack against North Korea.
October 9, 1950	UN forces capture the North Korean capital of Pyongyang and continue north to the hills overlooking the Yalu River.
January 4, 1951	North Korea, with China's help, retakes Seoul.
April 11, 1951	Truman dismisses MacArthur.
July 27, 1953	Armistice is signed on line roughly approximating the 38th parallel, where the war began.

South Korea's Long Road to Democracy (1953–2009)

1960	A student uprising begins the April Revolution, which overthrows the autocratic First Republic of South Korea; Syngman Rhee resigns and goes into exile.
May 16, 1961	Military forces, headed by General Park Chung Hee, overthrow the Second Republic of South Korea.
1966	Vietnam war accounts for 40% of South Korea's foreign exchange.
1970	Kyongbu Expressway (Seoul-Pusan) is completed and opened to traffic.
1972	Yushin Constitution further restricts civil liberties in South Korea.
October 26, 1979	President Park Chung Hee is assassinated by his intelligence chief.
1980	The Kwangju Uprising. Martial law is declared throughout the nation; The city of Kwangju becomes a battleground between dissenters and the armed forces (May 18–27).
1988	Democratic elections usher in the Sixth Republic of South Korea; military forbidden to exercise political role.
1988	24th Olympic Games held in Seoul.

1991	South Korea and North Korea join UN as two separate states.
1996	Chun Doo Hwan and Roh Tae Woo, two former South Korean presidents, are tried for corruption and murder.
1997	Asian financial crisis reaches South Korea; Kim Dae Jung, who had been jailed and narrowly escaped death under previous administrations, becomes president.
1998	Kim initiates Sunshine Policy of reconciliation with North Korea.
2000	The first summit between North and South Korean leaders is held, with Kim Dae Jung representing the south and Kim Jong Il the north; Kim Dae Jung is awarded the Nobel Peace Prize.
2007	The second summit between North and South Korean leaders is held, with Roh Moo Hyun representing the South and Kim Jong Il the North.
2008	Lee Myung Bak, a conservative, is elected president of South Korea.
2009	Roh Moo Hyun commits suicide after admitting that he had taken bribes; Kim Dae Jung dies of natural causes at age 85.

North Korea, the Democratic People's Republic of Korea (1945–2009)

1953	Kim Il Sung purges leading members of the South Korean Workers Party for acting as spies for the "American imperialists."
1956	Nikita Khrushchev gives "secret speech" denouncing Stalin; Kim Il Sung rejects de-Stalinization and renews purges of Soviet and Chinese factions in the Korean Workers Party.
1968	North Korea captures U.S. spy ship *Pueblo* and holds its crew captive for one year.
1974	North Korea faces an oil shock.
1982	Books on the *juche* philosophy are published in Kim Jong Il's name.
1983	North Korea attempts to assassinate South Korean president Chun Doo Hwan while he is on a visit

	to Burma; a bomb kills 21 people including members of the South Korean cabinet.
1987	North Korean agents plant a bomb on Korean Airlines flight 858; it explodes, killing all 115 people on board.
1991	North Korea and South Korea sign joint declaration on denuclearization of the Korean Peninsula.
1994	Kim Il Sung dies, and his son Kim Jong Il is acknowledged to be in control of the state; United States, North Korea, South Korea, and Japan sign Agreed Framework.
1996	North Korea, suffering widespread famine, accepts international aid.
1998	Kumgang (Diamond) Mountain resort near the east coast is opened to South Korean and international tourists.
2000	The first summit between North and South Korean leaders is held in Pyongyang, with Kim Dae Jung representing the South and Kim Jong Il the North; Kim Dae Jung is awarded the Nobel Peace Prize.
2002	George W. Bush calls North Korea a member of the "axis of evil."
2007	The second summit between North and South Korean leaders is held, with Roh Moo Hyun representing the South and Kim Jong Il the North.
2007	Tours of Kaesong area opened to South Korean and international tourists.
2008	A South Korean tourist to North Korea's Kumgang Mountain resort is shot when she wanders into a restricted zone, bringing a close to tourist trips to the mountain resort.
2009	Kim Jong Il suffers a stroke; his youngest son, 25-year old Kim Jong Un, emerges as his likely successor; a missile test in April and another nuclear test in May lead to international condemnation and calls for further sanctions.

Appendix 4

Bibliography

Benson, Sonia. *Korean War Almanac.* New York: Gale Group, 2002.

Best, Jonathan W. "Diplomatic and Cultural Contacts between Paekche and China." *Harvard Journal of Asiatic Studies* 42, no. 2 (1982): 443–501.

———. "Buddhism and Polity in Early Sixth-Century Paekche." *Korean Studies* 26, no. 2 (2002): 165–215.

Bluth, Christopher. *Korea.* Cambridge, U.K.: Polity Press, 2008.

Bnet Business Network. "100 N. Koreans reunited with families in Seoul." Bnet Business Network. August 21, 2000. Available online. URL: http://findarticles.com/p/articles/mi_m0WDQ/is_2000_August_21/ai_64528217?tag=content;col1. Retrieved February 2, 2009.

Buzo, Adrian. *The Guerrilla Dynasty: Politics and Leadership in North Korea.* Boulder, Colo.: Westview Press, 1999.

Chira, Susan. "Seoul Scandal: Day and Night Drama." *New York Times,* 10 November 1988.

Ch'oe, Yong-ho. *The Civil Examinations and the Social Structure in Early Yi Dynasty Korea, 1392–1600.* Seoul: Korean Research Center, 1987.

Choe Sang-Hun. "Hyundai in quagmire of North Korea politics." *International Herald Tribune,* 26 October 2005. Available online. URL: http://www.iht.com/articles/2005/10/25/business/hyundai.php. Retrieved January 28, 2009.

———. "North Korea threatens to expel South Koreans." *International Herald Tribune,* 3 August 2008. Available online. URL: http://www.iht.com/articles/2008/08/03/asia/04korea.php. Retrieved January 28, 2009.

Choi Jan Jip. *Labor and the Authoritarian State: Labor Unions in South Korean Manufacturing Industries.* Honolulu: University of Hawaii Press, 1979.

Clark, Donald N. "Choson's Founding Fathers: A Study of Merit Subjects in the Early Yi Dynasty." *Korean Studies* 6 (1982): 17–40.

———. "Sino-Korean Tributary Relations under the Ming." In Vol. 8, pt. 2 of *The Cambridge History of China, The Ming Dynasty, 1368–1644*. Edited by Denis Twitchett and Frederick W. Mote. Cambridge: Cambridge University Press, 1998.

Collins, J. Lawton. *War in Peacetime: The History and Lessons of Korea*. Boston: Houghton Mifflin Co., 1969.

Cook, Harold. *Korea's 1884 Incident: Its Background and Kim Okkyun's Elusive Dream*. Seoul: Royal Asiatic Society, Korea Branch, 1972.

Cumings, Bruce. *Korea's Place in the Sun: A Modern History*. New York: Norton, 2005.

———. *The Origins of the Korean War*. Studies of the East Asian Institute. Princeton, N.J.: Princeton University Press, 1990.

Deane, Hugh. *The Korean War: 1945–1953*. San Francisco: China Books, 1999.

Deuchler, Martina. *Confucian Gentlemen and Barbarian Envoys: The Opening of Korea, 1875–1885*. Seattle: University of Washington Press, 1977.

Duncan, John B. "The Formation of the Central Aristocracy in Early Koryo." *Korean Studies* 12 (1988): 39–61.

———. "The Korean Adoption of Neo-Confucianism: The Social Background." In *Confucianism and the Family*, edited by Walter H. Slote and George A. De Vos. Albany: State University of New York Press, 1998.

———. "The Social Background to the Founding of the Choson Dynasty: Change or Continuity?" *Journal of Korean Studies* 6 (1988–89): 39–79.

Duus, Peter. *The Abacus and the Sword: The Japanese Penetration of Korea, 1895–1910*. Berkeley: University of California Press, 1995.

Eckert, Carter J., and Ki-baek Yi. *Korea, Old and New: A History*. Seoul: Published for the Korea Institute, Harvard University by Ilchokak, 1990.

Edwards, Paul M. *Korean War Almanac*. New York: Facts On File, 2006.

Fairbank, John King, Edwin O. Reischauer, and Albert M. Craig. *East Asia, the Modern Transformation*. Boston: Houghton Mifflin, 1965.

Farris, William Wayne. "Ancient Japan's Korean Connection." *Korean Studies* 20 (1996): 1–22.

French, Paul. *North Korea: The Paranoid Peninsula—A Modern History*. New York: Zed Books, 2005.

Gabriel, Richard A., and Donald W. Boose. "The Korean Way of War: Salsu River." In *The Great Battles of Antiquity: A Strategic and Tactical*

Guide to Great Battles that Shaped the Development of War, edited by Richard A. Gabriel and Donald W. Boose. Westport, Conn.: Greenwood Press, 1994.

Grayson, James H. "Mimana, A Problem in Korean Historiography." *Korea Journal* 17, no. 8 (August 1977): 65–69.

Haboush, JaHyun Kim. "Constructing the Center: The Ritual Controversy and the Search for a New Identity in Seventeenth-Century Korea." In *Culture and the State in Late Choson Korea,* edited by JaHyun Kim Haboush and Martina Deuchler. Cambridge, Mass.: Harvard University Asia Center, 1999.

Halberstam, David. *The Coldest Winter: America and the Korean War.* New York: Hyperion, 2007.

Haliday, Jon, and Bruce Cumings. *Korea: The Unknown War.* New York: Viking, 1988.

Han Woo-keun. *The History of Korea.* Seoul: Euel-Yoo Publishing, 1970.

Hastings, Max. *The Korean War.* New York: Simon & Schuster, 1987.

Hejtmanek, Milan. "Chiphyonjon." In *King Sejong the Great: The Light of 15th Century Korea,* edited by Young-Key Kim-Renaud. Washington, D.C.: International Circle of Korean Linguistics, 1992.

Hicks, George. *The Comfort Women: Japan's Brutal Regime of Enforced Prostitution in the Second World War.* New York: Norton, 1994.

Hurst, G. Cameron III. "'The Good, The Bad and The Ugly': Personalities in the Founding of the Koryo Dynasty." *Korean Studies Forum* 7 (Summer–Fall 1981): 1–27.

Ienaga, Saburo. *The Pacific War: World War II and the Japanese, 1931–1945.* New York: Pantheon, 1978.

Jorgensen, John. "Who Was the Author of the Tan'gun Myth." In *Perspectives on Korea,* edited by Sang-Oak Lee and Duk-Soo Park, 222–255. Sydney: Wild Peony, 1998.

Kang, Hildi. *Under the Black Umbrella: Voices from Colonial Korea.* Ithaca, N.Y.: Cornell University Press, 2001.

Kang Man-gil. "Reflections on the Centenary of the Opening of Korea." *Korea Journal* (February 1976).

———. *A History of Contemporary Korea.* Folkestone, U.K.: Global Oriental, 2005.

Kaufman, Burton I. *The Korean Conflict.* Westport, Conn.: Greenwood Press, 1999.

Kim, Jung-Bae. "Formation of the Ethnic Korean Nation and the Emergence of Its Ancient Kingdom States." In *Korean History: Discovery of Its Characteristics and Developments,* edited by Korean National Commission for UNESCO. Elizabeth, N.J.: Hollym, 2004.

Kim, Sung Moon. "Between Confucian Ideology and the State: A New Approach to Understanding the Literati Purge of 1519." *Review of Korean Studies* 5, no. 2 (December 2002): 233–260.

Kim, Taik-kyoo. "Civil and Military Administration: Government Structure in Pre-Modern Korea." *Senri Ethnological Studies* 25 (1989): 87–110.

Kim, Won-yong. "Kyongju: The Homeland of Korean Culture." *Korea Journal* 22, no. 9 (September 1982): 25–32.

Kim, Young-duk. "The Great Tumulus of Whangnam." *Transactions of the Korea Branch of the Royal Asiatic Society* 72 (1997): 35–42.

Kim-Renaud, Young-Key, ed. *King Sejong the Great: The Light of Fifteenth Century Korea.* Washington, D.C.: The International Circle of Korean Linguistics, 1992.

Kim Young-sik. "The Left-Right Confrontation in Korea—It's Origin." Association for Asian Research. Available online. URL: http://www.asianresearch.org/articles/1636.html. Retrieved January 5, 2009.

Lankov, Andrei. *From Stalin to Kim Il Sung: The Formation of North Korea 1945–1960.* London: Hurst & Company, 2002.

Ledyard, Gari. "Confucianism and War: The Korean Security Crisis of 1598." *Journal of Korean Studies* 6 (1988–89): 81–119.

———. "The Mongol Campaigns in Korea and the Dating of *The Secret History of the Mongols.*" *Central Asiatic Journal* 9 (1964): 1–22.

Lee, Chong-wuk. "The Formation and Growth of Paekche." *Korea Journal* 18, no. 10 (October 1978): 35–40.

Lee, Ki-baik. "Confucian Political Ideology in the Silla Unification and Early Koryo Periods." *Journal of Social Sciences and Humanities* 42 (December 1975): 1–23.

Lee, Ki-dong. "Bureaucracy and Kolp'um System in the Middle Age of Silla." *Journal of Social Sciences and Humanities* 52 (December 1980): 31–58.

Lee, Song Mu. "The *Gwageo* Examination System during the Goryeo and Early Joseon Periods." In *Korean History: Discovery of Its Characteristics and Developments,* edited by Korean National Commission for UNESCO. Elizabeth, N.J.: Hollym, 2004.

Lee, Young-sik. "Recent Research Trends on the History of Kaya in Korea." *International Journal of Korean History* 1 (2000): 1–16.

Lew, Young Ick. "Yuan Shih-kai's Residency and the Korean Enlightenment Movement, 1885–94." *Journal of Korean Studies* 5 (1984): 63–108.

Mai Denawa. "Behind the Accounts of the Great Kanto Earthquake of 1923." Brown University Library Center for Digital Initiatives, fall 2005. Available online. URL: http://dl.lib.brown.edu/kanto/. Retrieved January 2, 2009.

Manwoo Lee. *The Odyssey of Korean Democracy.* New York: Praeger, 1990.

McBride, Richard D. "The Hwarang Segi Manuscripts: An In-Progress Colonial Period Fiction." *Korea Journal* 45, no. 3 (Autumn 2005): 230–260.

Millett, Allan R. *The War for Korea: 1945–1950: A House Burning.* Lawrence: University of Kansas Press, 2005.

Nam, Koon Woo. *The North Korean Communist Leadership, 1945–1960: A Study in Factionalism and Political Consolidation.* University: University of Alabama Press, 1974.

Nanto, Dick K. "The 1997–98 Asian Financial Crisis." CRS Report for Congress, 6 February 1998. Available online. URL: http://www.fas. org/man/crs/crs-asia2.htm. Retrieved January 22, 2009.

Nelson, Sarah M. "The Effects of Rice Agriculture on Prehistoric Korea." *Journal of Asian Studies* 41, no. 3 (May 1982): 531–543.

New York Times. "Korea Makes Protest." 30 June 1907. Available online. URL: http://query.nytimes.com/mem/archive-free/pdf?res=940CE0D F1F30E233A25753C3A9609C 946697D6CF. Retrieved December 22, 2008.

———. "Open Rebellion in Corea." 1 July 1894. Available online. URL: http://query.nytimes.com/mem/archive-free/pdf?res=9E01E4 DF1730E033A25752C0A9619C94659ED7CF. Retrieved December 22, 2008.

———. "Revolt in Corea Grows." 20 January 1895. Available online. URL: http://query.nytimes.com/mem/archive-free/pdf?res=9804E5D D103AE533A25753C2A9679C94649ED7CF. Retrieved December 22, 2008.

Nha, Il-Seong. "Silla's Cheomseongdae." *Korea Journal* 41, no. 4 (Winter 2001): 269–281.

Oberdorfer, Don. *The Two Koreas: A Contemporary History.* Basic Books, 2001.

Ogle, George E. *South Korea: Dissent within the Economic Miracle.* London: Zed Books, 1990.

Oh, Kong Dan, and Ralph C. Hassig. *North Korea through the Looking Glass.* Washington, D.C.: Brookings Institution Press, 2000.

Palais, James B. *Politics and Policy in Traditional Korea.* Cambridge, Mass.: Harvard East Asian Monograph, 1991.

———. "Slavery and Slave Society in the Koryo Period." *Journal of Korean Studies* 5 (1984): 173–190.

Park, Ki-Joo, and Donghyu Yang. "Standard of Living in the Choson Dynasty Korea in the 17th to the 19th Centuries." Available online. URL:

http://findarticles.com/p/articles/mi_qa5411/is_200710/ai_n21297026/
pg_17?tag=artBody;col1. Retrieved December 19, 2008.

Patterson, Orlando. *Slavery and Social Death: A Comparative Study.*
Cambridge, Mass.: Harvard University Press, 1982.

Pearlman, Michael D. "Truman and MacArthur: The Winding Road
to Dismissal." Combat Studies Institute, U.S. Army Command and
General Staff College. Available online. URL: http://www.cgsc.army.
mil/carl/download/csipubs/pearlman2.pdf. Retrieved June 12, 2009.

Peterson, Mark. "The Sejong Sillok." In Young-Key Kim-Renaud, ed.
King Sejong the Great: The Light of 15th Century Korea. Washington,
D.C.: International Circle of Korean Linguistics, 1992.

Reischauer, Edwin O. *Ennin's Diary: The Record of a Pilgrimage to China
in Search of the Law.* New York: Ronald Press, 1955.

Roy, Denny. *China's Foreign Relations.* Lanham, Md.: Rowman &
Littlefield, 1998.

Shim, Jae-Hoon. "A New Understanding of Kija Choson as a Historical
Anachronism." *Harvard Journal of Asiatic Studies* 62, no. 2 (December
2002): 271–305.

Shultz, Edward J. "Ch'oe Chunghon and Minamoto Yoritomo." *Japan
Review* 11 (1999): 31–53.

———. "Military Revolt in Koryo: The 1170 Coup d'Etat." *Korean
Studies* 3 (1979): 19–48.

Song, Ho Jung. "The Formation of Gojoseon and Its Social Characteristics."
Review of Korean Studies 7, no. 1 (March 2004): 95–114.

Song, Ki-ho. "The Dual Status of Parhae: Kingdom and Empire." *Seoul
Journal of Korean Studies* 12 (1999): 104–123.

Tikhonov, Vladimir. "*Hwarang* Organization: Its Functions and Ethics."
Korea Journal 38, no. 2 (Summer 1998): 318–338.

Totman, Conrad. *A History of Japan.* Oxford: Blackwell, 2000.

Wagner, Edward W. "The Literati Purges: Political Conflict in Early
Yi Korea." Harvard East Asia Series. Cambridge, Mass.: Harvard
University Press, 1975.

Yang Chu-dong. *Koga yongu* (Research on Ancient Songs [hyangga]).
Seoul: Ilchogak, 1965; rev. ed., 1983.

Yi, Seon Bok. "Aspects of Middle-Upper Paleolithic Transition in
Northeast Asia." *Seoul Journal of Korean Studies* 15 (2002): 75–100.

Yi, U-song. "A Study of the Period of the Northern and Southern
States." *Korea Journal* 17, no. 1 (January 1977): 28–33.

Youn, Moo-byong. "Archaeological Sites of Kyongju." In *Kyongju:
City of Millenial History,* edited by Korean National Commission for
UNESCO. Elizabeth, N.J.: Hollym, 1998.

Young, Carl. "Tonghak in the Aftermath of the Tonghak Rebellion, 1895–1901." In *Korea: The Past and the Present: Selected Papers from the British Association for Korean Studies BAKS Papers Series, 1991–2005.* Vol. 1, edited by Susan Pares. Kent, U.K.: Global Oriental, 2008.

Young Back Choi, Yesook Merrill, Yung Y. Yang, and Semoon Chang. *Perspectives on Korean Unification and Economic Integration.* Northhampton, Mass.: Edward Elgar Publishing, 2001.

Appendix 5

Suggested Reading

General Works

Chang, Yun-shik, Donald L. Baker, Hur Nam-lin, and Ross King, eds. *Korea between Tradition and Modernity: Selected Papers from the Fourth Pacific and Asian Conference on Korean Studies.* Vancouver: Institute of Asian Research, University of British Columbia, 2000.

Connor, Mary E. *The Koreas: A Global Studies Handbook.* Santa Barbara, Calif.: ABC-Clio Press, 2002.

Ham, Sok Hon. *Queen of Suffering: A Spiritual History of Korea.* Philadelphia: Friends World Committee for Consultation, 1985.

Hogarth, Hyun-key Kim. "Matrifocality in Korean Society: Past, Present and Future." *Papers of the British Association for Korean Studies* 7 (2000): 217–226.

Kidder, Sam. "Seoul." *Transactions of the Royal Asiatic Society, Korea Branch* 68 (1993): 45–56.

Kim, Dok-Ju. "A Study on the Name 'The Japan Sea.'" *Korean Observations on Foreign Relations* 2, no. 1 (April 2000): 152–165.

Lee, Ki-baik. *A New History of Korea.* Translated by Edward W. Wagner, with Edward J. Shultz. Cambridge, Mass.: Harvard University Press, 1984.

Lee, Kyong-hee. *World Heritage in Korea.* Seoul: Hak Go Jae, 1998.

Lewis, James, and Amadu Sesay, eds. *Korea and Globalization: Politics, Economics and Culture.* London: Routledge Curzon, 2002.

Pettid, Michael J. *Korean Cuisine: An Illustrated History.* London: Reaktion Books, 2008.

Pratt, Keith, ed. *Korea: A Cultural and Historical Dictionary.* Surrey, U.K.: Curzon Press, 1998.

From Early Settlements to the Silla Unification of Korea (Prehistory–668)

Best, Jonathan W. "Tales of Three Paekche Monks Who Traveled Afar in Search of the Law." *Harvard Journal of Asiatic Studies* 51, no. 1 (June 1991): 139–198.

Choi, Mong-Lyong, and Song-Nai Rhee. "Korean Archaeology for the 21st Century: From Prehistory to State Formation." *Seoul Journal of Korean Studies* 14 (2001): 116–148.

Choi, Mou-Chang. "The Paleolithic of Korea." *Anthropology* 91, no. 3 (1987): 755–786.

Choi, Sung-rak. "The Iron Age Culture in Southern Korea and Its Chinese Connection." *Korea Journal* 36, no. 4 (Winter 1996): 28–38.

Farris, William Wayne. *Sacred Texts and Buried Treasures: Issues in the Historical Archaeology of Ancient Japan.* Honolulu: University of Hawaii Press, 1998.

———. *Ancient Japan's Korean Connection.* Durham, N.C.: Duke University, Asian/Pacific Studies Institute, 1995.

Gabriel, Richard A., and Donald W. Boose. "The Korean Way of War: Salsu River." In *The Great Battles of Antiquity: A Strategic and Tactical Guide to Great Battles That Shaped the Development of War.* Westport, Conn.: Greenwood Press, 1994.

Grayson, James H. "Some Structural Patterns of the Royal Families of Ancient Korea." *Korea Journal* 16, no. 6 (June 1976): 27–32.

Han, Pyong-sam. "Important Prehistoric Sites." *Korea Journal* 17, no. 4 (April 1977): 14–17.

Hatada, Takashi. "An Interpretation of the King Kwanggaet'o Inscription." *Korean Studies* 3 (1979): 1–17.

Hong, Wontack. *Paekche of Korea and the Origin of Yamato Japan.* Seoul: Kudara International, 1994.

Im, Hyo-Jai. "Korean Neolithic Chronology: A Tentative Model." *Korea Journal* 24, no. 9 (September 1984): 11–22.

———. "The Korean Neolithic Age and Its Cultural Relationship to Northeast China." *Korea Journal* 36, no. 4 (Winter 1996): 5–16.

Kim, Song-ho. "Origins of the Japanese Polity: A Textual Reconsideration of the Horse-Rider Theory." *Korea Journal* 15, no. 12 (December 1985): 4–23.

Kim, Won-yong. "Wall Paintings of Koguryo Tombs." *Korea Journal* 3, no. 7 (July 1963): 19–21.

———. "Korea before History: A Brief Survey." *Korea Journal* 6, no. 1 (January 1966): 12–16.

———. "Discoveries of Rice in Prehistoric Sites in Korea." *Journal of Asian Studies* 41, no. 3 (May 1982): 513–518.

———. "Impact of Ancient Korean Culture upon Japan." *Korea Journal* 12, no. 6 (June 1972): 34–35.

Kim, Yong-duk. "Japan's Korean Roots." *Transactions of the Korea Branch of the Royal Asiatic Society* 76 (2001): 13–29.

———. "Wae Japan as a Tamno of Paekche." *Transactions of the Korea Branch of the Royal Asiatic Society* 71 (1996): 1–8.

———. "In Search of Japan's Origin." *Transactions of the Korea Branch of the Royal Asiatic Society* 73 (1998): 89–99.

Kirkland, J. Russell. "The 'Horseriders' in Korea: A Critical Evaluation of a Historical Theory." *Korean Studies* 5 (1981): 109–128.

Ledyard, Gari. "Galloping along with the Horseriders: Looking for the Founders of Japan." *Journal of Japanese Studies* 1, no. 2 (Spring 1975): 217–254.

Lee, Hong Jik. "The Relationship of Korea and Japan in the Earliest Period of Their Histories." *Koreana Quarterly* 5, no. 2 (Summer 1963): 140–145.

Lee, Yong-bum. "Korea's Political Power in Ancient Japan." *Korea Journal* 12, no. 6 (June 1972): 30–34.

Miller, Roy Andrew. "A Korean Poet in Eighth-Century Japan." *Korea Journal* 25, no. 11 (November 1985): 4–21.

———. "Early Korea and Early Japan." *Asian and Pacific Quarterly of Cultural and Social Affairs* 19, no. 1 (Spring 1987): 1–4.

Nelson, Sarah M. "The Effects of Rice Agriculture on Prehistoric Korea." *Journal of Asian Studies* 41, no. 3 (May 1982): 531–543.

———. "Korean Archaeological Sequences from the First Ceramics to the Introduction of Iron." In *Chronologies in Old World Archaeology.* Vol. 1, 2, 3d ed., edited by R. W. Ehrich. Chicago: University of Chicago Press, 1992.

———. *The Archaeology of Korea.* Cambridge, U.K.: Cambridge University Press, 1993.

Park, Chung H. *The Historic Long Deep Korean Roots in Japan.* New York: Vantage Press, 2004.

Pearson, Richard J. "The Prehistory of Korea: An Introduction." In *The Traditional Culture and Society of Korea: Prehistory,* edited by Richard J. Pearson. Occasional Papers No. 3. Honolulu: Center for Korean Studies, University of Hawaii, 1975.

———. "Korean Prehistory: An Overview." *Korea Journal* 15, no. 12 (December 1975): 4–11.

Sasse, Werner. "The Shilla Stone Inscription from Naengsu-ri, Yongil-gun." *Korea Journal* 31, no. 3 (Autumn 1991): 31–53.

Szczesniak, Boleslaw. "Japanese-Korean Wars in A.D. 391–407 and Their Chronology." *Journal of the Royal Asiatic Society* (April 1946): 54–66.

Yi, Pyong Do, and Tae-Young Choe. *An Introduction to the History of Ancient Korea.* Fairbanks, AK: Korean Studies Program, University of Alaska, 1990.

Yoon, Nae-Hyun. "True Understanding of Old Choson." *Korea Journal* 27, no. 12 (December 1987): 23–40.

Unified Silla (668–935) and Koryo (918–1392)

Hamada, Kosaku. "Sovereignty and Maritime Power: Chang Pogo's Ch'onghae Garrison and Pirates." *Interaction and Transformations* 1 (2003): 131–145.

Harrell, Mark. "Sokkuram: Buddhist Monument and Political Statement in Korea." *World Archaeology* 27, no. 2 (February 1995): 318–335.

Kim, Kumja Paik, ed. *Goryeo Dynasty: Korea's Age of Enlightenment, 918 to 1392.* San Francisco: Asian Art Museum, 2003.

Kim, J. Y. "The Kwanggaeto Stele Inscription." In *Contemporary European Writing on Japan: Scholarly Views from Eastern and Western Europe,* edited by Ian Nish. Kent, U.K.: Paul Norbury Publishers, 1988.

Shultz, Edward J. "Korea: A Hermit Nation?" *Review of Korean Studies* 10, no. 1 (March 2007): 107–117.

Song, Ki-ho. "Several Questions in Studies of the History of Palhae." *Korea Journal* 30, no. 6 (June 1990): 4–20.

———. "Current Trends in the Research of Palhae History." *Seoul Journal of Korean Studies* 3 (December 1990): 157–174.

———. "The Dual Status of Parhae: Kingdom and Empire." *Seoul Journal of Korean Studies* 12 (1999): 104–123.

———. "Several Questions in Historical Studies of Balhae." In *Korean History: Discovery of Its Characteristics and Developments,* edited by Korean National Commission for UNESCO. Elizabeth, N.J.: Hollym, 2004.

Yi, U-song. "A Study of the Period of the Northern and Southern States." *Korea Journal* 17, no. 1 (January 1977): 28–33.

Yuan, Waiming George. "Ko Son-ji (Kao Hsien-Chih): A Korean in the Chinese Military Service." *Asea yongu* 13, no. 3 (1970:9): 153–164.

The Early and Middle Choson (1392–1636)

Choe, Yong-ho. *The Civil Examinations and the Social Structure in Early Yi Dynasty Korea, 1392–1600.* Seoul: Korean Research Center, 1987.

Clark, Donald N. "Choson's Founding Fathers: A Study of Merit Subjects in the Early Yi Dynasty." *Korean Studies* 6 (1982): 17–40.

———. "Sino-Korean Tributary Relations under the Ming." In *The Ming Dynasty, 1368–1644.* Vol. 8, part 2 of *The Cambridge History of China,* edited by Denis Twitchett and Frederick W. Mote. Cambridge: Cambridge University Press, 1998.

Duncan, John B. "The Social Background to the Founding of the Choson Dynasty: Change or Continuity?" *Journal of Korean Studies* 6 (1988–89): 39–79.

———. *The Origins of the Choson Dynasty.* Seattle: University of Washington Press, 2000.

Kim, Chun-sung. "The Significance and Construction Beauty of Chongmyo, the Royal Ancestral Shrine." (*Kyonghui taehakkyo kwang-wang sanop chongbo yonguwon*) *Kwangwang sanop chongbo nonjip* 1 (1999:12): 83–104.

Kim, Dong-Uk. "Chongmyo." *Korea Journal* 40, no. 3 (Autumn 2000): 284–298.

Kim, Sung Moon. "Between Confucian Ideology and the State: A New Approach to Understanding the Literati Purge of 1519." *Review of Korean Studies* 5, no. 2 (December 2002): 233–260.

Kim-Renaud, Young-Key, ed. *King Sejong the Great: The Light of 15th Century Korea.* Washington, D.C.: International Circle of Korean Linguistics, 1992.

Ledyard, Gari. "Confucianism and War: The Korean Security Crisis of 1598." *Journal of Korean Studies* 6 (1988–89): 81–119.

Lee, Peter H., ed. *From Early Times to the Sixteenth Century.* Vol. 1 of *Sourcebook of Korean Civilization.* New York: Columbia University Press, 1993.

Peterson, Mark. "The Sejong Sillok." In *King Sejong the Great: The Light of 15th Century Korea,* edited by Young-Key Kim-Renaud. Washington, D.C.: International Circle of Korean Linguistics, 1992.

Turnbull, Stephen. *Fighting Ships of the Far East (2): Japan and Korea A.D. 612–1639.* London: Osprey Publishing, 2003.

Wagner, Edward W. "Two Early Genealogies and Women's Status in Early Yi Dynasty Korea." In *Korean Women: View from the Inner Room,* edited by Laurel Kendall and Mark Peterson. New Haven, Conn.: East Rock Press, 1983.

———. "The Literati Purges: Political Conflict in Early Yi Korea." Harvard East Asia Series, 1975.

———. "Social Background of Early Yi Dynasty Neo-Confucianists." (*Kyongbuk taehakkyo T'oegye yonguso*) *Hanguk ui ch'olhak* 10 (1982): 131–151.

———. "An Inquiry into the Origin, Development and Fate of Chapkwa-Chungin Lineage." In *Kuknaeoe e issoso Hangukhak ui hyonjae wa mirae*. Taejon: Inha taehakkyo Hangukhak yonguso, 1987.

Late Choson (1636–1910)

Baek, Seung-ch'ol. "The Development of Local Markets and the Establishment of a New Circulation System in Late Choson Society." *Seoul Journal of Korean Studies* 12 (1999): 152–176.

Cook, Harold. *Korea's 1884 Incident: Its Background and Kim Okkyun's Elusive Dream*. Seoul: Royal Asiatic Society, Korea Branch, 1972.

Chandra, Vipan. *Imperialism, Resistance, and Reform in Late Nineteenth-Century Korea: Enlightenment and the Independence Club*. Berkeley: University of California, Berkeley, Institute of East Asian Studies, Center for Korean Studies, 1988.

Deuchler, Martina. *Confucian Gentlemen and Barbarian Envoys: The Opening of Korea, 1875–1885*. Seattle: University of Washington Press, 1977.

Haboush, JaHyun Kim. *The Confucian Kingship in Korea: Yongjo and the Politics of Sagacity*. New York: Columbia University Press, 2001.

———. "Filial Emotions and Filial Values: Changing Patterns in the Discourse of Filiality in Late Choson Korea." *Harvard Journal of Asiatic Studies* 55, no. 1 (June 1995): 129–177.

———. "Dead Bodies in the Postwar Discourse of Identity in Seventeenth-Century Korea: Subversion and Literary Production in the Private Sector." *Journal of Asian Studies* 62, no. 2 (May 2003): 415–442.

Jun, Seong Ho, and James B. Lewis. "Wages, Rents, and Interest Rates in Southern Korea, 1700 to 1900." In *Research in Economic History*, Vol. 24, edited by Alexander J. Field, Gregory Clark, and William Sundstrom. Amsterdam: Elsevier, 2006.

Karlsson, Anders. "Challenging the Dynasty: Popular Protest, Chonggamnok and the Ideology of the Hong Kyongnae Rebellion." *International Journal of Korean History* 2 (2001): 255–277.

———. "*Chonggamnok* and the Ideology of the Hong Kyongnae Rebellion." In *History, Language and Culture in Korea: Proceedings of the 20th Conference of the Association of Korean Studies in Europe*

(AKSE), compiled by Youngsook Pak and Jaehoon Yeon. London: Eastern Art Publishing, 2001.

Kawashima, Fujiya. *What Is Yangban?: A Legacy for Modern Korea.* Seoul: Institute for Modern Korean Studies, Yonsei University, 2002.

———. "A Study of the *Hyangan*: Kin Groups and Aristocratic Localism in the Seventeenth- and Eighteenth-Century Korean Countryside." *Journal of Korean Studies* 5 (1984): 3–38.

———. "A Yangban Organization in the Countryside: The Tansong *Hyang'an* of Mid-Choson Dynasty Korea." *Journal of Korean Studies* 8 (1992): 3–35.

———. "Yangban Legacy: Cultural Localism and Korean Identity." In *Korean Cultural Roots: Religion and Social Thoughts,* edited by Ho-Youn Kwon. Chicago: Integrated Technical Resources, 1995.

Larsen, Kirk W. *Tradition, Treaties, and Trade: Qing Imperialism and Choson Korea, 1850–1910.* Cambridge, Mass.: Harvard East Asia Center, 2008.

Lee, Peter H., ed. *From the Seventeenth Century to the Modern Period.* Vol. 2 of *Sourcebook of Korean Civilization.* New York: Columbia University Press, 1996.

Lew, Young Ick. "Yuan Shih-kai's Residency and the Korean Enlightenment Movement, 1885–94." *Journal of Korean Studies* 5 (1984): 63–108.

Palais, James B. *Politics and Policy in Traditional Korea.* Cambridge, Mass.: Harvard East Asian Monograph, 1991.

Park, Eugene. *Between Dreams and Reality: The Military Examinations in Late Choson Korea, 1600–1894.* Cambridge, Mass.: Harvard East Asia Monograph, 2006.

Peterson, Mark. "Women without Sons: A Measure of Social Change in Yi Dynasty Korea." In *Korean Women: View from the Inner Room,* edited by Laurel Kendall and Mark Peterson. New Haven, Conn.: East Rock Press, 1983.

Quinones, C. Kenneth. "Military Officials of Yi Korea: 1864–1910." In *Che-1 hoe Hangukhak kukche haksul hoeui nonmunjip: Papers of the 1st International Conference on Korean Studies.* Songnam: Hanguk chong-shin munhwa yonguwon, 1980.

Setton, Mark. "Factional Politics and Philosophical Development in the Late Choson." *Journal of Korean Studies* 8 (1992): 37–79.

Wagner, Edward W. "The Civil Examination Process as Social Leaven: The Case of the Northern Provinces in the Yi Dynasty." *Korea Journal* 17, no. 1 (January 1977): 22–27.

Yi, Tae-jin. "King Chongjo: Confucianism, Enlightenment, and Absolute Rule." *Korea Journal* 40, no. 4 (Winter 2000): 168–201.

———. *Dynamics of Confucianism and Modernization in Korean History.* Ithaca, N.Y.: Cornell East Asia Series, 2007.

Young, Carl. "Tonghak in the Aftermath of the Tonghak Rebellion, 1895–1901." In *Korea: The Past and the Present: Selected Papers from the British Association for Korean Studies BAKS Papers Series, 1991–2005,* Vol. 1, edited by Susan Pares. Kent, U.K.: Global Oriental, 2008.

The Japanese Colony (1910–1945)

Brooks, Barbara J. "Japanese Colonial Citizenship in Treaty Port China: The Location of Koreans and Taiwanese in the Imperial Order." In *New Frontiers: Imperialism's New Communities in East Asia, 1842–1953,* edited by Robert Bickers and Christian Henriot. Manchester, U.K.: Manchester University Press, 2000.

Caprio, Mark E. "Civilizing Koreans: The 1910 Debate over Korean Education." In *Embracing the Other: The Interaction of Korean and Foreign Cultures: Proceedings of the 1st World Congress of Korean Studies, II.* Songnam, Republic of Korea: Academy of Korean Studies, 2002.

Choi, Hyaeweol. "(En)Gendering a New Nation in Missionary Discourse: An Analysis of W. Arthur Noble's *Ewa.*" *Korea Journal* 46, no. 1 (Spring 2006): 139–169.

Clark, Donald N. "'Surely God Will Work Out Their Salvation': Protestant Missionaries in the March First Movement." *Korean Studies* 13 (1989): 42–75.

Grayson, James H. "The Shinto Shrine Conflict and Protestant Martyrs in Korea, 1938–1945." *Missiology* 29, no. 3 (July 2001): 287–305.

Hwang, Kyung Moon. *Beyond Birth; Social Status in the Emergence of Modern Korea.* Cambridge, Mass.: Harvard University Asia Center, 2004.

Kim, C. I., Eugene Mortimore, and Doretha E. Mortimore, eds. *Korea's Response to Japan: The Colonial Period, 1910–1945.* Kalamazoo, Mich.: Center for Korean Studies, Western Michigan University, 1977.

Kim, Han-Kyo. "Japanese Colonialism in Korea." In *Japan Examined: Perspectives on Modern Japanese History,* edited by Harry Wray and Hilary Conroy. Honolulu: University of Hawaii Press, 1983.

Kim, Hyung-chan. "Portrait of a Troubled Korean Patriot: Yun Ch'i-ho's Views of the March First Independence Movement and World War II." *Korean Studies* 13 (1989): 76–91.

Ku, Daeyeol. "The March First Movement: With Special Reference to Its External Implications and Reactions of the United States." *Korea Journal* 42, no. 3 (Autumn 2002): 219–256.

Ledyard, Gari. "Korea and the World 1860–1945." In *Korean Challenges and American Policy,* edited by Ilpyong J. Kim. New York: Paragon House, 1991.

McCann, David R. "Korea the Colony and the Poet Sowol." In *War, Occupation, and Creativity: Japan and East Asia 1920–1960,* edited by Marlene J. Mayo and J. Thomas Rimer, with H. Eleanor Kerkham. Honolulu: University of Hawaii Press, 2001.

McNamara, Dennis. "Comparative Colonial Response: Korea and Taiwan, 1895–1919." *Korean Studies* 10 (1986): 54–68.

Moffett, Samuel H. "The Independence Movement and the Missionaries." *Transactions of the Korea Branch of the Royal Asiatic Society* 54 (1979): 13–32.

Palmer, Spencer J. "Korean Christians and the Shinto Shrine Issue." In *Korea's Response to Japan: The Colonial Period, 1910–1945,* edited by C. I. Eugene Kim and Doretha E. Mortimore. Kalamazoo, Mich.: Center for Korean Studies, Western Michigan University, 1977.

Rhee, M. J. *The Doomed Empire: Japan in Colonial Korea.* Brookfield, Vt.: Ashgate, 1997.

Robinson, Michael. "Broadcasting, Cultural Hegemony, and Colonial Modernity in Korea, 1924–1945." In *Colonial Modernity in Korea,* edited by Gi-Wook Shin and Michael Robinson. Cambridge, Mass.: Harvard University Asia Center, 1999.

Schmid, Andre. *Korea between Empires.* New York: Columbia University Press, 2002.

Shin, Gi-Wook, and Michael Robinson, eds. *Colonial Modernity in Korea.* Cambridge, Mass.: Harvard University Asia Center, 1999.

Liberation, Division, and the Korean War (1945–1953)

Chandra, Vipan. "Korean-American Relations in Historical Perspective: Some Reflections." *Korean and Korean-American Studies* 2, no. 3 (Fall-Winter 1986): 3–5.

Kang, Shin-pyo. "Collapse of Traditional Culture and Confusion in Mass Culture: An Experience of Koreans since World War II." *Korea Journal* 16, no. 9 (September 1976): 55–59.

Kirk, Donald, and Choe Sang-Hun. *Korea Witness: 135 Years of War, Crisis and News in the Land of the Morning Calm.* Seoul: EunHaengNaMu, 2006.

Shin, Gi-Wook, James Freda, and Gihong Yi. "The Politics of Ethnic Nationalism in Divided Korea." *Nations and Nationalism* 5, no. 4 (October 1999): 465–484.

South Korea's Long Road to Democracy (1953–2009)

Abelmann, Nancy. *Echoes of the Past, Epics of Dissent: A South Korean Social Movement.* Berkeley: University of California Press, 1996.

Armstrong, Charles K. "The Cultural Cold War in Korea, 1945–1950." *Journal of Asian Studies* 62, no. 1 (February 2003): 71–99.

Cha, Myung Soo. "Facts and Myths about Korea's Economic Past." *Australian Economic History Review* 44, no. 3 (November 2004): 278–293.

Hahm, Pyong-choon. "Toward a New Theory of Korean Politics: A Reexamination of Traditional Factors." In *Korean Politics in Transition,* edited by Edward Reynolds Wright. Seattle: University of Washington Press, 1975.

Han, Pyo-Wook. *The Problem of Korean Unification: A Study of the Unification Policy of the Republic of Korea, 1948–1960.* Seoul: Research Center for Peace and Unification of Korea, 1987.

Henderson, Gregory. "Constitutional Changes from the First to the Sixth Republics: 1948 to 1967." In *Political Change in South Korea,* edited by Ilpyong J. Kim and Young Whan Kihl. New York: Paragon House Publishers, 1988.

Hoare, James. "The Korean Peninsula: Fifty Years of Uncertainty." *Asian Affairs* 33, no. 2 (June 2002): 232–237.

Hyun, Chang-sung, Young-hee Cho, Chan-sik Park, Seok-ji Hahn, and Chang-hoon Ko. "The Resistance of the People and the Government's Countermeasures: The Historical Flow and Significance of the Case Studies from the 1000 Years in Cheju." *Journal of Island Studies* 3, no. 1 (Spring-Summer 2000): 16–30.

Kim, Hak-joon. "The American Military Government in South Korea, 1945–1948: Its Formation, Policies, and Legacies." *Asian Perspective* 12, no. 1 (Spring-Summer 1988): 51–83.

Kim, Kwang-Joong, ed. *Seoul, 20th Century: Growth and Change of the Last 100 Years.* Seoul: Seoul Development Institute, 2003.

Kim, Quee-Young. "From Protest to Change of Regime: The 4–19 Revolt and the Fall of the Rhee Regime in South Korea." *Social Forces* 74, no. 4 (June 1996): 1,179–1,209.

Koo, Youngnok, and Sung-joo Han, eds. *The Foreign Policy of the Republic of Korea.* New York: Columbia University Press, 1985.

Lew, Young Ick. "A Historical Overview of Korean Perceptions of the United States: Five Major Stereotypes." *Korea Journal* 44, no. 1 (Spring 2004): 109–151.

Merrill, John. "The American Occupation of Korea." In *Korean Challenges and American Policy*, edited by Ilpyong J. Kim. New York: Paragon House, 1991.

Nahm, Andrew, and James E. Hoare. *Historical Dictionary of the Republic of Korea*, 2d ed. Lanham, Md.: Scarecrow Press, 2004.

Pang, Kie-chung, and Michael D. Shin, eds. *Landlords, Peasants and Intellectuals in Modern Korea.* Ithaca, N.Y.: Cornell East Asia Series, 2005.

Shin, Gi-wook. "The Historical Making of Collective Action: The Korean Peasant Uprisings of 1946." *American Journal of Sociology* 99, no. 6 (May 1994): 1,596–1,624.

Woo-Cumings, Meredith. "The Korean Bureaucratic State: Historical Legacies and Comparative Perspectives." In *Politics and Policy in the New Korean State: From Roh Tae-woo to Kim Young-sam*, edited by James Cotton. New York: St. Martin's Press, 1995.

Yang, Sung Chul. "South Korea's Top Bureaucratic Elites 1948–1993: Their Recruitment Patterns and Modal Characteristics." In *Korean Politics: Striving for Democracy and Unification*, edited by Korean National Commission for UNESCO. Elizabeth, N.J.: Hollym, 2002.

North Korea (1945–2009)

Abdrakhmanov, M. "Korea: Withdrawal of Chinese Volunteers." *International Affairs* 4 (April 1958): 92–93.

Armstrong, Charles K. *The North Korean Revolution, 1945–1950.* Ithaca, N.Y.: Cornell University Press, 2002.

Baik, Bong. *Kim Il-song: Biography.* 3 vols. Tokyo: Miraisha, 1969–1970.

Baldwin, Frank. "Patrolling the Empire: Reflections on the USS *Pueblo.*" *Bulletin of Concerned Asian Scholars* 4, no. 2 (Summer 1972): 54–74.

Ch'oe, Yong-ho. "Christian Background in the Early Life of Kim Il-song." *Asian Survey* 26, no. 10 (October 1986): 1,082–1,091.

Kim, Ilpyong J. *Historical Dictionary of North Korea.* Lanham, Md.: Scarecrow Press, 2003.

Kimura, Mitsuhiko. "Conditions of Agricultural Production in North Korea, 1946–1950." *Korea Journal* 40, no. 4 (Winter 2000): 266–299.

Kwon, Soyoung. "State Building in North Korea: From a 'Self-Reliant' to a 'Military-First' State." *Asian Affairs* 34, no. 3 (November 2003): 286–296.

Lankov, Andrei N. "Kim Il Sung's Campaign against the Soviet Faction in Late 1955 and the Birth of Chuch'e." *Korean Studies* 23 (1999): 43–67.

Lee, Chong-sik. *The Korean Workers' Party: A Short History.* Stanford, Calif.: Hoover Institution Press, 1978.

Lee, In Ho. "The Soviet Military Government in North Korea." *Korea Observer* 23, no. 4 (Winter 1991): 521–548.

Lee, Yong Sun. "Elites of the North Korean Regime: Their Social Backgrounds and Career Patterns." *Journal of East Asian Affairs* 3, no. 1 (Spring-Summer 1988): 42–72.

Nahm, Andrew C. "The United States and North Korea since 1945." In *Korean-American Relations 1866–1997,* edited by Yur-Bok Lee and Wayne Patterson. Albany: State University of New York Press, 1999.

Oh, Sung. "Economic Status According to the Distribution of Housing Size in Kaesong around 1900." *Korean Studies* 30 (2006): 23–39.

Satterwhite, David. "A Half-Century of United States-Korea Policy: Inching toward United States–DPRK Rapprochement." In *North Korea in the New World Order,* edited by Hazel Smith, Chris Rhodes, Diana Pritchard, and Kevin Magill. New York: St. Martin's Press, 1996.

Suh, Dae-Sook. *Korean Communism, 1945–1980: A Reference Guide to the Political System.* Honolulu: University of Hawaii Press, 1981.

———. *Kim Il Sung: The North Korean Leader.* New York: Columbia University Press, 1988.

Yang, Sung Chul. "A Study of North Korea's Ruling Elite, 1946–1990: Based on a Background Analysis of the Members of the Korean Workers' Party Central Committee." *Vantage Point* 14, no. 4 (April 1991): 1–15; 14, no. 5 (May 1991): 1–13.

Winfield, Betty H., and Doyle Yoon. "Historical Images at a Glance: North Korea in American Editorial Cartoons." *Newspaper Research Journal* 23, no. 4 (Fall 2002): 97–100.

Zhebin, Alexander. "A Political History of Soviet-North Korean Nuclear Cooperation." In *The North Korean Nuclear Program: Security, Strategy and New Perspectives from Russia,* edited by Alexandre Mansourov and James Clay Moltz. New York: Routledge, 1999.

INDEX

Note: **Boldface** page numbers indicate primary discussion of a topic. Page numbers in *italic* indicate illustrations. The letters *c* and *m* indicate chronology and maps, respectively.